Kinetic Theory-Based Methods in Fluid Dynamics

Kinetic Theory-Based Methods in Fluid Dynamics

Editors

Zhen Chen
Liangqi Zhang
Liming Yang

MDPI • Basel • Beijing • Wuhan • Barcelona • Belgrade • Manchester • Tokyo • Cluj • Tianjin

Editors
Zhen Chen
Shanghai Jiao Tong University
China

Liangqi Zhang
Chongqing University
China

Liming Yang
Nanjing University of Aeronautics and Astronautics
China

Editorial Office
MDPI
St. Alban-Anlage 66
4052 Basel, Switzerland

This is a reprint of articles from the Special Issue published online in the open access journal *Entropy* (ISSN 1099-4300) (available at: https://www.mdpi.com/journal/entropy/special_issues/kinetic_theory).

For citation purposes, cite each article independently as indicated on the article page online and as indicated below:

LastName, A.A.; LastName, B.B.; LastName, C.C. Article Title. *Journal Name* **Year**, *Volume Number*, Page Range.

ISBN 978-3-0365-6914-7 (Hbk)
ISBN 978-3-0365-6915-4 (PDF)

© 2023 by the authors. Articles in this book are Open Access and distributed under the Creative Commons Attribution (CC BY) license, which allows users to download, copy and build upon published articles, as long as the author and publisher are properly credited, which ensures maximum dissemination and a wider impact of our publications.

The book as a whole is distributed by MDPI under the terms and conditions of the Creative Commons license CC BY-NC-ND.

Contents

Zhen Chen, Liangqi Zhang and Liming Yang
Kinetic Theory-Based Methods in Fluid Dynamics
Reprinted from: *Entropy* **2023**, *25*, 255, doi:10.3390/e25020255 1

Xiang-Bo Feng, Shi-Fan Huo, Xiao-Tao Xu, Fei Liu and Qing Liu
Numerical Study on Heat-Transfer Characteristics of Convection Melting in Metal Foam under Sinusoidal Temperature Boundary Conditions
Reprinted from: *Entropy* **2022**, *24*, 1779, doi:10.3390/e24121779 3

Alexey Morozov and Vladimir Titarev
Planar Gas Expansion under Intensive Nanosecond Laser Evaporation into Vacuum as Applied to Time-of-Flight Analysis
Reprinted from: *Entropy* **2022**, *24*, 1738, doi:10.3390/e24121738 19

Qiaochu Song, Rongqian Chen, Shuqi Cao, Jinhua Lou, Ningyu Zhan and Yancheng You
A Simplified Linearized Lattice Boltzmann Method for Acoustic Propagation Simulation
Reprinted from: *Entropy* **2022**, *24*, 1622, doi:10.3390/e24111622 35

Xiaodi Wu and Song Zhou
Thermal Lattice Boltzmann Flux Solver for Natural Convection of Nanofluid in a Square Enclosure
Reprinted from: *Entropy* **2022**, *24*, 1448, doi:10.3390/e24101448 57

Alberto Megías and Andrés Santos
Kinetic Theory and Memory Effects of Homogeneous Inelastic Granular Gases under Nonlinear Drag
Reprinted from: *Entropy* **2022**, *24*, 1436, doi:10.3390/e24101436 75

Di Zhou, Bingchen Du, Tongqing Guo, Qiaozhong Li and Zhiliang Lu
Application of a Gas-Kinetic BGK Scheme in Thermal Protection System Analysis for Hypersonic Vehicles
Reprinted from: *Entropy* **2022**, *24*, 1325, doi:10.3390/e24101325 91

Jie Liu, Tao Zhang and Shuyu Sun
Study of the Imbibition Phenomenon in Porous Media by the Smoothed Particle Hydrodynamic (SPH) Method
Reprinted from: *Entropy* **2022**, *24*, 1212, doi:10.3390/e24091212 111

Zeren Yang, Sha Liu, Congshan Zhuo and Chengwen Zhong
Free-Energy-Based Discrete Unified Gas Kinetic Scheme for van der Waals Fluid
Reprinted from: *Entropy* **2022**, *24*, 1202, doi:10.3390/e24091202 125

Tianbai Xiao
A Well-Balanced Unified Gas-Kinetic Scheme for Multicomponent Flows under External Force Field
Reprinted from: *Entropy* **2022**, *24*, 1110, doi:10.3390/e24081110 147

Wenqiang Guo and Guoxiang Hou
Three-Dimensional Simulations of Anisotropic Slip Microflows Using the Discrete Unified Gas Kinetic Scheme
Reprinted from: *Entropy* **2022**, *24*, 907, doi:10.3390/e24070907 175

Tingting Qi, Jianzhong Lin and Zhenyu Ouyang
Hydrodynamic Behavior of Self-Propelled Particles in a Simple Shear Flow
Reprinted from: *Entropy* **2022**, *24*, 854, doi:10.3390/e24070854 . . . . **209**

Dingwu Jiang, Pei Wang, Jin Li and Meiliang Mao
Nonlinear Modeling Study of Aerodynamic Characteristics of an X38-like Vehicle at Strong Viscous Interaction Regions
Reprinted from: *Entropy* **2022**, *24*, 836, doi:10.3390/e24060836 . . . . **221**

Editorial

Kinetic Theory-Based Methods in Fluid Dynamics

Zhen Chen [1,*], Liangqi Zhang [2] and Liming Yang [3]

1. School of Naval Architecture, Ocean and Civil Engineering, Shanghai Jiao Tong University, Shanghai 200240, China
2. College of Aerospace Engineering, Chongqing University, Chongqing 400044, China
3. Department of Aerodynamics, Nanjing University of Aeronautics and Astronautics, Nanjing 210016, China
* Correspondence: zhen.chen@sjtu.edu.cn

Kinetic theory stems from the statistical mechanics established at the mesoscopic scale. In the area of fluid dynamics, kinetic theory outperforms macroscopic interpretations (represented by the Navier–Stokes equations) in multiple aspects: it provides theoretical generality with no restrictions from the continuum assumption, clear interpretation of the streaming and collision of fluid particles in a physical process, simple algebraic formulas instead of partial differential equations in numerical evolution, and convenient implementation in parallel computation. Various methods, such as the discrete velocity method, gas kinetic scheme, unified gas kinetic scheme, lattice Boltzmann method, etc., have been developed within the framework of kinetic theory. These methods play unique and important roles in almost all studies of fluid dynamics. However, their broader application to engineering problems is often hindered by intrinsic limitations. Kinetic theory-based methods usually consume larger virtual memory than macroscopic methods. Additionally, high-fidelity simulations of flows beyond the continuum regime are still time-consuming. Therefore, developing robust and efficient kinetic theory-based methods is an urgent need in the fluid dynamics community.

This Special Issue is a timely forum for presenting recent advances in the very active area of kinetic theory-based methods in fluid dynamics. After a year-long preparation and a rigorous peer-review process, 12 articles were finally accepted for publication in this Special Issue. These articles report the latest developments in kinetic-theory-related numerical schemes [1,2] and typical applications in multiphase flows [3], thermal flows [4], micro/nano flows [5,6], flows in porous media [7], and compressible flows [8,9], as well as other areas of fluid dynamics [10–12]. Specifically, Song et al. [1] proposed a simplified linearized Boltzmann method for the effective simulation of acoustic propagation with a lower cost of virtual memory. Xiao [2] developed a well-balanced unified gas-kinetic scheme to model the dynamics of multicomponent gaseous flows under gravity, which allows for evolving a gravitational system under any initial condition to the hydrostatic equilibrium, and thus could be a proper solver for long-term evolving systems such as galaxy formation. Yang et al. [3] managed to remove the force imbalance in the direct implementation of a lattice Boltzmann free-energy model on the discrete unified gas kinetic scheme and successfully derived a robust free-energy model for van der Waals fluid. Feng et al. [4] utilized the multiple-relaxation-time lattice Boltzmann method to investigate the thermal behaviors of convection melting in metal foam under sinusoidal temperature boundary conditions. Wu and Zhou [5] presented an application of the lattice Boltzmann flux solver to the modelling of the natural convection process within a square cavity filled by nanofluid. Guo and Hou [6] derived an anisotropic slip boundary condition based on nonlinear velocity profiles near the wall, consolidated this new boundary treatment into the discrete unified gas kinetic scheme, and investigated the effects of anisotropic slip on the two-sided orthogonal oscillating micro-lid-driven cavity flow through three-dimensional simulations. Liu et al. [7] carried out a series of simulations using the smoothed particle hydrodynamics method to shed light on the physics under the imbibition phenomenon

Citation: Chen, Z.; Zhang, L.; Yang, L. Kinetic Theory-Based Methods in Fluid Dynamics. *Entropy* **2023**, *25*, 255. https://doi.org/10.3390/e25020255

Received: 30 January 2023
Accepted: 30 January 2023
Published: 31 January 2023

Copyright: © 2023 by the authors. Licensee MDPI, Basel, Switzerland. This article is an open access article distributed under the terms and conditions of the Creative Commons Attribution (CC BY) license (https://creativecommons.org/licenses/by/4.0/).

in porous media. Zhou et al. [8] employed the gas-kinetic BGK scheme and performed a thorough analysis of the thermal protection system for vehicles operating in extreme conditions of hypersonic flows. Jiang et al. [9] investigated the aerodynamic characteristics of an X38-like vehicle considering strong viscous interactions and complicated rarified effects, which could be of reference value to engineering designs. Morozov and Titarev [10] utilized three numerical tools to study the dynamics of gas expansion due to intense nanosecond laser evaporation into vacuum, with specific attention paid to factors that are essential for experimental measurements. Megías and Santos [11] established a numerical model to interpret interactions between the dilute granular gases and a thermal bath made from smaller particles, and found that the Sonine approximation performs better than the Maxwellian approximation in revealing inelasticity, drag nonlinearity and memory effects. Qi et al. [12] employed an immersed boundary-lattice Boltzmann method to simulate self-propelled particles in a simple shear flow, and studied the effects of multiple flow parameters (swimming Reynolds number, flow Reynolds number and blocking rate) on the kinematics and flow patterns.

The Guest Editors would like to express their sincere gratitude to all authors for their valuable contributions which made this Special Issue possible, and to all anonymous referees for their valuable time and professional feedback which substantially improved the quality of this Special Issue. Special thanks are given to the editorial team of *Entropy* for their consistent support and valuable assistance.

Funding: This work was supported by the National Natural Science Foundation of China (Grant Nos. 52201329, 12102071, 12202191, 92271103).

Conflicts of Interest: The authors declare no conflict of interest.

References

1. Song, Q.; Chen, R.; Cao, S.; Lou, J.; Zhan, N.; You, Y. A Simplified Linearized Lattice Boltzmann Method for Acoustic Propagation Simulation. *Entropy* **2022**, *24*, 1622. [CrossRef]
2. Xiao, T. A Well-Balanced Unified Gas-Kinetic Scheme for Multicomponent Flows under External Force Field. *Entropy* **2022**, *24*, 1110. [CrossRef] [PubMed]
3. Yang, Z.; Liu, S.; Zhuo, C.; Zhong, C. Free-energy-based discrete unified gas kinetic scheme for van der waals fluid. *Entropy* **2022**, *24*, 1202. [CrossRef] [PubMed]
4. Feng, X.-B.; Huo, S.-F.; Xu, X.-T.; Liu, F.; Liu, Q. Numerical Study on Heat-Transfer Characteristics of Convection Melting in Metal Foam under Sinusoidal Temperature Boundary Conditions. *Entropy* **2022**, *24*, 1779. [CrossRef] [PubMed]
5. Wu, X.; Zhou, S. Thermal Lattice Boltzmann Flux Solver for Natural Convection of Nanofluid in a Square Enclosure. *Entropy* **2022**, *24*, 1448. [CrossRef]
6. Guo, W.; Hou, G. Three-Dimensional Simulations of Anisotropic Slip Microflows Using the Discrete Unified Gas Kinetic Scheme. *Entropy* **2022**, *24*, 907. [CrossRef] [PubMed]
7. Liu, J.; Zhang, T.; Sun, S. Study of the imbibition phenomenon in porous media by the smoothed particle hydrodynamic (SPH) method. *Entropy* **2022**, *24*, 1212. [CrossRef]
8. Zhou, D.; Du, B.; Guo, T.; Li, Q.; Lu, Z. Application of a Gas-Kinetic BGK Scheme in Thermal Protection System Analysis for Hypersonic Vehicles. *Entropy* **2022**, *24*, 1325. [CrossRef]
9. Jiang, D.; Wang, P.; Li, J.; Mao, M. Nonlinear Modeling Study of Aerodynamic Characteristics of an X38-like Vehicle at Strong Viscous Interaction Regions. *Entropy* **2022**, *24*, 836. [CrossRef] [PubMed]
10. Morozov, A.; Titarev, V. Planar Gas Expansion under Intensive Nanosecond Laser Evaporation into Vacuum as Applied to Time-of-Flight Analysis. *Entropy* **2022**, *24*, 1738. [CrossRef] [PubMed]
11. Megías, A.; Santos, A. Kinetic theory and memory effects of homogeneous inelastic granular gases under nonlinear drag. *Entropy* **2022**, *24*, 1436. [CrossRef]
12. Qi, T.; Lin, J.; Ouyang, Z. Hydrodynamic behavior of self-propelled particles in a simple shear flow. *Entropy* **2022**, *24*, 854. [CrossRef] [PubMed]

Disclaimer/Publisher's Note: The statements, opinions and data contained in all publications are solely those of the individual author(s) and contributor(s) and not of MDPI and/or the editor(s). MDPI and/or the editor(s) disclaim responsibility for any injury to people or property resulting from any ideas, methods, instructions or products referred to in the content.

Article

Numerical Study on Heat-Transfer Characteristics of Convection Melting in Metal Foam under Sinusoidal Temperature Boundary Conditions

Xiang-Bo Feng [1,2], Shi-Fan Huo [1], Xiao-Tao Xu [3,*], Fei Liu [4,*] and Qing Liu [5]

[1] Xi'an Key Laboratory of Advanced Photo-Electronics Materials and Energy Conversion Device, School of Science, Xijing University, Xi'an 710123, China
[2] Shanxi Key Laboratory of Safety and Durability of Concrete Structures, College of Civil Engineering, Xijing University, Xi'an 710123, China
[3] Xi'an Thermal Power Research Institute Co., Ltd., Xi'an 710054, China
[4] Department of Mechanics and Aerospace Engineering, Southern University of Science and Technology, Shenzhen 518055, China
[5] School of Resource Engineering, Xi'an University of Architecture and Technology, Xi'an 710055, China
* Correspondence: xuxiaotao@tpri.com.cn (X.-T.X.); liuf@sustech.edu.cn (F.L.)

Abstract: Convection melting in metal foam under sinusoidal temperature boundary conditions is numerically studied in the present study. A multiple-relaxation-time lattice Boltzmann method, in conjunction with the enthalpy approach, is constructed to model the melting process without iteration steps. The effects of the porosity, phase deviation, and periodicity parameter on the heat-transfer characteristics are investigated. For the cases considered in this work, it is found that the effects of the phase deviation and periodicity parameter on the melting rate are weak, but the melting front can be significantly affected by the sinusoidal temperature boundary conditions.

Keywords: convection melting; sinusoidal side wall temperature; lattice Boltzmann method; metal foams; latent heat storage

1. Introduction

Latent heat storage (LHS), which uses solid–liquid phase-change materials (PCMs) as thermal-energy storage media, has been widely employed in industrial waste heat utilization to build energy saving systems, solar thermal utilization systems, etc. LHS with solid–liquid PCMs has become an important research topic during the past 30 years, and numerous reviews about this topic have been published. Zalba et al. [1] carried out a comprehensive review of the materials, the heat transfer process, and applications of LHS using solid–liquid PCMs. Farid et al. [2] reviewed the efforts in developing new PCMs for LHS applications. In a recent review by Nazir et al. [3], the applications of various PCMs, based on their thermophysical properties, were summarized, and the strategies for improving the characteristics of thermal-energy storage through nanomaterial additives, as well as encapsulation, were discussed in detail.

LHS with the use of solid–liquid PCMs has gradually become the preferred thermal-energy storage pattern, as solid–liquid PCMs have some outstanding features, such as the energy storage density being very high and the temperature fluctuation being small. However, the thermal conductivities for most of the solid–liquid PCMs are low (0.1~0.6 W/(m·K) [4]). This serious shortcoming strongly slows down the charging and discharging rates of thermal energy. To improve the LHS system's thermal performance, three main kinds of enhancement approaches have been employed: improving the uniformity of heat-transfer process, enhancing the thermal conductivity of PCMs, and extending the heat-transfer surface [5]. Among these enhancement approaches, enhancing the thermal conductivity performance of PCMs is an efficient way to improve the LHS system's thermal performance. High-porosity metal foams attract great attention for LHS applications because of their attractive advantages, such as high thermal conductivity and large specific surface areas.

In recent decades, numerous numerical studies on the characteristics of solid–liquid phase change in metal foams (porous media) have been performed. Weaver and Viskanta [6] numerically and experimentally investigated the melting process of ice in a cylindrical capsule filled with glass or aluminum beads. Beckermann and Viskanta [7] studied the melting and solidification processes of gallium in a square cavity filled with glass beads. They found that the shape of the interface can be considerably influenced by the convection effect in the liquid region. Tong et al. [8] performed a numerical study on the melting and freezing of a water–aluminum matrix system in a cylindrical annulus. They found that the heat-transfer rates of enhanced cases were increased by one order of magnitude, compared with that of the base case without an aluminum matrix.

In the numerical studies [6–8], the local thermal equilibrium (LTE) assumption is adopted, as the thermal conductivity of the solid matrix is low. However, for high-thermal-conductivity metal foams, such as copper or aluminum foam, the local thermal non-equilibrium (LTNE) effect (temperature difference) between a PCM and a metal matrix during the melting process should be considered. Harris et al. [9] developed an approximate theoretical enthalpy model (LTNE model) in which a temperature difference between the PCM and the walls of the pores was maintained. Based on the approximate model, the conditions for the occurrence of LTE were analyzed. Mesalhy et al. [10] developed a two-temperature model to analyze the LTNE effect between the PCM and the metal matrix, and a parametric study was performed to investigate the effects of thermal conductivity and porosity. Krishnan et al. [11] also proposed an LTNE model for simulating convection melting in metal foams, and the merits of using metal foam for enhancing thermal storage systems' effective thermal conductivity were discussed. An LTNE model regarding the volume change of the PCM was proposed by Yang and Garimella [12], and the effects of volume expansion/shrinkage were analyzed. Li et al. [13] investigated the melting of paraffin embedded in open-cell copper foam, and the effects of the morphology parameters of the metal foam on the temperature distributions were investigated. Zhao et al. [14] performed a numerical investigation on melting and solidification in copper foam, and the kinetic undercooling of solidification was analyzed. Wang et al. [15] studied the pore-scale melting in metal foams; different metal foams combined with paraffin and other PCMs were investigated to obtain the composite materials' effective thermal conductivity.

The above literature review indicates that many numerical studies have been carried out on the heat-transfer performance of PCMs in metal foams based on an LTNE model. Moreover, our literature survey with respect to improving an LHS system's thermal performance using metal foams found that nearly all of the numerical studies were conducted under constant wall heat flux or constant wall temperatures (uniform thermal boundary conditions). A fundamental understanding of the heat-transfer characteristics of melting in metal foams under non-uniform thermal boundary conditions is still lacking, and more studies are required. For natural convection in enclosures, previous studies indicated that non-uniform thermal boundary conditions (e.g., sinusoidal temperature boundary conditions) can significantly affect the flow structures and heat-transfer characteristics [16–18]. As expected, new heat-transfer characteristics can be created in the solid–liquid phase change of PCMs under sinusoidal temperature boundary conditions. Hence, this work aimed to study the heat-transfer characteristics of convection melting in metal foam under sinusoidal temperature boundary conditions. A multiple-relaxation-time (MRT) lattice Boltzmann (LB) method, in conjunction with the enthalpy approach, was constructed to model the melting process without iteration steps. This work will help in providing a valuable reference for improving the thermal performance of LHS systems.

2. Model Description

2.1. Physical Model

The problem considered in this work is shown in Figure 1. Initially, the temperatures of the PCM and metal foam are equal to T_i ($T_i < T_{\text{melt}}$). At $t = 0$, a sinusoidally varying temperature $T = T_h + \Delta T \sin(2k\pi y/L + \varphi)$ ($T_h > T_{\text{melt}}$) is imposed on the left wall, and then the PCM begins to melt. Note that the average temperature of the left wall is T_h, $\Delta T = T_h - T_{\text{melt}}$ is the characteristics temperature, k is the periodicity parameter, and φ is the phase deviation (phase of the sinusoidal profile).

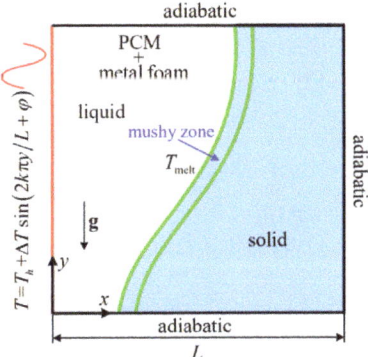

Figure 1. Physical model.

2.2. Governing Equations

For convection melting of solid–liquid PCMs embedded in metal foams, the following assumptions are made: (1) metal foam (m) is homogeneous and the pore diameter is uniform; (2) the flow (liquid region) is incompressible and laminar; (3) the volume change is neglected, i.e., $\rho_f = \rho_l = \rho_s$ (the subscript f denotes PCM, l denotes liquid PCM and s denotes solid PCM). Based on the LTNE model, the governing equations are provided by [11,19–21]

$$\nabla \cdot \mathbf{u} = 0 \tag{1}$$

$$\frac{\partial \mathbf{u}}{\partial t} + (\mathbf{u} \cdot \nabla)\left(\frac{\mathbf{u}}{\phi}\right) = -\frac{1}{\rho_f} \nabla(\phi p) + v_e \nabla^2 \mathbf{u} + \mathbf{F} \tag{2}$$

$$\frac{\partial}{\partial t}\left(\phi \rho_f c_{pf} T_f\right) + \nabla \cdot \left(\rho_l c_{pl} T_f \mathbf{u}\right) = \nabla \cdot \left(k_{ef} \nabla T_f\right) + h_{mf} a_{mf}\left(T_m - T_f\right) - \frac{\partial}{\partial t}(\phi \rho_l L_a f_l) \tag{3}$$

$$\frac{\partial}{\partial t}\left[(1-\phi)\rho_m c_{pm} T_m\right] = \nabla \cdot (k_{em} \nabla T_m) + h_{mf} a_{mf}\left(T_f - T_m\right) \tag{4}$$

where $\mathbf{u}$ and p are the velocity and pressure in the liquid region, respectively; ρ_f is the density; T is the temperature; ϕ is the metal foam's porosity; c_p is the specific heat; v_e is the effective kinematic viscosity; k_e is the effective thermal conductivity; h_{mf} is the interfacial heat-transfer coefficient; a_{mf} is the specific surface area of metal matrix; f_l is the liquid fraction; and L_a is the PCM's latent heat.

The total body force $\mathbf{F}$ is determined by [22,23]

$$\mathbf{F} = -\frac{\phi v}{K}\mathbf{u} - \frac{\phi F_\phi}{\sqrt{K}}|\mathbf{u}|\mathbf{u} + \phi\,\mathbf{G} \tag{5}$$

where v is the liquid PCM's kinematic viscosity and K and F_ϕ are the metal foam's permeability and inertia coefficient, respectively. $\mathbf{G}$ is the buoyancy force approximated by

$$\mathbf{G} = -\mathbf{g}\beta\left(T_f - T_0\right)f_l \tag{6}$$

where **g** is the gravitational acceleration, T_0 is the reference temperature, and β is the thermal-expansion coefficient.

For metal foams (e.g., aluminum or copper foam), the correlations of F_ϕ and K can be found in [24,25]. The effective thermal conductivities k_{ef} and k_{em} can be determined by analytical models [25,26]. In previous studies, the correlation for convection heat transfer through a bank of staggered cylinders proposed by Churchill and Chu [27] was widely employed to determine h_{mf}. The empirical formula for a_{mf} can be found in [25]. To determine the temperature-dependent (thermodynamic or dynamic mechanical) properties of complex materials, such as the cross-linking of polymers, the methods proposed by Likozar and Krajnc [28–30] can be employed.

3. Numerical Method

As a mesoscopic approach evolved from the lattice-gas automata [31], the LB method [32–34] has become an efficient numerical methodology for modeling solid–liquid phase-change problems [35,36]. In this section, the MRT-LB method, in conjunction with the enthalpy approach, is introduced to model the melting process without iteration steps.

3.1. MRT-LB Equation for Flow Field

For the 2D problem considered in this work, the D2Q9 lattice is employed [34]

$$\mathbf{e}_i = \begin{cases} (0,0), & i=0 \\ (\cos[(i-1)\pi/2], \sin[(i-1)\pi/2])c, & i=1 \sim 4 \\ (\cos[(2i-9)\pi/4], \sin[(2i-9)\pi/4])\sqrt{2}c, & i=5 \sim 8 \end{cases} \quad (7)$$

where $c = \delta_x/\delta_t$ is the lattice speed (δ_x is the lattice step and δ_t is the time step). In this work, c is set to 1 ($\delta_x = \delta_t$).

The MRT-LB equation for the flow field can be written as [37–39]

$$f_i(\mathbf{x}+\mathbf{e}_i\delta_t,\ t+\delta_t) = f_i(\mathbf{x},\ t) - \overline{\Lambda}_{ij}\left(f_j - f_j^{eq}\right)\Big|_{(x,\ t)} + \delta_t\left(\widetilde{S}_i - 0.5\overline{\Lambda}_{ij}\widetilde{S}_j\right) \quad (8)$$

where $f_i(\mathbf{x},\ t)$ is the density distribution function, $f_i^{eq}(\mathbf{x},\ t)$ is the equilibrium value of $f_i(\mathbf{x},\ t)$, $\overline{\Lambda} = [\overline{\Lambda}_{ij}]$ is the collision matrix, and $\widetilde{S}_i$ is the forcing term.

The MRT-LB Equation (8) can be divided into two parts: a collision part and a streaming part. By multiplying a transformation matrix **M**, the collision part can be carried out in moment space as

$$\mathbf{m}^*(\mathbf{x},\ t) = \mathbf{m}(\mathbf{x},\ t) - \Lambda(\mathbf{m}-\mathbf{m}^{eq})\Big|_{(x,\ t)} + \delta_t\left(\mathbf{I} - \frac{\Lambda}{2}\right)\mathbf{S} \quad (9)$$

The streaming part is performed in velocity space as

$$f_i(\mathbf{x}+\mathbf{e}_i\delta_t,\ t+\delta_t) = f_i^*(\mathbf{x},\ t) \quad (10)$$

where Λ is the relaxation matrix ($\Lambda = \mathbf{M}\overline{\Lambda}\mathbf{M}^{-1} = \mathrm{diag}(1,\ 1,\ s_e,\ s_v,\ s_v,\ s_q,\ s_q,\ s_\epsilon)$), $\mathbf{m} = |m\rangle = \mathbf{Mf}$, $\mathbf{m}^{eq} = |m^{eq}\rangle = \mathbf{Mf}^{eq}$, $\mathbf{S} = |S\rangle = \mathbf{M}\widetilde{\mathbf{S}}$, in which $\mathbf{f} = |f\rangle$, $\mathbf{f}^{eq} = |f^{eq}\rangle$, and $\widetilde{\mathbf{S}} = |\widetilde{S}\rangle$. Here, Dirac notation $|\cdot\rangle$ denotes a nine-dimensional column vector, e.g., $|m\rangle = (m_0, m_1, \ldots, m_8)^T$. f_i^* is determined by $\mathbf{f}^* = |f^*\rangle = \mathbf{M}^{-1}\mathbf{m}^*$.

M is a non-orthogonal transformation matrix [39]

$$\mathbf{M} = \begin{bmatrix} 1 & 1 & 1 & 1 & 1 & 1 & 1 & 1 & 1 \\ 0 & 1 & 0 & -1 & 0 & 1 & -1 & -1 & 1 \\ 0 & 0 & 1 & 0 & -1 & 1 & 1 & -1 & -1 \\ 0 & 1 & 1 & 1 & 1 & 2 & 2 & 2 & 2 \\ 0 & 1 & -1 & 1 & -1 & 0 & 0 & 0 & 0 \\ 0 & 0 & 0 & 0 & 0 & 1 & -1 & 1 & -1 \\ 0 & 0 & 0 & 0 & 0 & 1 & 1 & -1 & -1 \\ 0 & 0 & 0 & 0 & 0 & 1 & -1 & -1 & 1 \\ 0 & 0 & 0 & 0 & 0 & 1 & 1 & 1 & 1 \end{bmatrix} \quad (11)$$

The equilibrium moments $\left\{m_i^{eq}\right\}$ are determined by

$$\begin{array}{l} m_0^{eq} = \rho_f,\ m_1^{eq} = \rho_f u_x,\ m_2^{eq} = \rho_f u_y,\ m_3^{eq} = \frac{2}{3}\rho_f + \frac{\rho_f\left(u_x^2+u_y^2\right)}{\phi},\ m_4^{eq} = \frac{\rho_f\left(u_x^2-u_y^2\right)}{\phi} \\ m_5^{eq} = \rho_f u_x u_y,\ m_6^{eq} = \frac{1}{3}\rho_f u_y,\ m_7^{eq} = \frac{1}{3}\rho_f u_x,\ m_8^{eq} = \frac{1}{9}\rho_f + \frac{1}{3}\frac{\rho_f\left(u_x^2+u_y^2\right)}{\phi} \end{array} \quad (12)$$

The source terms $\{S_i\}$ are determined by

$$\begin{array}{l} S_0 = 0,\ S_1 = \rho_f F_x,\ S_2 = \rho_f F_y,\ S_3 = \frac{2\rho_f\left(u_x F_x + u_y F_y\right)}{\phi},\ S_4 = \frac{2\rho_f\left(u_x F_x - u_y F_y\right)}{\phi} \\ S_5 = \frac{\rho_f\left(u_x F_y + u_y F_x\right)}{\phi},\ S_6 = \frac{1}{3}\rho_f F_y,\ S_7 = \frac{1}{3}\rho_f F_x,\ S_8 = \frac{2}{3}\frac{\rho_f\left(u_x F_x + u_y F_y\right)}{\phi} \end{array} \quad (13)$$

To implement the non-slip velocity boundary condition on the phase interface accurately, the volumetric LB scheme [40] is employed; then, a new density distribution function is defined:

$$f_i^+ = f_l f_i + (1 - f_l) f_i^{eq}\left(\rho_f, \mathbf{u}_s\right) \quad (14)$$

In Equation (14), the superscript "+" denotes that the solid-phase effect has been considered, and $\mathbf{u}_s = 0$ (the solid phase is static). Accordingly, ρ_f and **u** are defined as

$$\rho_f = \sum_{i=0}^{8} f_i \quad (15)$$

$$\rho_f \mathbf{u} = \sum_{i=0}^{8} \mathbf{e}_i f_i^+ + \frac{\delta_t}{2} \rho_f \mathbf{F} \quad (16)$$

p is defined as $p = \rho c_s^2/\phi$ ($c_s = 1/\sqrt{3}$ is the sound speed). Explicitly, **u** can be calculated via [41]

$$\mathbf{u} = \frac{\mathbf{v}}{l_0 + \sqrt{l_0^2 + l_1|\mathbf{v}|}} \quad (17)$$

where

$$\rho_f \mathbf{v} = \sum_{i=0}^{8} \mathbf{e}_i f_i^+ + \frac{\delta_t}{2} \rho_f \phi \mathbf{G} \quad (18)$$

$$l_0 = \frac{1}{2}\left(1 + \phi\frac{\delta_t}{2}\frac{v}{K}\right),\ l_1 = \phi\frac{\delta_t}{2}\frac{F_\phi}{\sqrt{K}} \quad (19)$$

The kinetic viscosity $v = c_s^2\left(s_v^{-1} - 0.5\right)\delta_t$ and the bulk viscosity $\xi = c_s^2\left(s_e^{-1} - 0.5\right)\delta_t$.

3.2. MRT-LB Equation for the Temperature Field of the PCM

Equation (3) can be rewritten as

$$\frac{\partial H_f}{\partial t} + \nabla \cdot \left(\frac{c_{pl} T_f \mathbf{u}}{\phi}\right) = \nabla \cdot \left(\frac{k_{ef}}{\phi \rho_l} \nabla T_f\right) + \frac{h_{mf} a_{mf} (T_m - T_f)}{\phi \rho_l} \quad (20)$$

where $H_f = \sigma c_{pl} T_f + L_a f_l$ is the effective enthalpy and $\sigma = \frac{\rho_f c_{pf}}{\rho_l c_{pl}} = \frac{f_l \rho_l c_{pl} + (1-f_l) \rho_s c_{ps}}{\rho_l c_{pl}}$ is the heat-capacity ratio. When $f_l = 1$ (liquid region), $H_f = c_{pl} T_f + L_a$ and $\sigma_l = 1$; when $f_l = 0$ (solid region), $H_f = \sigma_s c_{pl} T_f$ and $\sigma_s = \frac{\rho_s c_{ps}}{\rho_l c_{pl}}$.

For the temperature field of the PCM, governed by Equation (20), the D2Q5 lattice is adopted and $\{\mathbf{e}_i | i = 0, \ldots, 4\}$ are provided in Equation (7). The enthalpy-based MRT-LB equation is determined by

$$\mathbf{g}(\mathbf{x} + \mathbf{e}\delta_t, t + \delta_t) = \mathbf{g}(\mathbf{x}, t) - \mathbf{N}^{-1}\mathbf{\Theta}\left(\mathbf{n}_g - \mathbf{n}_g^{eq}\right)\Big|_{(\mathbf{x}, t)} + \delta_t \mathbf{N}^{-1} \mathbf{S}_{\text{PCM}} \quad (21)$$

where g_i is the enthalpy distribution function and $\mathbf{\Theta} = \text{diag}(1, \zeta_\alpha, \zeta_\alpha, \zeta_e, \zeta_e)$ is the relaxation matrix.

Through the transformation matrix $\mathbf{N}$, the collision part of the MRT-LB Equation (21) is carried out in moment space as

$$\mathbf{n}_g^*(\mathbf{x}, t) = \mathbf{n}_g(\mathbf{x}, t) - \mathbf{\Theta}\left(\mathbf{n}_g - \mathbf{n}_g^{eq}\right)\Big|_{(\mathbf{x}, t)} + \delta_t \mathbf{S}_{\text{PCM}} \quad (22)$$

The streaming part is performed in velocity space as

$$g_i(\mathbf{x} + \mathbf{e}_i \delta_t, t + \delta_t) = g_i^*(\mathbf{x}, t) \quad (23)$$

where $\mathbf{n}_g = \mathbf{N}\mathbf{g}$ is the moment, and $\mathbf{n}_g^{eq} = \mathbf{N}\mathbf{g}^{eq}$ is the corresponding equilibrium moment. Here, g_i^{eq} is the equilibrium value of g_i, and $\mathbf{g}^* = \mathbf{N}^{-1}\mathbf{n}_g^*$.

$\mathbf{N}$ is a non-orthogonal transformation matrix [39]

$$\mathbf{N} = \begin{bmatrix} 1 & 1 & 1 & 1 & 1 \\ 0 & 1 & 0 & -1 & 0 \\ 0 & 0 & 1 & 0 & -1 \\ 0 & 1 & 1 & 1 & 1 \\ 0 & 1 & -1 & 1 & -1 \end{bmatrix} \quad (24)$$

The equilibrium moment $\mathbf{n}_g^{eq}$ is

$$\mathbf{n}_g^{eq} = \left(H_f, \frac{c_{pl} T_f u_x}{\phi}, \frac{c_{pl} T_f u_y}{\phi}, \varpi_1 c_{pl} T_f, 0\right)^T \quad (25)$$

where $\varpi_1 \in (0, 1)$. Correspondingly, g_i^{eq} is given by

$$g_i^{eq} = \begin{cases} H_f - \varpi_1 c_{pl} T_f, & i = 0 \\ \frac{1}{4} \varpi_1 c_{pl} T_f \left(1 + \frac{\mathbf{e}_i \cdot \mathbf{u}}{c_{sf}^2 \phi}\right), & i = 1 \sim 4 \end{cases} \quad (26)$$

where $c_{sf} = \sqrt{\varpi_1/2}$ is the sound speed.

The source term $\mathbf{S}_{\text{PCM}}$ is chosen as

$$\mathbf{S}_{\text{PCM}} = S_{\text{PCM}}(1, 0, 0, 0, 0)^T \quad (27)$$

where $S_{\text{PCM}} = Sr_f + \frac{1}{2}\delta_t \partial_t Sr_f$ and $Sr_f = h_{mf} a_{mf}(T_m - T_f)/(\phi \rho_l)$.

H_f is defined as

$$H_f = \sum_{i=0}^{4} g_i \qquad (28)$$

T_f can be determined via the following equation:

$$T_f = \begin{cases} H_f/(\sigma_s c_{pl}), & H_f \leq H_{fs} \\ T_{fs} + \frac{H_f - H_{fs}}{H_{fl} - H_{fs}}(T_{fl} - T_{fs}), & H_{fs} < H_f < H_{fl} \\ T_{fl} + (H_f - H_{fl})/(\sigma_l c_{pl}), & H_f \geq H_{fl} \end{cases} \qquad (29)$$

where T_{fs} is solidus temperature and T_{fl} is liquidus temperature ($T_{fs} \leq T_{fl}$); H_{fs} (H_{fl}) is the effective enthalpy corresponding to T_{fs} (T_{fl}).

f_l is determined by

$$f_l = \begin{cases} 0, & H_f \leq H_{fs} \\ \frac{H_f - H_{fs}}{H_{fl} - H_{fs}}, & H_{fs} < H_f < H_{fl} \\ 1, & H_f \geq H_{fl} \end{cases} \qquad (30)$$

α_{ef} is defined as

$$\alpha_{ef} = \frac{k_{ef}}{\phi \rho_l c_{pl}} = c_{sf}^2 \left(\zeta_\alpha^{-1} - \frac{1}{2} \right) \delta_t \qquad (31)$$

3.3. MRT-LB Equation for the Temperature Field of Metal Foam

Equation (4) can be rewritten as

$$\frac{\partial (c_{pm} T_m)}{\partial t} = \nabla \cdot \left(\frac{k_{em}}{(1-\phi)\rho_m} \nabla T_m \right) + \frac{h_{mf} a_{mf}(T_f - T_m)}{(1-\phi)\rho_m} \qquad (32)$$

For the temperature field of metal foam, governed by Equation (32), the MRT-LB equation based on D2Q5 lattice is as follows:

$$\mathbf{h}(\mathbf{x} + \mathbf{e}\delta_t, t + \delta_t) = \mathbf{h}(\mathbf{x}, t) - \mathbf{N}^{-1}\mathbf{Q}\left(\mathbf{n}_h - \mathbf{n}_h^{eq}\right)\Big|_{(\mathbf{x}, t)} + \delta_t \mathbf{N}^{-1} \mathbf{S}_{\text{metal}} \qquad (33)$$

where $h_i(\mathbf{x}, t)$ is the temperature distribution function, $\mathbf{Q} = \text{diag}(1, \eta_\alpha, \eta_\alpha, \eta_e, \eta_e)$ is the relaxation matrix, and $\mathbf{N}$ is given by Equation (24).

The collision part of the MRT-LB Equation (33) is performed in moment space as

$$\mathbf{n}_h^*(\mathbf{x}, t) = \mathbf{n}_h(\mathbf{x}, t) - \mathbf{Q}\left(\mathbf{n}_h - \mathbf{n}_h^{eq}\right)\Big|_{(\mathbf{x}, t)} + \delta_t \mathbf{S}_{\text{metal}} \qquad (34)$$

where $\mathbf{n}_h = \mathbf{N}\mathbf{h}$ is the moment, and $\mathbf{n}_h^{eq} = \mathbf{N}\mathbf{h}^{eq}$ is the corresponding equilibrium moment. Here, h_i^{eq} is the equilibrium value of h_i. The streaming step is carried out in the velocity space as follows:

$$h_i(\mathbf{x} + \mathbf{e}_i \delta_t, t + \delta_t) = h_i^*(\mathbf{x}, t) \qquad (35)$$

where $\mathbf{h}^* = \mathbf{N}^{-1}\mathbf{n}_h^*$. The equilibrium moment $\mathbf{n}_h^{eq}$ is defined as

$$\mathbf{n}_h^{eq} = \left(c_{pm} T_m, 0, 0, \varpi_2 c_{pm} T_m, 0 \right)^T \qquad (36)$$

where $\varpi_2 \in (0, 1)$. h_i^{eq} is determined by

$$h_i^{eq} = \begin{cases} (1 - \varpi_2) c_{pm} T_m, & i = 0 \\ \frac{1}{4} \varpi_2 c_{pm} T_m, & i = 1 \sim 4 \end{cases} \qquad (37)$$

The source term $\mathbf{S}_{metal}$ is chosen as

$$\mathbf{S}_{metal} = S_{metal}(1, 0, 0, 0, 0)^T \tag{38}$$

where $S_{metal} = Sr_m + \frac{1}{2}\delta_t \partial_t Sr_m$ and $Sr_m = h_{mf} a_{mf}\left(T_f - T_m\right)/[(1-\phi)\rho_m]$. T_m is defined by

$$T_m = \frac{1}{c_{pm}} \sum_{i=0}^{4} h_i \tag{39}$$

α_{em} is given by

$$\alpha_{em} = \frac{k_{em}}{(1-\phi)\rho_m c_{pm}} = c_{sm}^2 \left(\eta_\alpha^{-1} - \frac{1}{2}\right)\delta_t \tag{40}$$

where $c_{sm} = \sqrt{\varpi_2/2}$ is the sound speed.

4. Numerical Results

In this section, numerical simulations are performed to investigate the effects of the porosity, the phase deviation, and the periodicity parameter on the heat-transfer performance of the convection melting of solid–liquid PCM embedded in metal foam under sinusoidal temperature boundary conditions. The characteristic parameters include $Pr = v_{fl}/\alpha_{fl}$ (Prandtl number), $Ra = g\beta \Delta T L^3 / \left(v_{fl}\alpha_{fl}\right)$ (Rayleigh number), $Da = K/L^2$ (Darcy number), $J = v_e/v_{fl}$ (viscosity ratio), $\lambda = k_m/k_{fl}$ (thermal conductivity ratio), $\Gamma = \alpha_m/\alpha_{fl}$ (thermal diffusivity ratio), $\hat{\sigma} = \rho_m c_{pm}/\left(\rho_l c_{pl}\right)$ (metal foam to liquid PCM heat capacity ratio), $H_v = h_{mf} a_{mf} d_p^2/k_f$ (volumetric heat transfer coefficient), $Fo = t\alpha_{fl}/L^2$ (Fourier number), and $St = c_{pl}\Delta T/L_a$ (Stefan number), where $\alpha_f = k_f/(\rho c_p)_f$ is thermal diffusivity of PCM, $\alpha_m = k_m/(\rho c_p)_m$ is thermal diffusivity of metal foam, and d_p is mean pore diameter.

In simulations, the required parameters are chosen as follows: $Pr = 50$, $F_\phi = 0.068$, $Da = 10^{-4}$, $St = 1$, $\delta_x = \delta_y = \delta_t = 1$ ($c = 1$), $c_{pl} = c_{ps} = 1$, $J = \hat{\sigma} = 1$, $H_v = 5.9$, $\lambda = \Gamma = 10^3$, $d_p/L = 0.0135$, $k_f = 0.0005$ and $\varpi_1 = \varpi_2 = 1/2$. The relaxation rate ζ_e is determined by $\zeta_e = 2 - \zeta_\alpha$ to reduce the unphysical numerical diffusion [21,42]. The non-equilibrium extrapolation scheme [43] is adopted to realize the velocity and thermal boundary conditions. Numerical simulations are performed based on a grid size of $N_x \times N_y = 150 \times 150$. First, comparisons between the results predicted by the finite-volume method (FVM) [11] and the present method are made to validate the reliability of the present method. The predicted results are shown in Figures 2 and 3, where the melting front (solid–liquid interface) and temperature profiles ($\theta = (T - T_{melt})/\Delta T$) at different times for $Ra = 10^6$ and 10^8 with $\phi = 0.8$ are presented. In the figures, it can be seen that the present results match well with the results in [11]. In what follows, the effects of the porosity, the phase deviation, and the periodicity parameter on the heat-transfer performance are investigated.

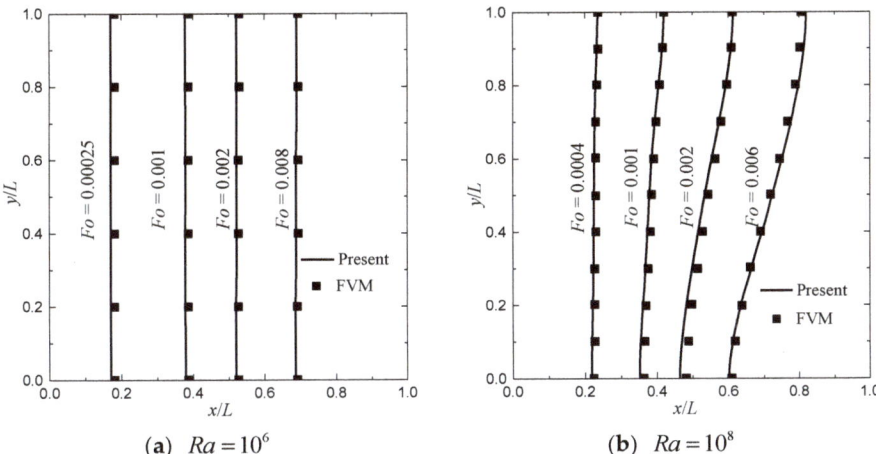

Figure 2. The melting front ($f_l = 0.5$) at different Fo.

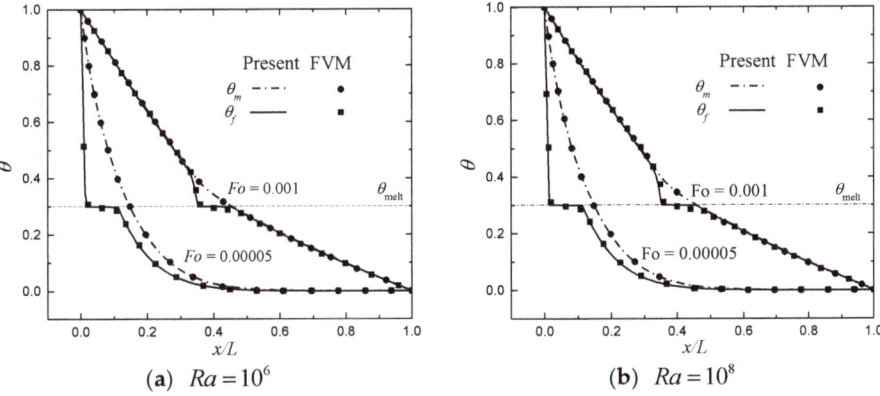

Figure 3. Temperature profiles ($y/L = 0.5$) at different Fo.

4.1. Effects of the Porosity and Phase Deviation

In this subsection, the effects of the porosity and the phase deviation are investigated. In Figure 4, the total liquid fractions for different ϕ with $Ra = 10^6$, $\varphi = \pi/4$ and $k = 0$ are shown. As can be seen in Figure 4, the melting rate decreases as ϕ increases. When $\phi = 0.8$, the completely melting time $Fo = 0.00485$. As ϕ increases to 0.9 and 0.95, the completely melting time Fo augments to 0.0103 and 0.0209, respectively. When ϕ increases from 0.8 to 0.9, the completely melting time increases by 112.37%; when ϕ increases from 0.9 to 0.95, the completely melting time increases by 102.91%. The influence of the porosity on the melting rate is induced by two factors: one is that the mass of the metal foam decreases as the porosity increases, which reduces the effective thermal conductivity, and consequently, the performance of heat transfer is deteriorated; the other is that the mass of the PCM increases as the porosity increases, which results in melting-time augmentation.

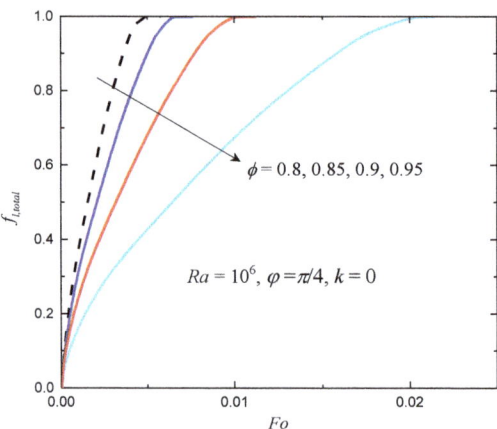

Figure 4. The total liquid fractions for different ϕ with $Ra = 10^6$, $\varphi = \pi/4$ and $k = 0$.

In Figure 5, the total liquid fractions for $\phi = 0.8$ and 0.95 under non-uniform ($T = T_h + \Delta T \sin(2\pi y/L + \pi/4)$ at $t = 0$) and uniform ($T = T_h$ at $t = 0$) thermal boundary conditions are presented. One can observe that the melting rate of the uniform case is only a little faster than that of the non-uniform case with the given parameters, as the characteristics temperatures are equal for the cases considered. In Figure 6, the total liquid fractions for different φ with $Ra = 10^6$ and $k = 0$ under non-uniform thermal boundary conditions are shown. It can be observed that the melting rate increases as φ increases from 0 to $\pi/2$. As shown in Figures 5 and 6, it seems that the effects of the phase deviation on the total liquid fraction are not very strong. This is because the average temperature of the left wall (with sinusoidally varying temperature) equals a constant.

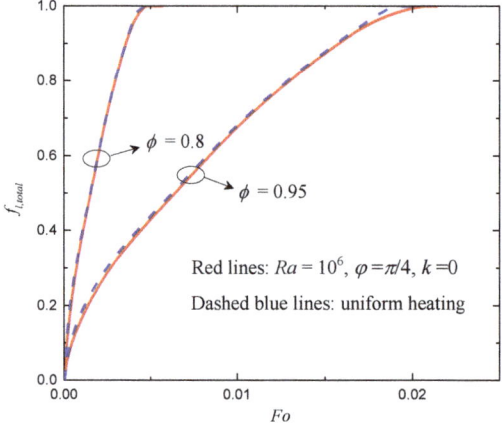

Figure 5. The total liquid fractions for $\phi = 0.8$ and 0.95 under non-uniform and uniform thermal boundary conditions.

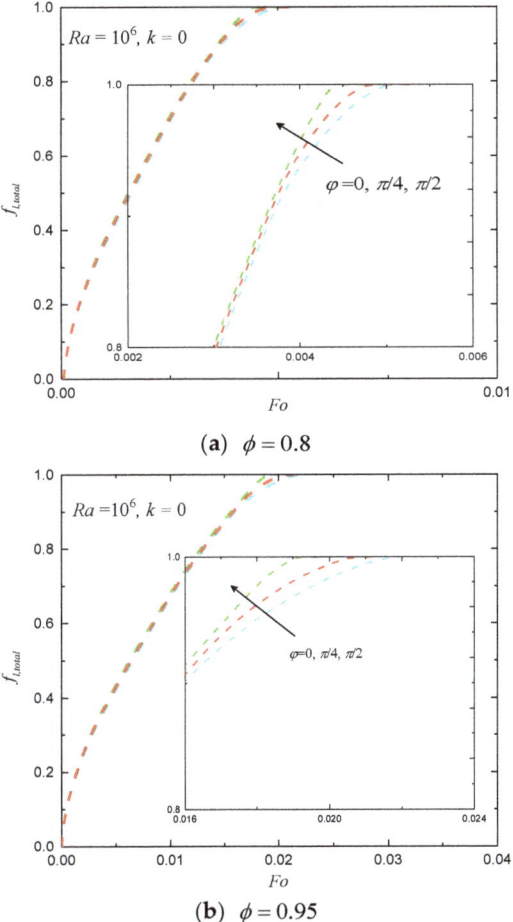

Figure 6. The total liquid fractions for different values of φ under non-uniform thermal boundary conditions.

In Figures 7 and 8, the liquid-fraction fields for different values of φ with $\phi = 0.8$ and 0.95 under non-uniform thermal boundary conditions are shown. As mentioned above, the effects of the phase deviation on the total liquid fraction are weak. However, in Figures 7 and 8 it can be clearly observed that the melting process can be significantly affected by the phase deviation. For the cases under uniform heating (Figures 7a and 8a), the melting front is almost parallel to the vertical walls, as the conduction effect dominates the heat-transfer process. For the cases under sinusoidal temperature boundary conditions, the phase interface is in a bending shape. This is because under the non-uniform thermal boundary condition, the convection effect in the related region is much stronger than that in the rest of the region. As shown in the figures, for $0 < \varphi < \pi/2$, the convective effect near the bottom wall is stronger and the melting front moves faster near the bottom wall. Obviously, this feature is rather valuable for practical LHS applications, as it offers a possible tool for controlling the melting front.

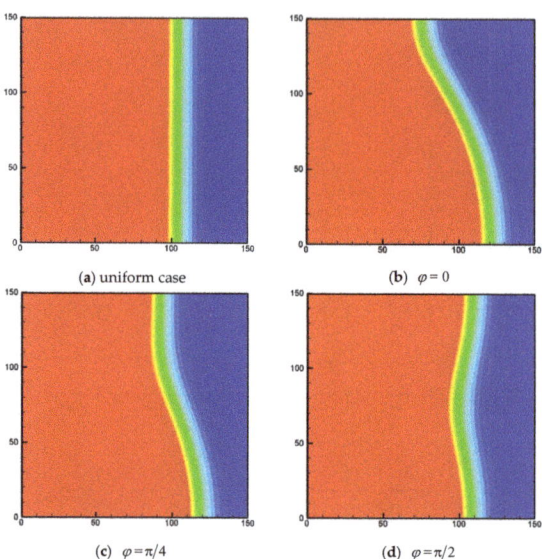

Figure 7. The liquid-fraction fields for different values of φ with $\Phi = 0.8$ under non-uniform thermal boundary conditions ($Fo = 0.0025$, $Ra = 10^6$, $k = 0$, $N_x \times N_y = 150 \times 150$).

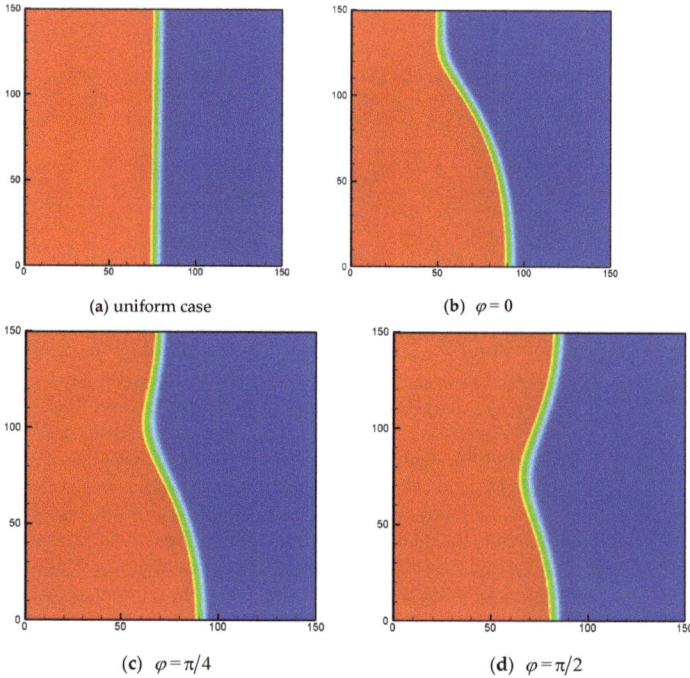

Figure 8. The liquid-fraction fields for different values of φ with $\Phi = 0.95$ under non-uniform thermal boundary conditions ($Fo = 0.0065$, $Ra = 10^6$, $k = 0$, $N_x \times N_y = 150 \times 150$).

4.2. Effects of the Periodicity Parameter

In this subsection, the effects of the periodicity parameter k on the performance of heat transfer are studied. In Figure 9, the total liquid fractions for different values of the periodicity parameter k with $Ra = 10^6$, $\phi = 0.9$ and $\varphi = 0$ are shown. As presented in the figure, the effects of the periodicity parameter on the total liquid fraction are weak. As k increases, the melting rate slightly increases, and approaches that of the uniform heating case. The liquid-fraction fields for different k at $Fo = 0.002$ under non-uniform thermal boundary conditions are presented in Figure 10, and one can observe that the melting front can also be affected by the periodicity parameter. As k increases to 4, the melting front is almost parallel to the vertical walls, which is similar to the situation of the uniform case.

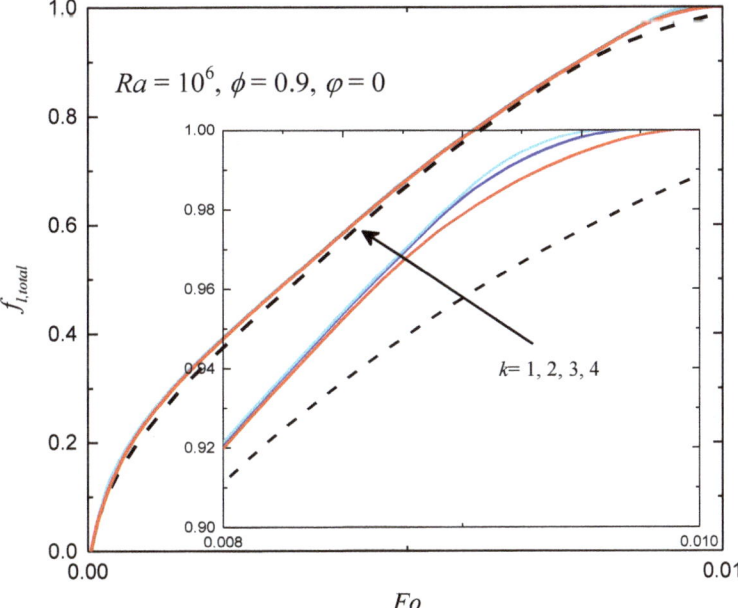

Figure 9. The total liquid fractions for different values of φ under non-uniform thermal boundary conditions ($Ra = 10^6$, $\Phi = 0.9$ and $\varphi = 0$).

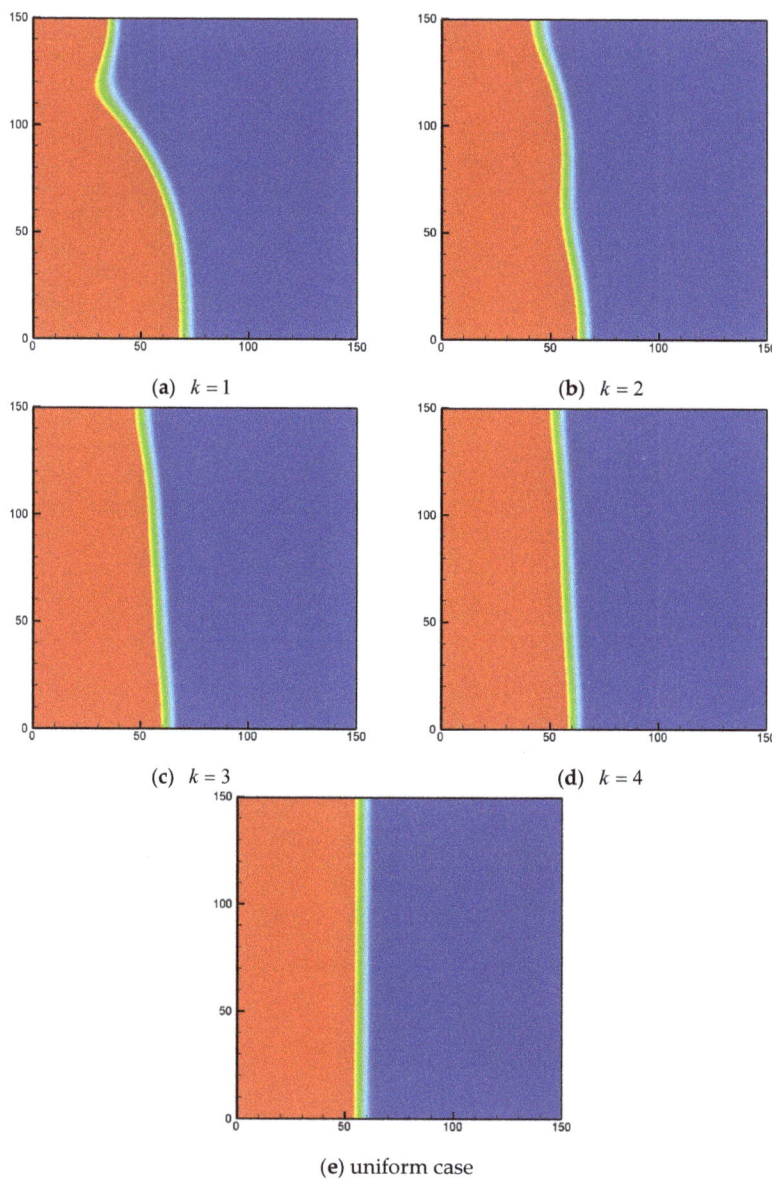

Figure 10. The liquid-fraction fields for different values of k under non-uniform thermal boundary conditions ($Fo = 0.002$, $Ra = 10^6$, $\Phi = 0.9$, $\varphi = 0$, $N_x \times N_y = 150 \times 150$).

5. Conclusions

An MRT-LB method in conjunction with the enthalpy approach was constructed for simulating convection melting in metal foam under sinusoidal temperature boundary conditions. The effects of the porosity, the phase deviation, and the periodicity parameter on the heat-transfer characteristics were investigated. The main conclusions are listed as follows:

(1) The melting rate decreases as ϕ increases. The influence of the porosity on the melting rate is induced by two factors: one is that the mass of the metal foam decreases as the porosity increases, which reduces the effective thermal conductivity; the other is that the mass of the PCM increases as the porosity increases, which results in melting time augmentation.
(2) The melting rate increases as the phase deviation increases from 0 to $\pi/2$. Although the effects of the phase deviation on the melting rate (total liquid fraction) are weak, the melting front can be significantly affected by the phase deviation.
(3) The effects of the periodicity parameter on the total liquid fraction are weak. However, the melting process can also be affected by the periodicity parameter. The above results provide a valuable reference for practical applications of LHS systems.

Author Contributions: Conceptualization, X.-B.F., X.-T.X. and F.L.; methodology, X.-B.F.; software, S.-F.H. and Q.L.; validation, X.-B.F., S.-F.H. and Q.L.; investigation, X.-B.F.; resources, X.-B.F.; data curation, S.-F.H.; writing—original draft preparation, X.-B.F. and S.-F.H.; writing—review and editing, X.-T.X. and F.L.; supervision, X.-T.X. and F.L.; funding acquisition, X.-T.X. and F.L. All authors have read and agreed to the published version of the manuscript.

Funding: This research was funded by the National Natural Science Foundation of China (No. 22008103) and the Natural Science Foundation of Shanxi Province (Nos. 2021JM-355 and 2020JQ-919).

Conflicts of Interest: The authors declare that there is no conflict of interest.

References

1. Zalba, B.; Marín, J.M.; Cabeza, L.F.; Mehling, H. Review on thermal energy storage with phase change: Materials, heat transfer analysis and applications. *Appl. Therm. Eng.* **2003**, *23*, 251–283. [CrossRef]
2. Farid, M.M.; Khudhair, A.M.; Razack, S.A.K.; Al-Hallaj, S. A review on phase change energy storage: Materials and applications. *Energy Convers. Manag.* **2004**, *45*, 1597–1615. [CrossRef]
3. Nazir, H.; Batool, M.; Osorio, F.J.B.; Isaza-Ruiz, M.; Xu, X.; Vignarooban, K.; Phelan, P.; Inamuddin; Kannan, A.M. Recent developments in phase change materials for energy storage applications: A review. *Int. J. Heat Mass Transf.* **2019**, *129*, 491–523. [CrossRef]
4. Pielichowska, K.; Pielichowski, K. Phase change materials for thermal energy storag. *Prog. Mater. Sci.* **2014**, *65*, 67–123. [CrossRef]
5. Tao, Y.B.; He, Y.L. A review of phase change material and performance enhancement method for latent heat storage syste. *Renew. Sust. Energy. Rev.* **2018**, *93*, 245–259. [CrossRef]
6. Weaver, J.A.; Viskanta, R. Melting of frozen, porous media contained in a horizontal or a vertical, cylindrical capsule. *Int. J. Heat Mass Transf.* **1986**, *29*, 1943–1951. [CrossRef]
7. Beckermann, C.; Viskanta, R. Natural convection solid/liquid phase change in porous media. *Int. J. Heat Mass Transf.* **1988**, *31*, 35–46. [CrossRef]
8. Tong, X.; Khan, J.A.; Amin, M.R. Enhancement of heat transfer by inserting a metal matrix into a phase change material. *Numer. Heat Transf. A* **1996**, *30*, 125–141. [CrossRef]
9. Harris, K.T.; Haji-Sheikh, A.; Nnanna, A.G.A. Phase-change phenomena in porous media—A non-local thermal equilibrium model. *Int. J. Heat Mass Transf.* **2001**, *44*, 1619–1625. [CrossRef]
10. Mesalhy; Lafdi, K.; Elgafy, A.; Bowman, K. Numerical study for enhancing the thermal conductivity of phase change material (PCM) storage using high thermal conductivity porous matrix. *Energy Convers. Manag.* **2005**, *46*, 847–867. [CrossRef]
11. Krishnan, S.; Murthy, J.Y.; Garimella, S.V. A two-temperature model for solid-liquid phase change in metal foams. *J. Heat Transf.* **2005**, *127*, 995–1004. [CrossRef]
12. Yang, Z.; Garimella, S.V. Melting of phase change materials with volume change in metal foams. *J. Heat Transf.* **2010**, *132*, 062301. [CrossRef]
13. Li, W.Q.; Qu, Z.G.; He, Y.L.; Tao, W.Q. Experimental and numerical studies on melting phase change heat transfer in open-cell metallic foams filled with paraffin. *Appl. Therm. Eng.* **2012**, *37*, 1–9. [CrossRef]
14. Zhao, Y.; Zhao, C.Y.; Xu, Z.G.; Xu, H.J. Modeling metal foam enhanced phase change heat transfer in thermal energy storage by using phase field method. *Int. J. Heat Mass Transf.* **2016**, *99*, 170–181. [CrossRef]
15. Wang, G.; Wei, G.S.; Xu, C.; Ju, X.; Yang, Y.; Du, X. Numerical simulation of effective thermal conductivity and pore-scale melting process of PCMs in foam metals. *Appl. Therm. Eng.* **2019**, *147*, 464–472. [CrossRef]
16. Deng, Q.H.; Chang, J.J. Natural convection in a rectangular enclosure with sinusoidal temperature distributions on both side walls. *Numer. Heat Transf. A* **2008**, *54*, 507–524. [CrossRef]
17. Sivasankaran, S.; Malleswaran, A.; Lee, J.; Sundar, P. Hydro-magnetic combined convection in a lid-driven cavity with sinusoidal boundary conditions on both sidewalls. *Int. J. Heat Mass Transf.* **2011**, *54*, 512–525. [CrossRef]

18. Wu, F.; Zhou, W.; Ma, X. Natural convection in a porous rectangular enclosure with sinusoidal temperature distributions on both side walls using a thermal non-equilibrium model. *Int. J. Heat Mass Transf.* **2015**, *85*, 756–771. [CrossRef]
19. Gao, D.; Tian, F.B.; Chen, Z.; Zhang, D. An improved lattice Boltzmann method for solid-liquid phase change in porous media under local thermal non-equilibrium conditions. *Int. J. Heat Mass Transf.* **2017**, *110*, 58–62. [CrossRef]
20. Gao, D.; Chen, Z.; Chen, L. A thermal lattice Boltzmann model for natural convection in porous media under local thermal non-equilibrium conditions. *Int. J. Heat Mass Transf.* **2014**, *70*, 979–989. [CrossRef]
21. Liu, Q.; He, Y.L.; Li, Q. Enthalpy-based multiple-relaxation-time lattice Boltzmann method for solid-liquid phase-change heat transfer in metal foams. *Phys. Rev. E* **2017**, *96*, 023303. [CrossRef] [PubMed]
22. Nithiarasu, P.; Seetharamu, K.N.; Sundararajan, T. Natural convective heat transfer in a fluid saturated variable porosity medium. *Int. J. Heat Mass Transf.* **1997**, *40*, 3955–3967. [CrossRef]
23. Hsu, C.T.; Cheng, P. Thermal dispersion in a porous medium. *Int. J. Heat Mass Transf.* **1990**, *33*, 1587–1597. [CrossRef]
24. Vafai, K. Convective flow and heat transfer in variable-porosity media. *J. Fluid Mech.* **1984**, *147*, 233–259. [CrossRef]
25. Calmidi, V.V. *Transport Phenomena in High Porosity Fibrous Metal Foams*; University of Colorado Denver: Denver, CO, USA, 1998.
26. Calmidi, V.V.; Mahajan, R.L. The effective thermal conductivity of high porosity fibrous metal foams. *J. Heat Transf.* **1999**, *121*, 466–471. [CrossRef]
27. Churchill, S.W.; Chu, H.H.S. Correlating equations for laminar and turbulent free convection from a horizontal cylinder. *Int. J. Heat Mass Transf.* **1975**, *18*, 1049–1053. [CrossRef]
28. Likozar, B.; Krajnc, M. Kinetic and heat transfer modeling of rubber blends' sulfur vulcanization with N-t-butylbenzothiazole-sulfenamide and N, N-di-t-butylbenzothiazole-sulfenamide. *J. Appl. Polym. Sci.* **2007**, *103*, 293–307. [CrossRef]
29. Likozar, B.; Krajnc, M. A study of heat transfer during molding of elastomers. *Chem. Eng. Sci.* **2008**, *63*, 3181–3192. [CrossRef]
30. Likozar, B.; Krajnc, M. Cross-linking of polymers: Kinetics and transport phenomena. *Ind. Eng. Chem. Res.* **2011**, *50*, 1558–1570. [CrossRef]
31. Frisch, U.; Hasslacher, B.; Pomeau, Y. Lattice-gas automata for the Navier-Stokes equation. *Phys. Rev. Lett.* **1986**, *56*, 1505–1508. [CrossRef]
32. McNamara, G.R.; Zanetti, G. Use of the Boltzmann equation to simulate lattice-gas automata. *Phys. Rev. Lett.* **1988**, *61*, 2332–2335. [CrossRef] [PubMed]
33. Higuera, F.J.; Succi, S.; Benzi, R. Lattice gas dynamics with enhanced collisions. *Europhys. Lett.* **1989**, *9*, 345–349. [CrossRef]
34. Qian, Y.H.; d'Humières, D.; Lallemand, P. Lattice BGK models for Navier-Stokes equation. *Europhys. Lett.* **1992**, *17*, 479–484. [CrossRef]
35. Li, Q.; Luo, K.H.; Kang, Q.J.; He, Y.L.; Chen, Q.; Liu, Q. Lattice Boltzmann methods for multiphase flow and phase-change heat transfer. *Prog. Energy Combust. Sci.* **2016**, *52*, 62–105. [CrossRef]
36. He, Y.L.; Liu, Q.; Li, Q.; Tao, W.Q. Lattice Boltzmann methods for single-phase and solid-liquid phase-change heat transfer in porous media: A review. *Int. J. Heat Mass Transf.* **2019**, *129*, 160–197. [CrossRef]
37. Lallemand, P.; Luo, L.-S. Theory of the lattice Boltzmann method: Dispersion, dissipation, isotropy, Galilean invariance, and stability. *Phys. Rev. E* **2000**, *61*, 6546–6562. [CrossRef]
38. McCracken, M.E.; Abraham, J. Multiple-relaxation-time lattice-Boltzmann model for multiphase flow. *Phys. Rev. E* **2005**, *71*, 036701. [CrossRef]
39. Liu, Q.; He, Y.L.; Li, D.; Li, Q. Non-orthogonal multiple-relaxation-time lattice Boltzmann method for incompressible thermal flows. *Int. J. Heat Mass Transf.* **2016**, *102*, 1334–1344. [CrossRef]
40. Huang, R.; Wu, H. Total enthalpy-based lattice Boltzmann method with adaptive mesh refinement for solid-liquid phase change. *J. Comput. Phys.* **2016**, *315*, 65–83. [CrossRef]
41. Guo, Z.; Zhao, T.S. Lattice Boltzmann model for incompressible flows through porous media. *Phys. Rev. E* **2002**, *66*, 036304. [CrossRef]
42. Huang, R.; Wu, H. Phase interface effects in the total enthalpy-based lattice Boltzmann model for solid-liquid phase change. *J. Comput. Phys.* **2015**, *294*, 346–362. [CrossRef]
43. Guo, Z.L.; Zheng, C.G.; Shi, B.C. Non-equilibrium extrapolation method for velocity and pressure boundary conditions in the lattice Boltzmann method. *Chin. Phys.* **2002**, *11*, 366.

Article

Planar Gas Expansion under Intensive Nanosecond Laser Evaporation into Vacuum as Applied to Time-of-Flight Analysis

Alexey Morozov [1,2] and Vladimir Titarev [2,*]

[1] Kutateladze Institute of Thermophysics of the Siberian Branch of the Russian Academy of Sciences, Lavrentyev Ave. 1, Novosibirsk 630090, Russia
[2] Federal Research Center "Computer Science and Control" of the Russian Academy of Sciences, Vavilova Str. 44/2, Moscow 119333, Russia
* Correspondence: vladimir.titarev@frccsc.ru

Abstract: A computational investigation of the dynamics of gas expansion due to intense nanosecond laser evaporation into vacuum has been carried out. The problem is solved in a one-dimensional approximation, which simplifies calculations and at the same time allows one to analyze the main features of the expansion dynamics. For analysis we use three different approaches. Two of them are based on kinetic analysis via the direct simulation Monte Carlo (DSMC) method and numerical solution of the model Bhatnagar–Gross–Krook (BGK) equation. The third one focuses on derivation of an analytical continuum solution. Emphasis is placed on the analysis of the velocity distribution function and the average energy of particles passing through the time-of-flight detector on the normal to the evaporation surface, which is important for interpreting experimental measurements. The formulated problem is quite difficult as the considered flow is time-dependent, contains discontinuities in boundary conditions and involves large variations of local Knudsen numbers as well as steep gradients of the velocity distribution function. Data were obtained on the particle energy in the time-of-flight distribution for the range of regimes from the free molecular flow to continuum one. The maximum attainable average energy of particles in the time-of-flight distribution is determined. The non-monotonicity of the energy increase was found, which is explained based on analysis of the velocity distribution of particles.

Keywords: DSMC; BGK model; gas expansion; pulsed laser evaporation; time-of-flight; rarefied gas; Nesvetay; LasInEx; discrete velocity scheme; ALE

1. Introduction

Various modern technologies for thin film deposition, nanoparticle synthesis, and surface treatment employ pulsed laser ablation of solid targets with nanosecond pulses of moderate intensity [1]. Such a process leads to the formation of a vapor cloud of the ablation products, which then expands into the surrounding space. Investigation of the dynamics of this process is useful in applications to control and monitor the gas phase.

In experiments, a small detector is usually located at a large distance from the target in the direction normal to the evaporation surface. One of the main instruments to experimentally control the laser ablation and desorption processes is the measurements of the so-called time-of-flight (TOF) distributions of particles passing through this detector [2–9]. By analyzing the TOF distributions, one can improve understanding of the ablation mechanism as well as estimate the temperature of the evaporating surface [6] and the composition of the surface material [10]. Correct interpretation of the TOF distributions can significantly advance the understanding of the processes accompanying pulsed laser ablation and hence facilitate the development of various laser ablation-based techniques.

The theoretical analysis of the problem in question is based mostly on various computational approaches. For low laser fluence the gas can be considered neutral since the effects of laser radiation absorption in the plume and gas ionization are negligible. Typically, the neutral plume expansion in vacuum is studied numerically using the direct simulation Monte Carlo (DSMC) method [11]. In the first works this method made it possible to study angular distributions of particles under pulsed desorption of a few monolayers based on one-dimensional calculations [12,13]. Later, based on two-dimensional calculations, the influence of the size of the evaporation spot on the expansion of particles was investigated [14] and the structure of the forming laser-induced plume and its expansion dynamics has been studied [15]. The influence of chemical reactions [16] and the interatomic interaction potential in the plume [17] on the expansion dynamics has been investigated as well. The effect of the pressure of the evaporated substance on the forming angular distributions of particles has been studied [18]. Special attention was paid to the effects of separation of the components of the gas mixture during ablation of multicomponent substances [10,19,20].

In a number of papers, the TOF distributions under pulsed laser evaporation into vacuums have been analyzed. The influence of the heat of vaporization and chemical reactions on the TOF distribution was studied [21]. Introduction of high-energy particles into the calculation to take into account the effect of ion recombination made it possible to describe TOF distributions under the conditions of plasma formation in the laser plume [22]. It was shown that using the calculated database of TOF distributions allows determining the irradiated surface temperature from the experimental TOF signals [23], while the commonly used fitting formulas greatly overestimate the surface temperature [24]. It was explained why the energy of particles in the TOF distribution can be several times higher than the energy of particles during evaporation and it was shown how this energy depends on the number of evaporated monolayers Θ [25,26]. It was shown that taking into account the time evolution of laser irradiation [27,28] and its spatial non-uniformity [29] has little effect on the energy and the velocity distribution function (VDF) of particles at the TOF detector.

However, the obtained data on the dependence of energy in the TOF distribution on the number of evaporated monolayers Θ were not completely clear and explainable. The previous calculations show a complicated dependence of the energy on the number of monolayers Θ with the formation of a bend [25,26] or even a flat-shaped region for large evaporation spots [28,29] for $1 < \Theta < 10$, followed by a further increase in energy at $10 < \Theta < 100$. This contradicts the general idea that, in the limit, the energy should approach to a certain value corresponding to the continuum solution.

Such a strange behavior of the energy dependence gave reason to assume that the calculations for $\Theta > 10$ were inaccurate. It would be interesting and useful to determine the maximum achievable energy in the continuum limit. However, it is very difficult to solve this problem in the axisymmetric formulation under intense evaporation (for $\Theta > 100$, when we approach the continuous regime), since this requires large computing resources. On the other hand, it is possible to derive an exact solution in the one-dimensional formulation and, on its basis, analyze the flow in the entire range of rarefaction, up to the continuous medium.

For nanosecond laser ablation, the radius of the spot is usually significantly larger than the plume length during the pulse action. As a result, the initial stage of the plume expansion can be considered as one-dimensional, which paves the way to commonly used simplified theoretical analysis [12,13,17,30–32]. This is vital because in laser ablation applications only a small amount of material typically evaporates and therefore the molecular collisions inside the plume occur only during the one-dimensional expansion. The subsequent three-dimensional expansion can be considered collisionless, greatly simplifying the analysis. Normally, the collisional stage of the gas expansion ends at a distance similar in size to the evaporation spot (~0.1 mm). Since the distance to the detector is much greater (~100 mm), the collisionless expansion can be regarded as if from a point source. Therefore, to estimate the energy of the particles on the TOF detector, it is enough to compute the energy of those particles that move along the normal to the surface inside a cone with a small opening angle. An analysis of the time evolution of this energy makes it possible to trace the transition to the collisionless stage of the gas expansion and to determine the energy of particles arriving at the TOF detector. The initial stage of the time evolution of the energy for a given duration of evaporation will be the same for both one-dimensional and three-dimensional calculations. The larger the evaporation spot is, the longer the three-dimensional calculation corresponds to the one-dimensional one.

Numerically, the formulated problem is quite difficult as the considered flow is time-dependent, contains discontinuities in boundary conditions and involves large variations of local Knudsen numbers as well as steep gradients of the VDF. To make our results more reliable and credible, in addition to the DSMC method, it is worth adding another modeling approach—the direct numerical solution of the model Bhatnagar–Gross–Krook (BGK) kinetic equation computed by the Nesvetay code [33,34]. Previously, good agreement has been obtained using this code both with the DSMC method and with the numerical solution of the exact Boltzmann equation for moderate evaporation (for the number of monolayers $\Theta < 100$) [33]. However, the question of solving the problem under conditions of nearly continuum regime remains open. Traditional discrete velocity methods (DVM) for kinetic equations are highly inefficient when applied to the problem under consideration. The recent incorporation [35] of the Arbitrary Lagrangian-Eulerian (ALE) methodology combined with the introduction of the special unstructured mixed-element velocity meshes [33] allows us now to compute the solution of the problem up to 100 times faster and hence has made it possible to significantly improve the accuracy of calculations and analyze the particle velocity distribution in the laser plume.

The present work focuses on the particular case of the plane expansion into vacuum during intense evaporation. The emphasis is made on the analysis of the VDF and the average energy of particles passing through the time-of-flight detector normal to the evaporation surface, which is important for interpreting experimental measurements. In our analysis we employ three methods. First, two methods are kinetic—the DSMC method and the numerical solution of the model BGK equation. The third method, which is only possible in the planar expansion case, is the analytical continuum solution, which approaches the kinetic solutions for the number of monolayers greater than 1000. The use of three independent analysis methods makes it possible to cross verify the results and increase the credibility of the analysis. The paper also demonstrates the good potential of using model kinetic equations to study flow problems, which need an accurate calculation of not just mean quantities (density, velocity, etc.), but also of the velocity distribution function.

2. Formulation of the Problem

A one-dimensional planar problem of pulsed evaporation of molecules into vacuum is considered. The laser-induced plume is assumed to be neutral. The mechanism of normal evaporation [36] is supposed when the relation between the surface temperature and the saturated gas pressure is described by the Clausius-Clapeyron equation. This mechanism is commonly considered to be adequate for describing experiments for moderate laser fluences for nanosecond ablation of different materials, e.g., metals, semiconductors, or graphite [37].

Molecules are evaporated with the energy corresponding to a surface temperature T_0. It is assumed that during time interval τ particle flux Ψ is constant and equal to $\Psi = n_0 u_T / 4$, where n_0 is the density of the saturated vapor corresponding to the temperature T_0, $u_T = 2u_0/\sqrt{\pi}$, $u_0 = \sqrt{2kT_0/m}$ is the most probable thermal speed, k is the Boltzmann constant, m is the mass of an evaporated molecule. All backscattered molecules which reach the evaporating surface are assumed to recondense on the surface. The monatomic gas is considered. The hard sphere model is used to simulate the process of particle collisions.

The concept of evaporated monolayers is often used [14,16,26] to describe the amount of evaporated material. One monolayer corresponds to such a number of particles that they cover the evaporating surface completely. The total number of evaporated molecules is equal to

$$N_{vap} = \tau \Psi_{vap} S, \qquad (1)$$

where $S = \pi R^2$ is the spot area. The number of evaporated monolayers is defined as

$$\Theta = \frac{N}{S/\Sigma} = \tau \Psi_{vap} \Sigma = \frac{\tau}{8\sqrt{2\pi}t_0}, \qquad (2)$$

where $\Sigma = \sigma/4$ is an area occupied by one molecule at the surface and $t_0 = \lambda_0/u_0$ is the average time between collisions in the saturated vapor with density n_0 and temperature T_0, λ_0 is the mean free path. Since we consider regimes up to the continuum medium, the interesting range of monolayers is $\Theta = 0.01$–$10{,}000$. To characterize the degree of rarefaction, one can determine the Knudsen number at the initial stage of expansion based on the plume length $L = u_T \tau$ as

$$Kn = \frac{\lambda_0}{L} = \frac{1}{16\sqrt{2\Theta}}. \qquad (3)$$

The indicated range of the number of monolayers Θ corresponds to the range of Knudsen numbers $Kn = 4$–4×10^{-6}. It is obviously that it ranges from a continuum solution to a free-molecular one.

Let us estimate the number of model particles required for simulating a typical near-continuum regime by the DSMC method in the axisymmetric formulation. The gas density near the evaporation surface during evaporation is close to density at the boundary of the Knudsen layer n_K. To correctly simulate the gas flow near the surface, the cell size should be no larger than the local mean free path $\Delta x = \lambda_K = \lambda_0 n_0 / n_K$. In addition, there must be at least one model particle in the smallest cell in the computational domain (cell size of Δx^3, near the flow axis). The maximum density and the maximum number of particles in the flow field are realized at the moment of time $t = \tau$. At this time, the total number of real molecules in the plume in the continuum limit can be estimated as $N_{mol} = n_K u_K \tau S$, where $u_K = c_K = \sqrt{\gamma k T_K / m}$ is velocity at the boundary of the Knudsen layer (where the Mach number $M = u/c = 1$), T_K is the temperature at the boundary of the Knudsen layer, $\gamma = (5+j)/(3+j)$ is the adiabatic exponent, and j is the number of internal degrees of freedom.

The total number of *model* particles in one-dimensional plane modeling can be estimated as the ratio of the total number of molecules in the plume to the number of molecules in the smallest cell near the surface:

$$N_{model,1D} = \frac{n_K u_K \tau \Delta x^2}{n_K \Delta x^3} = \frac{u_K \tau}{\lambda_K} = \frac{8 n_K \Theta}{n_0} \sqrt{\frac{\gamma \pi T_K}{T_0}} \approx 4.7 \cdot \Theta. \qquad (4)$$

Here, we use the data on the values at the Knudsen layer boundary obtained by the numerical solution of the model kinetic equation [38]

$$T_K/T_0 = 0.6434, \quad n_K/n_0 = 0.3225. \qquad (5)$$

To estimate the number of model particles in the axisymmetric calculation, it is necessary to compare the evaporation spot area $S = \pi R^2$ with the area of one cell $S_1 = \Delta x^2$. Expressing the spot radius in dimensionless form as $b = R/(u_T \tau)$, we obtain

$$\frac{S}{S_1} = \frac{\pi b^2 u_T^2 \tau^2}{\Delta x^2} = 512 \pi \left(\frac{n_K}{n_0}\right)^2 b^2 \Theta^2 = 167 \, b^2 \Theta^2. \qquad (6)$$

The total number of model particles in the axisymmetric calculation is

$$N_{model,3D} = \frac{S}{S_1} N_{model,1D} = 792 \, b^2 \Theta^3. \qquad (7)$$

For example, for a typical evaporation spot $b = 10$ and $\Theta = 1000$ we obtain $N_{model,3D} \approx 8 \times 10^{13}$, which is beyond the limits of possible computational possibilities, while for one-dimensional calculation the minimum number of model particles is only $N_{model,1D} \approx 5 \times 10^3$. It should be noted that the axisymmetric DSMC calculation requires the same large number of model particles as the corresponding three-dimensional calculation, and only the number of cells in physical space decreases. In principle, the number of model particles can be significantly reduced by using in the radial direction the cell size larger than the mean free path (and thus increasing the volume of the smallest cell) or by using weighting factors. However, such approaches are nontrivial and can also distort the calculation results. Sometimes, the cell size is set larger than the mean free path, which also makes it possible to reduce the number of model particles, but in this case, the accuracy of the resulting numerical solution requires a separate study [39]. Thus, it can be seen that the high-accurate numerical solution of this problem by the DSMC method in the axisymmetric formulation is exceedingly computational costly, if even possible, which explains the need to use the one-dimensional approach.

3. Methods of the Analysis

3.1. DSMC

The first of the two considered numerical approaches is the DSMC scheme. We use the standard version of the method [11] with some improvements borrowed from [40]. Broadly speaking, the DSMC approach works as follows. The gas cloud is described by the so-called model molecules. The state of each molecule is determined by its position in space and the velocity vector. Temporal evolution of the flow field during one time step is conducted via the so-called time splitting approach and consists of two stages. The first stage is collisionless movement of particles over the mesh in the physical domain, based on their position and velocity. The second stage involves the simulation of the interparticle collisions in accordance with the "no-time-counter" scheme.

The outlined computational DSMC algorithm was implemented by the first author in the parallel FORTRAN code LasInEx (Laser-Induced-Expansion) and has been successfully used in various studies, e.g., [15,20,26,34]. In the current work the computational domain in physical space is initially divided into cells of equal size. Its right boundary is pushed forward so that no particle can escape from the domain. At each moment of time when the domain length is updated and mesh is rebuilt, the maximum density in the computational region was calculated, and the cell size was set equal to the corresponding mean free path. Since the density decreases during the gas cloud plume expansion, the cell size grows accordingly.

3.2. BGK Model Equation

The second numerical approach is based on solving numerically the BGK model kinetic equation [41]. The state of the gas at position x at time moment t is described by the velocity distribution function $f(t, x, \xi)$ where $\xi = (\xi_1, \xi_2, \xi_3)$ are the components of the molecular velocity vector. Density, velocity, temperature, and pressure are defined by means of the integrals over the complete velocity space. For the considered one-dimensional problem the kinetic equation reads as follows:

$$\tfrac{\partial}{\partial t} f + \tfrac{\partial}{\partial x}(\xi_1 f) = \nu(f_M - f), \quad \nu = \tfrac{p}{\mu},$$
$$f_M = \tfrac{n}{(2\pi kT/m)^{3/2}} exp\left(-\tfrac{m(\xi-\mathbf{u})^2}{2kT}\right), p = nkT,$$

where ν is the collision frequency. For the hard sphere model, the viscosity coefficient is $\mu(T) \sim \sqrt{T}$.

The standard approach to solve a model kinetic equation for transient problems with sharp gradients is a discrete-velocity method (DVM). The essence of the method consists of replacing the infinite velocity domain by a finite integration domain and subsequently passing from the kinetic equation to the system of equations for finite set of integration points. The resulting system of kinetic equations can be solved by a variety of modern advection schemes [42,43]. However, the traditional DVM schemes are highly inefficient when applied to the problem under consideration. Instead, we use a recent ALE method [35], which uses deforming spatial meshes and expanding spatial domains. For the basic explanation of the ALE approach see, e.g., [44,45]. The test calculations, using the code Nesvetay developed by the second author [46–48], showed the ALE-DVM scheme to be up to 100 times more efficient as compared to the conventional DVM methods. It has been recently successfully used for studying gas expansion into background gas [34]. For flow into a vacuum, some modifications of the baseline scheme were made in order to improve its robustness. It is also important to note that to avoid division by zero the initial condition of vacuum is replaced by the background gas with the small number density value $10^{-15}\, n_0$. Background gas temperature value is not too important and for simplicity is set to be equal to T_0. Our numerical experiments have shown that the use of even smaller values does not change the outcome of the calculations. The initial value of the VDF is then set to be the locally Maxwellian function with the background gas density and temperature.

In the physical space, the initial domain extends up to 5 cm and is divided into 800 cells. During the calculations, it expands in such a way that the advancing wave never reaches the right boundary of the calculation domain. A specially constructed unstructured mixed-element velocity mesh, proposed in [33], is used in the velocity mesh. This is due the need to calculate the TOF distributions of particles, which involves the integration of the VDF over the cones with a small opening angle in the velocity space. Our approach to velocity mesh construction borrows ideas from computational astrophysics, see [49] and references therein. The mesh topology is different depending on the part of the velocity domain. For $\xi_1 > 0$, the mesh is constructed by extruding in the radial direction a triangular mesh on a unit sphere. This results in layers of prismatic cells together with one layer of tetrahedrons near the origin. For $\xi_1 < 0$, we use a conventional hexahedron mesh. Overall, the resulting velocity mesh contains 840 thousand cells and allows the integration for cones with half angles as low as $0.1°$.

To reduce the required computing time, the calculations by the Nesvetay code are run on parallel computers using two-level MPI+OpenMP approach. By default, 8 OpenMP threads are assigned to each MPI process.

3.3. Analytical Continuum Solution

To obtain a solution in the limiting case of the continuous medium, we use an analytical solution of the continuity and Euler's equations for pulsed adiabatic expansion of gas desorbing into vacuum [50]. The applicability of this solution to the considered problem is due to the fact that the adiabaticity assumption is violated only in a small subsonic layer near the evaporation surface, while in the rest of the flow field is well satisfied. On the other hand, the continuum description of the flow is violated only at the plume front or for evaporation of a small number of monolayers.

The position of the plume front $\widetilde{x}_f$ and the point of the maximum plume density x_{max} (for $t > \tau$) are determined by the relations

$$\widetilde{x}_f(\widetilde{t}) = \frac{\gamma+1}{\gamma-1}\widetilde{t},\ \widetilde{x}_{\max}(\widetilde{t}) = \frac{\gamma+1}{\gamma-1}\left(\widetilde{t} - \widetilde{t}^{\frac{3-\gamma}{\gamma+1}}\right), \tag{8}$$

where $\widetilde{t} = t/\tau$, $\widetilde{x} = x/(u_K \tau)$. Solution for the zone $\widetilde{x}_{max} < \widetilde{x} < \widetilde{x}_f$ is determined by the formulas for plane continuum unsteady expansion into vacuum [51]

$$\begin{cases} \widetilde{u}(\widetilde{x},\widetilde{t}) = 1 + \frac{2}{\gamma+1}\frac{\widetilde{x}}{\widetilde{t}}, \\ \widetilde{c}(\widetilde{x},\widetilde{t}) = 1 - \frac{\gamma-1}{\gamma+1}\frac{\widetilde{x}}{\widetilde{t}}, \end{cases} \tag{9}$$

where $\widetilde{u} = u/u_K$, $\widetilde{c} = c/c_K$, u is velocity, c is the speed of sound.

Solution in the zone $0 < \tilde{x} < \tilde{x}_{max}$ should be found separately for any particular case of γ [50]. For monatomic gas ($\gamma = 5/3$), the solution is

$$\begin{cases} \tilde{t}(\tilde{u}, \tilde{c}) = \frac{(18\tilde{c}^2 + 3\tilde{c}\tilde{u} - 12\tilde{c} - \tilde{u}^2 + 2\tilde{u} + 8)(3\tilde{c} + \tilde{u} + 2)}{108\tilde{c}^3}, \\ \tilde{x}(\tilde{u}, \tilde{c}) = -\frac{(9\tilde{c}^2 - \tilde{u}^2 + 4\tilde{u})(3\tilde{c} + \tilde{u} + 2)(3\tilde{c} - \tilde{u} - 2)}{108\tilde{c}^3}. \end{cases} \quad (10)$$

Further, assuming the adiabatic relation $n = \text{const} \cdot c^{2/(\gamma-1)}$, temperature and density can be calculated. To compare the DSMC calculation with the analytical solution, one should use known values of density and temperature (5) at the boundary of the Knudsen layer.

To calculate the energy of particles moving in a velocity cone with an angle α, an approach based on the Monte Carlo method is used. Based on the analytical solution (9)–(11), we calculate density, velocity, and temperature profiles. Then, at every point in space, the particle velocity components (u', v', w') are generated in accordance with the local Maxwellian VDF and for each particle it is determined whether it is inside the velocity cone with an angle α or not (i.e., whether the conditions $u' > 0$ and $\sqrt{v'^2 + w'^2}/u' < \text{tg}\alpha$ are satisfied). To calculate the average energy, integration is carried out over the entire space, taking into account density at each point.

4. Results and Discussion

4.1. Distribution of Molecules in the Velocity Cone

Figure 1 shows typical density and temperature profiles for various numbers of evaporated monolayers. With an increase in the number of evaporated monolayers, the plume is accelerated with a corresponding drop in temperature due to collisions between particles in the plume. So, for time 10τ, the maximum density value for $\Theta = 1000$ is 2 times smaller as compared to $\Theta = 0$, whereas the maximum temperature is 10 times smaller.

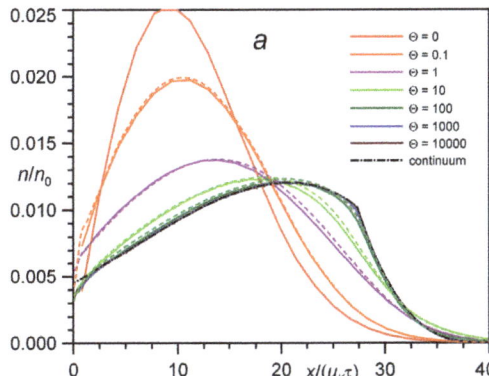 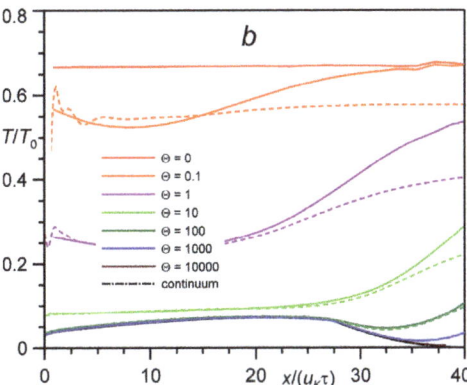

Figure 1. Profiles of density (**a**) and temperature (**b**) in time $t = 10\tau$ for different numbers of evaporated monolayers Θ: DSMC (*solid lines*) vs. BGK model (*dashed lines*) and continuum solution (*dash-dotted line*).

To analyze experimentally measured distributions of particles at a time-of-flight detector, we consider the distribution of particles moving inside a velocity cone with a given angle α. Figure 2 shows numerical results for particles moving along the x axis inside a velocity cone with an angle of 3° (i.e., particles for which $\sqrt{v'^2 + w'^2}/u' < \text{tg } 3°$, where ($u'$, v', w') are the components of the particle velocity vector). It is these particles that will arrive at the time-of-flight detector with a size of $L\text{tg}3°$ (here L is the distance to the detector) under the condition of collisionless expansion. The distribution differs significantly from the one shown in Figure 1a. With an increase in the number of monolayers, the fraction of particles that arrive at the time-of-flight detector increases strongly. It can be seen that faster particles from the plume front with a low temperature arrive at the detector, while slower particles from the plume back with a relatively high temperature move away to the sides. The fraction of particles that arrive at the detector is quite small. One can see that the maximum density of particles in the velocity cone in Figure 2 for $\Theta \geq 1000$ is 0.002, while the maximum particle density in Figure 1 is 0.012, i.e., 6 times higher. Particles at the plume front ($x > 30\ u_K\tau$) for a large number of monolayers move with almost zero temperature, strictly forward, so most of them will arrive at the detector.

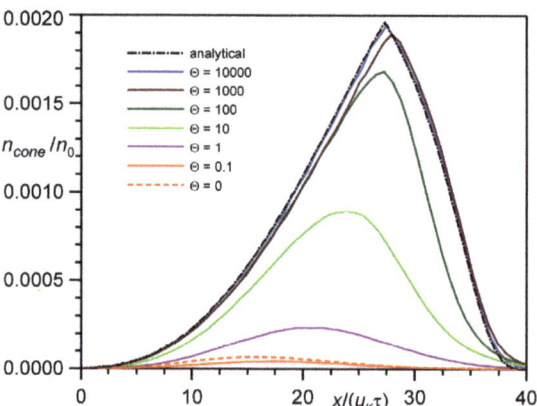

Figure 2. The DSMC calculated spatial distribution of particles moving along the x axis in the 3° velocity cone at time $t = 10\tau$.

Figure 3 shows the distribution of the fraction of particles that arrive at the detector with a size of $Ltg3°$. In fact, this is equivalent to the probability of a particle being inside the velocity cone with an angle of 3°. It can be seen that with an increase in the number of monolayers from $\Theta = 10$ to 10,000, the probability of a particle arriving at the detector increases from 0.1 to 0.95. For the continuum solution, the probability reaches unity. It is important to note that the numerical solution actually begins to coincide with the analytical continuum solution only for the number of monolayers $\Theta = 10,000$, which corresponds to an extremely small Knudsen number $Kn = 4 \times 10^{-6}$.

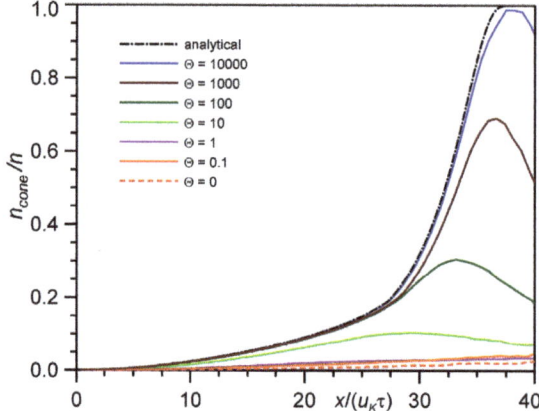

Figure 3. The DSMC calculated probability of a particle to be inside a 3° velocity cone at time $t = 10\ \tau$.

The number of particles moving in a velocity cone with an angle α and correspondingly arriving at the detector of size $Ltg\alpha$ depends on the number of evaporated monolayers Θ and the angle α and varies with time. Figure 4 shows the time evolution of the number of particles for different cone angles. To normalize this number, we use the area of the spherical segment $S' \sim 1 - \cos\alpha \approx \alpha^2/2$. The larger the number of monolayers Θ, the larger the number of collisions between particles during expansion and, correspondingly, the larger the number of particles moving along the normal in the velocity cone. It can be seen that for Θ = 100 for the angle α = 1°, 3% of the evaporated particles arrive at the detector, while for Θ = 1, only 0.2%.

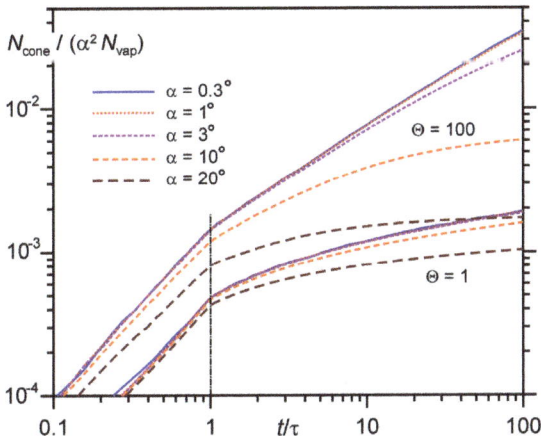

Figure 4. Time evolution of the number of particles moving along the x axis in the velocity cone with an angle α = 0.3°, 1°, 3°, 10°, 20° for the number of monolayers Θ = 1 and 100.

4.2. Temporal Evolution of Average Energy of Molecules

Figure 5 shows the time evolution of the average energy of particles moving in the velocity cone with different values of the cone angle α. One can see good agreement between the DSMC results and the kinetic equation for Θ > 1. The solution for the number of monolayers 10,000 agrees very well with the analytical continuum solution. For Θ < 1, there is a monotonic increase in energy with time. Similarly, for Θ > 1, the energy increases in the initial period of time, up to $t = (3–10)\tau$. This energy rise is caused by two factors, the gas-dynamic acceleration of the plume in the forward direction and the kinetic selection of high-speed particles [26]. In this case, due to separation of molecules for non-stationary expansion, collisions occur mostly between molecules with a close velocity component in the normal direction to the surface. This leads to the transfer of energy from the radial component (along the surface) to the axial component (parallel to the normal to the surface) and to the focusing of molecules in the direction of the normal. This effect has been seen in previous DSMC studies of pulsed evaporation in vacuum [12,14,26]. For Θ ≥ 1, after time $t = (3–10)\tau$, the energy begins to decrease. This effect can be explained as follows. With increase in the number of evaporated monolayers, the region of collisional expansion becomes larger. In this case, low-speed molecules, which move to the side at lower values of Θ, undergo additional collisions, which direct them in the forward direction. Thus, the low-speed "tail" of the VDF increases and the total energy decreases accordingly.

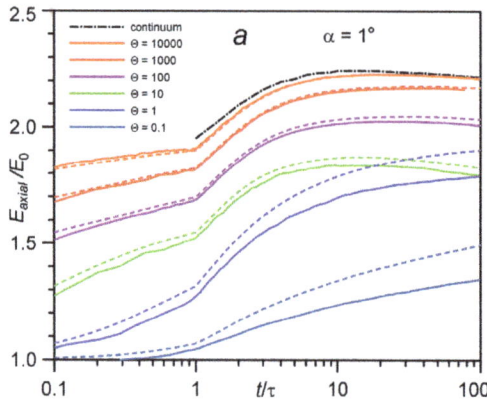
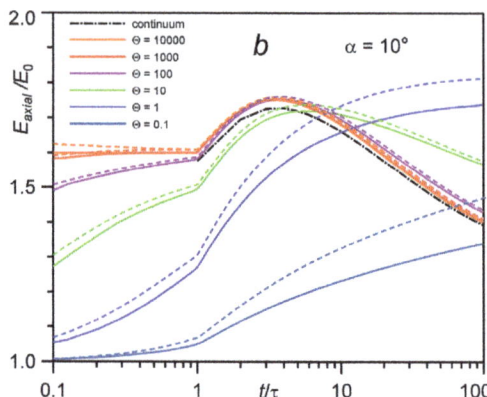

Figure 5. Time evolution of the average energy of particles moving inside a velocity cone with an angle of 1° (**a**) and 10° (**b**) for different numbers of evaporated monolayers Θ.

As an illustration, Figure 6 shows the distributions of those particles that move along the axis x inside a cone with an angle of 1° and 10°. The flow regime with strong effect is selected, for $\Theta = 100$. As shown in Figure 4, the number of molecules moving along the axis constantly increases with time. The VDF changes, on the one hand, due to a change in the velocities of molecules moving inside the cone, and on the other hand, due to the appearance of new molecules in the cone. To separate these processes, the function is normalized by the number of molecules in the cone at the end of the evaporation, as $\tilde{f}_{axial}(t, \alpha, u) = f_{axial}(t, \alpha, u) / \int_0^\infty f_{axial}(\tau, \alpha, u) du$. For $t = \tau$ this function coincides with the usual VDF.

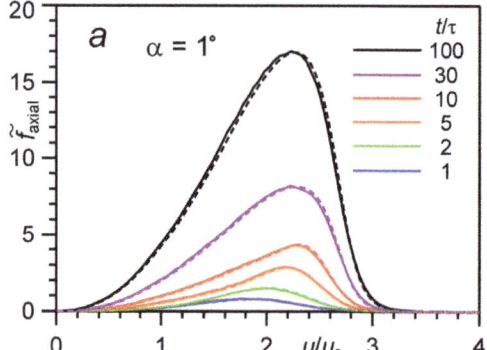
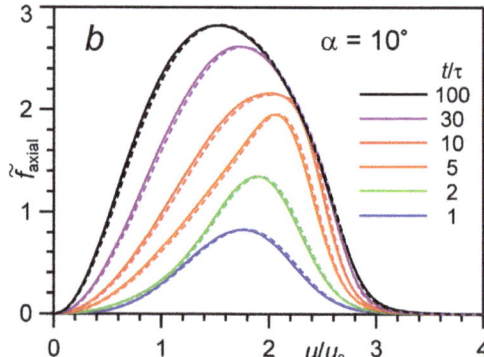

Figure 6. The velocity distribution function of molecules moving along the axis in the cone with angle $\alpha = 1°$ (**a**) and 10° (**b**) for the number of monolayers $\Theta = 100$: DSMC calculation (*solid lines*) in comparison with the BGK model (*dashed lines*).

There is a qualitative difference in the VDF evolution for the small angle ($\alpha = 1°$) and the large angle ($\alpha = 10°$). For the small angle initially up to a time of $t = 10\tau$ there is an increase in the number of high-speed molecules, which leads to an increase in the average energy of these particles. Later, for $t > 5\tau$, there is a proportional increase in the number of both fast and slow molecules, which results in the conservation of the average energy of the molecules. However, for the large angle the situation is qualitatively different. After a time of $t = 5\tau$, the number of low-speed molecules increases mostly, which considerably decreases the energy E_{axial}.

It should be noted that the total number of molecules moving inside the cone for $\alpha = 1°$ increases by a factor of 23 during expansion (from 0.0014 at time $t = \tau$ to 0.033 at time $t = 100\tau$, see Figure 4), while for $\alpha = 10°$ only by a factor of 5 (from 0.0012 to 0.006 over the same time interval). It should be expected that with an increase in the number of monolayers (in the continuum limit), with time approaching infinity, all particles should move strictly along the axis. As a result, the energy ratio approaches the unit value $E_{axial}/E_0 = 1$.

These data are vital for understanding the patterns observed in two-dimensional calculations. It was found out earlier that for a given number of monolayers with an increase in the size of the evaporation spot (increase in b up to 5), the corresponding rise in the energy of particles passing through the TOF detector takes place [25]. However, with further increasing the spot (for $b > 5$), some decreasing energy is observed. Since an increase in the spot size is equivalent to an increase in the duration of the one-dimensional flow regime, the presence of an energy maximum for relatively large spots ($b\sim5$) is equivalent to the presence of an energy maximum for a relatively long time of one-dimensional calculation ($t\sim5\tau$) and apparently has the same reason. In one-dimensional calculations, it is possible to obtain highly accurate numerical data for almost arbitrarily small angles of the cone and a large number of evaporated monolayers, thus revealing general trends. However, in two-dimensional calculations it is much more difficult due to the requirement of significant computational resources.

4.3. Generalizing Dependences on Average Energy of Molecules

Figure 7 depicts average axial energy computed at time $t/\tau = 10$ and 100 for different angles. Previously, similar dependences were obtained for $t/\tau = 25$ for the number of monolayers $\Theta < 100$ [33]. It can be seen that as the number of monolayers increases from 100 to 10,000, the energy tends to a certain limiting value, which coincides with the analytical continuum solution. At the same time, there is some curve bend in the Section 1 $<\Theta < 100$, and for the angle $\alpha \geq 5°$, there is even an energy maximum for $\Theta = 1$. These features are associated with an increase in the number of low-velocity particles in the velocity cone, as shown in Figure 6.

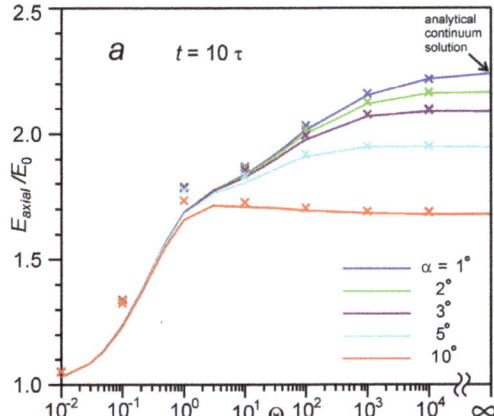
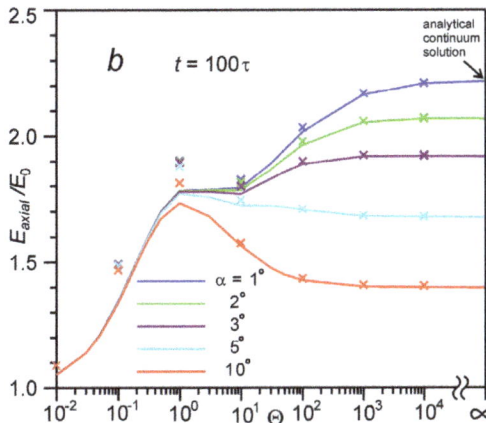

Figure 7. Average axial energy $E_{axial}(t, \alpha, \Theta)$ as a function of the number of evaporated monolayers Θ at time $t = 10\ \tau$ (**a**) and $100\ \tau$ (**b**): DSMC calculation (*solid lines*) in comparison with the BGK model (*crosses*).

The dependences of the average energy of particles in the time-of-flight distribution for $t = 10\tau$ are similar to those in axisymmetric calculations for a small evaporation spot ($b = 10$) [25,26]. The flat-shaped section of energy for $1 < \Theta < 10$ for $t = 100\tau$ in Figure 7b is in good agreement with the flat-shaped section for $1 < \Theta < 10$ for a large evaporation spot ($b \geq 30$) [28,29]. It can be concluded that the observed peculiarity of the energy change in the axisymmetric calculation is of the same nature as in our plane calculation. It can also be expected that with an increase of the number of monolayers in the axisymmetric calculation (which is technically difficult due to computational limitations), the energy of particles at the TOF detector should reach some limiting continuum value. This limiting value can be estimated on the basis of our one-dimensional calculations. Figure 8 shows the dependences of the average axial energy on the angle, calculated on the basis of the analytical continuum solution. It can be seen that as the angle decreases, the energy value reaches a certain limit value. Thus, a decrease in the angle from $\alpha = 1°$ to $0.1°$ leads to an increase in energy by only 4%. It is important to note that the energy value with decreasing angle depends very weakly on time. Increasing the time from 10τ to 100τ only increases the energy by 1%. The maximum achievable energy of particles at the TOF detector is $2.32\ E_0$. This corresponds to the case of evaporation from an infinitely large evaporation spot, and in the case of evaporation from any other spot, the energy at the TOF detector should not exceed this value. This is consistent with previous axisymmetric calculations in which the observed energy was less than this maximum value [25,26,28,29].

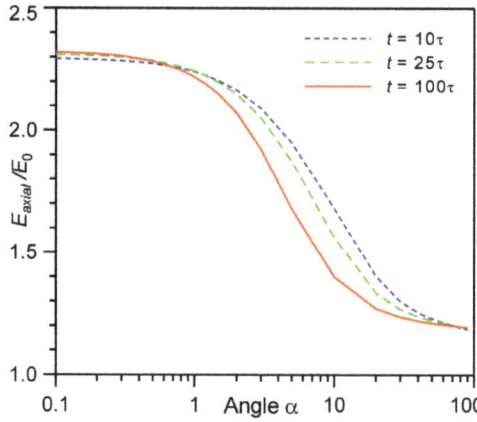

Figure 8. Average axial energy E_{axial} as a function of the angle α at time $t = 10, 25, 100\tau$ based on the analytical continuum solution.

For the largest possible angle (90°) in Figure 8 the particle energy in the plume is about $1.19 E_0$. This increase in energy is due to the fact that the total energy of the plume during expansion is not conserved since a considerable fraction of low-energy particles backscatters and recondenses at the evaporation surface [52–54]. It was shown that during evaporation of 1000 monolayers, the fraction of particles returning back to the evaporation surface for the entire time of expansion is $\beta = 0.275$, with the back flux during evaporation being $\beta_1 = 0.163$ and after evaporation being $\beta_2 = \beta - \beta_1 = 0.112$ [54]. The corresponding kinetic energies of backscattering particles can be estimated as $E_{\beta,1} \approx 0.6 E_0$ [52,53] and $E_{\beta,2} \approx 0.3 E_0$ [53]. Then, we can estimate the total plume kinetic energy as $E_{plume} \approx (E_0 - \beta_1 E_{b,1} - \beta_2 E_{b,2})/(1 - \beta) \approx 1.2 E_0$, which agrees well with our analytical estimation.

5. Conclusions

The dynamics of gas expansion under intense nanosecond laser evaporation into vacuum is studied. The use of two different kinetic approaches (the DSMC method and the solution of the model BGK equation) allowed obtaining a reliable solution that agrees well with the analytical continuum solution for a large number of monolayers. An analysis of the velocity distribution function and the average energy of particles passing through a time-of-flight detector on the normal to the evaporation surface is carried out. The use of the analytical continuum model made it possible to determine the maximum possible particle energy in the time-of-flight distribution. Based on the analysis of the distribution of particle velocities, the peculiarities of the energy increase in the time-of-flight distribution are explained. The data obtained are important for the interpretation of experimental time-of-flight measurements.

Author Contributions: Conceptualization, A.M. and V.T.; Methodology, V.T.; Software, V.T.; Validation, A.M.; Formal analysis, A.M.; Investigation, A.M. and V.T.; Resources, V.T.; Data curation, V.T.; Writing—original draft preparation, A.M.; Writing—review and editing, A.M. and V.T.; Visualization, A.M.; Supervision, V.T.; Project administration, V.T.; Funding acquisition, V.T. All authors have read and agreed to the published version of the manuscript.

Funding: This research was funded by Russian Science Foundation, project number 22-11-00078.

Acknowledgments: The research was carried out using the infrastructure of the Shared Research Facilities "High Performance Computing and Big Data" (CKP "Informatics" of Federal Research Center "Computer Science and Control" of the Russian Academy of Sciences (Moscow) and Joint Supercomputing Center of the Russian Academy of Sciences (http://www.jscc.ru/)).

Conflicts of Interest: The authors declare no conflict of interest.

References

1. Bäuerle, D. *Laser Processing and Chemistry*, 4th ed.; Springer: Berlin/Heidelberg, Germany, 2011.
2. Kell, R.; Dreyfus, R.W. On the effect of Knudsen-layer formation on studies of vaporization, sputtering, and desorption. *Surf. Sci.* **1988**, *198*, 263–276. [CrossRef]
3. Braun, R.; Hess, P. Time-of-flight investigation of infrared laser-induced multilayer desorption of benzene. *J. Chem. Phys.* **1993**, *99*, 8330–8340. [CrossRef]
4. Krajnovich, D.J. Laser sputtering of highly oriented pyrolytic graphite at 248 nm. *J. Chem. Phys.* **1995**, *102*, 726–743. [CrossRef]
5. Claeyssens, F.; Henley, S.J.; Ashfold, M.N.R. Comparison of the ablation plumes arising from ArF laser ablation of graphite, silicon, copper, and aluminum in vacuum. *J. Appl. Phys.* **2003**, *94*, 2203–2211. [CrossRef]
6. Morozov, A.A. Analytical formula for interpretation of time-of-flight distributions for neutral particles under pulsed laser evaporation in vacuum. *J. Phys. D Appl. Phys.* **2015**, *48*, 195501. [CrossRef]
7. Bauer, W.; Perram, G. Laser ablated Ti velocity distribution dynamics. *J. Opt. Soc. Am. B* **2018**, *35*, 27–37. [CrossRef]
8. Skočić, M.; Dojić, D.; Bukvić, S. Consideration of optical time of flight measurement in laser induced plasmas. *Spectrochim. Acta B* **2020**, *165*, 105786. [CrossRef]
9. Irimiciuc, S.A.; Chertopalov, S.; Lancok, J.; Craciun, V. Langmuir probe technique for plasma characterization during pulsed laser deposition process. *Coatings* **2021**, *11*, 762. [CrossRef]
10. Morozov, A.A.; Mironova, M.L. Numerical analysis of time-of-flight distributions of neutral particles for pulsed laser ablation of binary substances into vacuum. *Appl. Phys. A* **2017**, *123*, 783. [CrossRef]
11. Bird, G.A. *Molecular Gas Dynamics and Direct Simulation of Gas Flows*; Clarendon Press: Oxford, UK, 1994.
12. NoorBatcha, I.; Lucchese, R.R.; Zeiri, Y. Effects of gas-phase collisions on particles rapidly desorbed from surfaces. *Phys. Rev. B* **1987**, *36*, 4978–4981. [CrossRef]
13. Feil, H.; Baller, T.S.; Dieleman, J. Effects of post-desorption collisions on the energy distribution of SiCl molecules pulsed-laser desorbed from Cl-covered Si surfaces: Monte-Carlo simulations compared to experiments. *Appl. Phys. A* **1992**, *55*, 554–560. [CrossRef]
14. Sibold, D.; Urbassek, H.M. Effect of gas-phase collisions in pulsed-laser desorption: A three-dimensional Monte Carlo simulation study. *J. Appl. Phys.* **1993**, *73*, 8544–8551. [CrossRef]
15. Morozov, A.A. Dynamics of gas cloud expansion under pulsed laser evaporation into vacuum. *J. Phys. Conf. Ser.* **2018**, *1105*, 012116. [CrossRef]
16. Itina, T.E.; Tokarev, V.N.; Marine, W.; Autric, M. Monte Carlo simulation study of the effects of nonequilibrium chemical reactions during pulsed laser desorption. *J. Chem. Phys.* **1997**, *106*, 8905–8912. [CrossRef]
17. Petrov, V.A.; Ranjbar, O.A.; Zhilyaev, P.A.; Volkov, A.N. Kinetic simulations of laser-induced plume expansion from a copper target into a vacuum or argon background gas based on ab initio calculation of Cu–Cu, Ar–Ar, and Ar–Cu interactions. *Phys. Fluids* **2020**, *32*, 102010. [CrossRef]
18. Konomi, I.; Motohiro, T.; Kobayashi, T.; Asaoka, T. Considerations on the determining factors of the angular distribution of emitted particles in laser ablation. *Appl. Surf. Sci.* **2010**, *256*, 4959–4965. [CrossRef]
19. Urbassek, H.M.; Sibold, D. Gas-phase segregation effects in pulsed laser desorption from binary targets. *Phys. Rev. Lett.* **1993**, *70*, 1886–1889. [CrossRef]

20. Morozov, A.A.; Starinskiy, S.V.; Bulgakov, A.V. Pulsed laser ablation of binary compounds: Effect of time delay in component evaporation on ablation plume expansion. *J. Phys. D Appl. Phys.* **2021**, *54*, 175203. [CrossRef]
21. Itina, T.E.; Patrone, L.; Marine, W.; Autric, M. Numerical analysis of TOF measurements in pulsed laser ablation. *Appl. Phys. A* **1999**, *69*, S59–S65. [CrossRef]
22. Garrelie, F.; Aubreton, J.; Catherinot, A. Monte Carlo simulation of laser-induced plasma plume expansion under vacuum: Comparison with experiments. *J. Appl. Phys.* **1998**, *83*, 5075–5082. [CrossRef]
23. Morozov, A.A. Interpretation of time-of-flight distributions for neutral particles under pulsed laser evaporation using direct Monte Carlo simulation. *J. Chem. Phys.* **2013**, *139*, 234706. [CrossRef] [PubMed]
24. Bykov, N.Y.; Bulgakova, N.M.; Bulgakov, A.V.; Loukianov, G.A. Pulsed laser ablation of metals in vacuum: DSMC study versus experiment. *Appl. Phys. A* **2004**, *79*, 1097–1100. [CrossRef]
25. Morozov, A.A. Analysis of time-of-flight distributions under pulsed laser ablation in vacuum based on the DSMC calculations. *Appl. Phys. A* **2013**, *111*, 1107–1111. [CrossRef]
26. Morozov, A.A.; Evtushenko, A.B.; Bulgakov, A.V. Gas-dynamic acceleration of laser-ablation plumes: Hyperthermal particle energies under thermal vaporization. *Appl. Phys. Lett.* **2015**, *106*, 054107. [CrossRef]
27. Ellegaard, O.; Schou, J.; Urbassek, H.M. Monte–Carlo description of gas flow from laser-evaporated silver. *Appl. Phys. A* **1999**, *69*, S577–S581. [CrossRef]
28. Morozov, A.A. Effect of temporal evolution of the evaporation surface temperature on the plume expansion under pulsed laser ablation. *J. Phys. Conf. Ser.* **2020**, *1677*, 012143. [CrossRef]
29. Morozov, A.A. Effect of evaporation-flux nonuniformity along the irradiation-spot radius on the plume expansion dynamics during pulsed laser ablation in vacuum. *Thermophys. Aeromech.* **2022**, *29*, 437–448. [CrossRef]
30. Itina, T.E.; Marine, W.; Autric, M. Nonstationary effects in pulsed laser ablation. *J. Appl. Phys.* **1999**, *85*, 7905–7908. [CrossRef]
31. Gusarov, A.V.; Smurov, I. Influence of atomic collisions in vapour phase on pulsed laser ablation. *Appl. Surf. Sci.* **2000**, *168*, 96–99. [CrossRef]
32. Volkov, A.N. Splitting of laser-induced neutral and plasma plumes: Hydrodynamic origin of bimodal distributions of vapor density and plasma emission intensity. *J. Phys. D Appl. Phys.* **2021**, *54*, 37LT01. [CrossRef]
33. Morozov, A.A.; Frolova, A.A.; Titarev, V.A. On different kinetic approaches for computing planar gas expansion under pulsed evaporation into vacuum. *Phys. Fluids* **2020**, *32*, 112005. [CrossRef]
34. Morozov, A.A.; Titarev, V.A. Dynamics of planar gas expansion during nanosecond laser evaporation into a low-pressure background gas. *Phys. Fluids* **2022**, *34*, 096101. [CrossRef]
35. Titarev, V.A.; Morozov, A.A. Arbitrary Lagrangian-Eulerian discrete velocity method with application to laser-induced plume expansion. *Appl. Math. Comput.* **2022**, *429*, 127241. [CrossRef]
36. Miotello, A.; Kelly, R. Critical assessment of thermal models for laser sputtering at high fluences. *Appl. Phys. Lett.* **1995**, *67*, 3535–3537. [CrossRef]
37. Bulgakova, N.M.; Bulgakov, A.V. Pulsed laser ablation of solids: Transition from normal vaporization to phase explosion. *Appl. Phys. A* **2001**, *73*, 199–208. [CrossRef]
38. Sone, Y.; Sugimoto, H. Kinetic theory analysis of steady evaporating flows from a spherical condensed phase into a vacuum. *Phys. Fluids A* **1993**, *5*, 1491–1511. [CrossRef]
39. Titov, E.V.; Levin, D.A. Extension of the DSMC method to high pressure flows. *Int. J. Comput. Fluid Dyn.* **2007**, *21*, 351–368. [CrossRef]
40. Bird, G.A.; Gallis, M.A.; Torczynski, J.R.; Rader, D.J. Accuracy and efficiency of the sophisticated direct simulation Monte Carlo algorithm for simulating noncontinuum gas flows. *Phys. Fluids* **2009**, *21*, 017103. [CrossRef]
41. Bhatnagar, P.; Gross, E.; Krook, M. A model for collision processes in gases. I. Small amplitude processes in charged and neutral one-component systems. *Phys. Rev.* **1954**, *94*, 511–525. [CrossRef]
42. Drikakis, D.; Rider, W. *High Resolution Methods for Incompressible and Low Speed Flows*; Springer: Berlin/Heidelberg, Germany, 2005.
43. Toro, E.F. *Riemann Solvers and Numerical Methods for Fluid Dynamics*, 3rd ed.; Springer: Berlin/Heidelberg, Germany, 2009.
44. Hirt, C.W.; Amsden, A.A.; Cook, J.L. An arbitrary Lagrangian-Eulerian computing method for all flow speeds. *J. Comput. Phys.* **1974**, *14*, 227. [CrossRef]
45. Boscheri, W.; Loubère, R.; Dumbser, M. Direct Arbitrary-Lagrangian-Eulerian ADER-MOOD finite volume schemes for multidimensional hyperbolic conservation laws. *J. Comput. Phys.* **2015**, *292*, 56. [CrossRef]
46. Titarev, V. Efficient deterministic modelling of three-dimensional rarefied gas flows. *Commun. Comput. Phys.* **2012**, *12*, 162. [CrossRef]
47. Titarev, V.; Dumbser, M.; Utyuzhnikov, S. Construction and comparison of parallel implicit kinetic solvers in three spatial dimensions. *J. Comput. Phys.* **2014**, *256*, 17. [CrossRef]
48. Titarev, V. Application of the Nesvetay code for solving three-dimensional high-altitude aerodynamics problems. *Comput. Math. Math. Phys.* **2020**, *60*, 737. [CrossRef]
49. Florinski, V.; Balsara, D.; Garain, S.; Gurski, K. Technologies for supporting high-order geodesic mesh frameworks for and space sciences. *Comput. Astrophys. Cosmol.* **2020**, *7*, 1. [CrossRef]
50. Sibold, D.; Urbassek, H.M. Gas-dynamic study of pulsed desorption flows into a vacuum. *Phys. Fluids A* **1992**, *4*, 165–177. [CrossRef]

51. Stanukovich, K.P. *Unsteady Motion of Continuous Media*; Pergamon: New York, NY, USA, 1960.
52. Moizhes, B.Y.; Nemchinsky, V.A. Formation of a jet during vaporization in vacuum. *Sov. Phys. Tech. Phys.* **1982**, *27*, 438–441.
53. Morozov, A.A. Evolution of the back flux in the case of pulsed evaporation into vacuum. *Dokl. Phys.* **2004**, *49*, 134–137. [CrossRef]
54. Morozov, A.A. Thermal model of pulsed laser ablation: Back flux contribution. *Appl. Phys. A* **2004**, *79*, 997–999. [CrossRef]

Article

A Simplified Linearized Lattice Boltzmann Method for Acoustic Propagation Simulation

Qiaochu Song, Rongqian Chen *, Shuqi Cao, Jinhua Lou, Ningyu Zhan and Yancheng You

School of Aerospace Engineering, Xiamen University, Xiamen 361005, China
* Correspondence: rqchen@xmu.edu.cn

Abstract: A simplified linearized lattice Boltzmann method (SLLBM) suitable for the simulation of acoustic waves propagation in fluids was proposed herein. Through Chapman–Enskog expansion analysis, the linearized lattice Boltzmann equation (LLBE) was first recovered to linearized macroscopic equations. Then, using the fractional-step calculation technique, the solution of these linearized equations was divided into two steps: a predictor step and corrector step. Next, the evolution of the perturbation distribution function was transformed into the evolution of the perturbation equilibrium distribution function using second-order interpolation approximation of the latter at other positions and times to represent the nonequilibrium part of the former; additionally, the calculation formulas of SLLBM were deduced. SLLBM inherits the advantages of the linearized lattice Boltzmann method (LLBM), calculating acoustic disturbance and the mean flow separately so that macroscopic variables of the mean flow do not affect the calculation of acoustic disturbance. At the same time, it has other advantages: the calculation process is simpler, and the cost of computing memory is reduced. In addition, to simulate the acoustic scattering problem caused by the acoustic waves encountering objects, the immersed boundary method (IBM) and SLLBM were further combined so that the method can simulate the influence of complex geometries. Several cases were used to validate the feasibility of SLLBM for simulation of acoustic wave propagation under the mean flow.

Keywords: simplified linearized lattice Boltzmann method; immersed boundary method; computational aeroacoustics

1. Introduction

The phenomenon of acoustic waves propagating in complex flows such as shear layers or a vortex often exists in aerospace engineering [1–4]. Studies have shown that such flow structures will change the characteristics of acoustic wave propagation, leading to refraction, reflection, and scattering and thus affect the measurement and localization of sound source [5,6]. Therefore, it is of great significance to carry out research on the propagation of acoustic waves in the flow.

Numerical simulation is an important means for such research. The main method used is direct numerical simulation (DNS) [7,8], which combines acoustic disturbance and the mean flow and then simulates acoustic waves propagation directly by solving the Navier–Stokes equations. However, DNS requires a very fine grid and a small time step, making its computational cost extremely high. In addition, because acoustic disturbance is usually several orders of magnitude smaller than the mean flow, the calculation of the two parts combined smoothens out the effect of acoustic disturbance, resulting in large error. To overcome these shortcomings, methods of solving perturbation equations such as linearized Euler equations (LEE) [9–11] or linearized Navier–Stokes equations (LNSE) [12,13] have been proposed to simulate acoustic wave propagation. These methods essentially solve macroscopic equations, which require high-precision schemes to ensure accuracy. Therefore, the numerical simulation of acoustic wave propagation still needs further development.

Over the last few decades, the lattice Boltzmann method (LBM) has become a popular computational fluid dynamics method [14–18]. LBM is based on molecular dynamics theory, which abstracts fluid into a large number of microscopic particles that collide and migrate through discrete grids according to simple motion rules to illustrate the evolution of the flow field; it reveals macroscopic motion characteristics of a fluid using a particle-distribution function. LBM does not entail solving complex differential equations directly; it only requires solving algebraic equations, which make the calculation process simpler. It has been applied to computational aeroacoustics [19–22]. Studies have shown that LBM has lower dissipation under the same accuracy, and it is easy to carry out parallel calculations [23], which makes the method suitable for large-scale aeroacoustics simulation. However, in acoustic waves propagation simulation, LBM combines the calculation of acoustic disturbance and the mean flow, which can lead inaccuracies. To better simulate the propagation of acoustic disturbance, the linearized lattice Boltzmann method (LLBM) was established [24,25], which divides the distribution function into a mean component and perturbation parts. Based on the moment relationship between the perturbation distribution function and the perturbation macroscopic variables, the linearized lattice Boltzmann equation (LLBE) can be recovered to linearized macroscopic equations through Chapman–Enskog (C-E) expansion analysis and the evolution of the perturbation distribution function is realized using the standard LBM. It should be pointed out that because the standard LBM can only be applied to uniform grids; special methods are required if it is applied to nonuniform grids. At the same time, it stores the particle velocities and the distribution function of all lattice velocity directions at each grid point, which requires a lot of memory. These deficiencies make it difficult for standard LBM or LLBM to simulate acoustic wave propagation. To solve these deficiencies, Shu et al. proposed the lattice Boltzmann flux solver (LBFS) employing the finite volume method to calculate the flux at an interface [26–30]. Zhan et al. further developed a linearized lattice Boltzmann flux solver (LLBFS) suitable for acoustic propagation simulation [31], wherein the solution of the interface satisfies the lattice Boltzmann equation; this is more in line with physical laws, and the calculation load is comparable to the traditional flux scheme. However, LBFS and LLBFS involve two models, the finite volume method (FVM) and the LBM, which are inconvenient for researchers. Chen et al. recently proposed a simplified lattice Boltzmann method (SLBM) [32,33], which approximates the nonequilibrium part of the distribution function by second-order interpolation of the equilibrium distribution function at other locations and times, so that the evolution of the distribution function can be transformed into the evolution of the equilibrium distribution function. SLBM further simplifies the calculation, and, at the same time, the distribution function in the lattice velocity direction of each particle at each grid point does not need to be stored, which makes it less memory-demanding.

In this paper, a simplified linearized lattice Boltzmann method (SLLBM) that combines the advantages of LLBM and SLBM was proposed and used for acoustic wave propagation simulation. Through C-E expansion analysis, the LLBE was recovered to linearized macroscopic equations; this process was divided into a predictor step and a corrector step using the fractional-step calculation technique. Using second-order interpolation approximation of the perturbation equilibrium distribution function at other positions and times to represent the nonequilibrium part of the perturbation distribution function, the evolution of the latter was transformed into the evolution of the former, and the calculation formulas of SLLBM were deduced. SLLBM inherits the advantages of the LLBM, calculating acoustic disturbance and the mean flow separately so macroscopic variables of the mean flow do not affect the calculation of acoustic disturbance. At the same time, in the SLLBM, the perturbation macroscopic variables were directly evolved so that the evolution and storage of the perturbation distribution function were avoided, which implies only the perturbation macroscopic variables instead of the values of perturbation distribution functions along all lattice velocity directions at each grid point needing to be stored and the physical boundary conditions can be directly processed without converting the perturbation distribution function and perturbation macroscopic variables to each other according to the moment relationships. As a result, SLLBM requires less memory and is simpler to operate than the standard LBM. In addition, to simulate the scattering effect of acoustic waves encountering objects, the immersed boundary method (IBM) was introduced into the framework of SLLBM so that the method can simulate the influence of complex geometries.

The remainder of this paper is arranged as follows. In Section 2, theories related to SLLBM are introduced, including the LLBE and its recovered form, the derivation process of SLLBM, the IBM under the framework of SLLBM, boundary conditions, and the computational sequence. In Section 3, several cases are used to validate the feasibility of SLLBM for acoustic wave propagation simulation. Finally, conclusions are drawn in Section 4.

2. Methodology

2.1. LLBE and C-E Expansion Analysis

For the lattice Boltzmann equation, the density distribution function f can be divided into the steady mean component $\bar{f}$ and the perturbation part f', i.e., $f = \bar{f} + f'$. Using the perturbation distribution function, the LLBE with the Bhatnagar–Gross–Krook (BGK) approximation is obtained:

$$\frac{\partial f'_\alpha}{\partial t} + \xi_\alpha \cdot \nabla f'_\alpha = -\frac{1}{\tau}(f'_\alpha - f'^{eq}_\alpha) \qquad (1)$$

where $\tau = \frac{v}{c_s^2 \delta_t} + \frac{1}{2}$ is the nondimensional relaxation time, which is associated with the kinematic viscosity v of the fluid, ξ_α and f'_α represent the component of the lattice velocity and the perturbation distribution function f' in direction α, respectively; f'^{eq}_α is the perturbation equilibrium distribution function, which is given by [25]:

$$f'^{eq}_\alpha = \frac{\rho'}{\bar{\rho}} \bar{f}^{eq}_\alpha + \bar{\rho} w_\alpha \left(\frac{\xi_\alpha \cdot \mathbf{u}'}{c_s^2} + \frac{(\xi_\alpha \cdot \mathbf{u}')(\xi_\alpha \cdot \bar{\mathbf{u}})}{c_s^4} - \frac{\mathbf{u}' \cdot \bar{\mathbf{u}}}{c_s^2} \right) \qquad (2)$$

where $c_s = 1/\sqrt{3}$ is the speed of sound, w_α is the weight coefficient of the lattice in direction α; $\bar{\rho}$, $\bar{\mathbf{u}}$, and ρ', $\mathbf{u}'$ denote the macroscopic variables, which are divided into the mean flow and acoustic disturbance, respectively; $\bar{f}^{eq}_\alpha$ is the steady equilibrium distribution function:

$$\bar{f}^{eq}_\alpha = \bar{\rho} w_\alpha \left(1 + \frac{\xi_\alpha \cdot \bar{\mathbf{u}}}{c_s^2} + \frac{(\xi_\alpha \cdot \bar{\mathbf{u}})^2}{2c_s^4} - \frac{|\bar{\mathbf{u}}|^2}{2c_s^2} \right) \qquad (3)$$

The linearized macroscopic variables $\bar{\rho}$, $\bar{\mathbf{u}}$, and ρ', $\mathbf{u}'$ and mesoscopic variables have the following moment relationship:

$$\rho' = \sum_\alpha f'^{eq}_\alpha \qquad (4)$$

$$\bar{\rho} \mathbf{u}' + \rho' \bar{\mathbf{u}} = \sum_\alpha \xi_\alpha f'^{eq}_\alpha \qquad (5)$$

For two-dimensional problems, the LBM adopts the D2Q9 model; the lattice velocity ξ_α and weight coefficient w_α are given by:

$$\begin{array}{l} |\xi_0| = 0, \quad |\xi_{1-4}| = 1, \quad |\xi_{5-8}| = \sqrt{2} \\ w_0 = \frac{4}{9}, \quad w_{1-4} = \frac{1}{9}, \quad w_{5-8} = \frac{1}{36} \end{array} \qquad (6)$$

C-E expansion analysis is often used to link the kinetic theory of gases and the macroscopic equations of motion [24]. It can also be used to link LLBE and LNSE. By C-E expansion analysis, the perturbation distribution function, time derivative, and spatial derivative can be expanded into the following forms, respectively:

$$f'_\alpha = f'^{(0)}_\alpha + Kn f'^{(1)}_\alpha + Kn^2 f'^{(2)}_\alpha \tag{7}$$

$$\frac{\partial}{\partial t} = Kn \frac{\partial}{\partial t_0} + Kn^2 \frac{\partial}{\partial t_1} \tag{8}$$

$$\nabla = Kn \cdot \nabla_1 \tag{9}$$

where Kn is the Knudsen number.

By substituting Equations (7)–(9) into the Taylor expansion of LLBE (Equation (1)), the decomposition forms of different orders can be obtained:

$$O(Kn^0): \quad f'^{(0)}_\alpha = f'^{eq}_\alpha \tag{10}$$

$$O(Kn^1): \quad \left(\frac{\partial}{\partial t_0} + \xi_\alpha \cdot \frac{\partial}{\partial r_1}\right) f'^{(0)}_\alpha + \frac{1}{\tau} f'^{(1)}_\alpha = 0 \tag{11}$$

$$O(Kn^2): \quad \frac{\partial f'^{(0)}_\alpha}{\partial t_1} + \left(1 - \frac{1}{2\tau}\right)\left(\frac{\partial}{\partial t_0} + \xi_\alpha \cdot \nabla_1\right) f'^{(1)}_\alpha + \frac{1}{\tau \delta_t} f'^{(2)}_\alpha = 0 \tag{12}$$

Sum the zero-order moments and first-order moments of Equations (11) and (12) under the $O(Kn^1)$ and $O(Kn^2)$ orders in all lattice velocity directions and multiply the results with Kn and Kn^2, respectively; by adding the results separately, we obtain the governing equations of the LLBE recovered by C-E expansion analysis:

$$\frac{\partial \rho'}{\partial t} + \nabla \cdot \left(\sum_\alpha \xi_\alpha f'^{eq}_\alpha\right) = 0 \tag{13}$$

$$\frac{\partial (\rho' \overline{\mathbf{u}} + \overline{\rho} \mathbf{u}')}{\partial t} + \nabla \cdot \left(\sum_\alpha \xi^i_\alpha \xi^j_\alpha f'^{eq}_\alpha + \left(1 - \frac{1}{2\tau}\right) \sum_\alpha \xi^i_\alpha \xi^j_\alpha f'^{neq}_\alpha\right) = 0 \tag{14}$$

where $f'^{neq}_\alpha = Kn f'^{(1)}_\alpha = -\tau \delta_t D f'^{eq}_\alpha$ denotes the perturbation non-equilibrium distribution function, and it satisfies the following moment relationship:

$$\sum_\alpha f'^{neq}_\alpha = 0, \quad \sum_\alpha \xi_\alpha f'^{neq}_\alpha = 0 \tag{15}$$

In addition, to restore Equations (13) and (14) to LNSE, the mesoscopic and macroscopic variables need to satisfy the following moment relationship in addition to Equations (4) and (5):

$$\sum_\alpha \xi^i_\alpha \xi^j_\alpha f'^{eq}_\alpha = \rho' c_s^2 \delta_{i,j} + \overline{\rho} \mathbf{u}' \overline{\mathbf{u}} + \rho' \overline{\mathbf{u}\mathbf{u}} + \overline{\rho} \overline{\mathbf{u}} \mathbf{u}' \tag{16}$$

$$\sum_\alpha \xi^i_\alpha \xi^j_\alpha f'^{neq}_\alpha = -\overline{\mu}\left(\nabla \mathbf{u}' + (\nabla \mathbf{u}')^T\right) - \mu'\left(\nabla \overline{\mathbf{u}} + (\nabla \overline{\mathbf{u}})^T\right) \tag{17}$$

where $\mu = \overline{\mu} + \mu' = \tau \delta_t (\overline{\rho} + \rho') c_s^2$ is the dynamic viscosity of the fluid.

2.2. SLLBM

According to the fractional-step calculation technique, Equations (13) and (14) can be decomposed into two steps: a predictor step and a corrector step:

The predictor step is formulated as follows:

$$\frac{\partial \rho'}{\partial t} + \nabla \cdot \left(\sum_\alpha \xi_\alpha f'^{eq}_\alpha\right) = 0 \tag{18}$$

$$\frac{\partial(\rho'\bar{\mathbf{u}} + \bar{\rho}\mathbf{u}')}{\partial t} + \nabla \cdot \left(\sum_\alpha \xi_\alpha^i \xi_\alpha^j f_\alpha'^{eq} + \frac{1}{2\tau} \sum_\alpha \xi_\alpha^i \xi_\alpha^j f_\alpha'^{neq} \right) = 0 \qquad (19)$$

The corrector step is formulated as follows:

$$\frac{\partial \rho'}{\partial t} = 0 \qquad (20)$$

$$\frac{\partial(\rho'\bar{\mathbf{u}} + \bar{\rho}\mathbf{u}')}{\partial t} + \nabla \cdot \left(\left(1 - \frac{1}{\tau}\right) \sum_\alpha \xi_\alpha^i \xi_\alpha^j f_\alpha'^{neq} \right) = 0 \qquad (21)$$

In the predictor step, the solution can be advanced using the following relations:

$$\rho'^* = \sum_\alpha f_\alpha'^{eq}(\mathbf{r} - \xi_\alpha \delta_t, t - \delta_t) \qquad (22)$$

$$\bar{\rho}\mathbf{u}'^* + \rho'^*\bar{\mathbf{u}} = \sum_\alpha \xi_\alpha f_\alpha'^{eq}(\mathbf{r} - \xi_\alpha \delta_t, t - \delta_t) \qquad (23)$$

where δ_t is the time step and * is the intermediate value of the perturbation macroscopic variables obtained by solving the predictor step. It can be proven that Equations (22) and (23) can be used to accurately solve Equations (18) and (19).

The Taylor expansion of the perturbation equilibrium distribution function can be obtained by:

$$f_\alpha'^{neq}(\mathbf{r} - \xi_\alpha \delta_t, t - \delta_t) = f_\alpha'^{eq}(\mathbf{r}, t) - \delta_t D f_\alpha'^{eq}(\mathbf{r}, t) - \frac{\delta_t}{2\tau} D f_\alpha'^{neq}(\mathbf{r}, t) + O(\delta_t^3) \qquad (24)$$

By substituting Equation (24) into Equations (22) and (23) and combining the outcome with Equation (15), we obtain:

$$\rho'^* = \sum_\alpha f_\alpha'^{eq}(\mathbf{r}, t) - \delta_t \left[\frac{\partial}{\partial t} \sum_\alpha f_\alpha'^{eq}(\mathbf{r}, t) + \nabla \cdot \sum_\alpha \xi_\alpha f_\alpha'^{eq}(\mathbf{r}, t) \right] \\ - \frac{\delta_t}{2\tau} \left[\frac{\partial}{\partial t} \sum_\alpha f_\alpha'^{neq}(\mathbf{r}, t) + \nabla \cdot \sum_\alpha \xi_\alpha f_\alpha'^{neq}(\mathbf{r}, t) \right] + O(\delta_t^3) \qquad (25)$$

$$\bar{\rho}\mathbf{u}'^* + \rho'^*\bar{\mathbf{u}} = \sum_\alpha \xi_\alpha f_\alpha'^{eq}(\mathbf{r}, t) - \delta_t \left[\frac{\partial}{\partial t} \sum_\alpha \xi_\alpha f_\alpha'^{eq}(\mathbf{r}, t) + \nabla \cdot \sum_\alpha \xi_\alpha^i \xi_\alpha^j f_\alpha'^{eq}(\mathbf{r}, t) \right] \\ - \frac{\delta_t}{2\tau} \left[\nabla \cdot \sum_\alpha \xi_\alpha^i \xi_\alpha^j f_\alpha'^{neq}(\mathbf{r}, t) \right] + O(\delta_t^3) \qquad (26)$$

According to the moment relationship introduced in Section 1, Equations (25) and (26) are transformed into the following form:

$$\frac{\partial \rho'}{\partial t} + \nabla \cdot \left(\sum_\alpha \xi_\alpha f_\alpha'^{eq} \right) + O(\delta_t^2) = 0 \qquad (27)$$

$$\frac{\partial(\bar{\rho}\mathbf{u}' + \rho'\bar{\mathbf{u}})}{\partial t} + \nabla \cdot \left[\sum_\alpha \xi_\alpha^i \xi_\alpha^j f_\alpha'^{eq}(\mathbf{r}, t) + \frac{1}{2\tau} \sum_\alpha \xi_\alpha^i \xi_\alpha^j f_\alpha'^{neq} \right] + O(\delta_t^2) = 0 \qquad (28)$$

where $O(\delta_t^2)$ is a second-order small parameter, which can be ignored. Thus, Equations (27) and (28) can accurately recover the predictor step Equations (18) and (19).

For the linear continuous equation (Equation (13)), the predictor step can be used directly to solve without correction, i.e., $\rho'^{n+1} = \rho'^*$, where the superscript $n+1$ represents the perturbation macroscopic variables at the next time step. However, for the linear momentum equation (Equation (14)), there is still a deviation $\nabla \cdot \left[\left(1 - \frac{1}{\tau}\right) \sum_\alpha \xi_\alpha^i \xi_\alpha^j f_\alpha'^{neq} \right]$ between Equation (28) and Equation (14), i.e.,:

$$\overline{\rho}\mathbf{u}'^{n+1} + \rho'^{n+1}\overline{\mathbf{u}} = \overline{\rho}\mathbf{u}'^* + \rho'^*\overline{\mathbf{u}} - \nabla \cdot \left[\left(1 - \frac{1}{\tau}\right)\sum_\alpha \xi_\alpha^i \xi_\alpha^j f_\alpha'^{neq}\right] \qquad (29)$$

To calculate Equation (29), similar to the derivation of the predictor step, we can apply Equation (15) into the Taylor expansion of the perturbation nonequilibrium distribution function $f_\alpha'^{neq}(\mathbf{r} - \xi_\alpha \delta_t, t)$, and the following relationship can be deduced:

$$-\nabla \cdot \left[\left(1 - \frac{1}{\tau}\right)\sum_\alpha \xi_\alpha^i \xi_\alpha^j f_\alpha'^{neq}(\mathbf{r}, t)\right] = \left(1 - \frac{1}{\tau}\right)\frac{1}{\delta_t}\sum_\alpha \xi_\alpha f_\alpha'^{neq}(\mathbf{r} - \xi_\alpha \delta_t, t) \qquad (30)$$

By using Equation (30), Equation (29) can be written as:

$$\overline{\rho}\mathbf{u}'^{n+1} + \rho'^{n+1}\overline{\mathbf{u}} = \overline{\rho}\mathbf{u}'^* + \rho'^*\overline{\mathbf{u}} + \left(1 - \frac{1}{\tau}\right)\sum_\alpha \xi_\alpha f_\alpha'^{neq}(\mathbf{r} - \xi_\alpha \delta_t, t) \qquad (31)$$

We therefore obtained simplified calculation formulas for LLBM, which are summarized as follows:

For the linear continuous equation, the perturbation density at the next time step is directly calculated by:

$$\rho'^{n+1} = \sum_\alpha f_\alpha'^{eq}(\mathbf{r} - \xi_\alpha \delta_t, t - \delta_t) \qquad (32)$$

For the linear momentum equation, the perturbation velocity at the next time step is obtained through the predictor–corrector process as shown below:

It is obtained in the predictor step as follows:

$$\overline{\rho}\mathbf{u}'^* + \rho'^*\overline{\mathbf{u}} = \sum_\alpha \xi_\alpha f_\alpha'^{eq}(\mathbf{r} - \xi_\alpha \delta_t, t - \delta_t) \qquad (33)$$

It is obtained in the corrector step as follows:

$$\mathbf{u}'^{n+1} = \left(\overline{\rho}\mathbf{u}'^* + \rho'^*\overline{\mathbf{u}} + \left(1 - \frac{1}{\tau}\right)\sum_\alpha \xi_\alpha f_\alpha'^{neq}(\mathbf{r} - \xi_\alpha \delta_t, t) - \rho'^{n+1}\overline{\mathbf{u}}\right)/\overline{\rho} \qquad (34)$$

The perturbation nonequilibrium distribution function $f_\alpha'^{neq}$ is given by:

$$f_\alpha'^{neq}(\mathbf{r}, t) = -\tau \delta_t D f_\alpha'^{eq}(\mathbf{r}, t) = -\tau \left[f_\alpha'^{eq*}(\mathbf{r}, t) - f_\alpha'^{eq}(\mathbf{r} - \xi_\alpha \delta_t, t - \delta_t)\right] \qquad (35)$$

where $f_\alpha'^{eq*}(\mathbf{r}, t)$ denotes the perturbation equilibrium distribution function calculated by the intermediate value of the linear macroscopic variables.

2.3. IBM

The idea of the IBM is to imagine immersion of the solid in the fluid [34–39], and the interaction between the fluid and the solid wall is realized by adding a boundary force term to the right side of the linear momentum equation. Through this treatment, the linear momentum equation can be written as:

$$\frac{\partial(\overline{\rho}\mathbf{u}' + \rho'\overline{\mathbf{u}})}{\partial t} + \nabla \cdot (\overline{\rho}\mathbf{u}'\overline{\mathbf{u}} + \rho'\overline{\mathbf{u}\mathbf{u}} + \overline{\rho}\mathbf{u}\mathbf{u}') = \\ -\nabla(\rho' c_s^2) + \nabla \cdot \left[\overline{\mu}\left(\nabla \mathbf{u}' + (\nabla \mathbf{u}')^T\right) + \mu'\left(\nabla \overline{\mathbf{u}} + (\nabla \overline{\mathbf{u}})^T\right)\right] + \mathbf{f} \qquad (36)$$

$$\mathbf{f}(\mathbf{r}, t) = \int_\Gamma \mathbf{F}(s, t)\delta(\mathbf{r} - \mathbf{R}(s, t))ds \qquad (37)$$

where $\mathbf{r}$ and $\mathbf{R}$ represent the positions of the Euler point and the Lagrangian point, $\mathbf{f}$ and $\mathbf{F}$ represent the boundary force terms of the Euler point and the Lagrangian point, δ is the Dirac delta function, and s is the index of the Lagrangian point.

The key to wall boundary processing is to solve the boundary force term of the Lagrangian point. In this paper, the method of Chen et al. [37] was used to revise the perturbation velocity $\mathbf{u}'^{n+1}$. In the following derivation process, the revised result of the perturbation velocity $\mathbf{u}'^{n+1}$ is recorded as $\mathbf{u}'^{n+1}_I$, which can be evaluated by:

$$\mathbf{u}'^{n+1}_I = \mathbf{u}'^{n+1} + \Delta \mathbf{u}' \tag{38}$$

where $\Delta \mathbf{u}'$ denotes the revise of $\mathbf{u}'^{n+1}$.

The boundary force term $\mathbf{f}$ of the Euler point in Equation (36) can be related to $\Delta \mathbf{u}'$ according to the following formula:

$$\mathbf{f} = \rho'^{n+1} \frac{\Delta \mathbf{u}'}{\delta_t} \tag{39}$$

The no-slip boundary condition was adopted for perturbation velocity on the wall boundary, that is, the perturbation velocity of fluid at the Lagrangian point is the same as the perturbation velocity of the immersed object, which can be written as follows:

$$\mathbf{U}'^{n+1}_I(\mathbf{R}_l) = \mathbf{U}'_B(\mathbf{R}_l) \tag{40}$$

where $\mathbf{U}'^{n+1}_I$ and $\mathbf{U}'_B$ represent the perturbation velocity of the fluid and boundary, respectively, and the former is obtained by of the perturbation velocity of the Euler point as follows:

$$\mathbf{U}'^{n+1}_I(\mathbf{R}_l) = \sum_e \mathbf{u}'^{n+1}(r_e) K(r_e - \mathbf{R}_l) \delta_e^2 \\ l = 1,2,\ldots,N \quad e = 1,2,\ldots,M \tag{41}$$

where N and M represent the number of Lagrangian points and Euler points, respectively; δ_e is the grid scale of the Euler grid; and K is the kernel function related to the positions of Lagrangian points and Euler points, which is defined by:

$$K(r_e - \mathbf{R}_l) = \delta(r_{e1} - R_{l1}) \delta(r_{e2} - R_{l2}) \tag{42}$$

where δ is written as:

$$\delta(r) = \begin{cases} 1 + \frac{\cos(\pi |r|/2)}{4} & |r| \leq 2 \\ 0 & |r| > 2 \end{cases} \tag{43}$$

In Equation (38), the revised perturbation velocity is obtained by interpolating the perturbation velocity at the Lagrangian point, and the mathematical relationship that satisfies the no-slip boundary condition is as follows:

$$\Delta \mathbf{u}'(r_e) = \sum_l \delta \mathbf{u}'_l K(r_e - \mathbf{R}_l) \delta_l \quad l = 1,2,\ldots,N \quad e = 1,2,\ldots,M \tag{44}$$

where δ_l is the scale of the Lagrangian grid.

Combining Equations (38)–(44), a linear system for solving the correction velocity at Lagrangian points can be obtained:

$$\mathbf{A} \cdot \mathbf{X} = \mathbf{B} \tag{45}$$

where

$$\mathbf{A} = \delta_e^2 \begin{bmatrix} K_{11} & K_{12} & \cdots & K_{1M} \\ K_{21} & K_{22} & \cdots & K_{2M} \\ \vdots & \vdots & \ddots & \vdots \\ K_{N1} & K_{N2} & K_{N3} & K_{NM} \end{bmatrix} \cdot \begin{bmatrix} K_{11} & K_{12} & \cdots & K_{1N} \\ K_{21} & K_{22} & \cdots & K_{2N} \\ \vdots & \vdots & \ddots & \vdots \\ K_{M1} & K_{M2} & K_{M3} & K_{MN} \end{bmatrix} \tag{46}$$

$$\mathbf{X} = \left[\delta \mathbf{u}'^1_l \delta^1_l, \delta \mathbf{u}'^2_l \delta^2_l, \ldots, \delta \mathbf{u}'^N_l \delta^N_l \right]^T \tag{47}$$

$$\mathbf{B} = \begin{bmatrix} \mathbf{U}'^{1}_{B} \\ \mathbf{U}'^{2}_{B} \\ \vdots \\ \mathbf{U}'^{N}_{B} \end{bmatrix} - \begin{bmatrix} K_{11} & K_{12} & \cdots & K_{1M} \\ K_{21} & K_{22} & \cdots & K_{2M} \\ \vdots & \vdots & \ddots & \vdots \\ K_{N1} & K_{N2} & K_{N3} & K_{NM} \end{bmatrix} \begin{bmatrix} \mathbf{u}'^{*}_{1} \\ \mathbf{u}'^{*}_{2} \\ \vdots \\ \mathbf{u}'^{*}_{M} \end{bmatrix} \quad (48)$$

2.4. Boundary Conditions

2.4.1. Periodic Boundary Condition

Here, we adopted the periodic boundary condition [40]. Taking the two-dimensional flow shown in Figure 1 as an example, the fluid flows in from the left and out to the right. There are two layers of virtual grid points x_0 and x_{N+1} outside the entrance x_1 on the left and the exit x_N on the right, respectively; the periodic boundary conditions are:

$$q'_{1,5,8}(x_0, j, t) = q'_{1,5,8}(x_N, j, t) \quad (49)$$

$$q'_{3,6,7}(x_{N+1}, j, t) = q'_{3,6,7}(x_1, j, t) \quad (50)$$

where q' represents the perturbation macroscopic variables.

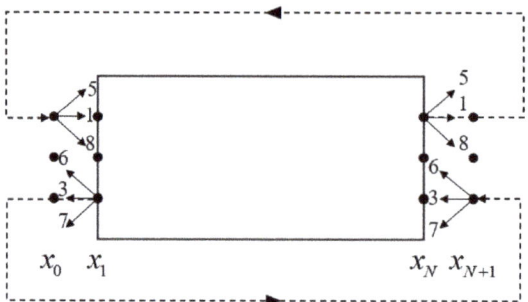

Figure 1. Schematic model of periodic boundary condition.

2.4.2. Nonequilibrium Extrapolation Boundary

To process the perturbation nonequilibrium distribution function at the boundary, this paper adopts a nonequilibrium extrapolation boundary condition, which is obtained by interpolating two grid points inside the boundary:

$$f'^{neq}_i(x_0) = f'^{neq}_i(x_1) + \left[f'^{neq}_i(x_1) - f'^{neq}_i(x_2)\right] \frac{x_{i0} - x_{i1}}{x_{i1} - x_{i2}} \quad (51)$$

where x_0, x_1, and x_2 represent the boundary points and the grid points of the first layer and the second layer adjacent to the boundary, respectively. Because the calculation adopts a uniform grid, Equation (51) can be expressed as:

$$f'^{neq}_i(x_0) = 2f'^{neq}_i(x_1) - f'^{neq}_i(x_2) \quad (52)$$

2.5. Computational Sequence

The computational steps of the SLLBM can be summarized as follows:

(1) Determine the mesh size parameters δ_x and the time step δ_t and then calculate the relaxation time τ.
(2) Calculate the predictor step of the linear governing equations by Equation (33) and obtain the intermediate value of the perturbation macroscopic variables q'^{*} of the new time step.
(3) According to Equation (35), calculate the perturbation nonequilibrium distribution function f'^{neq}_α, selecting appropriate boundary conditions for f'^{neq}_α.

(4) Use Equation (34) to calculate the corrector step of the linear momentum equation, and obtain the perturbation velocity $\mathbf{u}'^{n+1}$ of the next time step.
(5) Implement appropriate boundary conditions for the perturbation macroscopic variables and repeat the above process until the results convergent.

For the sound propagation problem that needs to calculate the interaction between the fluid and the solid wall in the fluid, it is necessary to use the IBM derived in Section 1. In this case, the perturbation velocity needs to be revised after step 5. The specific process is as follows:

(1) Solve Equation (45) to obtain the perturbation velocity revision term at the Lagrangian point.
(2) According to the perturbation velocity obtained by Equation (34), combined with Equations (38) and (44), the perturbation velocity of the Euler grid point at the next moment $\mathbf{u}'^{n+1}_I$ can be obtained.

2.6. Memory Cost

As can be seen from the introduction in Section 2.2, in the SLLBM, the perturbation macroscopic variables were directly evolved so that the evolution and storage of the perturbation distribution function were avoided, which implies only the perturbation macroscopic variables, instead of the values of perturbation distribution functions along all lattice velocity directions at each grid point, need to be stored. As a result, SLLBM requires less memory than the standard LBM.

For instance, during the simulation of the acoustic wave propagation in the two-dimensional imcompressible isothermal flow by the D2Q9 model, only six variables including the present values and the intermediate values of perturbation velocity and density need to be stored at each grid point. Compared with the standard LBM, the number of variables to be stored at each grid point was reduced from 9 to 6, implying the SLLBM can theoretically save about 33.3% of memory [32]. In the simulation of the three-dimensional problem by D3Q19 model, the number of variables to be stored at each grid point was reduced from 19 to 8, which means the SLLBM can theoretically save about 57.9% of memory [41].

3. Numerical Examples

In this section, some numerical examples are used to verify the correctness of the SLLBM for the simulation of acoustic waves propagation in the fluid; we consider the following scenarios: (1) propagation of a Gaussian pulse, (2) propagation of a time-periodic sound sources, (3) propagation of plane wave, (4) a Gaussian pulse interacting with a solid wall, and (5) a Gaussian pulse scattered by a stationary circular cylinder.

Cases (1), (2), and (3) test the feasibility and accuracy of SLLBM through the simulation of three different sound sources. Case (4) evaluates the feasibility of SLLBM for calculating the acoustic reflections by a solid wall. Case (5) is used to test the feasibility of introducing the IBM into the SLLBM framework to study the interaction between acoustic waves and complex boundaries.

In these examples, the variables are all nondimensionalized, and the nondimensional parameters of density, velocity, and pressure are ρ_∞, c_∞, and $\rho_\infty c_\infty^2$, respectively.

3.1. Case 1: Propagation of a Gaussian Pulse

As shown in Figure 2, the computational domain of Gaussian pulse propagation is $[-200, 200] \times [-200, 200]$, the grid points are uniformly arranged, the grid scale $\delta_x = 1.0$, the time step $\delta_t = 1.0$, and the relaxation time $\tau = 0.5$. At the initial moment, a Gaussian pulse was applied with the following formula:

$$\begin{cases} \rho'(x,y,0) = \varepsilon \exp(-\beta(x^2+y^2)) & \bar{\rho} = \rho_0 \\ u'(x,y,0) = 0 & \bar{u} = u_0 \\ v'(x,y,0) = 0 & \bar{v} = v_0 \end{cases} \quad (53)$$

where $\rho_0 = 1.0$ represents the density of the uniform mean flow, $\varepsilon = 0.01$ is the density pulse amplitude; and β is the source shape factor obtained by $\beta = \ln 2/b^2$, where $b = 8$ representing the half-width Gaussian factor. For this form of Gaussian impulse propagation, the exact solution for the perturbation density ρ' is described by [42]:

$$\rho'(x,y,t) = \frac{\varepsilon}{2\beta} \int_0^\infty \exp\left(-\psi^2/4\beta\right) \cos(c_s t \psi) J_0(\psi \eta) \psi d\psi \tag{54}$$

where $\eta = \left[(x - u_0 t_0)^2 + y^2\right]^{\frac{1}{2}}$, and $J_0(\cdot)$ is the zero-order Bessel function of the first kind. For both cases of stationary medium $\bar{u} = 0.0$ and moving medium $\bar{u} = 0.3$, Figure 3 shows the contours of instantaneous perturbation density at $t = 80$, and Figure 4 shows a comparison of the instantaneous perturbation density and the exact solution along the centerline at $y = 0$. The calculation results of the SLLBM are in good agreement with the exact solutions regardless of whether there is the convective effect, which shows that SLLBM can simulate the acoustic waves propagation problems in stationary and moving medium.

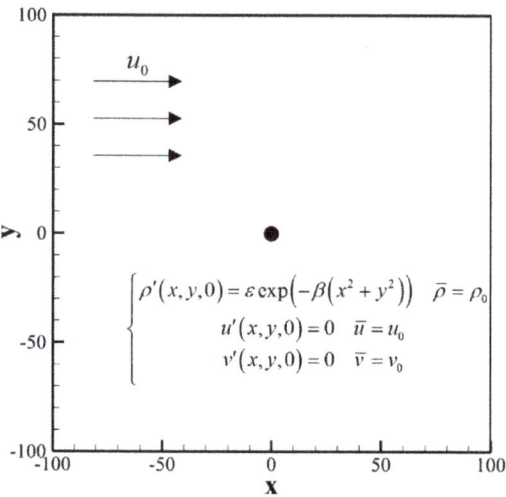

Figure 2. Computational model of a Gaussian pulse propagation.

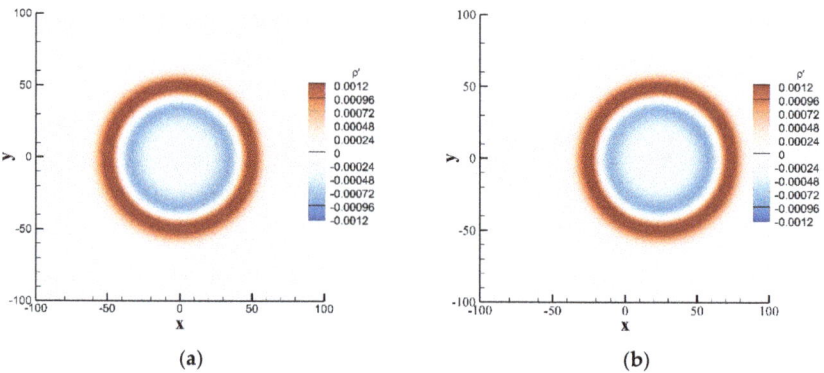

Figure 3. Instantaneous perturbation density contours of a Gaussian pulse obtained by the SLLBM at $t = 80$. (**a**) stationary medium ($\bar{u} = 0.0$), (**b**) moving medium ($\bar{u} = 0.3$).

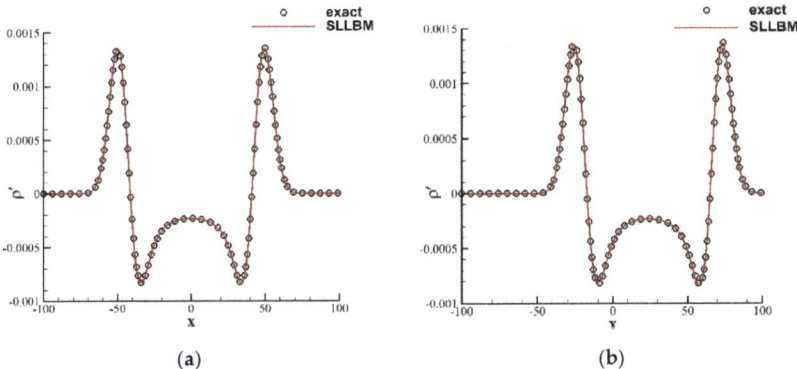

Figure 4. Instantaneous perturbation density distribution along the centerline at $y = 0$ for $t = 80$. (**a**) stationary medium ($\bar{u} = 0.0$), (**b**) moving medium ($\bar{u} = 0.3$).

3.2. Case 2: Propagation of a Time-Periodic Acoustic Source

As the second case, we simulate the propagation of a time-periodic acoustic source in a stationary medium. The acoustic source is given by the following formula:

$$\begin{cases} \rho'(x,y,0) = \varepsilon \sin(\omega t) & \bar{\rho} = \rho_0 \\ u'(x,y,0) = 0 & \bar{u} = u_0 \\ v'(x,y,0) = 0 & \bar{v} = v_0 \end{cases} \quad (55)$$

where $\varepsilon = 0.01$ is the density pulse amplitude, $\omega = \pi/10$ represents the frequency of the time-periodic acoustic source; and $(\rho_0, u_0, v_0) = (1.0, 0.0, 0.0)$ are the variables in the stationary flow. The computation domain is a $[-50, 50] \times [-50, 50]$ square, and a uniform grid is used, giving the grid spacing and the time step of 1.0.

For the static medium, Figure 5 shows the instantaneous perturbation density contours of the time-periodic acoustic source in the stationary medium at $t = 75$ for two relaxation times $\tau = 0.6$ and 1.0. The SLLBM clearly captures the sound wave generated at the origin and as it propagates outward, and the attenuation speed of the acoustic waves amplitude is significantly greater when $\tau = 1.0$. For quantitative analysis, Figure 6 shows a comparison of the instantaneous perturbation density curve along the centerline at $t = 75$ with the exact solution [43]. As can be seen, the results calculated by SLLBM are in good agreement with the exact solution.

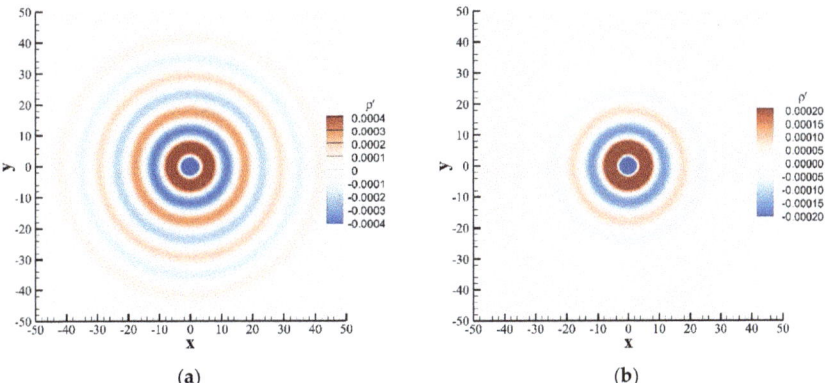

Figure 5. Instantaneous perturbation density contours of a time-periodic acoustic source in a stationary flow obtained by the SLLBM at $t = 75$. (**a**) $\tau = 0.6$, (**b**) $\tau = 1.0$.

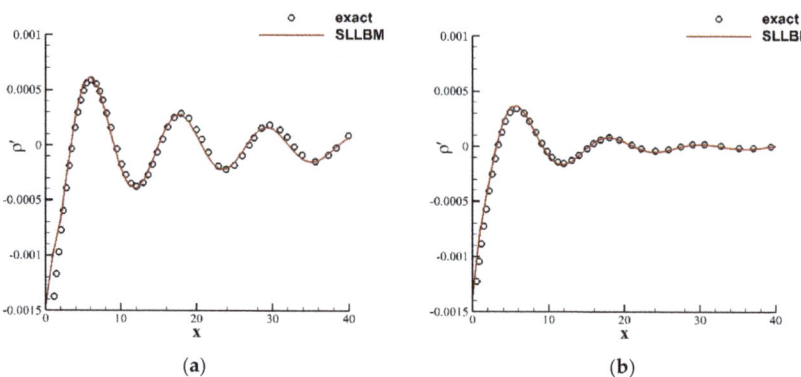

Figure 6. Instantaneous perturbation density distribution along centerline at $t = 75$ for $y = 0$. (a) $\tau = 0.6$, (b) $\tau = 1.0$.

For the moving medium, the Mach number of the uniform flow was set as 0.1 or 0.2, and relaxation time as $\tau = 0.6$. Figure 7 shows the perturbation density contours at $t = 100$. It can be seen that the wavelengths were shorter in the left and longer in the right of the sound source because of the Doppler effect. The wavelengths of acoustic waves located on the left and right sides of the sound source should be [43]:

$$\lambda_{left,right} = (c_s \mp \overline{u})T \tag{56}$$

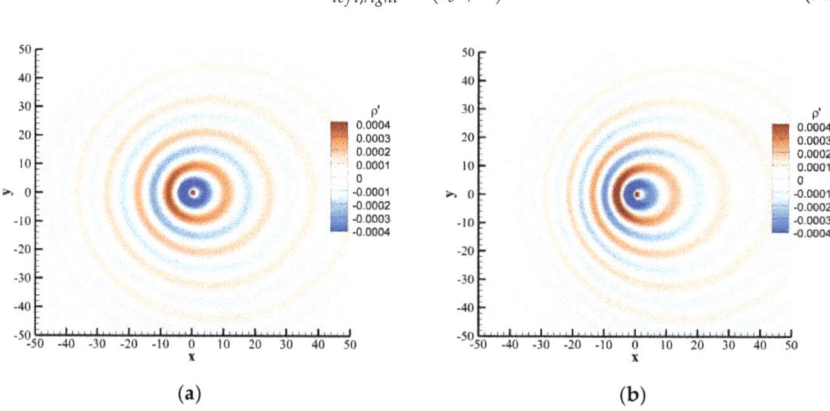

Figure 7. Instantaneous perturbation density contours of a time-periodic acoustic source in a uniform flow obtained by the SLLBM at $t = 100$. (a) $\overline{u} = 0.1$, (b) $\overline{u} = 0.2$.

Since $T = \frac{2\pi}{\omega} = 20$, $c_s = 0.586$, and $\overline{u} = 0.1$ or 0.2, the wavelengths of acoustic waves located on the left sides of the sound source should be 9.72 and 7.72, and the wavelengths on the right side should be 13.72 and 15.72, respectively. For quantitative analysis, the instantaneous perturbation density curves along the centerline at $t = 100$ are shown in Figure 8, from which the Doppler effect is clear. It can be seen that the wavelengths of acoustic waves located on the left sides of the sound source $\lambda_{left} \approx 9.64$ or 7.80, and the wavelengths on the right side $\lambda_{right} \approx 13.57$ or 15.73, which shows that SLLBM can also well simulate the convection effect of the moving medium.

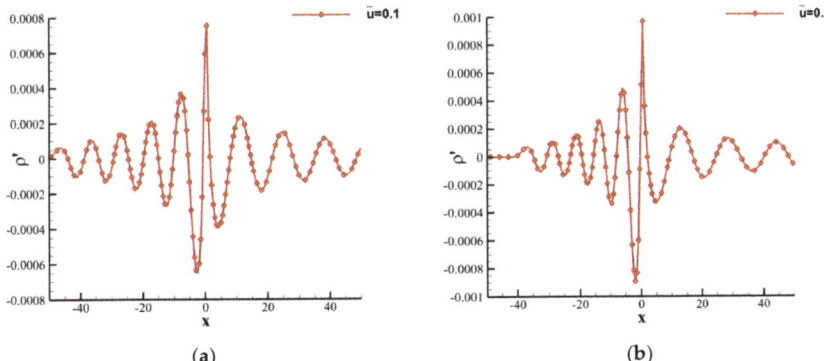

Figure 8. Instantaneous perturbation density distribution along centerline at $t = 100$ for $y = 0$. (a) $\bar{u} = 0.1$, (b) $\bar{u} = 0.2$.

3.3. Case 3: Propagation of Plane Wave

In this case, we simulate the propagation of a one-dimensional plane wave. The calculation model is shown in Figure 9. On the top and bottom boundaries, a periodic boundary was applied, the right side is a nonequilibrium extrapolation boundary, and the left side is a sound source, which is given by the following formula:

$$\begin{cases} \rho'(x,y,0) = \varepsilon \sin(\omega t) & \bar{\rho} = \rho_0 \\ u'(x,y,0) = c_s \varepsilon \sin(\omega t)/\bar{\rho} & \bar{u} = u_0 \\ v'(x,y,0) = 0 & \bar{v} = v_0 \end{cases} \quad (57)$$

where $\varepsilon = 0.01$, $(\rho_0, u_0, v_0) = (1.0, 0.0, 0.0)$ are the variables in the stationary flow, $\omega = 2\pi c_s/\lambda$ represents the frequency of the sound source, and λ denotes the wavelength. For this defined one-dimensional plane wave propagation, the exact solution for the perturbation velocity u' is given by:

$$u'(x,t) = \frac{c_s \varepsilon}{\rho_0} e^{-\varphi x} \sin(\omega t - kx) \quad (58)$$

where $\varphi = 4\pi^2 v/c_s \lambda^2$ represents the attenuation coefficient of the acoustic wave. The calculation domain was set at $[0, 20] \times [0, 1000]$, the calculation grid adopts a uniform grid, the grid scale $\delta_x = 1.0$, and the time step $\delta_t = 1.0$.

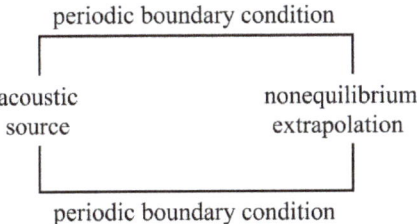

Figure 9. Schematic model of the plane wave calculation model.

Figure 10 provides the perturbation density contours for different kinematic viscosities and different wavelengths at $t = 75$. The plane wave propagates in the form of a band, and the larger the wavelength and the smaller the kinematic viscosity, the slower the acoustic waves decays during the propagation process. To specifically judge the influence of wavelength and kinematic viscosity on the propagation of the one-dimensional plane wave, Figure 11 plots the comparison of the instantaneous perturbation velocity u' distribution with the exact solution at the position $y = 10$. During the propagation of a one-dimensional plane wave, the wavelength determines the phase of the acoustic wave, and the kinematic viscosity determines the amplitude. For plane wave propagation with different kinematic viscosities or wavelengths, the results obtained by SLLBM are in good agreement with the exact solutions.

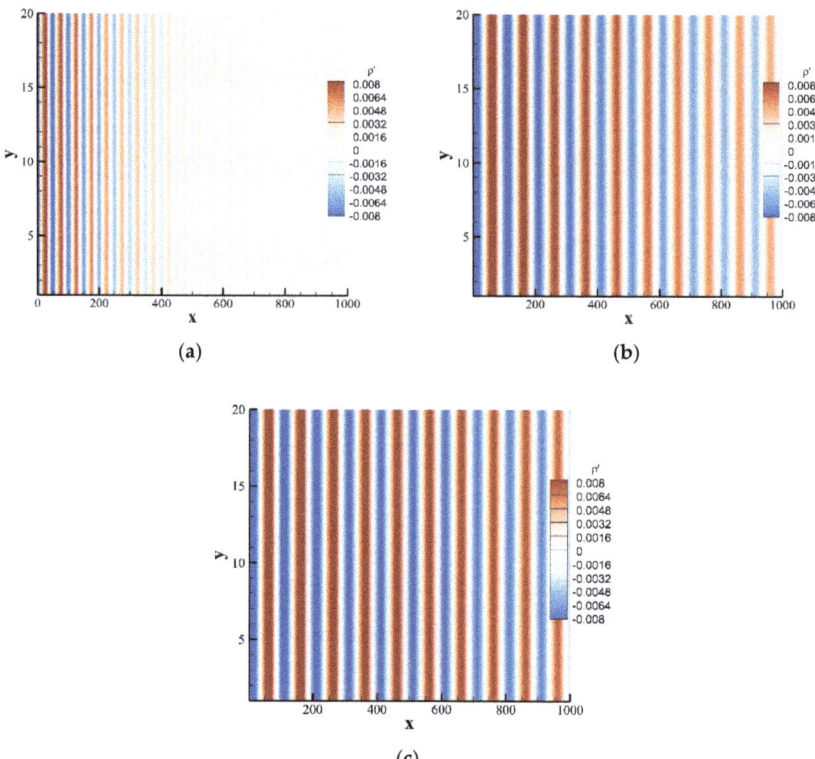

Figure 10. Instantaneous perturbation density contours of plane wave obtained by the SLLBM at $t = 5000$. (**a**) $(v, \lambda) = (0.1, 50)$, (**b**) $(v, \lambda) = (0.1, 100)$, (**c**) $(v, \lambda) = (0.05, 100)$.

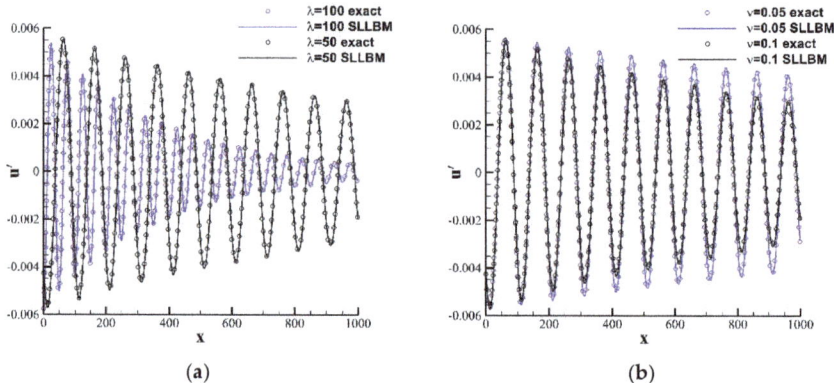

Figure 11. Instantaneous perturbation density distribution along the centerline $y = 10$ at $t = 5000$. (**a**) $v = 0.1$, (**b**) $\lambda = 100$.

3.4. Case 4: Propagation of a Gaussian Pulse with Wall Reflection

This case simulates the propagation of a Gaussian pulse with wall reflections by SLLBM. The calculation model is shown in Figure 12 and the sound source is defined by:

$$\begin{cases} \rho'(x,y,0) = \varepsilon \exp\left(-\beta\left((x-0)^2 + (y+75)^2\right)\right) & \bar{\rho} = \rho_0 \\ u'(x,y,0) = 0 & \bar{u} = u_0 \\ v'(x,y,0) = 0 & \bar{v} = v_0 \end{cases} \quad (59)$$

where $\varepsilon = 0.01$, $(\rho_0, u_0, v_0) = (1.0, 0.0, 0.0)$ are the variables in the stationary flow and $\beta = \ln 2/3^2$. The calculation domain was set at $[-100, 100] \times [-100, 100]$, the calculation adopts a uniform grid, the grid scale $\delta_x = 0.5$, and the time step $\delta_t = 0.5$, and the relaxation time $\tau = 0.5$. The exact solution for the perturbation density ρ' is defined by:

$$\rho'(x,y,t) = \frac{\varepsilon}{\beta} \int_0^\infty \exp\left(-\psi^2/4\beta\right) \cos(c_s t \psi)[J_0(\psi \eta_1) + J_0(\psi \eta_2)]\psi d\psi \quad (60)$$

where $\eta_1 = \left[(x - u_0 t)^2 + (y+75)^2\right]^{0.5}$, $\eta_2 = \left[(x - u_0 t)^2 + (y+125)^2\right]^{0.5}$.

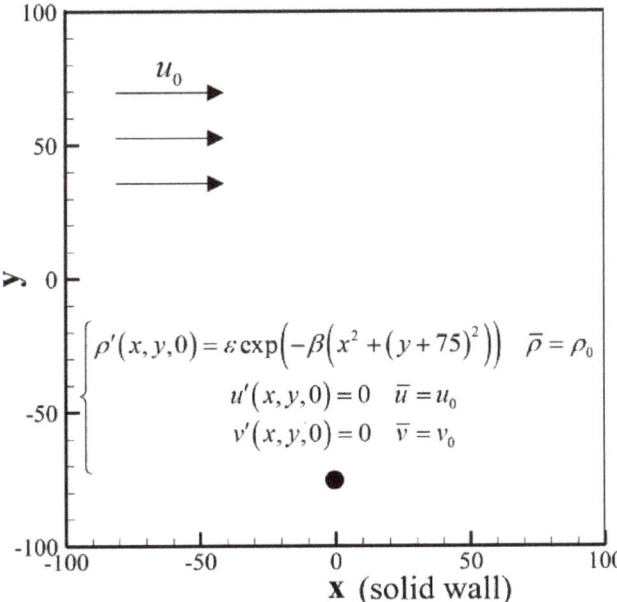

Figure 12. Computational model of Gaussian pulse propagation with wall reflection.

Figure 13 shows the perturbation density contours at $t = 26, 120$, and 160 obtained by the SLLBM. Figure 14 shows the perturbation density distributions along the reflecting wall $y = -100$ and $x = y + 100$ at these three moments calculated by the SLLBM and compared with the exact solution. There are two peaks along $x = y + 100$ at $t = 120, 160$, the inner peak is generated by the reflection of the pulse with the wall, and the outer one is generated by the propagation of the pulse. The numerical solutions are in good agreement with the exact solution, which shows that SLLBM can simulate the problem of acoustic waves encountering wall reflections.

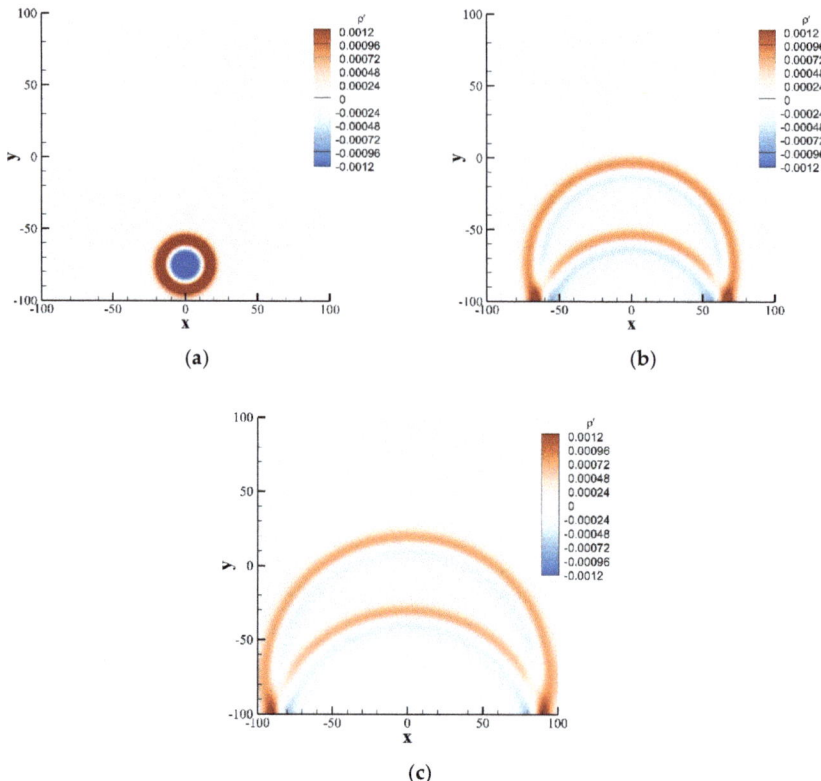

Figure 13. Instantaneous perturbation density contours of a Gaussian pulse with wall reflection obtained by the SLLBM. (**a**) $t = 26$, (**b**) $t = 120$, (**c**) $t = 160$.

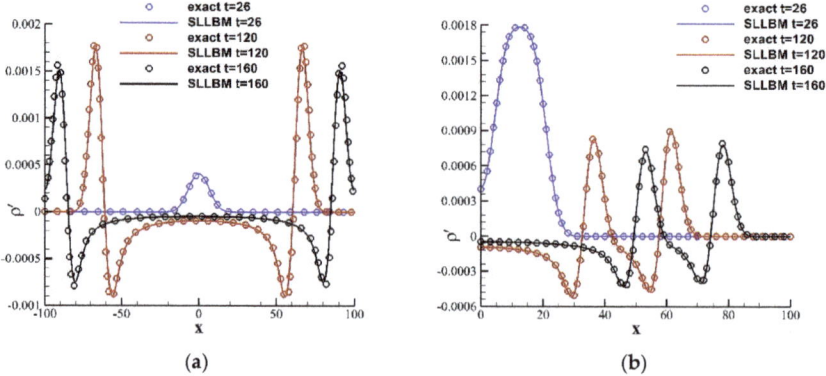

Figure 14. Instantaneous perturbation density distribution at different locations at $t = 26, 120, 160$. (**a**) $y = -100$, (**b**) $x = y + 100$.

3.5. Case 5: A Gaussian Pulse Scattered by a Stationary Cylinder

In this problem, a stationary circular cylinder (radius $R = 10$) is located at the origin. At the initial moment, the sound source is applied as follows (Figure 15):

$$\begin{cases} \rho'(x,y,0) = \varepsilon \exp\left(-\beta\left((x-400.0)^2 + (y-0.0)^2\right)\right), & \bar{\rho} = \rho_0 \\ u'(x,y,0) = 0 & \bar{u} = u_0 \\ v'(x,y,0) = 0 & \bar{v} = v_0 \end{cases} \quad (61)$$

where $\varepsilon = 0.01$, $(\rho_0, u_0, v_0) = (1.0, 0.0, 0.0)$, and $\beta = \ln 2$. The calculation grid adopts a uniform grid, the grid scale $\delta_x = 1.0$, and the time step $\delta_t = 1.0$. The circular cylinder was treated using the immersion boundary method, the surface is described by 150 uniform Lagrangian points, and the far-field was treated using the nonequilibrium extrapolation method. Three monitoring points A, B, and C are located at $(0,5)$, $(5\cos(3\pi/4), 5\sin(3\pi/4))$, $(-5,0)$ in the computational domain. Figure 16 shows the instantaneous density contours at $tc_s = 4$, $tc_s = 6$, $tc_s = 10$, and $tc_s = 12$. The propagation of the pulse wave and the interaction with the circular cylinder are shown. Figure 17 shows a comparison of the perturbation density at the three monitoring points with the exact solution. The numerical solution calculated by SLLBM-IBM is in good agreement with the exact solution [44], which quantitatively verifies the correctness of this method.

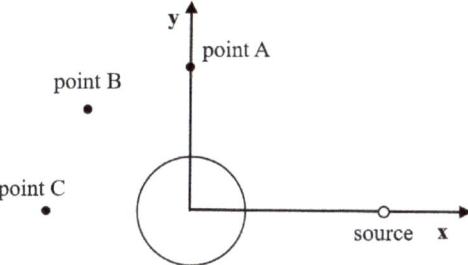

Figure 15. Computational model of a Gaussian pulse scattered by a stationary circular cylinder.

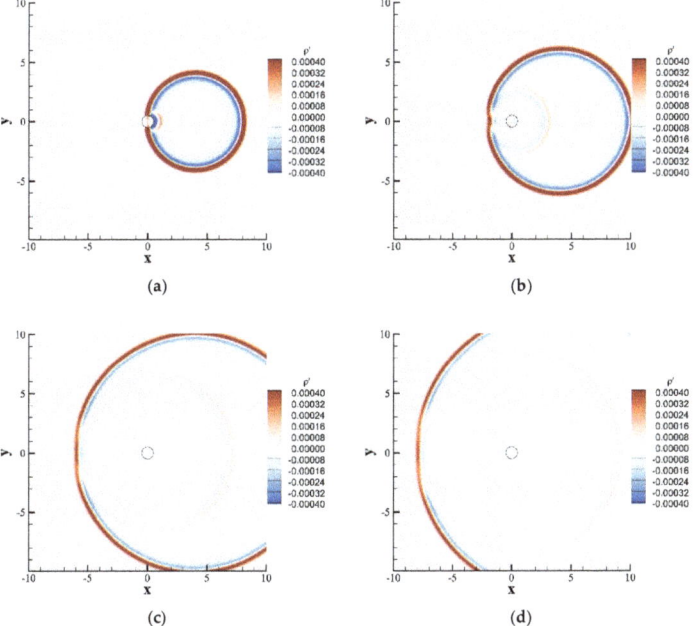

Figure 16. Disturbance density contours of Gaussian pulse scattering with a circular cylinder obtained by the SLLBM-IBM. (**a**) $tc_s = 4$, (**b**) $tc_s = 6$, (**c**) $tc_s = 10$, (**d**) $tc_s = 12$.

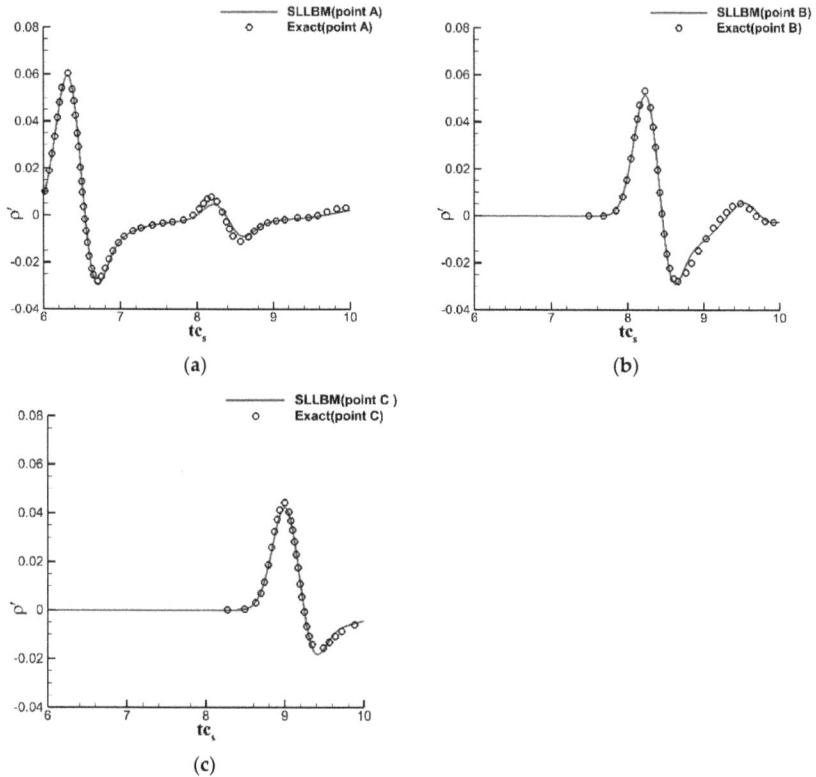

Figure 17. Disturbance density curves of a Gaussian pulse scattering with a circular cylinder obtained by the SLLBM-IBM. (**a**) point A, (**b**) point B, (**c**) point C.

4. Conclusions

SLLBM was proposed and applied to the simulation of acoustic wave propagation in fluids. This method recovered the LLBE to LNSE by C-E expansion analysis, and adopted the fractional-step calculation technique; the predictor-corrector formula of SLLBM was derived. Because the perturbation nonequilibrium distribution function can be approximated by second-order interpolation of the perturbation equilibrium distribution function at other positions and times, the evolution of the perturbation distribution function could be transformed into the evolution of the perturbation equilibrium distribution function. Compared with standard LBM, SLLBM calculates the acoustic disturbance and the mean flow separately, so macroscopic variables of the mean flow do not affect the calculation of acoustic disturbance. At the same time, SLLBM has other advantages: the calculation process is simpler, and the cost of computing memory is reduced. In addition, to simulate the scattering effect of acoustic waves encountering objects, the immersed boundary method (IBM) is within the framework of SLLBM so that the method can simulate the influence of complex geometries.

Various numerical cases, including the propagation of a Gaussian pulse and the interaction with a wall or cylinder, the propagation of a time-periodic acoustic source, and plane wave, were simulated to validate the accuracy of SLLBM. The results obtained by SLLBM are in good agreement with the exact solutions, which proves the accuracy and feasibility of SLLBM in the simulation of acoustic wave propagation.

Author Contributions: Conceptualization, R.C.; methodology, Q.S., R.C.; software, Q.S., S.C.; formal analysis, Q.S., N.Z.; investigation, S.C.; resources, R.C.; data curation, N.Z.; writing—original draft preparation, Q.S.; writing—review and editing, R.C., J.L.; visualization, Q.S., J.L.; supervision, Y.Y.; funding acquisition, R.C. All authors have read and agreed to the published version of the manuscript.

Funding: The research was funded by the Aeronautical Science Foundation of China under Grant number 20200057068001; Laboratory of Aerodynamic Noise Control under Grant number ANCL20210201; National Key Laboratory of Science and Technology on Aerodynamic Design and Research under Grant number 614220121030202; National Natural Science Foundation of China under Grant number 11602209.

Institutional Review Board Statement: Not applicable.

Data Availability Statement: Not applicable.

Acknowledgments: The authors are very much indebted to the editors and referees for their most valuable comments and suggestions, which helped us to improve the quality of the paper.

Conflicts of Interest: The authors declare no conflict of interest.

Abbreviations

c_s	speed of sound	ξ	lattice velocity
f	density distribution function	w	weight coefficient of the lattice
f	boundary force terms of the Euler point	ρ	denisity
F	boundary force terms of the Lagrangian point	v	kinematic viscosity
K	kernel function	μ	dynamic viscosity
Kn	Knudsen number	τ	relaxation time
M	number of the Euler points		
N	number of the Lagrangian point	\multicolumn{2}{l	}{Superscripts}
r	position of the Euler point	$'$	perturbation part
s	index of the Lagrangian point	$-$	steady mean part
u	velocity vector	eq	equilibrium distribution function
U$_I$	velocity of the fluid	neq	non-equilibrium distribution function
U$_B$	velocity of the immersed boundary	$*$	intermediate variables
R	position of the Lagrangian point	$n+1$	variables at the next time step
δ_t	time step		
δ_x	lattice spacing	\multicolumn{2}{l	}{Subscripts}
δ_e	scale of the Euler grid	α	direction
δ_l	scale of the Lagrangian grid	e	Euler grid point
λ	wavelength	l	Lagrangian grid point

References

1. Labbé, R.; Pinton, J.-F. Propagation of sound through a turbulent vortex. *Phys. Rev. Lett.* **1998**, *81*, 1413. [CrossRef]
2. Astley, R.J. Numerical methods for noise propagation in moving flows, with application to turbofan engines. *Acoust. Sci. Technol.* **2009**, *30*, 227–239. [CrossRef]
3. Tam, C.K.W.; Parrish, S.A.; Envia, E.; Chien, E.W. Physical processes influencing acoustic radiation from jet engine inlets. *J. Fluid Mech.* **2013**, *725*, 152–194. [CrossRef]
4. Wang, L.; Chen, R.; You, Y.; Qiu, R. Investigation of acoustic propagation and source localization in a hot jet flow. *J. Sound Vib.* **2021**, *492*, 115801.
5. Campos, L.; Kobayashi, M. On the reflection and transmission of sound in a thick shear layer. *J. Fluid Mech.* **2000**, *424*, 303–326. [CrossRef]
6. Xu, G.; Shi, Y.; Zhao, Q. New research progress in helicopter rotor aerodynamic noise. *Acta Aeronaut. Et Astronaut. Sin.* **2017**, *38*, 520991.
7. Moore, P.; Slot, H.; Boersma, B.J. Simulation and measurement of flow generated noise. *J. Comput. Phys.* **2007**, *224*, 449–463. [CrossRef]
8. Sandberg, R.; Sandham, N.; Joseph, P. Direct numerical simulations of trailing-edge noise generated by boundary-layer instabilities. *J. Sound Vib.* **2007**, *304*, 677–690. [CrossRef]
9. Gréverie, L.; Bailly, C. Formulation of an acoustic wave operator based on linearized Euler equations. *Comptes Rendus L'Acad. Sci. Ser. IIB Mec. Phys. Chim. Astron.* **1998**, *11*, 741–746.

10. Bailly, C.; Juve, D. Numerical solution of acoustic propagation problems using linearized Euler equations. *AIAA J.* **2000**, *38*, 22–29.
11. Sun, Y.; Fattah, R.; Zhong, S.; Zhang, X. Stable time-domain CAA simulations with linearised governing equations. *Comput. Fluids* **2018**, *167*, 187–195. [CrossRef]
12. Gikadi, J.; Föller, S.; Sattelmayer, T. Impact of turbulence on the prediction of linear aeroacoustic interactions: Acoustic response of a turbulent shear layer. *J. Sound Vib.* **2014**, *333*, 6548–6559.
13. Berggren, M.; Bernland, A.; Noreland, D. Acoustic boundary layers as boundary conditions. *J. Comput. Phys.* **2018**, *371*, 633–650. [CrossRef]
14. Qian, Y.-H.; d'Humières, D.; Lallemand, P. Lattice BGK models for Navier-Stokes equation. *EPL (Europhys. Lett.)* **1992**, *17*, 479. [CrossRef]
15. Guo, Z.; Shi, B.; Wang, N. Lattice BGK model for incompressible Navier–Stokes equation. *J. Comput. Phys.* **2000**, *165*, 288–306. [CrossRef]
16. Aidun, C.K.; Clausen, J.R. Lattice-Boltzmann method for complex flows. *Annu. Rev. Fluid Mech.* **2010**, *42*, 439–472. [CrossRef]
17. Frapolli, N.; Chikatamarla, S.; Karlin, I. Theory, analysis, and applications of the entropic lattice Boltzmann model for compressible flows. *Entropy* **2020**, *22*, 370.
18. Wang, L.; Zhang, X.; Zhu, W.; Xu, K.; Wu, W.; Chu, X.; Zhang, W. Accurate Computation of Airfoil Flow Based on the Lattice Boltzmann Method. *Appl. Sci.* **2019**, *9*, 2000. [CrossRef]
19. Dhuri, D.B.; Hanasoge, S.M.; Perlekar, P.; Robertsson, J.O. Numerical analysis of the lattice Boltzmann method for simulation of linear acoustic waves. *Phys. Rev. E* **2017**, *95*, 043306.
20. Casalino, D.; Hazir, A.; Mann, A. Turbofan broadband noise prediction using the lattice Boltzmann method. *AIAA J.* **2018**, *56*, 609–628. [CrossRef]
21. Daroukh, M.; Le Garrec, T.; Polacsek, C. Low-speed turbofan aerodynamic and acoustic prediction with an isothermal lattice Boltzmann method. *AIAA J.* **2022**, *60*, 1152–1170.
22. Schäfer, R.; Böhle, M. Validation of the Lattice Boltzmann Method for Simulation of Aerodynamics and Aeroacoustics in a Centrifugal Fan. *Acoustics* **2020**, *2*, 735–752. [CrossRef]
23. Latt, J.; Malaspinas, O.; Kontaxakis, D.; Parmigiani, A.; Lagrava, D.; Brogi, F.; Belgacem, M.B.; Thorimbert, Y.; Leclaire, S.; Li, S. Palabos: Parallel lattice Boltzmann solver. *Comput. Math. Appl.* **2021**, *81*, 334–350. [CrossRef]
24. Vergnault, E.; Malaspinas, O.; Sagaut, P. A lattice Boltzmann method for nonlinear disturbances around an arbitrary base flow. *J. Comput. Phys.* **2012**, *231*, 8070–8082.
25. Pérez, J.M.; Aguilar, A.; Theofilis, V. Lattice Boltzmann methods for global linear instability analysis. *Theor. Comput. Fluid Dyn.* **2017**, *31*, 643–664.
26. Wang, Y.; Yang, L.; Shu, C. From Lattice Boltzmann Method to Lattice Boltzmann Flux Solver. *Entropy* **2015**, *17*, 7713–7735.
27. Yang, L.; Shu, C.; Wu, J. A hybrid lattice Boltzmann flux solver for simulation of viscous compressible flows. *Adv. Appl. Math. Mech.* **2016**, *8*, 887–910.
28. Zhang, L.; Chen, Z.; Shu, C.; Zhang, M. A kinetic theory-based axisymmetric lattice Boltzmann flux solver for isothermal and thermal swirling flows. *J. Comput. Phys.* **2019**, *392*, 141–160. [CrossRef]
29. Liu, Y.; Shu, C.; Zhang, H.; Yang, L. A high order least square-based finite difference-finite volume method with lattice Boltzmann flux solver for simulation of incompressible flows on unstructured grids. *J. Comput. Phys.* **2020**, *401*, 109019. [CrossRef]
30. Yang, L.; Shu, C.; Chen, Z.; Hou, G.; Wang, Y. An improved multiphase lattice Boltzmann flux solver for the simulation of incompressible flow with large density ratio and complex interface. *Phys. Fluids* **2021**, *33*, 033306. [CrossRef]
31. Zhan, N.; Chen, R.; You, Y. Linear lattice Boltzmann flux solver for simulating acoustic propagation. *Comput. Math. Appl.* **2022**, *114*, 21–40. [CrossRef]
32. Chen, Z.; Shu, C.; Wang, Y.; Yang, L.; Tan, D. A simplified lattice Boltzmann method without evolution of distribution function. *Adv. Appl. Math. Mech.* **2017**, *9*, 1–22. [CrossRef]
33. Chen, Z.; Shu, C.; Tan, D.; Wu, C. On improvements of simplified and highly stable lattice Boltzmann method: Formulations, boundary treatment, and stability analysis. *Int. J. Numer. Methods Fluids* **2018**, *87*, 161–179. [CrossRef]
34. Griffith, B.E.; Patankar, N.A. Immersed methods for fluid–structure interaction. *Annu. Rev. Fluid Mech.* **2020**, *52*, 421. [PubMed]
35. Abalakin, I.V.; Zhdanova, N.y.S.; Kozubskaya, T.K. Immersed boundary method for numerical simulation of inviscid compressible flows. *Comput. Math. Math. Phys.* **2018**, *58*, 1411–1419. [CrossRef]
36. Kim, J.; Kim, D.; Choi, H. An immersed-boundary finite-volume method for simulations of flow in complex geometries. *J. Comput. Phys.* **2001**, *171*, 132–150. [CrossRef]
37. Chen, Z.; Shu, C.; Tan, D. Immersed boundary-simplified lattice Boltzmann method for incompressible viscous flows. *Phys. Fluids* **2018**, *30*, 053601. [CrossRef]
38. Dupuis, A.; Chatelain, P.; Koumoutsakos, P. An immersed boundary–lattice-Boltzmann method for the simulation of the flow past an impulsively started cylinder. *J. Comput. Phys.* **2008**, *227*, 4486–4498. [CrossRef]
39. Mittal, R.; Iaccarino, G. Immersed boundary methods. *Annu. Rev. Fluid Mech.* **2005**, *37*, 239–261. [CrossRef]
40. Sukop, M.; Thorne, D.T., Jr. *Lattice Boltzmann Modeling*; Springer: Berlin/Heidelberg, Germany, 2006.
41. Chen, Z.; Shu, C. Simplified lattice Boltzmann method for non-Newtonian power-law fluid flows. *Int. J. Numer. Methods Fluids* **2020**, *92*, 38–54. [CrossRef]

42. Tam, C.K.; Webb, J.C. Dispersion-relation-preserving finite difference schemes for computational acoustics. *J. Comput. Phys.* **1993**, *107*, 262–281. [CrossRef]
43. Viggen, E.M. The lattice Boltzmann method with applications in acoustics. Master Thesis, NTNU, Trondheim, Norway, 2009.
44. Tam, C.K.; Hardin, J.C. Second computational aeroacoustics (CAA) workshop on benchmark problems. In Proceedings of the Second Computational Aeroacoustics (CAA) Workshop on Benchmark Problems, Tallahassee, FL, USA, 1 January 1997.

Article

Thermal Lattice Boltzmann Flux Solver for Natural Convection of Nanofluid in a Square Enclosure

Xiaodi Wu [1] and Song Zhou [2,*]

[1] School of Ocean Engineering and Technology, Sun Yat-sen University, Zhuhai 519082, China
[2] School of Aerospace Engineering and Applied Mechanics, Tongji University, Shanghai 200092, China
* Correspondence: zhousong@tongji.edu.cn

Abstract: In the present study, mathematical modeling was performed to simulate natural convection of a nanofluid in a square enclosure using the thermal lattice Boltzmann flux solver (TLBFS). Firstly, natural convection in a square enclosure, filled with pure fluid (air and water), was investigated to validate the accuracy and performance of the method. Then, influences of the Rayleigh number, of nanoparticle volume fraction on streamlines, isotherms and average Nusselt number were studied. The numerical results illustrated that heat transfer was enhanced with the augmentation of Rayleigh number and nanoparticle volume fraction. There was a linear relationship between the average Nusselt number and solid volume fraction. and there was an exponential relationship between the average Nusselt number and *Ra*. In view of the Cartesian grid used by the immersed boundary method and lattice model, the immersed boundary method was chosen to treat the no-slip boundary condition of the flow field, and the Dirichlet boundary condition of the temperature field, to facilitate natural convection around a bluff body in a square enclosure. The presented numerical algorithm and code implementation were validated by means of numerical examples of natural convection between a concentric circular cylinder and a square enclosure at different aspect ratios. Numerical simulations were conducted for natural convection around a cylinder and square in an enclosure. The results illustrated that nanoparticles enhance heat transfer in higher Rayleigh number, and heat transfer of the inner cylinder is stronger than that of the square at the same perimeter.

Keywords: natural convection; nanofluid; thermal lattice Boltzmann flux solver; immersed boundary method

1. Introduction

Natural convection has received widespread attention by many researchers because it is relevant to many engineering applications, such as heat exchangers, solar energy and nuclear reactors. Conventional fluids, such as water and ethylene glycol mixture, are not effective heat transfer medias, due to low thermal conductivity. Therefore, nanofluids have gained attention as an alternative and effective heat transfer medium, due to having higher thermal conductivities [1]. There are two main research approaches for studying nanofluids: experiments and numerical simulations. In view of experiments, Song et al. [2] measured the thermal performance of SiC nanofluid in a water pool boiling experiment, and investigated the enhancement for critical heat flux. Nikhah et al. [3] carried out an experimental investigation on the convective boiling of dilute CuO-water nanofluids in an upward flow inside a conventional heat exchanger. Alkasmoul et al. [4] investigated the turbulent flow of Al_2O_3-water, TiO_2-water and CuO-water nanofluids in a heated, horizontal tube with a constant heat flux. The results showed that the efficiency of nanofluids in enhancing heat transfer was not high for turbulent flows. Qi et al. [5] carried out an experimental study on boiling heat transfer of an α-Al_2O_3-water nanofluid.

More researchers have applied numerical methods to study the performance of nanofluids. Khanafer et al. [6] directly solved the macroscopic governing equations to investigate heat transfer enhancement in a two-dimensional enclosure utilizing nanofluids for various pertinent parameters, including Grashof numbers and volume fractions. The results indicated that heat transfer increased with the volumetric fraction of the copper nanoparticles in water at any given Grashof number. Fattahi et al. [7] carried out a study on water-based nanofluid, containing Al_2O_3 or Cu nanoparticles, in a square cavity for Rayleigh number 10^3–10^6 and solid volume fraction 0–0.05, by means of the lattice Boltzmann method. The results indicated that the average Nusselt number increased by increasing the solid volume fraction and the effects of solid volume fraction on Cu were stronger than on Al_2O_3. He et al. [8] applied the single-phase lattice model to simulate convection heat transfer utilizing Al_2O_3-water nanofluid in a square cavity. Qi et al. [9] applied the two-phase lattice Boltzmann model for natural convection of nanofluid. From the above analysis, the lattice Boltzmann method (LBM) has obtained remarkable achievements in simulating incompressible viscous laminar nanoflow. Saadat et al. [10] developed a compressible LB model on standard lattices to solve supersonic flows involving shock waves, based on the consistent D2Q9 LB model, and with the help of appropriate correction terms introduced into the kinetic equations to compensate for deviations in the hydrodynamic limit. Huang et al. [11] improved the lattice Boltzmann model with a self-tuning equation of state to simulate the thermal flows beyond the Boussinesq and ideal-gas approximations. Hosseini et al. [12] derived the appropriate form of the correction term for the space- and time-discretized LB equations, through a Chapman–Enskog analysis for different orders of the equilibrium distribution function. As a mesoscopic approach, LBM can easily solve the macroscopic variables used by distribution functions and the linear streaming and collision processes can effectively simulate the nonlinear convection and diffusion effects in the macroscopic state. With the development of Lattice models in recent years, LBM can solve various flow problems successfully, including incompressible, compressible and thermal flows, by introducing a variety of applicable models. However, the solutions of flow for High Mach number and turbulence problems of complex shape are limited because the standard LBM is strictly limited to using the uniform Cartesian mesh due to the lattice uniformity for flow.

Recently, the idea of coupling the LBM and conventional methods (including finite difference method and finite volume method) has been proposed for computational fluid dynamics. It effectively combines the merits of macroscopic and mesoscopic methods. The coupling algorithm can be divided into the whole region coupling algorithm and the partition coupling algorithm. The whole region coupling algorithm solves the different variables used by different numerical algorithms. Nie et al. [13] and Mezrhab et al. [14] used the LBM-FDM coupling method to solve natural convection problems, in which LBM solved flow problems and FDM analyzed heat transfer. Chen et al. [15] used the LBM-FDM coupling method to solve the two-phase interface convection problem, in which LBM solved the velocity field and FDM solved the concentration field. Mishra et al. [16] used LBM-FVM to solve heat conduction and radiation problems. Sun and zhang [17] used LBM-FVM for conduction and radiation in irregular geometry. The partition coupling algorithm divides the whole region into several sub-regions and realizes the coupling function through information transfer between the sub-regions. Luan et al. [18–20] simulated complex flows in porous media using LBM-FVM. Chen et al. [21–23] used LBM-FVM to study the multiscale flow, multi-component mass transfer, proton conduction and electrochemical reaction processes. Li et al. [24,25] used LBM-FVM to study natural convection and the solid–liquid variation problem. Feng et al. [26] developed a thermal lattice Boltzmann model with a hybrid recursive regularization collision operator on standard lattices for simulation of subsonic and sonic compressible flows without shock by LBM-FVM. Essentially, the main advantage of the above two coupling methods is to improve the calculation efficiency of LBM and expand the applications of macroscopic computational fluid dynamics.

A new coupling idea gas been proposed in the past five years. This coupling method adopts the finite volume method to discretize macroscopic governing equations and uses local lattice Boltzmann equation solutions to calculate interface flux, on the basis of considering migration and collision processes. This method realizes the coupling of the macroscopic method and the mesoscopic model and is named the lattice Boltzmann flux solver (LBFS). Yang et al. [27,28] proposed LBFS based on compressible models, which is suitable for calculating viscous and compressible multi-component flows. Shu et al. [29] and Wang et al. [30–32] developed LBFS for incompressible viscous flow problems. This method integrates the advantages of the macroscopic method and the mesoscopic model, to not only realize the unified solution of non-viscous flux and viscous flux, but also to improve calculation efficiency without using a uniform grid in the whole calculation domain. Based on the above development, Wang et al. [33] developed the thermal lattice Boltzmann flux solver (TLBFS) and successfully used it to simulate the natural convection problem. Cao [34] proposed a variable property-based lattice Boltzmann flux solver (VPLBFS) for thermal flows with partial or total variation in fluid properties in the low Mach number limit.

In this paper, we attempted to build mathematical modeling to simulate the natural convection of Al_2O_3/water nanofluid in a square enclosure using the thermal lattice Boltzmann flux solver (TLBFS), which is a coupling method combining the finite volume method to discretize the macroscopic governing equations in space, and reconstructed flux solutions at the interface between two adjacent cell centers by using the single-relaxation-time Lattice Boltzmann model. The top mpotivating priority of this paper was to establish a simple and effective numerical calculation method to solve natural convection problems. Therefore, it was necessary to introduce the boundary treatment technique in the solver. Tong et al. [35] applied the multiblock lattice Boltzmann method with a fixed Eulerian mesh, and the fouling layer was represented by an immersed boundary with Lagrangian points. The shape change of the fouling layer could be carried out by deforming the immersed boundary, while keeping the mesh of flow simulation unchanged. Suzuki et al. [36] simulated lift and thrust generation by a butterfly-like flapping wing body model by means of immersed boundary lattice Boltzmann simulations. The immersed boundary method is an effective and simple method to treat solid surface boundary conditions and the numerical method based on a non-body-fitted grid can avoid the abundant work involved in grid generation. Therefore, the immersed boundary method was applied to implement the no-slip boundary condition and Dirichlet boundary condition was applied for natural convection around a bluff body in a square enclosure with the purpose of effective treatment of surface boundaries. Natural convection problems were investigated at different Rayleigh numbers and nanoparticle volume fractions. Influences of the Rayleigh number and nanoparticle volume fraction on the streamlines, isotherms and average Nusselt number were studied.

2. Governing Equations and Numerical Method

2.1. The Macroscopic Governing Equations

For incompressible thermal nanofluid, in consideration of single phase and constant properties flow conditions, the macroscopic governing equations of natural convection in a two-dimensional enclosure can be written as follows:

Continuity equation;

$$\frac{\partial \rho_{nf}}{\partial t} + \nabla \cdot \rho_{nf} u = 0 \tag{1}$$

Momentum equation;

$$\frac{\partial}{\partial t}\left(\rho_{nf} u\right) + \nabla\left(\rho_{nf} uu\right) = -\nabla p + \mu_{nf}\nabla\left[\left(\nabla u + (\nabla u)^T\right)\right] + F_{nf} \tag{2}$$

Energy equation;

$$\frac{\partial}{\partial t}\left(\rho_{nf} e\right) + \nabla\left(\rho_{nf} ue\right) = \chi_{nf}\nabla^2\left(\rho_{nf} e\right) \tag{3}$$

where ρ, u, p and m represent fluid density, velocity, pressure, dynamic viscosity coefficient, respectively; e stands for internal energy defined as $e = DRT/2$, where D is the dimension, R is the gas constant and T represents the temperature; χ is the thermal diffusivity. The subscript nf denotes the nanofluid.

Natural convection heat transfer in nanofluids is studied in a two-dimensional enclosure. Nanoparticles considered to be spherical and frictional forces are neglected. The flow is assumed as laminar with a single-phase homogeneous mixture. The buoyancy force always plays an essential role as an external force. Using the Boussinesq approximation, the force source term can be defined as:

$$F_{nf} = \rho_{nf} \beta_{nf} g (T - T_m) j \qquad (4)$$

where g represents the gravity acceleration, β is the thermal expansion coefficient and T_m is the average temperature.

According to Chapman-Enskog analysis, the relationships can be established between the fluxes and the distribution functions of the lattice Boltzmann model. Based on the thermal lattice Boltzmann flux solver (TLBFS), the governing Equations (1)–(3) can be rewritten as:

$$\frac{\partial \rho_{nf}}{\partial t} + \nabla \cdot \left(\sum_\alpha e_\alpha f_\alpha^{eq} \right) = 0 \qquad (5)$$

$$\frac{\partial \rho_{nf} u}{\partial t} + \nabla \cdot \prod_1 = F_{nf} \qquad (6)$$

$$\frac{\partial \rho_{nf} e}{\partial t} + \nabla \cdot \prod_2 = 0 \qquad (7)$$

where

$$\prod_1 = \sum_{\alpha=0}^{N} (e_\alpha)_\beta (e_\alpha)_\gamma \left[f_\alpha^{eq} + (I - \frac{1}{2\tau_v}) f_\alpha^{neq} \right] \qquad (8)$$

$$\prod_2 = \sum_{\alpha=0}^{N} e_\alpha \left[g_\alpha^{eq} + (I - \frac{1}{2\tau_c}) g_\alpha^{neq} \right] \qquad (9)$$

$$\tau_v = \mu_{nf} / (\rho_{nf} c_s^2 \delta_t) + 0.5 \qquad (10)$$

$$\tau_c = \chi_{nf} / \left(2 c_s^2 \delta_t \right) + 0.5 \qquad (11)$$

From the above process, the macroscopic flow variables and fluxes can be computed by equilibrium and non-equilibrium distribution functions of the lattice model for the governing equations of nanofluid. Equations (8) and (9) are used to solve the macroscopic flow variables, and fluxes can be evaluated by the thermal lattice Boltzmann flux solver, which is introduced in detail in the next section. The force source term is added at the cell center during the calculation process.

2.2. Thermal Lattice Boltzmann Flux Solver

The discrete term of the governing Equations (5)–(7) by finite volume method:

$$\frac{dW_i}{dt} = \frac{1}{\Delta V_i} \sum_k R_k dS_k + F \qquad (12)$$

where $W = [\rho_{nf}, \rho_{nf} u, \rho_{nf} v, \rho_{nf} e]^T$; dV_i and dS_k are the volume of ith control volume and the area of the kth interface. For the 2D case, the D2Q9 lattice velocity model [37] is used for momentum and energy fluxes. The expression of the fluxes R_k at the cell interfaces is as followed:

$$R_k = \begin{pmatrix} n_x\left(f_1^{eq} - f_3^{eq} + f_5^{eq} - f_6^{eq} - f_7^{eq} + f_8^{eq}\right) + n_y\left(f_2^{eq} - f_4^{eq} + f_5^{eq} + f_6^{eq} - f_7^{eq} - f_8^{eq}\right) \\ n_x\left(\hat{f}_1 + \hat{f}_3 + \hat{f}_5 + \hat{f}_6 + \hat{f}_7 + \hat{f}_8\right) + n_y\left(\hat{f}_5 - \hat{f}_6 + \hat{f}_7 - \hat{f}_8\right) \\ n_x\left(\hat{f}_5 - \hat{f}_6 + \hat{f}_7 - \hat{f}_8\right) + n_y\left(\hat{f}_2 + \hat{f}_4 + \hat{f}_5 + \hat{f}_6 + \hat{f}_7 + \hat{f}_8\right) \\ n_x\left(\hat{g}_1 - \hat{g}_3 + \hat{g}_5 - \hat{g}_6 - \hat{g}_7 + \hat{g}_8\right) + n_y\left(\hat{g}_2 - \hat{g}_4 + \hat{g}_5 + \hat{g}_6 - \hat{g}_7 - \hat{g}_8\right) \end{pmatrix} \tag{13}$$

$$\hat{f}_\alpha = f_\alpha^{eq} + \left(1 - \frac{1}{2\tau_v}\right) f_\alpha^{neq} \tag{14}$$

$$\hat{g}_\alpha = g_\alpha^{eq} + \left(1 - \frac{1}{2\tau_c}\right) g_\alpha^{neq} \tag{15}$$

From Equations (13)–(15), it can be seen that the important segment to solve fluxes is to accurately evaluate the f_α^{eq}, $\hat{f}_\alpha$ and $\hat{g}_\alpha$ terms.

The simplified thermal lattice Boltzmann model with BGK approximation can be written as:

$$f_\alpha(\mathbf{r} + \mathbf{e}_\alpha \delta_t, t + \delta_t) - f_\alpha(\mathbf{r}, t) = -\frac{1}{\tau_v}\left[f_\alpha(\mathbf{r}, t) - f_\alpha^{eq}(\mathbf{r}, t)\right] \tag{16}$$

$$g_\alpha(\mathbf{r} + \mathbf{e}_\alpha \delta_t, t + \delta_t) - g_\alpha(\mathbf{r}, t) = -\frac{1}{\tau_c}\left[g_\alpha(\mathbf{r}, t) - g_\alpha^{eq}(\mathbf{r}, t)\right] \tag{17}$$

In which equilibrium density distribution function and equilibrium internal energy distribution function is given as:

$$f_\alpha^{eq}(\mathbf{r}, t) = \rho w_\alpha \left[1 + \frac{\mathbf{e}_\alpha \cdot \mathbf{u}}{c_s^2} + \frac{(\mathbf{e}_\alpha \cdot \mathbf{u})^2 - (c_s|\mathbf{u}|)^2}{2c_s^4}\right] \tag{18}$$

$$g_\alpha^{eq}(\mathbf{r}, t) = \begin{cases} -\frac{2\rho}{3}\frac{|\mathbf{u}|^2}{c^2}, & \alpha = 0 \\ \frac{\rho e}{9}\left[\frac{3}{2} + \frac{3}{2}\cdot\frac{\mathbf{e}_\alpha \cdot \mathbf{u}}{c^2} + \frac{9}{2}\cdot\frac{(\mathbf{e}_\alpha \cdot \mathbf{u})^2}{c^4} - \frac{3}{2}\cdot\frac{|\mathbf{u}|^2}{c^2}\right], & \alpha = 1,2,3,4 \\ \frac{\rho e}{36}\left[3 + 6\cdot\frac{\mathbf{e}_\alpha \cdot \mathbf{u}}{c^2} + \frac{9}{2}\cdot\frac{(\mathbf{e}_\alpha \cdot \mathbf{u})^2}{c^4} - \frac{3}{2}\cdot\frac{|\mathbf{u}|^2}{c^2}\right], & \alpha = 5,6,7,8 \end{cases} \tag{19}$$

Using the second-order Taylor series expansion, Equations (16) and (17) can be transformed as below:

$$\delta_t\left(\frac{\partial}{\partial t} + \mathbf{e}_\alpha \cdot \nabla\right)f_\alpha + \frac{\delta_t^2}{2}\left(\frac{\partial}{\partial t} + \mathbf{e}_\alpha \cdot \nabla\right)^2 f_\alpha + \frac{1}{\tau}\left(f_\alpha - f_\alpha^{eq}\right) + O(\delta_t^3) = 0 \tag{20}$$

$$\delta_t\left(\frac{\partial}{\partial t} + \mathbf{e}_\alpha \cdot \nabla\right)g_\alpha + \frac{\delta_t^2}{2}\left(\frac{\partial}{\partial t} + \mathbf{e}_\alpha \cdot \nabla\right)^2 g_\alpha + \frac{1}{\tau}\left(g_\alpha - g_\alpha^{eq}\right) + O(\delta_t^3) = 0 \tag{21}$$

By the multi-scale Chapman-Enskog expansion, the distribution function, the temporal and spatial derivatives, the non-equilibrium density and energy distribution functions can be transformed into an expression only related to the equilibrium distribution functions and can be derived from:

$$f_\alpha^{neq}(\mathbf{r}, t) = -\tau_v\left[f_\alpha^{eq}(\mathbf{r}, t) - f_\alpha^{eq}(\mathbf{r} - \mathbf{e}_\alpha \delta_t, t - \delta_t)\right] \tag{22}$$

$$g_\alpha^{neq}(\mathbf{r}, t) = -\tau_c\left[g_\alpha^{eq}(\mathbf{r}, t) - g_\alpha^{eq}(\mathbf{r} - \mathbf{e}_\alpha \delta_t, t - \delta_t)\right] \tag{23}$$

From Figure 1, the flow properties of eight vertices of the D2Q9 model can be evaluated by interpolation with the given flow properties at the cell centers of two adjacent control volumes. The values r_i, r_{i+1} and r are defined as the physical positions of the two cell centers and their interfaces, respectively. The interpolation formulation can be given as:

$$\psi(\mathbf{r} - \mathbf{e}_\alpha \delta_t, t - \delta_t) = \begin{cases} \psi(\mathbf{r}_i) + (\mathbf{r} - \mathbf{e}_\alpha \delta_t - \mathbf{r}_i)\cdot \nabla \psi(\mathbf{r}_i) & \mathbf{r} - \mathbf{e}_\alpha \delta_t \text{ in } \Omega_i \\ \psi(\mathbf{r}_{i+1}) + (\mathbf{r} - \mathbf{e}_\alpha \delta_t - \mathbf{r}_{i+1})\cdot \nabla \psi(\mathbf{r}_{i+1}) & \mathbf{r} - \mathbf{e}_\alpha \delta_t \text{ in } \Omega_{i+1} \end{cases} \tag{24}$$

where ψ stands for the flow properties, including ρ, u, v and e. $f_\alpha^{eq}(r - e_\alpha \delta_t, t - \delta_t)$ and $g_\alpha^{eq}(r - e_\alpha \delta_t, t - \delta_t)$ can be obtained by the corresponding equilibrium density distribution function and energy distribution function. Then, the flow properties of the cell interface can be written as:

$$\rho(r,t) = \sum_{\alpha=0} f_\alpha^{eq}(r - e_\alpha \delta_t, t - \delta_t) \qquad (25)$$

$$\rho(r,t)u(r,t) = \sum_{\alpha=0} e_\alpha f_\alpha^{eq}(r - e_\alpha \delta_t, t - \delta_t) \qquad (26)$$

$$\rho(r,t)e(r,t) = \sum_{\alpha=0} g_\alpha^{eq}(r - e_\alpha \delta_t, t - \delta_t) \qquad (27)$$

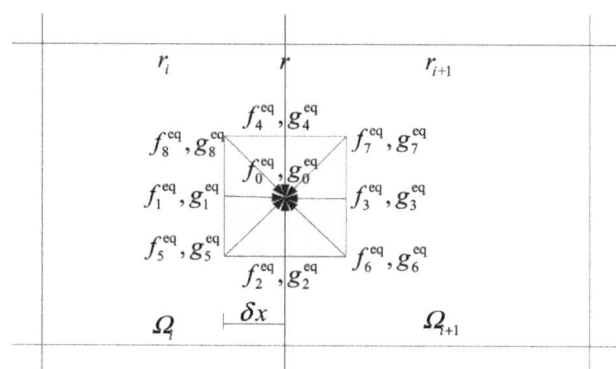

Figure 1. Local flux reconstruction at cell interface.

Next, $f_\alpha^{eq}(r, t)$ and $g_\alpha^{eq}(r, t)$ can also be easily solved by distribution functions. After obtaining the equilibrium distribution functions, the fluxes can be evaluated according to Equation (13).

2.3. Computational Sequence

The complete numerical simulation procedures for each time step of the proposed method are summarized below.

1. According to the fluid properties of the nanofluid, determine initial velocity and temperature field;
2. Based on the grid size, identify a streaming time step at each interface and then the single relaxation parameters, including dynamic viscosity and the thermal diffusivity;
3. Apply the D2Q9 model to compute the density and energy equilibrium distribution functions $f_\alpha^{eq}(r - e_\alpha \delta_t, t - \delta_t)$ and $g_\alpha^{eq}(r - e_\alpha \delta_t, t - \delta_t)$ around the middle point r of each interface;
4. Compute the macroscopic flow properties of nanofluid at the cell interface and then compute $f_\alpha^{eq}(r, t)$ and $g_\alpha^{eq}(r, t)$ by the equilibrium distribution functions of the D2Q9 model;
5. Compute $\hat{f}_\alpha$ and $\hat{g}_\alpha$ terms, then the fluxes at the cell interface can be solved by Equation (13);
6. Calculate the force source term and add this term to the fluxes;
7. Solve Equations (5)–(7) to obtain the macroscopic flow properties of the nanofluid;
8. Repeat steps (3)–(7) until the following convergence criterion is satisfied.

3. Numerical Examples of Natural Convection in a Square Enclosure

3.1. Problem Description

The computational domain and boundary conditions are shown in Figure 2. From this figure, it can be seen that the no slip boundary condition was applied on four walls. The adiabatic condition was set on the top and bottom walls and temperatures of 1 and 0 were applied on the left and right walls, respectively. The non-dimensional parameters, Prandtl number Pr and Rayleigh number Ra, were applied to determine the dynamic similarity as follows:

$$Pr = \nu/\chi \tag{28}$$

$$Ra = \frac{V_c^2 \cdot L^2}{\nu \cdot \chi} \tag{29}$$

where $L = 1$ is the characteristic length of the square cavity and V_c is the characteristic thermal velocity which is constrained by the low Mach number limit. In the present simulations, $V_c = 0.1$ was set in order to ensure incompressible viscous flow.

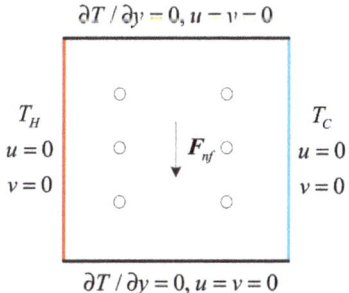

Figure 2. Computational domain and boundary conditions.

In the present study, Al$_2$O$_3$/water nanofluid was used. The thermophysical properties of the water and nanoparticles are listed in Table 1. The homogeneous model for nanofluid was adopted. Physical properties of the nanofluids, including density, specific heat and thermal expansion coefficient, were obtained using the classical formula developed for conventional solid–liquid mixtures as follows:

$$\rho_{nf} = (1-\phi)\rho_f + \phi\rho_s \tag{30}$$

$$(\rho c_p)_{nf} = (1-\phi)(\rho c_p)_f + \phi(\rho c_p)_s \tag{31}$$

$$\beta_{nf} = (1-\phi)\beta_f + \phi\beta_s \tag{32}$$

where ϕ refers to the volume concentration of nanoparticles and the subscripts s, f denote the particle and base fluids.

Table 1. Thermophysical properties of fluid and nanoparticles.

Properties	Fluid Phase (Water)	Solid Phase (Al$_2$O$_3$)
ρ (kg/m^3)	997	3880
c_p (J/kg·K)	4179	765
β (1/K)	0.00021	0.0000085
k (W/m·K)	0.613	40
μ (kg/m·s)	0.000855	-

The effective viscosity and thermal conductivity of the nanofluid strongly affect the heat transfer rate and flow characteristics of nanofluids. The effective viscosity could be estimated by experimental correlation for 47 nm Al$_2$O$_3$/water nanofluid by Angue Mintsa et al. [38] and thermal conductivity was given by Gherasim et al. [39] as follows:

$$\mu_{nf} = 0.904 e^{14.8\phi} \mu \tag{33}$$

$$\kappa_{nf} = (1.72\phi + 1.0)\kappa_f \tag{34}$$

In the present simulations, the convergence criterion for flow field and temperature field were respectively given as follows:

$$Error1 = \frac{\sum_{ij} \left| \sqrt{(u(i,j,t+\delta_t))^2 + (v(i,j,t+\delta_t))^2} - \sqrt{(u(i,j,t))^2 + (v(i,j,t))^2} \right|}{\sum_{ij} \sqrt{(u(i,j,t+\delta_t))^2 + (v(i,j,t+\delta_t))^2}} \leq 1 \times 10^{-7} \tag{35}$$

$$Error2 = \frac{\sum_{ij} |T(i,j,t+\delta_t) - T(i,j,t)|}{\sum_{ij} T(i,j,t+\delta_t)} \leq 1 \times 10^{-7} \tag{36}$$

3.2. Natural Convection of Pure Fluid in a Square Enclosure

To testify as to the accuracy and performance of the lattice Boltzmann flux solver based on the population model, the classical natural convection in a square enclosure filled with air and water was studied at $Ra = 10^3$, 10^4, 10^5 and 10^6.

Firstly, a grid independent study was conducted on five different uniform grids of 101×101, 151×151, 201×201, 251×251 and 301×301 for the natural convection problem at $Ra = 10^6$ and $Pr = 0.7$. As shown in Table 2, when the mesh size was 201×201, or even larger, the average Nusselt number did not change much and the value was between the benchmark solutions of Davis [40] and Hortmann et al. [41]. When the mesh size was larger than 151×151, the maximum horizontal velocity on the vertical mid-plane, the maximum vertical velocity on the horizontal mid-plane and their locations were in agreement with the benchmark solutions of Davis [40]. The above results illustrated grid independence on uniform grids of 201×201, for the case of $Ra = 10^6$.

Table 2. Grid independent study on uniform of natural convection at $Ra = 10^6$.

Method	Grids	Nu_{avg}	y	u_{max}	x	v_{max}
	101×101	8.788	0.855	64.22	0.0350	217.60
	151×151	8.809	0.850	64.66	0.0367	219.32
Present	201×201	8.816	0.853	64.99	0.0375	220.05
	251×251	8.819	0.854	66.18	0.0380	220.17
	301×301	8.819	0.852	66.99	0.0383	220.14
De Vahl Davis [40]		8.800	0.850	64.63	0.0397	219.36
Hortmann et al. [41]		8.825	-	-	-	-

Based on the above results, the grid independent study was conducted on non-uniform grids by using the size of less than 201×201. Table 3 shows the numerical results of six different non-uniform grids of natural convection at $Ra = 10^6$. From this table, the results were close to the data of uniform grids of 201×201 when the non-uniform mesh was more than 121×121. In order to ensure the accuracy and efficiency of numerical simulations, the non-uniform grid of 141×141 was chosen to simulate natural convection in a square enclosure.

Table 3. Grid independent study on non-uniform of natural convection at $Ra = 10^6$.

Grids	Nu_{avg}	y	u_{max}	x	v_{max}
81×81	8.803	0.856	64.77	0.0358	218.98
101×101	8.811	0.855	64.99	0.0349	219.16
121×121	8.816	0.854	65.04	0.0400	219.37
141×141	8.818	0.853	65.03	0.0388	220.15
161×161	8.819	0.853	65.03	0.0379	220.14
181×181	8.820	0.853	65.06	0.0372	220.22

The average Nusselt number results at different Rayleigh numbers are listed in Table 4, and it can be seen that the numerical simulation results were in good agreement with previous literature results at different Rayleigh numbers. This illustrated the accuracy of the present method for natural convection.

Table 4. Comparison of average Nusselt numbers at different Rayleigh numbers.

Ra	Air				Water		
	Present	Davis [40]	Khanafer et al. [6]	Qi [9]	Present	Kahveci [42]	Lai and Yang [1]
10^3	1.118	1.118	1.118	1.118	1.119	-	1.128
10^4	2.246	2.243	2.245	2.247	2.278	2.274	2.286
10^5	4.522	4.519	4.522	4.522	4.725	4.722	4.729
10^6	8.818	8.800	8.826	8.808	9.204	9.230	9.173

Figure 3 shows the temperature distribution at horizontal midsections of the enclosure. For the enclosure filled with air, the results of $Ra = 10^5$ were compared with the numerical results of Khanafer et al. [6] and the experimental results of Krane and Jessee [43]. For the enclosure filled with water, the results were compared with numerical results of Lai and Yang [1]. It was noted from the comparisons that the solutions were in excellent agreement. This illustrated that the method in this paper could capture the temperature field very well.

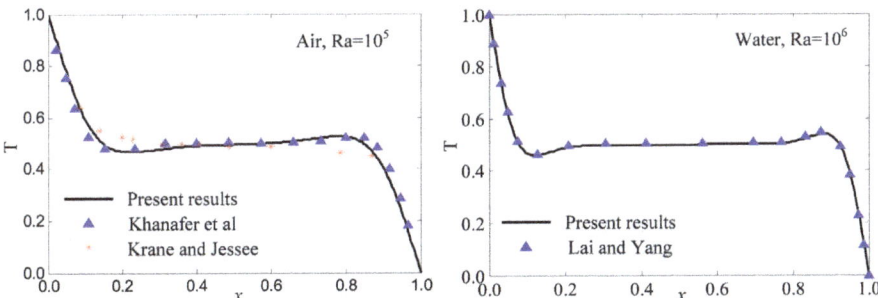

Figure 3. Comparison of temperature distribution at horizontal midsections with previous literatures.

The streamlines and isotherms of air and water at various Rayleigh numbers are shown in Figures 4 and 5, respectively. It can be seen that the natural convection and heat transfer between the wall and fluid were enhanced as Ra increased. For $Ra \leq 10^4$, the flow characteristic was to appear as a central vortex. For $Ra > 10^4$, the central vortex became more expanded and finally broke up into two vortices so that temperature boundary layers were formed. The above phenomenon agreed well with previous studies.

3.3. Natural Convection of Nanofluid in a Square Enclosure

After validating the numerical method for natural convection in a square enclosure filled with pure fluid, the natural convection in a square enclosure filled with Al_2O_3-water nanofluid of nanoparticles having volume fraction ϕ = 1–4% at $Ra = 10^3$–10^6 was simulated to validate the present numerical algorithm. The presented averaged Nusselt numbers were compared with the numerical results of Lai and Yang [1] and listed in Table 5. It shows that there was a good agreement and the relative errors were less than 0.8%, which further illustrated that the present numerical method could simulate the natural convection of nanofluid at different Rayleigh numbers and nanoparticle volume fractions.

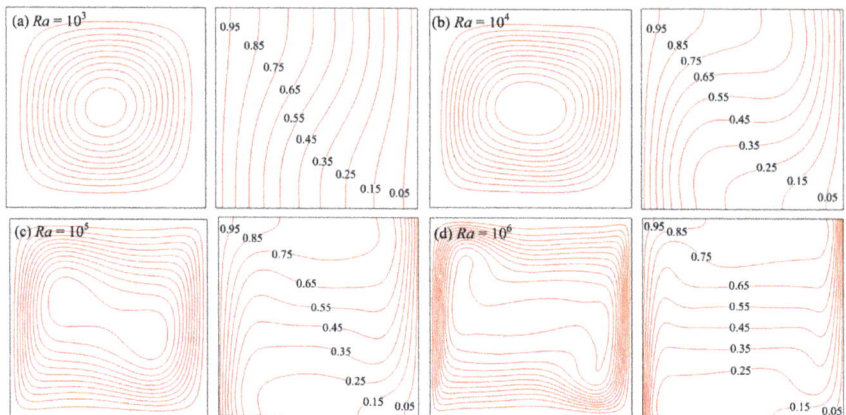

Figure 4. Streamlines and isotherms of air at various Rayleigh numbers.

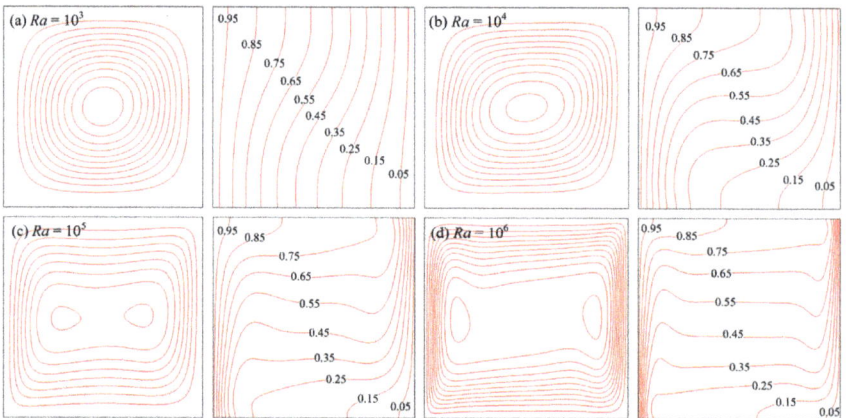

Figure 5. Streamlines and isotherms of water at various Rayleigh numbers.

Table 5. Comparison of average Nusselt numbers with the previous studies.

Ra	ϕ	Present	Ref [1]	Relative Error (%)
10^3	0.01	1.139	1.147	0.697
	0.02	1.158	1.167	0.771
	0.03	1.177	1.186	0.756
	0.04	1.196	1.206	0.829
10^4	0.01	2.317	2.326	0.387
	0.02	2.357	2.366	0.380
	0.03	2.396	2.406	0.416
	0.04	2.435	2.445	0.409
10^5	0.01	4.807	4.811	0.008
	0.02	4.890	4.894	0.008
	0.03	4.972	4.977	0.010
	0.04	5.054	5.059	0.010
10^6	0.01	9.366	9.331	0.375
	0.02	9.528	9.492	0.386
	0.03	9.688	9.653	0.363
	0.04	9.849	9.813	0.367

In the present numerical simulations, the effect of nanoparticle suspensions (Al$_2$O$_3$-water) on flow and temperature characteristics for $Ra = 10^3$–10^6 and nanoparticles volume fraction ϕ = 0–10% were studied. The variation of average Nusselt number against solid volume fraction for different Rayleigh numbers is shown in Figure 6a and the variation of average Nusselt number against Rayleigh number for different solid volume fractions is shown in Figure 6b.

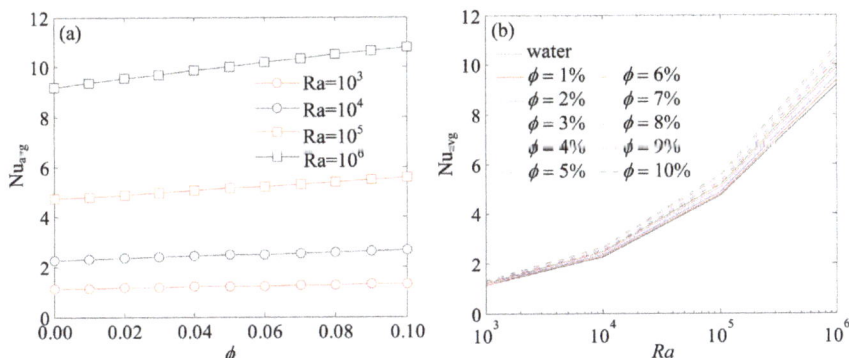

Figure 6. Variation of average Nusselt number against (**a**) solid volume fraction for different Rayleigh number; (**b**) Rayleigh number for different solid volume fraction.

Numerical results indicated that average Nusselt number increased with the increase of Ra and ϕ. This illustrated that the function of heat transfer was enhanced with the augmentation of nanofluid thermal conductivity, which indicated that the major mechanism of heat transfer in flowing fluid was thermal dispersion. At the same Ra, the relationship of the average Nusselt number and solid volume fraction was almost linear. At the same solid volume fraction, the relationship of the average Nusselt number and Ra presented an exponential form. At higher Rayleigh number, the greater the heat transfer rate that could be obtained.

Figures 7 and 8 indicate the isotherms and streamlines of nanofluid (Al$_2$O$_3$-water) at $Ra = 10^3$–10^6 and ϕ = 0%, 5% and 10%, which show the effect of volume fraction and Ra on flow field and temperature field very well. From Figure 7, it can be seen that heat transfer between the wall and fluid were enhanced as Ra increased. As the volume fraction of nanoparticles increased, the isotherm changed slightly. That was because the mixture flow became more viscous, due to the nanoparticles. The velocity of flow fluid reduced and then natural convection weakened. However, the function of heat transfer in total computational domain was enhanced, which was attributed to the augmentation of nanofluid thermal conductivity.

From Figure 8, it can be observed that the flow appeared as a central vortex for lower Ra. As Ra increased, the central vortex became more expanded and finally broke up into two vortices, so that temperature boundary layers were formed. For pure fluid, the vortex formed in the enclosure as a result of the buoyancy effect. By increasing the volume fraction of nanoparticles, the intensity of streamlines increased, due to the high energy transport through the flow as a result of irregular motion of the ultra-fine particles.

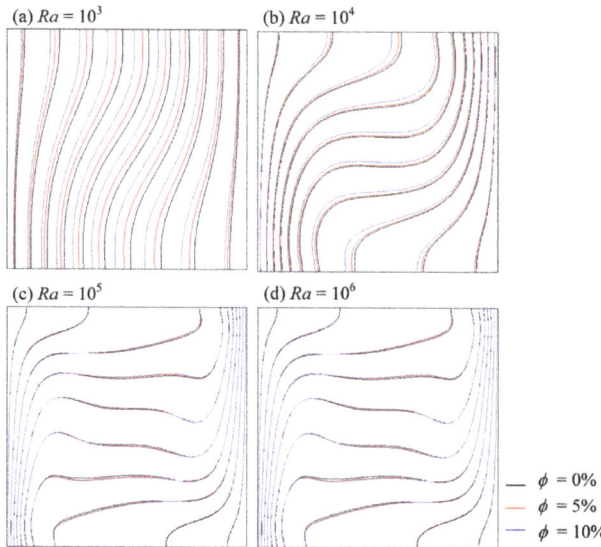

Figure 7. Isotherms of nanofluid at various Ra and ϕ.

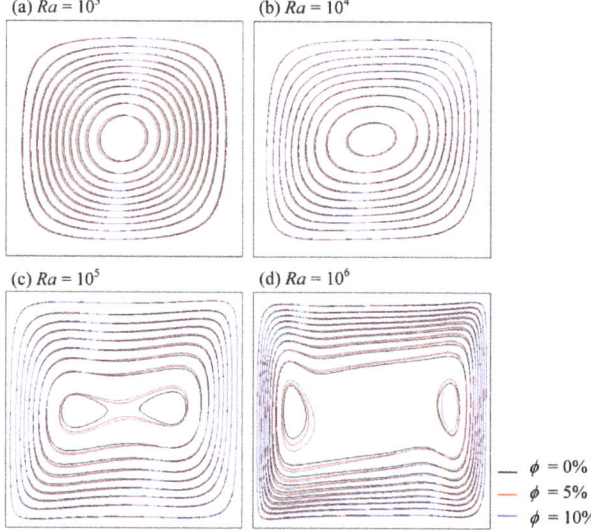

Figure 8. Streamlines of nanofluid at various Ra and ϕ.

4. Numerical Examples of Natural Convection around Bluff Body in a Square Enclosure

4.1. Problem Description

The boundary condition-enforced immersed boundary method was chosen for treatment of the solid boundary conditions. Based on the immersed boundary method and thermal lattice Boltzmann flux solver (IB-TLBFS), the macroscopic governing equations can be rewritten as:

$$\frac{\partial \rho_{nf}}{\partial t} + \nabla \cdot \left(\sum_{\alpha} e_{\alpha} f_{\alpha}^{eq} \right) = 0 \tag{37}$$

$$\frac{\partial \rho_{nf} u}{\partial t} + \nabla \cdot \prod_1 = F_{nf} + f_b \tag{38}$$

$$\frac{\partial \rho_{nf} e}{\partial t} + \nabla \cdot \prod_2 = q_b \tag{39}$$

where the force source term f_b and the heat source term q_b are both generated by the immersed boundary. To solve the governing equations, the calculation process is divided into two steps: the first step predicts the state variables without taking account of the boundary function and the second step corrects velocity and temperature by the immersed boundary method.

In this work, the implicit velocity correction scheme proposed by Wang et al. [44] was be applied in view of satisfaction of the no slip boundary. The implicit heat source scheme proposed by Ren et al. [15] was applied for the Dirichlet boundary conditions of the temperature field.

Natural convection of a heated bluff body in a square enclosure was studied. The physical models, computational domain and boundary conditions are presented in Figure 9. All boundaries were no-slip and isothermal boundary conditions. The flow was assumed to be laminar and driven by the temperature difference.

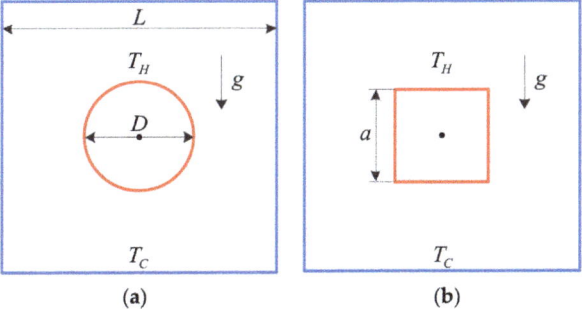

Figure 9. The physical models, computational domain and boundary conditions between bluff body and square enclosure. (a) Cylinder (b) Square.

Numerical investigations were carried on two types of bluff bodies, a circular cylinder and a square. The four side walls of the outer square enclosure were cooled isothermally at T_C and the side length was L. The wall of the inner bluff body was heated isothermally at T_H and D and a represent the diameter of the circular cylinder and the side length of the square, respectively. For fixed Rayleigh number, numerical simulation cases were designed to have a fixed perimeter for different bluff bodies and the influences of geometry on the heat transfer is discussed in detail.

4.2. Natural Convection in the Annulus between Concentric Circular Cylinder and Square Enclosure

After validating the numerical algorithm of the thermal lattice Boltzmann flux solver, natural convection in the annulus between concentric circular cylinder and square enclosure at $Ra = 10^4$, 10^5 and 10^6 were simulated to validate the immersed boundary method and code implementation. Numerical simulations were conducted for three different aspect ratios (Ar = 1.67, 2.5 and 5.0). The average Nusselt number was also computed and compared with reference data in the literature.

The computed average Nusselt numbers are compared in Table 6 with those of Ren et al. [45], Shu et al. [46] and Moukalled et al. [47]. From this table, it can be seen that the present results of the method combining IBM and TLBFS agreed very well with reference data. Besides this, the results revealed that the average Nusselt number greatly depended on Rayleigh number and aspect ratio. Due to buoyancy-induced convection, the average Nusselt number increased with increase of Ra, while it decreased with increase of Ar, due to the effect of annulus gap space.

Table 6. Comparison of average Nusselt numbers at different Ra and Ar.

Ra	Ar	Present	Ren et al. [45]	Shu and Zhu [46]	Moukalled and Acharya [47]
	1.67	5.425	5.303	5.40	5.826
10^4	2.50	3.256	3.161	3.24	3.331
	5.00	2.090	2.051	2.08	2.071
	1.67	6.285	6.171	6.21	6.212
10^5	2.50	4.954	4.836	4.86	5.080
	5.00	3.809	3.704	3.79	3.825
	1.67	11.943	11.857	12.00	11.620
10^6	2.50	9.002	8.546	8.90	9.374
	5.00	6.110	5.944	6.11	6.107

The streamlines and isotherms in the annulus at various Rayleigh numbers and aspect ratios are shown in Figure 10. Conduction dominated the flow field and a relatively weak convective flow could be observed in the annulus at the lower Ra. As the Rayleigh number increased, the strength of the convective flow grew and the center of the recirculation eddy changed its position. When $Ra = 10^6$, a relatively stronger convective flow dominated the fluid field and a higher temperature gradient could be observed. In contrast, stronger convective flow and higher temperature gradient could be observed in the case of lower values of Ar.

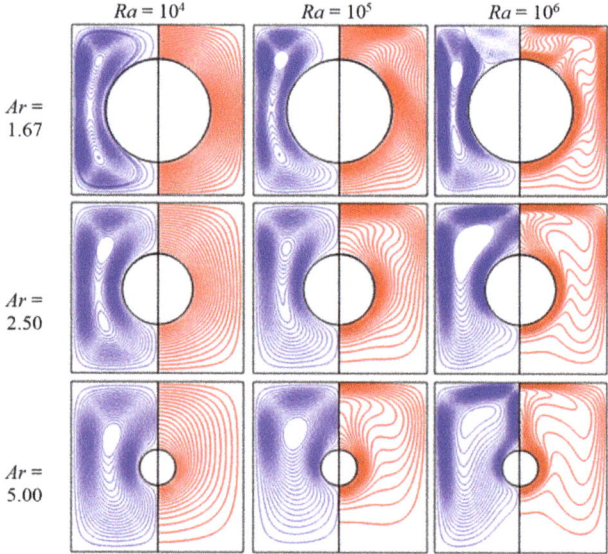

Figure 10. Streamlines and isotherms at various Ra and Ar.

4.3. Natural Convection of Nanofluid between Bluff Body and Square Enclosure

In the present study, numerical investigations of natural convection between heated bluff body and square enclosure were conducted for nanoparticles having volume fractions of $\phi = 0\%$, 2% and 4% and Rayleigh numbers of $Ra = 10^4$, 10^5 and 10^6.

The averaged Nusselt numbers are listed in Table 7. The numerical simulation results indicated that average Nusselt number increased with increase of Ra and ϕ, which was the same as occurred in natural convection of square enclosure. By comparison, the averaged

Nusselt number of the natural convection around a circular cylinder in an enclosure was greater than that of the square at the same calculation conditions. This illustrated that a smooth geometrical shape was beneficial to heat transfer.

Table 7. Comparison of average Nusselt numbers at various Ra and ϕ.

ϕ	Cylinder			Square		
	$Ra = 10^4$	$Ra = 10^5$	$Ra = 10^6$	$Ra = 10^4$	$Ra = 10^5$	$Ra = 10^6$
0.00	3.131	5.080	9.144	2.9432	4.8675	8.6541
0.02	3.132	5.098	9.200	2.9447	4.8884	8.7186
0.04	3.134	5.117	9.263	2.9463	4.9103	8.7883

Figures 11 and 12 present the distribution of the isotherms for different Rayleigh numbers ($Ra = 10^5$ and 10^6) and values of nanoparticle volume fractions ($\phi = 0$ and 0.04). An overview of this figure indicated that the thermal fields strongly depended on Rayleigh number. When $Ra = 10^5$ or even lower, the isotherms of $\phi = 0$ were almost close to that of $\phi = 0.04$, which illustrated that nanoparticle volume fraction played a smaller role in heat transfer and flow pattern. When $Ra = 10^6$, there were significant differences between the isotherms of $\phi = 0$ and $\phi = 0.04$, which illustrated that nanoparticle volume fraction played a role in heat transfer and flow pattern for high Ra. The thickness of the thermal boundary layer decreased as the volume fraction increased, which was due to the increasing conduction heat transfer by adding nanoparticle volume fraction.

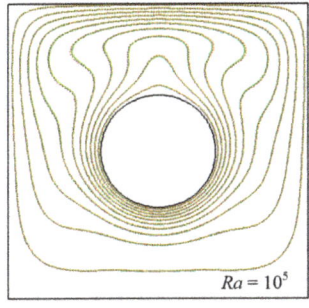
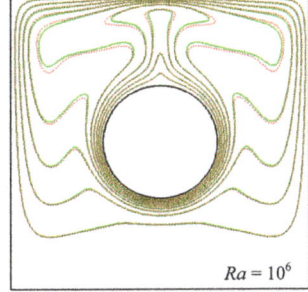

Figure 11. Isotherms for natural convection around cylinder at different nanoparticles volume fraction. Green line: $\phi = 0.00$, red line: $\phi = 0.04$.

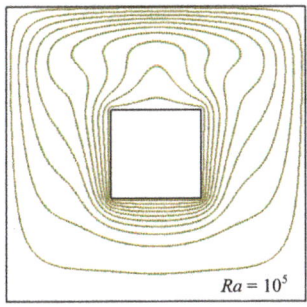
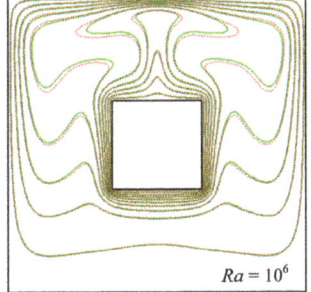

Figure 12. Isotherms for natural convection around square at different nanoparticles volume fraction. Green line: $\phi = 0.00$, red line: $\phi = 0.04$.

Figure 13 shows the streamlines for natural convection around a circular cylinder and square at nanoparticle volume fractions $\phi = 0.04$ and $Ra = 10^6$. From Table 7, it can be seen that the preferable heat transfer effect could be acquired by the cylinder in comparison with the square at the same perimeter. That was because the velocity and temperature gradients around the sharp corners of the square dramatically changed, which prevented the heat transfer effect.

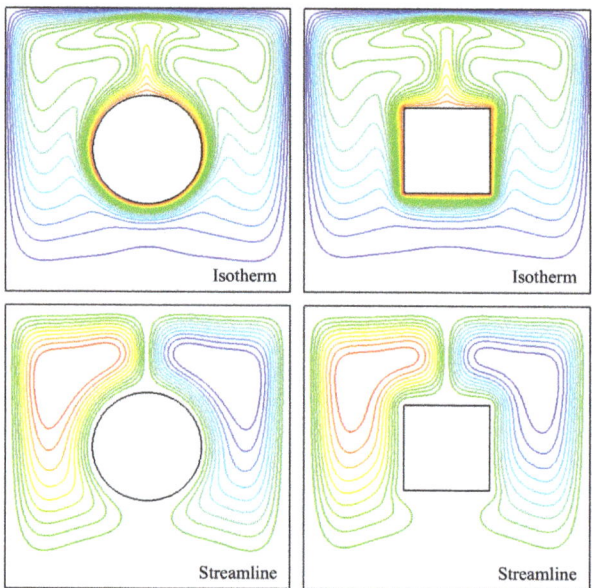

Figure 13. Isotherms and streamlines for natural convection at nanoparticles volume fraction $\phi = 0.04$ and $Ra = 10^6$.

5. Conclusions

The thermal lattice Boltzmann flux solver (TLBFS) was applied to simulate natural convection of nanofluid in a square enclosure. This method couples the finite volume method and lattice Boltzmann models to realize the solution of incompressible thermal flow. To validate the accuracy and performance of this method, natural convection in a square enclosure filled with pure fluid (air and water) was first studied. There were good agreements with previous literature. Numerical investigations of fluid flow and convective heat transfer were performed. The effects of some parameters, such as the Rayleigh number (Ra), and volume fraction of nanoparticles (ϕ), on natural convection were analyzed. With increase in the Rayleigh number and nanoparticle volume fraction, the heat transfer rate increased and the nanofluid flow became more viscous and this led to a decrease in nanofluid motion velocity. The average Nusselt number was an increasing exponential function of the Rayleigh number and an increasing linear function of the nanoparticle volume fraction. Then, natural convection around a bluff body in a square enclosure was studied by a method combining TLBFS and immersed boundary method. Natural convection problems in the annulus between concentric circular cylinder and square enclosure without nanofluid were simulated, which validated the feasibility of the numerical algorithm and code implement. Numerical investigations of natural convection between heated bluff body (cylinder and square) and square enclosure were conducted for different nanoparticle volume fractions and Rayleigh numbers. The numerical results illustrated that heat transfer effect increased with increase of Ra and ϕ. At lower Ra, the function of heat transfer with the augmentation of nanofluid thermal conductivity was counteracted by the more viscous flow. Nevertheless, nanoparticles played a better role in enhancing natural convection at higher Ra. The above results declare that the TLBFS is a promising method for heat transfer of nanofluids of the future.

Author Contributions: Methodology, X.W.; Project administration, S.Z.; Validation, X.W.; Writing—original draft, X.W.; Writing—review & editing, S.Z. All authors have read and agreed to the published version of the manuscript.

Funding: This work is supported by the National Key Research and Development Program of China (NO. 2020YFB0311500), to which the authors are most grateful.

Conflicts of Interest: The authors declare no conflict of interest.

References

1. Lai, F.H.; Yang, Y.T. Lattice Boltzmann simulation of natural convection heat transfer of Al_2O_3/water nanofluids in a square enclosure. *Int. J. Therm. Sci.* **2011**, *50*, 1930–1941. [CrossRef]
2. Song, S.L.; Lee, J.H.; Chang, S.H. CHF enhancement of SiC nanofluid in pool boiling experiment. *Exp. Therm. Fluid Sci.* **2014**, *52*, 12–18. [CrossRef]
3. Nikkhah, V.; Sarafraz, M.M.; Hormozi, F.; Peyghambarzadeh, S.M. Particulate fouling of CuO-water nanofluid at isothermal diffusive condition inside the conventional heat exchanger-experimental and modeling. *Exp. Therm. Fluid Sci.* **2015**, *60*, 83–95. [CrossRef]
4. Alkasmoul, F.S.; Al-Asadi, M.T.; Myers, T.G.; Thompson, H.M.; Wilson, M.C.T. A practical evaluation of the performance of Al_2O_3-water, TiO_2-water and CuO-water nanofluids for convective cooling. *Int. J. Heat Mass Transf.* **2018**, *126*, 639–651. [CrossRef]
5. Qi, C.; He, Y.; Hu, Y.; Jiang, B.; Luan, T.; Ding, Y. Experimental Study on Boiling Heat Transfer of α-Al_2O_3-Water Nanofluid. *Nanosci. Nanotechnol. Lett.* **2013**, *5*, 895–901. [CrossRef]
6. Khanafer, K.; Vafai, K.; Lightstone, M. Buoyancy-driven heat transfer enhancement in a two-dimensional enclosure utilizing nanofluids. *Int. J. Heat Mass Transf.* **2003**, *46*, 3639–3653. [CrossRef]
7. Fattahi, E.; Farhadi, M.; Sedighi, K.; Nemati, H. Lattice Boltzmann simulation of natural convection heat transfer in nanofluids. *Int. J. Therm. Sci.* **2012**, *52*, 137–144. [CrossRef]
8. He, Y.; Qi, C.; Hu, Y.; Qin, B.; Li, F.; Ding, Y. Lattice Boltzmann simulation of alumina-water nanofluid in a square cavity. *Nanoscale Res. Lett.* **2011**, *6*, 184. [CrossRef] [PubMed]
9. Qi, C.; He, Y.; Yan, S.; Tian, F.; Hu, Y. Numerical simulation of natural convection in a square enclosure filled with nanofluid using the two-phase Lattice Boltzmann method. *Nanoscale Res. Lett.* **2013**, *8*, 56. [CrossRef] [PubMed]
10. Saadat, M.H.; Bösch, F.; Karlin, I.V. Lattice Boltzmann model for compressible flows on standard lattices: Variable Prandtl number and adiabatic exponent. *Phys. Rev. E* **2019**, *99*, 013306. [CrossRef]
11. Huang, R.; Lan, L.; Li, Q. Lattice Boltzmann simulations of thermal flows beyond the Boussinesq and ideal-gas approximations. *Phys. Rev. E* **2020**, *102*, 043304. [CrossRef]
12. Hosseini, S.A.; Darabiha, N.; Thévenin, D. Compressibility in lattice Boltzmann on standard stencils: Effects of deviation from reference temperature. *Philos. Trans. R. Soc. London Ser. A Math. Phys. Eng. Sci.* **2020**, *378*, 20190399. [CrossRef]
13. Nie, X.; Shan, X.; Chen, H. Lattice-Boltzmann/Finite-Difference Hybrid Simulation of Transonic Flow. In Proceedings of the 47th AIAA Aerospace Sciences Meeting including the New Horizons Forum and Aerospace Exposition, Orlando, FL, USA, 5–8 January 2009.
14. Mezrhab, A.; Bouzidi, M.; Lallemand, P. Hybrid lattice-Boltzmann finite-difference simulation of convective flows. *Comput. Fluids* **2004**, *33*, 623–641. [CrossRef]
15. Chen, W.; Chen, S.; Yuan, X.; Zhang, H.; Yu, K. Three-dimensional simulation of interfacial convection in CO_2–ethanol system by hybrid lattice Boltzmann method with experimental validation. *Chin. J. Chem. Eng.* **2015**, *23*, 356–365. [CrossRef]
16. Mishra, S.C.; Roy, H.K. Solving transient conduction and radiation heat transfer problems using the lattice Boltzmann method and the finite volume method. *J. Comput. Phys.* **2007**, *223*, 89–107. [CrossRef]
17. Sun, Y.; Zhang, X. A hybrid strategy of lattice Boltzmann method and finite volume method for combined conduction and radiation in irregular geometry. *Int. J. Heat Mass Transf.* **2018**, *121*, 1039–1054. [CrossRef]
18. Luan, H.; Xu, H.; Chen, L.; Feng, Y.; He, Y.; Tao, W. Coupling of finite volume method and thermal lattice Boltzmann method and its application to natural convection. *Int. J. Numer. Methods Fluids* **2012**, *70*, 200–221. [CrossRef]
19. Luan, H.B.; Xu, H.; Chen, L.; Sun, D.L.; Tao, W.Q. Numerical Illustrations of the Coupling Between the Lattice Boltzmann Method and Finite-Type Macro-Numerical Methods. *Numer. Heat Transf. Part B Fundam.* **2010**, *57*, 147–171. [CrossRef]
20. Luan, H.B.; Xu, H.; Chen, L.; Sun, D.L.; He, Y.L.; Tao, W.Q. Evaluation of the coupling scheme of FVM and IBM for fluid flows around complex geometries. *Int. J. Heat Mass Transf.* **2011**, *54*, 1975–1985. [CrossRef]
21. Chen, L.; He, Y.-L.; Kang, Q.; Tao, W.-Q. Coupled numerical approach combining finite volume and lattice Boltzmann methods for multi-scale multi-physicochemical processes. *J. Comput. Phys.* **2013**, *255*, 83–105. [CrossRef]
22. Chen, L.; Feng, Y.-L.; Song, C.-X.; He, Y.-L.; Tao, W.-Q. Multi-scale modeling of proton exchange membrane fuel cell by coupling finite volume method and lattice Boltzmann method. *Int. J. Heat Mass Transf.* **2013**, *63*, 268–283. [CrossRef]

23. Chen, L.; Luan, H.; Feng, Y.; Song, C.; He, Y.-L.; Tao, W.-Q. Coupling between finite volume method and lattice Boltzmann method and its application to fluid flow and mass transport in proton exchange membrane fuel cell. *Int. J. Heat Mass Transf.* **2012**, *55*, 3834–3848. [CrossRef]
24. Li, Z.; Yang, M.; Zhang, Y. Hybrid Lattice Boltzmann and Finite Volume Method for Natural Convection. *J. Thermophys. Heat Transf.* **2014**, *28*, 68–77. [CrossRef]
25. Li, Z.; Yang, M.; Zhang, Y. A Hybrid Lattice Boltzmann and Finite-Volume Method for Melting with Convection. *Numer. Heat Transf. Part B Fundam.* **2014**, *66*, 307–325. [CrossRef]
26. Feng, Y.; Boivin, P.; Jacob, J.; Sagaut, P. Hybrid recursive regularized thermal lattice Boltzmann model for high subsonic compressible flows. *J. Comput. Phys.* **2019**, *394*, 82–99. [CrossRef]
27. Yang, L.; Shu, C.; Wu, J. Extension of lattice Boltzmann flux solver for simulation of 3D viscous compressible flows. *Comput. Math. Appl.* **2016**, *71*, 2069–2081. [CrossRef]
28. Yang, L.M.; Shu, C.; Wu, J. A Hybrid Lattice Boltzmann Flux Solver for Simulation of Viscous Compressible Flows. *Adv. Appl. Math. Mech.* **2016**, *8*, 887–910. [CrossRef]
29. Shu, C.; Wang, Y.; Teo, C.J.; Wu, J. Development of Lattice Boltzmann Flux Solver for Simulation of Incompressible Flows. *Adv. Appl. Math. Mech.* **2014**, *6*, 436–460. [CrossRef]
30. Wang, Y.; Shu, C.; Teo, C.J. Development of LBGK and incompressible LBGK-based lattice Boltzmann flux solvers for simulation of incompressible flows. *Int. J. Numer. Methods Fluids* **2014**, *75*, 344–364. [CrossRef]
31. Wang, Y.; Shu, C.; Huang, H.; Teo, C. Multiphase lattice Boltzmann flux solver for incompressible multiphase flows with large density ratio. *J. Comput. Phys.* **2015**, *280*, 404–423. [CrossRef]
32. Wang, Y.; Shu, C.; Teo, C.J. A fractional step axisymmetric lattice Boltzmann flux solver for incompressible swirling and rotating flows. *Comput. Fluids* **2014**, *96*, 204–214. [CrossRef]
33. Wang, Y.; Shu, C.; Teo, C. Thermal lattice Boltzmann flux solver and its application for simulation of incompressible thermal flows. *Comput. Fluids* **2014**, *94*, 98–111. [CrossRef]
34. Cao, Y. Variable property-based lattice Boltzmann flux solver for thermal flows in the low Mach number limit. *Int. J. Heat Mass Transf.* **2016**, *103*, 254–264. [CrossRef]
35. Tong, Z.X.; Li, M.J.; Li, D.; Gu, Z.L.; Tao, W.Q. Two-dimensional numerical model for predicting fouling shape growth based on immersed boundary method and lattice Boltzmann method. *Appl. Therm. Eng.* **2020**, *179*, 115755. [CrossRef]
36. Suzuki, K.; Minami, K.; Inamuro, T. Lift and thrust generation by a butterfly-like flapping wing–body model: Immersed boundary–lattice Boltzmann simulations. *J. Fluid Mech.* **2015**, *767*, 659–695. [CrossRef]
37. Qian, Y.H.; D'Humières, D.; Lallemand, P. Lattice BGK Models for Navier-Stokes Equation. *Eur. Lett.* **1992**, *17*, 479–484. [CrossRef]
38. Mintsa, H.A.; Roy, G.; Nguyen, C.T.; Doucet, D. New temperature dependent thermal conductivity data for water-based nanofluids. *Int. J. Therm. Sci.* **2009**, *48*, 363–371. [CrossRef]
39. Gherasim, I.; Roy, G.; Nguyen, C.T.; Vo-Ngoc, D. Experimental investigation of nanofluids in confined laminar radial flows. *Int. J. Therm. Sci.* **2009**, *48*, 1486–1493. [CrossRef]
40. De Vahl Davis, G. Natural convection of air in a square cavity: A bench mark numerical solution. *Int. J. Numer. Methods Fluids* **1983**, *3*, 249–264. [CrossRef]
41. Hortmann, M.; Perić, M.; Scheuerer, G. Finite volume multigrid prediction of laminar natural convection: Bench-mark solutions. *Int. J. Numer. Methods Fluids* **1990**, *11*, 189–207. [CrossRef]
42. Kahveci, K. Buoyancy Driven Heat Transfer of Nanofluids in a Tilted Enclosure. *J. Heat Transf.* **2010**, *132*, 062501. [CrossRef]
43. Krane, R.J.; Jessee, J. Some detailed field measurements for a natural convection flow in a vertical square enclosure. In Proceedings of the 1st ASME-JSME Thermal Engineering Joint Conference, Honolulu, HI, USA, 20–24 March 1983; Volume 1, pp. 323–329.
44. Wang, Y.; Shu, C.; Teo, C.; Wu, J. An immersed boundary-lattice Boltzmann flux solver and its applications to fluid–structure interaction problems. *J. Fluids Struct.* **2015**, *54*, 440–465. [CrossRef]
45. Ren, W.; Shu, C.; Wu, J.; Yang, W. Boundary condition-enforced immersed boundary method for thermal flow problems with Dirichlet temperature condition and its applications. *Comput. Fluids* **2012**, *57*, 40–51. [CrossRef]
46. Shu, C.; Zhu, Y.D. Efficient computation of natural convection in a concentric annulus between an outer square cylinder and an inner circular cylinder. *Int. J. Numer. Methods Fluids* **2002**, *38*, 429–445. [CrossRef]
47. Moukalled, F.; Acharya, S. Natural convection in the annulus between concentric horizontal circular and square cylinders. *J. Thermophys. Heat Transf.* **1996**, *10*, 524–531. [CrossRef]

Article

Kinetic Theory and Memory Effects of Homogeneous Inelastic Granular Gases under Nonlinear Drag

Alberto Megías [1] and Andrés Santos [2,*]

[1] Departamento de Física, Universidad de Extremadura, E-06006 Badajoz, Spain
[2] Departamento de Física and Instituto de Computación Científica Avanzada (ICCAEx), Universidad de Extremadura, E-06006 Badajoz, Spain
* Correspondence: andres@unex.es

Abstract: We study a dilute granular gas immersed in a thermal bath made of smaller particles with masses not much smaller than the granular ones in this work. Granular particles are assumed to have inelastic and hard interactions, losing energy in collisions as accounted by a constant coefficient of normal restitution. The interaction with the thermal bath is modeled by a nonlinear drag force plus a white-noise stochastic force. The kinetic theory for this system is described by an Enskog–Fokker–Planck equation for the one-particle velocity distribution function. To get explicit results of the temperature aging and steady states, Maxwellian and first Sonine approximations are developed. The latter takes into account the coupling of the excess kurtosis with the temperature. Theoretical predictions are compared with direct simulation Monte Carlo and event-driven molecular dynamics simulations. While good results for the granular temperature are obtained from the Maxwellian approximation, a much better agreement, especially as inelasticity and drag nonlinearity increase, is found when using the first Sonine approximation. The latter approximation is, additionally, crucial to account for memory effects such as Mpemba and Kovacs-like ones.

Keywords: granular gases; kinetic theory; Enskog–Fokker–Planck equation; direct simulation Monte Carlo; event-driven molecular dynamics

1. Introduction

Since the late 20th century, the study of granular materials has become of great importance in different branches of science, such as physics, engineering, chemistry, and mathematics, motivated by either fundamental or industrial reasons. It is well known that rapid flows in granular gases in the dilute regime are well described by a modified version of the classical Boltzmann's kinetic theory for hard particles. The most widely used model for the granular particles is the inelastic hard-sphere (IHS) one, in which particles are assumed to be hard spheres (or, generally, hard d-spheres) that lose energy due to inelasticity, as parameterized by a constant coefficient of normal restitution.

Theoretical predictions have been tested by different experimental setups in the freely evolving case [1,2]. However, it is rather difficult to experimentally replicate the latter granular gaseous systems due to the fast freezing implied by the dissipative interactions. Then, energy injection is very common in granular experiments [3–10]. In addition, granular systems are never found in a vacuum on Earth. From a quick but attentive glance at our close environment, grains might be found, for example, in the form of dust or pollen suspended in the air, sand, or dirtiness, diving down or browsing through a river, or even forming part of more complex systems such as soils. Therefore, fundamental knowledge about driven granular flows contributes to the understanding of a great variety of phenomena in nature. This is one of the reasons why the study of driven granular flows has become quite important, besides its intrinsic interest at physical and mathematical levels. Consequently, modeling driven granular flows constitutes a solid part of granular matter research, with theorists combining different collisional models and distinct interactions with the surroundings [11–20].

Recent works [21–23] introduced a model for a molecular gas in which the interaction of the particles with a background fluid is described by a stochastic force and a drag force whose associated drag coefficient has a quadratic dependence on the velocity modulus. This latter dependence is motivated by situations where the particle masses in the gas and the background fluid are not disparate [24–26]. The nonlinearity of the drag force implies an explicit coupling of the temperature with higher-order moments of the velocity distribution function (VDF) of the gas, implying the existence of interesting memory effects, such as Mpemba or Kovacs-like ones, as well as nonexponential relaxations [21–23]. On the other hand, the elastic property of the molecular particles implies that the system ends in an equilibrium state described by the common Maxwell–Boltzmann VDF, unlike granular gases, both driven and freely evolving [11,12,14,17,18,27–30], where a coupling of the hydrodynamic quantities with the cumulants of the VDF is always present. To imagine a real situation, one might possibly consider, for example, a microgravity experiment of pollen grains in a dust cloud.

Throughout this work, we study the properties of homogeneous states of a dilute inelastic granular gas immersed in a background fluid made of smaller particles, the influence of the latter on the former being accounted for at a coarse-grained level by the sum of a deterministic nonlinear drag force and a stochastic force. This gives rise to a competition between the pure effects of the bath and the granular energy dissipation. In fact, we look into expected nonGaussianities from a Sonine approximation of the VDF, commonly used in granular gases. The theoretical results are tested against computer simulations, with special attention on the steady-state properties and memory effects.

The paper is organized as follows. We introduce the model for this system and the associated kinetic-theory evolution equations in Section 2. In Section 3, the Maxwellian and first Sonine approximations are constructed, and the steady-state values are theoretically evaluated. Then, Section 4 collects simulation results from the direct simulation Monte Carlo (DSMC) method and the event-driven molecular dynamics (EDMD) algorithm, which are compared to the theoretical predictions for steady and transient states, including memory effects. Finally, some conclusions of this work are exposed in Section 5.

2. The Model

We consider a homogeneous, monodisperse, and dilute granular gas of identical inelastic hard d-spheres of mass m and diameter σ, immersed in a background fluid made of smaller particles. In a coarse-grained description, the interactions between the grains and the fluid particles can be effectively modeled by a drag force plus a stochastic force acting on the grains. If the mass ratio between the fluid and granular particles is not very small, the drag force becomes a nonlinear function of the velocity [24–26]. The model, as said in Section 1, has previously been studied in the case of elastic collisions [21–23] but not, to our knowledge, in the context of the IHS model. Figure 1 shows an illustration of the system and its modeling.

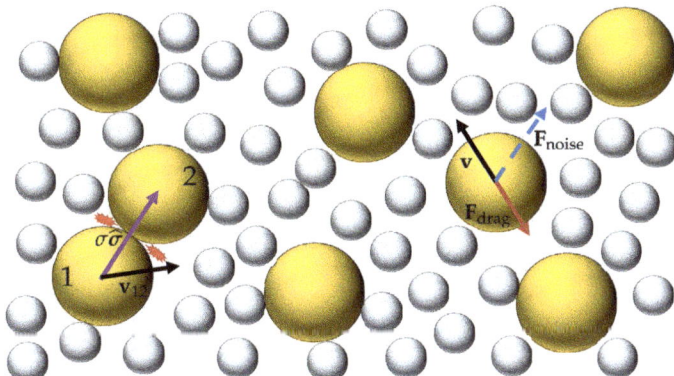

Figure 1. Illustration of the system considered in this paper. A granular gas of hard particles (represented by large yellowish spheres) is coupled to a thermal bath (made of particles represented by the small grayish spheres) via a drag force $\mathbf{F}_{\text{drag}} = -m\zeta(v)\mathbf{v}$, where $\zeta(v)$ is a velocity-dependent drag coefficient, and a stochastic force $\mathbf{F}_{\text{noise}} = m\chi(v)\boldsymbol{\eta}$, where $\boldsymbol{\eta}$ is a Gaussian white-noise term. In addition, the granular particles are subjected to binary inelastic collisions, represented by the red gleam-like lines.

2.1. Enskog–Fokker–Planck Equation

The full dynamics of the system can be studied from the inelastic homogeneous Enskog–Fokker–Planck equation (EFPE),

$$\partial_t f(\mathbf{v};t) - \partial_\mathbf{v} \left[\zeta(v)\mathbf{v} + \frac{\chi^2(v)}{2}\partial_\mathbf{v} \right] f(\mathbf{v};t) = J[\mathbf{v}|f,f], \tag{1}$$

where f is the one-particle VDF, so that $n = \int d\mathbf{v} f(\mathbf{v};t)$ is the number density, and $J[\mathbf{v}|f,f]$ is the usual Enskog–Boltzmann collision operator defined by

$$J[\mathbf{v}_1|f,f] \equiv \sigma^{d-1}g_c \int d\mathbf{v}_2 \int_+ d\widehat{\boldsymbol{\sigma}} \, (\mathbf{v}_{12} \cdot \widehat{\boldsymbol{\sigma}}) \left[\alpha^{-2} f(\mathbf{v}_1'')f(\mathbf{v}_2'') - f(\mathbf{v}_1)f(\mathbf{v}_2) \right]. \tag{2}$$

Here, α is the coefficient of normal restitution (see below), $\mathbf{v}_{12} = \mathbf{v}_1 - \mathbf{v}_2$ is the relative velocity, $\widehat{\boldsymbol{\sigma}} = (\mathbf{r}_1 - \mathbf{r}_2)/\sigma$ is the intercenter unit vector at contact, $g_c = \lim_{r \to \sigma^+} g(r)$ is the contact value of the pair correlation function $g(r)$, $\int_+ d\widehat{\boldsymbol{\sigma}} \equiv \int d\widehat{\boldsymbol{\sigma}} \Theta(\mathbf{v}_{12} \cdot \widehat{\boldsymbol{\sigma}})$, Θ being the Heaviside step-function and $\mathbf{v}_i''$ refers to the precollisional velocity of the particle i. Within the IHS model, the collisional rules are expressed by [18,30]

$$\mathbf{v}_{1/2}'' = \mathbf{v}_{1/2} \mp \frac{1 + \alpha^{-1}}{2}(\mathbf{v}_{12} \cdot \widehat{\boldsymbol{\sigma}})\widehat{\boldsymbol{\sigma}}. \tag{3}$$

From Equation (3), one gets $(\mathbf{v}_{12} \cdot \widehat{\boldsymbol{\sigma}}) = -\alpha(\mathbf{v}_{12}'' \cdot \widehat{\boldsymbol{\sigma}})$; this relation defines the coefficient of normal restitution, which is assumed to be constant.

The second term on the left-hand side of Equation (1) represents the action of a net force $\mathbf{F} = \mathbf{F}_{\text{drag}} + \mathbf{F}_{\text{noise}}$ describing the interaction with the particles of the background fluid. The deterministic nonlinear drag force is $\mathbf{F}_{\text{drag}} = -m\zeta(v)\mathbf{v}$, where the drag coefficient $\zeta(v)$ depends on the velocity. In turn, $\mathbf{F}_{\text{noise}} = m\chi^2(v)\boldsymbol{\eta}$ is a stochastic force, where $\chi^2(v)$ measures its intensity, and $\boldsymbol{\eta}$ is a stochastic vector with the properties of a zero-mean Gaussian white noise with a unit covariance matrix, i.e.,

$$\langle \eta_i(t) \rangle = 0, \quad \langle \eta_i(t)\eta_j(t') \rangle = \mathbb{I}\delta_{ij}\delta(t-t'), \tag{4}$$

where i and j are particle indices, and I is the $d \times d$ unit matrix so that different Cartesian components of $\boldsymbol{\eta}_i(t)$ are uncorrelated. The functions $\xi(v)$ and $\chi^2(v)$ are constrained to follow the fluctuation-dissipation theorem as

$$\chi^2(v) = v_b^2 \xi(v), \qquad (5)$$

$v_b = \sqrt{2T_b/m}$ being the thermal velocity associated with the background temperature T_b.

The drag coefficient ξ is commonly assumed to be independent of the velocity. However, a dependence on v cannot be ignored if the mass of a fluid particle is not much smaller than that of grain [24–26]. The first correction to $\xi = $ const is a quadratic term [21–23], namely

$$\xi(v) = \xi_0 \left(1 + 2\gamma \frac{v^2}{v_b^2}\right), \qquad (6)$$

where ξ_0 is the drag coefficient in the zero-velocity limit and γ controls the degree of nonlinearity of the drag force.

2.2. Dynamics

It is well known that, in the case of driven granular gases [11,12,14,17–19,31,32], there exists a competition between the loss and gain of energy due to inelasticity and the action of the thermal bath, respectively. This eventually leads the granular gas to a steady state, in contrast to the freely cooling case [18].

The basic macroscopic quantity characterizing the time evolution of the system is the granular temperature, defined analogously to the standard temperature in kinetic theory as

$$T(t) = \frac{m}{dn} \int d\mathbf{v} \, v^2 f(\mathbf{v}; t). \qquad (7)$$

While in the case of elastic collisions, the asymptotic steady state is that of equilibrium at temperature T_b, i.e., $\lim_{t \to \infty} T(t) = T_b$, in the IHS model, the steady state is a nonequilibrium one and, moreover, $\lim_{t \to \infty} T(t) = T^{\text{st}} < T_b$. From the EFPE, one can derive the evolution equation of the granular temperature, which is given by

$$\frac{\partial_t T}{\xi_0} = 2(T_b - T)\left[1 + (d+2)\gamma \frac{T}{T_b}\right] - 2(d+2)\gamma \frac{T^2}{T_b} a_2 - \frac{\zeta}{\xi_0} T, \qquad (8)$$

where

$$\zeta(t) \equiv -\frac{m}{dT(t)n} \int d\mathbf{v} \, v^2 J[\mathbf{v}, f, f] \qquad (9)$$

is the cooling rate and

$$a_2(t) \equiv \frac{d}{d+2} \frac{n \int d\mathbf{v} \, v^4 f(\mathbf{v}; t)}{[\int d\mathbf{v} \, v^2 f(\mathbf{v}; t)]^2} - 1 \qquad (10)$$

is the excess kurtosis (or fourth cumulant) of the time-dependent VDF. The coupling of $T(t)$ to $a_2(t)$ is a direct consequence of the quadratic term in the drag coefficient. As for the cooling rate $\zeta(t)$, it is a consequence of inelasticity and, therefore, vanishes in the elastic case (conservation of energy). Insertion of Equation (2) into Equation (9) yields [18]

$$\zeta(t) = (1 - \alpha^2) \frac{\nu(t)}{\sqrt{2}dn^2} \frac{\Gamma\left(\frac{d}{2}\right)}{\Gamma\left(\frac{d+3}{2}\right)} \int d\mathbf{v}_1 \int d\mathbf{v}_2 \left[\frac{v_{12}}{v_{\text{th}}(t)}\right]^3 f(\mathbf{v}_1; t) f(\mathbf{v}_2; t). \qquad (11)$$

Here, $v_{\text{th}}(t) = \sqrt{2T(t)/m}$ is the time-dependent thermal velocity and

$$\nu(t) = g_c K_d n \sigma^{d-1} v_{\text{th}}(t), \quad K_d \equiv \frac{\pi^{d-1}}{\sqrt{2}\Gamma(d/2)}, \qquad (12)$$

is the time-dependent collision frequency.

Let us rewrite Equation (8) in dimensionless form. First, we introduce the reduced quantities

$$t^* \equiv \nu_b t, \quad \theta(t^*) \equiv \frac{T(t)}{T_b}, \quad \zeta_0^* \equiv \frac{\zeta_0}{\nu_b}, \quad \mu_\ell(t^*) \equiv -\frac{1}{n\nu(t)} \int d\mathbf{v} \left[\frac{v}{v_{\text{th}}(t)}\right]^\ell J[\mathbf{v}|f,f], \quad (13)$$

where $\nu_b = g_c K_d n\sigma^{d-1} v_b$ is the collision frequency associated with the background temperature T_b. Note that the control parameter ζ_0^* measures the ratio between the characteristic times associated with collisions and drag. In the molecular case, ζ_0^* depends on the bath-to-grain density, size, and mass ratios, but otherwise, it is independent of T_b [21,26]. In terms of the quantities defined in Equation (13), Equation (8) becomes

$$\frac{\dot{\theta}}{\zeta_0^*} = 2(1-\theta)[1 + (d+2)\gamma\theta] - 2(d+2)\gamma\theta^2 a_2 - \frac{2\mu_2}{d}\frac{\theta^{3/2}}{\zeta_0^*}, \quad (14)$$

where henceforth, a dot over a quantity denotes a derivative with respect to t^*, and we have taken into account that $\zeta(t)/\nu(t) = 2\mu_2(t^*)/d$ and $\nu(t)/\nu_b = \theta^{1/2}(t^*)$.

Equation (14) is not a closed equation since it is coupled to the full VDF through a_2 and μ_2. More generally, taking velocity moments on the EFPE, an infinite hierarchy of moment equations can be derived. In dimensionless form, it reads

$$\frac{\dot{M}_\ell}{\zeta_0^*} = \ell \left\{ \left[(\ell-2)\gamma + \frac{\mu_2}{d}\frac{\sqrt{\theta}}{\zeta_0^*} + (d+2)\gamma\theta(1+a_2) - \frac{1}{\theta}\right] M_\ell - 2\gamma\theta M_{\ell+2} + \frac{d+\ell-2}{2}\frac{M_{\ell-2}}{\theta} \right\}$$
$$- \mu_\ell \frac{\sqrt{\theta}}{\zeta_0^*}, \quad (15)$$

where $M_\ell(t^*) \equiv n^{-1} \int d\mathbf{v} [v/v_{\text{th}}(t)]^\ell f(\mathbf{v};t)$. In particular, $M_0 = 1$, $M_2 = \frac{d}{2}$, $M_4 = \frac{d(d+2)}{4}(1+a_2)$, and $M_6 = \frac{d(d+2)(d+4)}{8}(1+3a_2-a_3)$, a_3 being the sixth cumulant.

Equation (15) is trivial for $\ell = 0$ and $\ell = 2$. The choice $\ell = 4$ yields

$$\frac{\dot{a}_2}{\zeta_0^*} = 4\gamma\theta \left[\frac{2(1+a_2)}{\theta} + (d+2)(1+a_2)^2 - (d+4)(1+3a_2-a_3)\right] - 4\frac{a_2}{\theta}$$
$$+ \frac{4}{d}\left[\mu_2(1+a_2) - \frac{\mu_4}{d+2}\right]\frac{\sqrt{\theta}}{\zeta_0^*}. \quad (16)$$

Equations (14)–(16) are formally exact in the context of the EFPE, Equation (1). Nevertheless, they cannot be solved because of the infinite nature of the hierarchy (15) and the highly nonlinear dependence of the collisional moments μ_ℓ on the velocity moments of the VDF. This forces us to devise tractable approximations in order to extract information about the dynamics and steady state of the system.

3. Approximate Schemes

3.1. Maxwellian Approximation

The simplest approximation consists of assuming that the VDF remains very close to a Maxwellian during its time evolution so that the excess kurtosis a_2 can be neglected in Equation (14), and the reduced cooling rate μ_2 can be approximated by [11,12,17,18,28,33,34]

$$\mu_2 \approx \mu_2^{(0)} = 1 - \alpha^2. \quad (17)$$

In this Maxwellian approximation (MA), Equation (14) becomes

$$\frac{\dot\theta}{\zeta_0^*} \approx 2(1-\theta)[1+(d+2)\gamma\theta] - \frac{2(1-\alpha^2)}{d}\frac{\theta^{3/2}}{\zeta_0^*}. \tag{18}$$

This is a closed equation for the temperature ratio $\theta(t^*)$ that can be solved numerically for any initial temperature. The steady-state value θ^{st} in the MA is obtained by equating to zero the right-hand side of Equation (18), which results in a fourth-degree algebraic equation.

3.2. First Sonine Approximation

As we will see later, the MA given by Equation (18) provides a simple and, in general, rather accurate estimate of $\theta(t^*)$ and θ^{st}. However, since the evolution of temperature is governed by its initial value only, the MA is unable to capture memory phenomena, such as Mpemba- or Kovacs-like effects, which are observed even in the case of elastic particles [21–23]. This is a consequence of the absence of any coupling of θ with some other dynamical variable(s).

The next simplest approximation beyond the MA consists of incorporating a_2 into the description but assuming it is small enough as to neglect nonlinear terms involving this quantity, as well as higher-order cumulants, i.e., $a_2^k \to 0$ for $k \geq 2$ and $a_\ell \to 0$ for $\ell \geq 3$. This represents the so-called first Sonine approximation (FSA), according to which Equations (14) and (16) become

$$\frac{\dot\theta}{\zeta_0^*} \approx 2(1-\theta)[1+(d+2)\gamma\theta] - 2(d+2)\gamma\theta^2 a_2 - \frac{2\left[\mu_2^{(0)}+\mu_2^{(1)}a_2\right]}{d}\frac{\theta^{3/2}}{\zeta_0^*}, \tag{19a}$$

$$\frac{\dot a_2}{\zeta_0^*} \approx 4\gamma\theta\left[2\frac{1+a_2}{\theta}+(d+2)(1+2a_2)-(d+4)(1+3a_2)\right] - 4\frac{a_2}{\theta}$$
$$+\frac{4}{d}\left\{\mu_2^{(0)}-\frac{\mu_4^{(0)}}{d+2}+\left[\mu_2^{(0)}+\mu_2^{(1)}-\frac{\mu_4^{(1)}}{d+2}\right]a_2\right\}\frac{\sqrt\theta}{\zeta_0^*}, \tag{19b}$$

where we have used [11,12,17,18,28,33,34]

$$\mu_2 \approx \mu_2^{(0)} + \mu_2^{(1)}a_2, \quad \mu_4 \approx \mu_4^{(0)} + \mu_4^{(1)}a_2, \tag{20}$$

with

$$\mu_2^{(1)} = \frac{3}{16}\mu_2^{(0)}, \quad \mu_4^{(0)} = \left(d+\frac{3}{2}+\alpha^2\right)\mu_2^{(0)}, \tag{21a}$$

$$\mu_4^{(1)} = \frac{3}{32}\left(10d+39+10\alpha^2\right)\mu_2^{(0)} + (d-1)(1+\alpha). \tag{21b}$$

Equations (19) make a set of two coupled differential equations. In contrast to the MA, now the evolution of $\theta(t^*)$ is governed by the initial values of both θ and a_2. This latter fact implies that the evolution of temperature depends on the initial preparation of the whole VDF, this being a determinant condition for the emergence of memory effects, which will be explored later in Section 4.1.

3.2.1. Steady-State Values

The steady-state values θ^{st} and a_2^{st} in the FSA are obtained by equating to zero the right-hand sides of Equations (19), i.e.,

$$\dot{\theta} = 0 \Rightarrow F_0(\theta^{\text{st}}) + F_1(\theta^{\text{st}}) a_2^{\text{st}} = \left[\mu_2^{(0)} + \mu_2^{(1)} a_2^{\text{st}}\right] \frac{(\theta^{\text{st}})^{3/2}}{\zeta_0^*}, \quad (22a)$$

$$\dot{a}_2 = 0 \Rightarrow G_0(\theta^{\text{st}}) + G_1(\theta^{\text{st}}) a_2^{\text{st}} = \left\{\frac{\mu_4^{(0)}}{d+2} - \mu_2^{(0)} + \left[\frac{\mu_4^{(1)}}{d+2} - \mu_2^{(0)} - \mu_2^{(1)}\right] a_2^{\text{st}}\right\} \frac{(\theta^{\text{st}})^{3/2}}{\zeta_0^*}, \quad (22b)$$

where

$$F_0(\theta) = d(1-\theta)[1 + (d+2)\gamma\theta], \quad F_1(\theta) = -d(d+2)\gamma\theta^2, \quad (23a)$$
$$G_0(\theta) = 2d\gamma\theta(1-\theta), \quad G_1(\theta) = d\gamma\theta[2 - \theta(d+8)] - d. \quad (23b)$$

Eliminating a_2^{st} in Equation (22), one gets a closed nonlinear equation for θ^{st} in our FSA. Once numerically solved, a_2^{st} is simply given by either Equation (22a) or Equation (22b). For instance, Equation (22a) gives

$$a_2^{\text{st}} = -\frac{F_0(\theta^{\text{st}}) - \mu_2^{(0)}(\theta^{\text{st}})^{3/2}/\zeta_0^*}{F_1(\theta^{\text{st}}) - \mu_2^{(1)}(\theta^{\text{st}})^{3/2}/\zeta_0^*}. \quad (24)$$

Figure 2 compares the MA and FSA predictions of θ^{st} for three- and two-dimensional granular gases with $\zeta_0^* = 1$. We observe that the breakdown of equipartition (as measured by $1 - \theta^{\text{st}}$) is stronger in 2D than 3D and increases with increasing inelasticity but decreases as the nonlinearity of the drag force grows. Apart from that, the deviations of the MA values with respect to the FSA ones increase with increasing nonlinearity and inelasticity, the MA values tending to be larger (i.e., closer to equipartition) than the FSA ones.

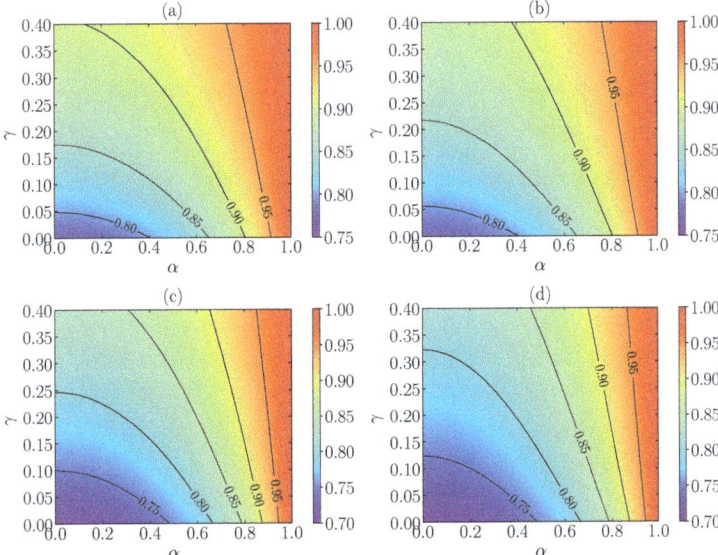

Figure 2. Theoretical predictions for the steady-state value of the reduced temperature θ^{st} as a function of the coefficient of normal restitution α and of the nonlinearity control parameter γ with $\zeta_0^* = 1$. Panels (**a**,**c**) correspond to the MA, while panels (**b**,**d**) correspond to the FSA. The dimensionality of the system is $d = 3$ in panels (**a**,**b**) and $d = 2$ in panels (**c**,**d**). The contour lines are separated by an amount of $\Delta\theta^{\text{st}} = 0.05$.

The FSA predictions of a_2^{st} are displayed in Figure 3. First, it is quite apparent that the departure from the Maxwellian VDF (as measured by the magnitude of a_2^{st}) is higher in 2D than 3D. It is also noteworthy that a_2^{st} starts growing with increasing γ, reaches a maximum at a certain value $\gamma = \gamma_{\max}(\alpha, \xi_0^*)$, and then it decreases as γ increases beyond $\gamma_{\max}(\alpha, \xi_0^*)$; this effect is more pronounced for small α.

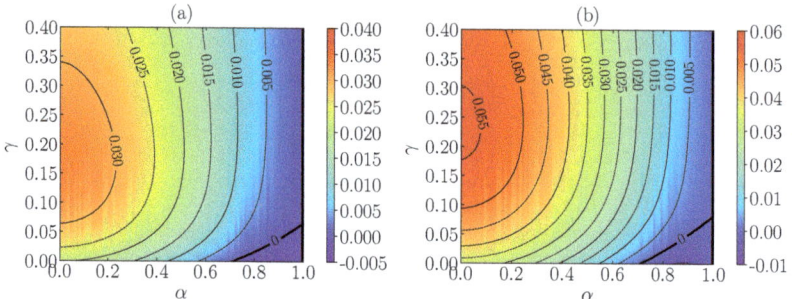

Figure 3. FSA predictions for the steady-state value of the excess kurtosis a_2^{st} as a function of the coefficient of normal restitution α and of the nonlinearity control parameter γ with $\xi_0^* = 1$. The dimensionality of the system is $d = 3$ in panel (**a**) and $d = 2$ in panel (**b**). The contour lines are separated by an amount of $\Delta a_2^{st} = 0.005$. The thickest black line corresponds to the contour $a_2^{st} = 0$.

Another interesting feature is that a_2^{st} takes negative values (in the domain of small inelasticity) only if γ is smaller than a certain value γ_c. Of course, $a_2^{st}(\alpha, \gamma)|_{\alpha=1} = 0$ for any γ (since the steady state with $\alpha = 1$ is that of equilibrium), but $\partial_\alpha a_2^{st}(\alpha, \gamma)|_{\alpha=1} < 0$ if $\gamma < \gamma_c$ and $\partial_\alpha a_2^{st}(\alpha, \gamma)|_{\alpha=1} > 0$ if $\gamma > \gamma_c$. Thus, the critical value γ_c is determined by the condition $\partial_\alpha a_2^{st}(\alpha, \gamma_c)|_{\alpha=1} = 0$. Interestingly, the result obtained from the FSA, Equation (24), is quite simple, namely

$$\gamma_c = \frac{1}{3(d+2)}, \tag{25}$$

which is independent of ξ_0^*.

3.2.2. Special Limits

Absence of Drag

Let us first define a *noise temperature* T_n as $T_n = T_b \xi_0^{*2/3} \propto (\xi_0 T_b)^{2/3}$, so that $\theta^{3/2}/\xi_0^* = (T/T_n)^{3/2}$. Now we take the limit of zero drag, $\xi_0 \to 0$, with finite noise temperature T_n. This implies $T_b \to \infty$, and thus, the natural temperature scale of the problem is no longer T_b but T_n, i.e., $\theta^{st} \to 0$ but $T^{st}/T_n =$ finite. From Equations (23) we see that $F_0(0) = d$, $F_1(0) = 0$, $G_0(0) = 0$, and $G_1(0) = -d$. Therefore, Equations (22) reduce to

$$\dot{\theta} = 0 \Rightarrow d\left(\frac{T_n}{T^{st}}\right)^{3/2} = \mu_2^{st}, \tag{26a}$$

$$\dot{a}_2 = 0 \Rightarrow -d\left(\frac{T_n}{T^{st}}\right)^{3/2} a_2^{st} = \frac{\mu_4^{st}}{d+2} - \mu_2^{st}(1 + a_2^{st}), \tag{26b}$$

where, for the sake of generality, we have undone the linearizations with respect to a_2^{st}. By the elimination of $(T_n/T^{st})^{3/2}$, one simply gets $(d+2)\mu_2^{st} = \mu_4^{st}$, from which one can then obtain a_2^{st} upon linearization [11,12]. The steady-state temperature is given by $T^{st}/T_n = (d/\mu_2^{st})^{2/3}$.

Homogeneous Cooling State

If, in addition to $\zeta_0 \to 0$, we take the limit $T_n \to 0$, the asymptotic state becomes the homogeneous cooling state. In that case, T does not reach a true stationary value, but a_2 does. As a consequence, Equation (26a) is not applicable, but Equation (26b), with $T_n = 0$, can still be used to get $(d+2)\mu_2^{st}(1 + a_2^{st}) = \mu_4^{st}$, as expected [11,12,17].

Linear Drag Force

If the drag force is linear in velocity (i.e., $\gamma = 0$), we have $F_0(\theta) = d(1 - \theta)$, $F_1(\theta) = 0$, $G_0(\theta) = 0$, and $G_1(\theta) = -d$. Using Equation (22b), a_2^{st} is given by

$$a_2^{st} = -\frac{\mu_4^{(0)} - (d+2)\mu_2^{(0)}}{\mu_4^{(0)} - (d+2)\left[\mu_2^{(0)} + \mu_2^{(1)} - d\zeta_0^*/(\theta^{st})^{3/2}\right]}, \quad (27)$$

thus recovering previous results [31,32].

Collisionless Gas

If the collision frequency ν_b is much smaller than the zero-velocity drag coefficient ζ_0, the granular dynamics is dominated by the interaction with the background fluid and the grain–grain collisions can be neglected; therefore, the grains behave as Brownian particles. In that case, the relevant dimensionless time is no longer $t^* = \nu_b t$ but $\tau = \zeta_0 t = \zeta_0^* t^*$ and the evolution equations (19) become

$$\frac{d\theta}{d\tau} \approx 2(1 - \theta)[1 + (d+2)\gamma\theta] - 2(d+2)\gamma\theta^2 a_2, \quad (28a)$$

$$\frac{da_2}{d\tau} \approx 4\gamma\theta\left[2\frac{1 + a_2}{\theta} + (d+2)(1 + 2a_2) - (d+4)(1 + 3a_2)\right] - 4\frac{a_2}{\theta}, \quad (28b)$$

It is straightforward to check that the steady-state solution is $\theta^{st} = 1$ and $a_2^{st} = 0$, regardless of the value of γ, as expected.

4. Comparison with Computer Simulations

We have carried out DSMC and EDMD computer simulations to validate the theoretical predictions. The DSMC method is based on the acceptance-rejection Monte Carlo Metropolis decision method [35] but adapted to solve the Enskog–Boltzmann equation [36,37], and the algorithm is, consequently, adjusted to agree with the inelastic collisional model [12,17] and reflect the interaction with the bath [23]. On the other hand, the EDMD algorithm is based on the one exposed in Ref. [23], but is adequated to the IHS collisional model. The main difference between DSMC and EDMD is that the latter does not follow any statistical rule to solve the Boltzmann equation but solves the equations of motion of the hard particles. Simulation details about the characteristics of the schemes and numerical particularities can be found in Appendix A.

In Figure 4, results from simulations are compared with the theoretical predictions of θ^{st} (from MA and FSA) and of a_2^{st} (from FSA) in a three-dimensional ($d = 3$) IHS system with $\zeta_0^* = 1$. It can be observed that both the DSMC and EDMD results agree with each other. From Figure 4a, one can conclude that, as expected, FSA works in the prediction of θ^{st} much better than MA for values of γ close to $\gamma_{max}(\alpha, \zeta_0^*)$ (which corresponds to the maximum magnitude of a_2^{st}). Moreover, FSA gives reasonably good estimates for the values of a_2^{st}, although they get worse for increasing inelasticity, i.e., decreasing α. One might also think that the increase in γ produces a poorer approach; however, according to the theory, the performance of FSA improves if $\gamma > \gamma_{max}(\alpha, \zeta_0^*)$, which corresponds to a decrease in $|a_2^{st}|$. Of course, nonlinear terms or higher-order cumulants might play a role that is not accounted for within FSA.

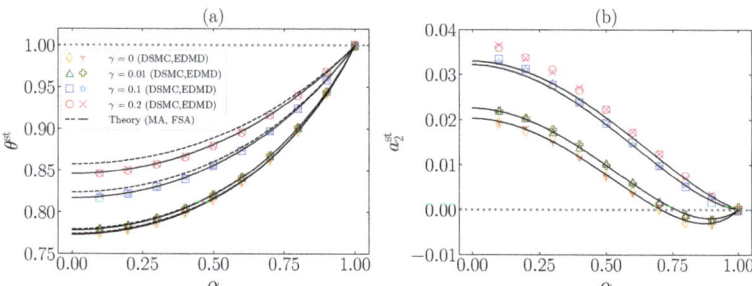

Figure 4. Plots of the steady-state values of (**a**) the temperature ratio θ^{st} and (**b**) the excess kurtosis a_2^{st} vs. the coefficient of normal restitution α for $\xi_0^* = 1$, $d = 3$, and different values of the nonlinear parameter: $\gamma = 0, 0.01, 0.1, 0.2$. The symbols stand for DSMC ($\diamond$, $\triangle$, $\square$, $\circ$) and EDMD (Y, +, *, ×) simulation results, respectively. Dashed (– –) and solid (——) lines refer to MA (only in panel (**a**)) and FSA predictions, respectively. The horizontal gray dotted lines ($\cdots$) correspond to the steady-state values in the elastic limit. As representative values, note that, at $\xi_0^* = 1$, one has $\gamma_{max} = 0.25, 0.19, 0.17$ for $\alpha = 0.8, 0.5, 0.2$, respectively.

Apart from the steady-state values, we have studied the temporal evolution of θ and a_2, starting from a Maxwellian VDF at temperature T_b, i.e., $\theta(0) \equiv \theta^0 = 1$ and $a_2(0) \equiv a_2^0 = 0$. Note that this state is that of equilibrium in the case of elastic collisions ($\alpha = 1$), regardless of the value of the nonlinearity parameter γ. The theoretical and simulation results are displayed in Figure 5 for $d = 3$, $\xi_0^* = 1$, and some characteristic values of α and γ.

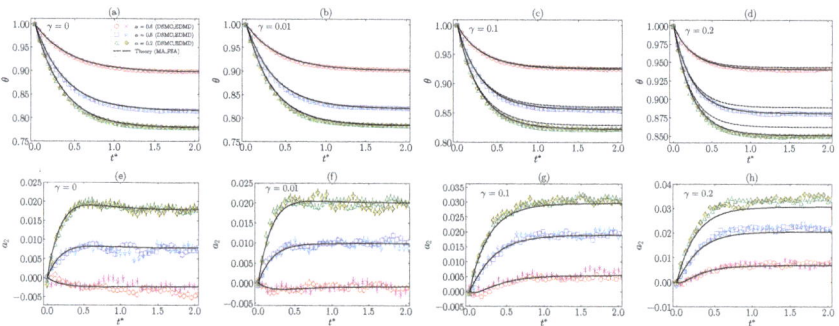

Figure 5. Plots of the time evolution of (**a**–**d**) the temperature ratio $\theta(t^*)$ and (**e**–**h**) the excess kurtosis $a_2(t^*)$ for $\xi_0^* = 1$, $d = 3$, and different values of the coefficient of normal restitution ($\alpha = 0.8, 0.5, 0.2$) and the nonlinearity parameter: (**a**,**e**) $\gamma = 0$, (**b**,**f**) $\gamma = 0.01$, (**c**,**g**) $\gamma = 0.1$, and (**d**,**h**) $\gamma = 0.2$. The symbols stand for DSMC ($\circ$, $\square$, $\triangle$) and EDMD (×, *, +) simulation results, respectively. Dashed (– –) and solid (——) lines refer to MA (only in panels (**a**–**d**)) and FSA predictions, respectively. All states are initially prepared with a Maxwellian VDF at the bath temperature, i.e., $\theta^0 = 1$ and $a_2^0 = 0$.

We observe that the relaxation of θ is accurately predicted by MA, except for the later stage with small α and/or large γ, in accordance with the discussion of Figure 4. This is remedied by FSA, which exhibits an excellent agreement with simulation results in the case of θ and a fair agreement in the case of a_2, again in accordance with the discussion of Figure 4. It is also worth mentioning the good mutual agreement between DSMC and EDMD data, even though fluctuations are much higher in a_2 than in θ because of the rather small values of $|a_2|$.

4.1. Memory Effects

Whereas the temperature relaxation from Maxwellian initial states is generally accurate from MA, it misses the explicit dependence of the temperature evolution on the fourth cumulant (see Equation (14)), which, however, is captured by FSA (see Equation (19a)). This coupling of θ to a_2 is a signal of preparation dependence of the system, hence, a signal of memory effects, as occurs in the elastic case reported in Refs. [21–23].

4.1.1. Mpemba Effect

We start the study of memory effects with the Mpemba effect [38–42]. This counterintuitive phenomenon refers to situations in which an initially hotter sample (A) of a fluid—or, more generally, a statistical-mechanical system—cools down sooner than an initially colder one (B) in a cooling experiment. We will refer to this as the direct Mepmba effect (DME). Analogously, the inverse Mpemba effect (IME) occurs in heating experiments if the initially colder sample (B) heats up more rapidly than the initially hotter one (A) [21,23,40,41,43]. In the special case of a molecular gas (i.e., $\alpha = 1$), an extensive study of both DME and IME has recently been carried out [21,23].

Figure 6a,b present an example of DME and IME, respectively. As expected, FSA describes the evolution and crossing for temperatures of samples A and B very well. On the contrary, MA does not predict this memory effect. In addition, from Figure 6c,d we can conclude that FSA captures the relaxation of a_2 toward $a_2^{st} \neq 0$ quite well.

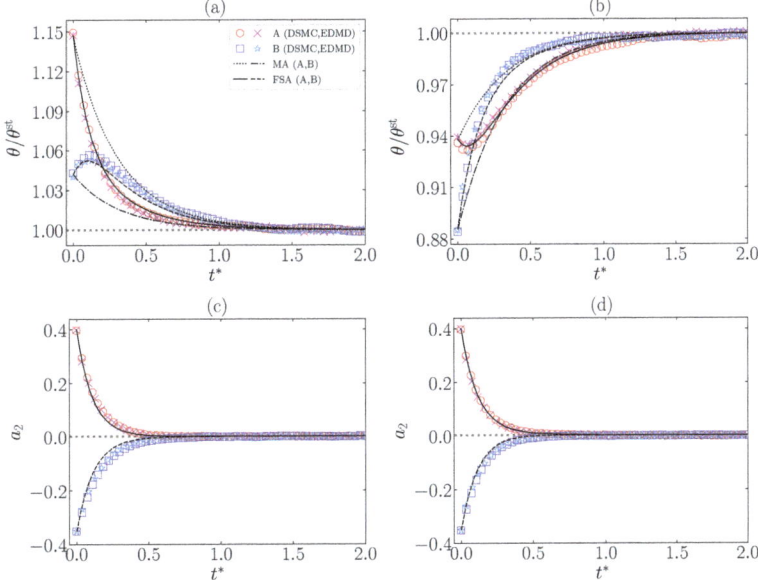

Figure 6. Time evolution of (**a**,**b**) $\theta(t^*)/\theta^{st}$ and (**c**,**d**) $a_2(t^*)$ for two samples (A and B) with $\alpha = 0.9$, $\xi_0^* = 1$, $d = 3$, and $\gamma = 0.1$. Panels (a, c) illustrate the DME with initial conditions $\theta_A^0 = 1.1 \simeq 1.15\theta^{st}$, $a_{2A}^0 = 0.4$, $\theta_B^0 = 1 \simeq 1.04\theta^{st}$, $a_{2B}^0 = -0.35$, while panels (b, d) illustrate the IME with initial conditions $\theta_A^0 = 0.9 \simeq 0.94\theta^{st}$, $a_{2A}^0 = 0.4$, $\theta_B^0 = 0.85 \simeq 0.89\theta^{st}$, $a_{2B}^0 = -0.35$. The symbols stand for DSMC (○, □) and EDMD (×, ∗) simulation results, respectively. Solid (----) and dashed (- -) lines correspond to FSA predictions for samples A and B, respectively, whereas black dotted (· · ·) and dash-dotted (- · -) lines in panels (**a**,**b**) refer to MA predictions for samples A and B, respectively. The gray thin horizontal lines correspond to the steady-state values. Note that $a_2^{st} \neq 0$, despite what panels (**c**,**d**) seem to indicate because of the vertical scale.

4.1.2. Kovacs Effect

Next, we turn to another interesting memory effect: the Kovacs effect [44,45]. In contrast to the Mpemba effect, the Kovacs effect has a well-defined two-stage protocol and does not involve a comparison between two samples. In the context of our system, the protocol proceeds as follows. First, the granular gas is put in contact with a bath at temperature T_{b1} and initialized at a temperature $T^0 > T_1^{st}$, $T_1^{st} = \theta^{st} T_{b1}$ being the corresponding steady-state temperature (note that θ^{st} is independent of T_{b1} at fixed ξ_0^*). The system is allowed to relax to the steady state during a time window $0 < t < t_K$, but then, at $t = t_K$, the bath temperature is suddenly modified to a new value T_b, such that $T(t_K) = T^{st}$, $T^{st} = \theta^{st} T_b$ being the new steady-state value. If the system did not retain a memory of its previous history, one would have $T(t) = T^{st}$ for $t > t_K$, and this is, in fact, the result given by the MA. However, the temperature exhibits a hump for $t > t_K$, before relaxing to T^{st}. This hump is a consequence of the dependence of $\partial_t T$ on the additional variables of the system. According to Equation (14), and maintained in the FSA, Equation (19a), the first relevant quantity to be responsible for a possible hump is the excess kurtosis of the VDF, as occurs in the elastic limit [22]. In fact, at time $t^* = t_K^*$, such that $\theta(t_K^*) = \theta^{st}$, the slope of the temperature according to FSA, Equation (19a), reads

$$\dot\theta(t_K^*) \approx 2\theta^{st}\left[(d+2)\xi_0^*\gamma\theta^{st} + \frac{\mu_2^{(1)}}{d}\sqrt{\theta^{st}}\right]\left[a_2^{st} - a_2(t_K^*)\right]. \qquad (29)$$

Thus, a nonzero difference $a_2^{st} - a_2(t_K^*)$ implies the existence of a Kovacs-like hump, its sign being determined by that of this difference; that is, we will obtain an upward hump if $a_2(t_K^*) < a_2^{st}$ or a downward hump if $a_2(t_K^*) > a_2^{st}$.

For simplicity, in our study of the Kovacs-like effect, we replace the first stage of the protocol ($0 < t^* < t_K^*$) by just generating the state at $t^* = t_K^*$ with $\theta(t_K^*) = \theta^{st}$ and $a_2(t_K^*) \neq a_2^{st}$ (see Appendix A). The effect is illustrated in Figure 7 for the same system as in Figure 6 with the choices $a_2(t_K^*) = -0.35 < a_2^{st}$ and $a_2(t_K^*) = 0.4 > a_2^{st}$. Again, the DSMC and EDMD results agree with each other and with the theoretical predictions. However, in the case $a_2(t_K^*) = -0.35$ (upward hump), Figure 7a, we observe that the theoretical curve lies below the simulation results. This might be caused by a nonnegligible value of the sixth cumulant $a_3(t_K^*) = -0.375$, as reported in Ref. [23] in the elastic case. Apart from this small discrepancy, FSA captures the magnitude and sign of the humps, as well as the relaxation of the fourth cumulant, very well.

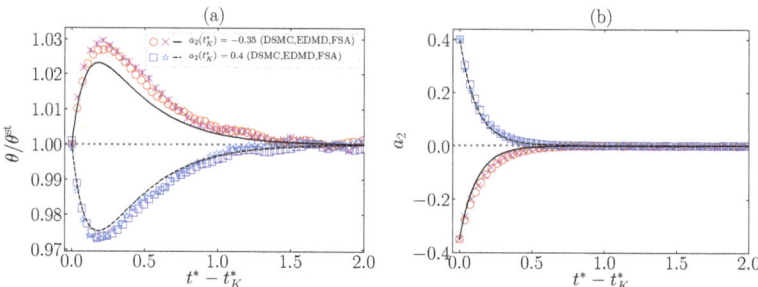

Figure 7. Time evolution for $t^* > t_K^*$ of (a) $\theta(t^*)/\theta^{st}$ and (b) $a_2(t^*)$ for a system with $\alpha = 0.9$, $\xi_0^* = 1$, $d = 3$, and $\gamma = 0.1$. The figure illustrates Kovacs-like effects with conditions $\theta(t_K^*) = \theta^{st}$ and either $a_2(t_K^*) = -0.35$ (○, □, —) or $a_2(t_K^*) = 0.4$) (×, ∗, - - -). The symbols stand for DSMC and EDMD simulation results, while the lines refer to FSA predictions.

5. Conclusions

In this work, we have looked into the dynamics of a dilute granular gas immersed in a thermal bath (at temperature T_b) made of smaller particles but with masses comparable to those of the grains. To mathematically characterize this system, we have worked under the assumptions of Boltzmann's kinetic theory, describing the system by the one-particle VDF, whose evolution is monitored by the EFPE, Equation (1), for the IHS model of hard d-spheres. The action of the bath on the dynamics of the granular gas is modeled by a nonlinear drag force and an associated stochastic force. At a given dimensionality d, the control parameters of the problem are the coefficient of normal restitution (α), the (reduced) drag coefficient at zero velocity (ξ_0^*), and the nonlinearity parameter (γ).

After a general presentation of the kinetic theory description in Section 2, we obtained the evolution equation of the reduced temperature $\theta(t^*) \equiv T(t)/T_b$ (Equation (14)), which is coupled explicitly with the excess kurtosis, a_2, and depends on every velocity moment through the second collisional moment μ_2 (which is nonzero due to inelasticity). Therefore, the whole dynamics in the context of the EFPE is formally described by Equation (14) and the infinite hierarchy of moment equations given by Equation (15). In order to give predictions, we proposed two approximations. The first one is MA, which consists of assuming a Maxwellian form for the one-particle VDF, whereas the second one, FSA consists of truncating the Sonine expansion of the VDF up to the first nontrivial cumulant a_2. Their evolution equations are given by Equations (18) and (19), respectively. The predictions for the steady-state values are exposed in Figures 2 and 3, which show some small discrepancies in θ^{st} between MA and FSA as we increase the inelasticity (decreasing α). Moreover, we observed that, for fixed α and ξ_0^*, a_2^{st} gets its maximum value when the nonlinearity parameter is $\gamma = \gamma_{max}(\alpha, \xi_0^*)$. Another interesting feature is the existence of a critical value γ_c, such that for $\gamma > \gamma_c$, the values of a_2^{st} are always positive for every value of α, while for $\gamma < \gamma_c$, we find $a_2^{st} < 0$ for inelasticities small enough. Interestingly, the value of γ_c given by Equation (25) is found to be independent of ξ_0^*. In addition, some already known limits are recovered in Section 3.2.2.

Furthermore, in order to check the predictions from MA and FSA equations, we carried out DSMC and EDMD simulations for hard spheres ($d = 3$) with fixed $\xi_0^* = 1$ (which corresponds to comparable time scales associated with drag and collisions). First, from Figure 4a, we can conclude that, whereas MA provides good predictions of θ^{st}, except for large inelasticities and values of γ close to γ_{max}, FSA is much more accurate because it takes into account the influence of a_2^{st}. The latter approach is generally reliable for a_2^{st}, as observed in Figure 4b, although, not unexpectedly, it slightly worsens as $|a_2^{st}|$ grows. Relaxation curves starting from a Maxwellian initial state in Figure 5 show that FSA agrees very well with both DSMC and EDMD; however, MA exhibits good agreement during the first stage of the evolution but becomes less reliable as the steady state is approached.

A relevant feature of these systems, as already studied in the elastic case [21–23], is the emergence of memory effects, which are not contemplated by MA. FSA predicts the emergence of the Mpemba effect very well for both DME and IME, as can be seen in Figure 6. Analogously, Kovacs-like humps, both upward and downward, are correctly described by FSA, as observed in Figure 7, although the FSA humps are slightly less pronounced (especially the upward one) than the simulation ones. This is presumably due to the role played by a_3 and higher-order cumulants, as occurs in the elastic limit reported in Ref. [23].

To conclude, we expect that this work will motivate research about this type of system and the emergence of memory effects. For instance, one can extend the study to other collisional models (such as that of rough spheres), to nonhomogeneous states, or to a more detailed description of the memory effects observed.

Author Contributions: A.M. worked out the approximations and performed the simulations. A.S. supervised the work. Both authors participated in the analysis and discussion of the results and worked on the revision and writing of the final manuscript. All authors have read and agreed to the published version of the manuscript.

Funding: The authors acknowledge financial support from Grant No. PID2020-112936GB-I00 funded by MCIN/AEI/10.13039/501100011033, and from Grants No. IB20079 and No. GR21014 funded by Junta de Extremadura (Spain) and by ERDF "A way of making Europe". A.M. is grateful to the

Spanish Ministerio de Ciencia, Innovación y Universidades for a predoctoral fellowship FPU2018-3503.

Institutional Review Board Statement: Not applicable.

Data Availability Statement: The data presented in this study are available in the online repository: https://github.com/amegiasf/GranularNonlinearDrag.

Acknowledgments: The authors are grateful to the computing facilities of the Instituto de Computación Científica Avanzada of the University of Extremadura (ICCAEx), where the simulations were run.

Conflicts of Interest: The authors declare no conflict of interest.

Abbreviations

The following abbreviations are used in this manuscript:

DME	Direct Mpemba effect
DSMC	Direct simulation Monte Carlo
EDMD	Event-driven molecular dynamics
EFPE	Enskog–Fokker–Planck equation
FSA	First Sonine approximation
IHS	Inelastic hard spheres
IME	Inverse Mpemba effect
MA	Maxwellian approximation
VDF	Velocity distribution function

Appendix A. Simulation Details

Throughout the elaboration of this work, we have used two different algorithms to simulate the considered system: DSMC and EDMD methods. Whereas the former is based on statistical properties and subjected to the assumptions of the Boltzmann equation, such as *Stosszahlansatz*, the latter solves the trajectory of each particle without any extra assumption. On the other hand, the original algorithms are slightly modified for the proper collisional model and the interaction with the thermal bath, as explained below.

In general, the simulation results shown in this work are obtained from averaging over 100 samples in both simulation schemes, and steady-state results come from averaging over 50 points in the mean trajectory once stationary behavior is observed.

Appendix A.1. Direct Simulation Monte Carlo

The DSMC algorithm used in this work is based on the original works of G.A. Bird [36,37], but modified for the IHS collisional model and the implementation of the nonlinear drag. As we considered homogeneous states, only the velocities of the N granular particles, $\{\mathbf{v}_i\}_{i=1}^N$, are used to numerically solve the EFPE. Whereas initial velocities for results in Figures 4 and 5 were drawn from a Maxwellian VDF with $\theta^0 = 1$; in the case of Figures 6 and 7, velocities were initialized from a Gamma VDF (see Refs. [23,30] for additional details). After initialization, particles were updated with a fixed time step, Δt, much smaller than the mean free time. The method is properly divided into two stages: collision and free streaming [12].

In the collision stage, a number $\lfloor \frac{1}{2} N \omega_{\max} \Delta t \rfloor$ of pairs are randomly chosen with equiprobability—the ignored decimals in the rounding are saved for the next iterative step—$\omega_{\max}$ being an upper bound estimate for the one-particle collision rate. Then, given a chosen pair ij, a collision is accepted with probability $\Theta(\mathbf{v}_{ij} \cdot \widehat{\sigma}_{ij})\omega_{ij}/\omega_{\max}$, where $\widehat{\sigma}_{ij}$ is a random vector drawn from a uniform probability distribution in the unit d-sphere, and $\omega_{ij} = \frac{2\pi^{d/2}}{\Gamma(d/2)} g_c n \sigma^{d-1} |\mathbf{v}_{ij} \cdot \widehat{\sigma}_{ij}|$. Acceptance implies that the velocities are updated according to the collisional rules in Equation (3), i.e., $\mathbf{v}_{i/j}(t) \to \mathbf{v}_{i/j}(t + \Delta t) = \mathbf{v}_{i/j} \pm \frac{1+\alpha}{2}(\mathbf{v}_{ij} \cdot \widehat{\sigma}_{ij})$.

In the free-streaming stage, each particle velocity is updated according to an Euler numerical algorithm of a Langevin-like equation derived from an Itô interpretation of the Fokker–Planck part of the EFPE (see Ref. [23]),

$$\mathbf{v}_i(t) \to \mathbf{v}_i(t + \Delta t) = \mathbf{v}_i(t) - [\xi(v_i(t)) - 2\xi_0\gamma]\mathbf{v}_i\Delta t + \chi(v_i(t))\sqrt{\Delta t}\mathbf{Y}_i, \quad (A1)$$

where $\mathbf{Y}_i$ is a random vector drawn from a Gaussian probability distribution with unit variance, $P(\mathbf{Y}) = (2\pi)^{-d/2}e^{-Y^2/2}$.

In the implementations of the DSMC algorithm, we used $N = 10^4$ hard spheres ($d = 3$) and a time step $\Delta t = 10^{-2}\lambda/v_b$, $\lambda = (\sqrt{2}\pi n\sigma^2)^{-1}$ being the mean free path.

Appendix A.2. Event-Driven Molecular Dynamics

EDMD methods compute the evolution of particles driven by events: particle–particle collisions, boundary effects, or other more complex interactions. Analogously to the splitting described in the DSMC algorithm, free streaming of particles occurs between two consecutive events. Here, we need to consider the influence of the stochastic and drag forces not only in the velocities but also in the positions of the N granular particles, $\{\mathbf{r}_i\}_{i=1}^N$. In order to account for this, we followed the *approximate Green Function* algorithm proposed in Ref. [46]. Whereas the velocities are updated according to Equation (A1), the positions follow

$$\mathbf{r}_i(t) \to \mathbf{r}_i(t + \Delta t) = \mathbf{r}_i(t) + \mathbf{v}_i(t)\Delta t\left[1 - \Delta t\frac{\xi(v_i(t)) - 2\gamma\xi_0}{2}\right] + \frac{1}{2}\chi(v_i(t))\Delta t^{3/2}\mathbf{W}_i, \quad (A2)$$

where $\mathbf{W}_i = \mathbf{Y}_i + \sqrt{5/3}\mathbf{Y}'_i$, $\mathbf{Y}'_i$ being another random vector drawn from $P(\mathbf{Y}) = (2\pi)^{-d/2}e^{-Y^2/2}$.

In the EDMD simulations, we defined a set of $N = 8 \times 10^3$ hard spheres ($d = 3$), with a reduced number density $n\sigma^3 = 10^{-3}$, implying a box length $L/\sigma = 2 \times 10^2$, and used a time step $\Delta t \approx 10^{-3}\lambda/v_b$. Periodic boundary conditions were imposed, and no inhomogeneities were observed.

References

1. Tatsumi, S.; Murayama, Y.; Hayakawa, H.; Sano, M. Experimental study on the kinetics of granular gases under microgravity. *J. Fluid Mech.* **2009**, *641*, 521–539. [CrossRef]
2. Yu, P.; Schröter, M.; Sperl, M. Velocity Distribution of a Homogeneously Cooling Granular Gas. *Phys. Rev. Lett.* **2020**, *124*, 208007. [CrossRef] [PubMed]
3. Pouliquen, O.; Nicolas, M.; Weidman, P.D. Crystallization of non-Brownian Spheres under Horizontal Shaking. *Phys. Rev. Lett.* **1997**, *79*, 3640–3643. [CrossRef]
4. Tennakoon, S.G.K.; Behringer, R.P. Vertical and Horizontal Vibration of Granular Materials: Coulomb Friction and a Novel Switching State. *Phys. Rev. Lett.* **1998**, *81*, 794–797. [CrossRef]
5. Metcalfe, G.; Tennakoon, S.G.K.; Kondic, L.; Schaeffer, D.G.; Behringer, R.P. Granular friction, Coulomb failure, and the fluid-solid transition for horizontally shaken granular materials. *Phys. Rev. E* **2002**, *65*, 031302. [CrossRef]
6. Huan, C.; Yang, X.; Candela, D.; Mair, R.W.; Walsworth, R.L. NMR experiments on a three-dimensional vibrofluidized granular medium. *Phys. Rev. E* **2004**, *69*, 041302. [CrossRef]
7. Schröter, M.; Goldman, D.I.; Swinney, H.L. Stationary state volume fluctuations in a granular medium. *Phys. Rev. E* **2005**, *71*, 030301. [CrossRef]
8. Abate, A.R.; Durian, D.J. Approach to jamming in an air-fluidized granular bed. *Phys. Rev. E* **2006**, *74*, 031308. [CrossRef]
9. Eshuis, P.; van der Meer, D.; Alam, M.; van Gerner, H.J.; van der Weele, K.; Lohse, D. Onset of Convection in Strongly Shaken Granular Matter. *Phys. Rev. Lett.* **2010**, *104*, 038001. [CrossRef]
10. Michael, B.; Simon, M.; Gustavo, C.; Eric, F. Wave spectroscopy in a driven granular material. *Proc. R. Soc. A* **2022**, *476*, 20220014. [CrossRef]
11. van Noije, T.P.C.; Ernst, M.H. Velocity distributions in homogeneous granular fluids: The free and the heated case. *Granul. Matter* **1998**, *1*, 57–64. [CrossRef]
12. Montanero, J.M.; Santos, A. Computer simulation of uniformly heated granular fluids. *Granul. Matter* **2000**, *2*, 53–64. [CrossRef]
13. Garzó, V.; Chamorro, M.G.; Vega Reyes, F. Transport properties for driven granular fluids in situations close to homogeneous steady states. *Phys. Rev. E* **2013**, *87*, 032201. Erratum in *Phys. Rev. E* **2013**, *87*, 059906. [CrossRef]

14. Vega Reyes, F.; Santos, A. Steady state in a gas of inelastic rough spheres heated by a uniform stochastic force. *Phys. Fluids* **2015**, *27*, 113301. [CrossRef]
15. Brey, J.J.; Buzón, V.; Maynar, P.; García de Soria, M.I. Hydrodynamics for a model of a confined quasi-two-dimensional granular gas. *Phys. Rev. E* **2015**, *91*, 052201. [CrossRef]
16. Garzó, V.; Brito, R.; Soto, R. Enskog kinetic theory for a model of a confined quasi-two-dimensional granular fluid. *Phys. Rev. E* **2018**, *98*, 052904. [CrossRef]
17. Santos, A.; Montanero, J.M. The second and third Sonine coefficients of a freely cooling granular gas revisited. *Granul. Matter* **2009**, *11*, 157–168. [CrossRef]
18. Garzó, V. *Granular Gaseous Flows. A Kinetic Theory Approach to Granular Gaseous Flows*; Springer Nature: Cham, Switzerland, 2019.
19. Megías, A.; Santos, A. Driven and undriven states of multicomponent granular gases of inelastic and rough hard disks or spheres. *Granul. Matter* **2019**, *21*, 49. [CrossRef]
20. Gómez González, R.; Garzó, V. Kinetic theory of granular particles immersed in a molecular gas. *J. Fluid Mech.* **2022**, *943*, A9. [CrossRef]
21. Santos, A.; Prados, A. Mpemba effect in molecular gases under nonlinear drag. *Phys. Fluids* **2020**, *32*, 072010. [CrossRef]
22. Patrón, A.; Sánchez-Rey, B.; Prados, A. Strong nonexponential relaxation and memory effects in a fluid with nonlinear drag. *Phys. Rev. E* **2021**, *104*, 064127. [CrossRef] [PubMed]
23. Megías, A.; Santos, A.; Prados, A. Thermal versus entropic Mpemba effect in molecular gases with nonlinear drag. *Phys. Rev. E* **2022**, *105*, 054140. [CrossRef] [PubMed]
24. Ferrari, L. Particles dispersed in a dilute gas: Limits of validity of the Langevin equation. *Chem. Phys.* **2007**, *336*, 27–35. [CrossRef]
25. Ferrari, L. Particles dispersed in a dilute gas. II. From the Langevin equation to a more general kinetic approach. *Chem. Phys.* **2014**, *428*, 144–155. [CrossRef]
26. Hohmann, M.; Kindermann, F.; Lausch, T.; Mayer, D.; Schmidt, F.; Lutz, E.; Widera, A. Individual Tracer Atoms in an Ultracold Dilute Gas. *Phys. Rev. Lett.* **2017**, *118*, 263401. [CrossRef]
27. Brilliantov, N.; Pöschel, T. Deviation from Maxwell distribution in granular gases with constant restitution coefficient. *Phys. Rev. E* **2000**, *61*, 2809–2812. [CrossRef]
28. Brilliantov, N.V.; Pöschel, T. *Kinetic Theory of Granular Gases*; Oxford University Press: Oxford, UK, 2004.
29. Vega Reyes, F.; Santos, A.; Kremer, G.M. Role of roughness on the hydrodynamic homogeneous base state of inelastic spheres. *Phys. Rev. E* **2014**, *89*, 020202(R). [CrossRef]
30. Megías, A.; Santos, A. Kullback–Leibler divergence of a freely cooling granular gas. *Entropy* **2020**, *22*, 1308. [CrossRef]
31. Chamorro, M.G.; Vega Reyes, F.; Garzó, V. Homogeneous states in granular fluids driven by thermostats. *AIP Conf. Proc.* **2012**, *1501*, 1024–1030. [CrossRef]
32. Chamorro, M.G.; Vega Reyes, F.; Garzó, V. Homogeneous steady states in a granular fluid driven by a stochastic bath with friction. *J. Stat. Mech.* **2013**, P07013. [CrossRef]
33. Goldshtein, A.; Shapiro, M. Mechanics of collisional motion of granular materials. Part 1. General hydrodynamic equations. *J. Fluid Mech.* **1995**, *282*, 75–114. [CrossRef]
34. Brilliantov, N.; Pöschel, T. Breakdown of the Sonine expansion for the velocity distribution of granular gases. *Europhys. Lett.* **2006**, *74*, 424–430. Erratum in *Europhys. Lett.* **2006**, *75*, 188. [CrossRef]
35. Metropolis, N.; Rosenbluth, A.W.; Rosenbluth, M.N.; Teller, A.H.; Teller, E. Equation of State Calculations by Fast Computing Machines. *J. Chem. Phys.* **1953**, *21*, 1087–1092. [CrossRef]
36. Bird, G.A. *Molecular Gas Dynamics and the Direct Simulation of Gas Flows*; Clarendon: Oxford, UK, 1994.
37. Bird, G.A. *The DSMC Method*; CreateSpace Independent Publishing Platform: Scotts Valley, CA, USA, 2013.
38. Mpemba, E.B.; Osborne, D.G. Cool? *Phys. Educ.* **1969**, *4*, 172–175. [CrossRef]
39. Burridge, H.C.; Linden, P.F. Questioning the Mpemba effect: Hot water does not cool more quickly than cold. *Sci. Rep.* **2016**, *6*, 37665. [CrossRef]
40. Lu, Z.; Raz, O. Nonequilibrium thermodynamics of the Markovian Mpemba effect and its inverse. *Proc. Natl. Acad. Sci. USA* **2017**, *114*, 5083–5088. [CrossRef]
41. Lasanta, A.; Vega Reyes, F.; Prados, A.; Santos, A. When the Hotter Cools More Quickly: Mpemba Effect in Granular Fluids. *Phys. Rev. Lett.* **2017**, *119*, 148001. [CrossRef]
42. Bechhoefer, J.; Kumar, A.; Chétrite, R. A fresh understanding of the Mpemba effect. *Nat. Rev. Phys.* **2021**, *3*, 534–535. [CrossRef]
43. Gómez González, R.; Khalil, N.; Garzó, V. Mpemba-like effect in driven binary mixtures. *Phys. Fluids* **2021**, *33*, 053301. [CrossRef]
44. Kovacs, A.J. Transition vitreuse dans les polymères amorphes. Etude phénoménologique. *Fortschr. Hochpolym.-Forsch.* **1963**, *3*, 394–507. [CrossRef]
45. Kovacs, A.J.; Aklonis, J.J.; Hutchinson, J.M.; Ramos, A.R. Isobaric volume and enthalpy recovery of glasses. II. A transparent multiparameter theory. *J. Polym. Sci. Polym. Phys. Ed.* **1979**, *17*, 1097–1162. [CrossRef]
46. Scala, A. Event-driven Langevin simulations of hard spheres. *Phys. Rev. E* **2012**, *86*, 026709. [CrossRef] [PubMed]

Article

Application of a Gas-Kinetic BGK Scheme in Thermal Protection System Analysis for Hypersonic Vehicles

Di Zhou, Bingchen Du, Tongqing Guo *, Qiaozhong Li and Zhiliang Lu

Key Laboratory of Unsteady Aerodynamics and Flow Control, Ministry of Industry and Information Technology, Nanjing University of Aeronautics and Astronautics, Nanjing 210016, China
* Correspondence: guotq@nuaa.edu.cn

Abstract: One major problem in the development of hypersonic vehicles is severe aerodynamic heating; thus, the implementation of a thermal protection system is required. A numerical investigation on the reduction of aerodynamic heating using different thermal protection systems is conducted using a novel gas-kinetic BGK scheme. This method adopts a different solution strategy from the conventional computational fluid dynamics technique, and has shown a lot of benefits in the simulation of hypersonic flows. To be specific, it is established based on solving the Boltzmann equation, and the obtained gas distribution function is used to reconstruct the macroscopic solution of the flow field. Within the finite volume framework, the present BGK scheme is specially designed for the evaluation of numerical fluxes across the cell interface. Two typical thermal protection systems are investigated by using spikes and opposing jets, separately. Both their effectiveness and mechanisms to protect the body surface from heating are analyzed. The predicted distributions of pressure and heat flux, and the unique flow characteristics brought by spikes of different shapes or opposing jets of different total pressure ratios all verify the reliability and accuracy of the BGK scheme in the thermal protection system analysis.

Keywords: gas-kinetic scheme; BGK model; thermal protection system; hypersonic flow

1. Introduction

Increasing attention is being paid to hypersonic vehicles within the aerospace community because of their fast access to space, rapid military response at long ranges, and fast means of commercial air travel. In the long-term development of hypersonic vehicles, one of the most important problems is severe aerodynamic heating at the nose of the vehicle [1]. This makes the design and use of a thermal protection system (TPS) essential, especially for sustained long-range maneuverable flights.

Currently, many thermal protection systems have been constructed. These can be categorized into two types: active method and passive method. Active methods protect the body surface from heating by using injection gases or mechanical devices, such as evaporation cooling [2], film cooling [3], opposing jet [4], mechanical spike [5], and directed energy air spike [6]. Passive methods generally use heat protection materials [7] and ablators [8]. In the present study, active thermal protection systems are considered for their reusability and fine controllability. As the design of such TPS largely depends on the aero-thermal loads acting on the vehicle, accurate prediction of aerodynamic heating plays a vital role [9].

Hypersonic flows are usually characterized with a thin shock layer, complex wave structures, and various shock–boundary interactions. This demands higher requirements from the numerical methods. In conventional computational fluid dynamics (CFD) technology, the total fluxes across the cell interface are split into inviscid and viscous parts, and different solution strategies are adopted for them. Over the past few years, a variety of important numerical algorithms have been developed specifically to deal with inviscid fluxes. Most of them are constructed based on the mathematical and physical properties of the Euler equations and can work well for flows at moderate Mach numbers. However, they may exhibit different numerical behaviors in hypersonic flows. For instance, the JST scheme has gained popularity in aircraft design due to its lower cost, but it may encounter instabilities and accuracy degradation at a higher Mach number. The Van Leer's flux-vector splitting scheme works very well in the case of Euler equations, but may provide inaccurate stagnation temperatures for hypersonic viscous flows. The Roe's flux-difference splitting upwind scheme shows a high resolution in the boundary layers and a good solution for shocks, but the well-known "carbuncle" phenomenon may occur in multi-dimensional and high-speed problems. Even for the AUSM-family schemes that are very popular in hypersonic flow simulation, sometimes local pressure oscillations are found in the vicinity of shocks and in cases where the flow is aligned with the grid. Considering these defects, many improvements have been proposed to enhance the modeling capabilities, mostly through some mathematical or artificial corrections [10–12]. However, as has been pointed out by Xu [13], these numerical difficulties are inherently due to the deficiencies of the Euler equations at describing the realistic flow evolution process around the cell interface. Using some special modifications not only brings uncertainties and inconveniences to computations, but also covers up this inherent defect.

In the last decade, many attempts have been made to develop numerical schemes based on solving more fundamental governing equations of physics, e.g., the Boltzmann equation. Particularly, the gas-kinetic Bhatnagar–Gross–Krook (BGK) scheme [14,15] has been shown to be a promising Boltzmann-type method. Its main advantages are the following. First, using the BGK collision model gives superior dissipation characteristics, which are important for capturing flow discontinuities. Second, the BGK scheme has been proven to satisfy the entropy condition and thus avoids unphysical solutions such as the "carbuncle" phenomenon. Third, its inherent positive property ensures good robustness in low-density regions. Furthermore, from the perspective of implementation, the BGK scheme allows for calculating the total fluxes in a unified way. In a pioneering study, Xu et al. [16] proposed a multi-dimensional BGK scheme for accurately predicting viscous stress and heat flux, where flow gradients in both parallel and perpendicular directions are considered. Later, Li et al. [17] developed a BGK method with kinetic boundary conditions and applied it to the numerical study of hypersonic flow past a hollow cylinder flare model. Recently, by introducing effective relaxation time into the BGK equation, Tan et al. [18] extended the method for hypersonic turbulence simulations. Other notable works include those of Li and Fu [19], Li and Zhang [20], Yang and co-workers [21,22], to mention only a few. All of the above studies show the good prospect of the BGK scheme in hypersonic applications.

The goal of this paper is to apply the gas-kinetic BGK scheme to thermal protection system analysis, which has rarely been seen in the literatures to the best of our knowledge. This is also a further extension of the previous work [23] on the algorithm improvement of the original method. Here, two commonly used active TPSs were chosen to be studied, i.e., the spike and the opposing jet. As the implementation of both will greatly increase the complexity of hypersonic flow fields and bring a lot of new aerodynamic and aerothermal phenomena, the capabilities of the BGK scheme for hypersonic flow simulation in the presence of TPS are highlighted. It is also noted that changes in the spike configurations (spike length, shape, etc.) or opposing jet parameters (mass flow rate, total pressure ratio, etc.) could produce diverse flow fields and significantly affect the performance of the TPS; thus, the abilities of the BGK scheme to capture these characteristics were also examined.

This paper is organized as follows: Section 2 describes the BGK model for the concerned governing equations. Section 3 describes the construction and implementation of the BGK scheme. Section 4 presents the numerical results and an analysis of the typical thermal protection systems using the developed method. The last section is the conclusion.

2. BGK Model for the Governing Equations

Because the thermal protection systems studied in this work are axisymmetric with respect to the geometry and flow conditions, the two-dimensional (2D) axisymmetric Navier-Stokes (N-S) equations are solved, which can be written as

$$\frac{\partial}{\partial t}\int_\Omega W d\Omega + \frac{1}{y}\oint_{\partial\Omega} y F dS = \int_\Omega Q d\Omega \qquad (1)$$

where t is time, Ω is the control volume, and y is the coordinate in the radial direction. The vectors of conservative variables W, total fluxes F, and source terms Q are given by

$$W = \begin{bmatrix} \rho \\ \rho u \\ \rho v \\ \rho E \end{bmatrix}, \quad F = \begin{bmatrix} \rho V \\ \rho u V + n_x p - n_x \tau_{xx} - n_y \tau_{xy} \\ \rho v V + n_y p - n_x \tau_{yx} - n_y \tau_{yy} \\ (\rho E + p)V - n_x \Theta_x - n_y \Theta_y \end{bmatrix}, \quad Q = \begin{bmatrix} 0 \\ 0 \\ p - \tau_{\theta\theta} \\ 0 \end{bmatrix} \qquad (2)$$

where ρ, u, v, E, and p denote the density, the velocity components in the axial and radial direction, the total energy per unit mass, and the pressure, respectively. The contravariant velocity is defined as $V = n_x u + n_y v$, with n_x, n_y being components of the unit normal vector. The notations τ_{xx}, τ_{xy}, τ_{yx}, τ_{yy}, $\tau_{\theta\theta}$ represent components of the viscous stress tensor and Θ_x, Θ_y are the terms describing the work of the viscous stresses and heat conduction. Details of their formulations can be seen in [10].

It should be noted that the axisymmetric equations can be transformed to the 2D planar N-S equations by removing the terms related to the radius and the additional source term.

The present BGK scheme is designed to discretize the fluxes F by reconstructing the gas distribution function f at the cell interface. The time evolution of f is governed by the 2D Boltzmann equation with the BGK collision model

$$\frac{\partial f}{\partial t} + \xi_x \frac{\partial f}{\partial x} + \xi_y \frac{\partial f}{\partial y} = -\frac{1}{\tau}(f - g) \qquad (3)$$

where ξ_x and ξ_y denote the particle streaming velocities, τ is the collision time, and g is the equilibrium distribution function approached by f. The equilibrium state is generally assumed to be a Maxwellian distribution

$$g = \rho \left(\frac{\lambda}{\pi}\right)^{\frac{K+2}{2}} e^{-\lambda((\xi_x - u)^2 + (\xi_y - v)^2 + \zeta^2)} \qquad (4)$$

where $\lambda = \rho/2p$ for perfect gases, K denotes the number of degrees of the internal variables ζ and is equal to 3 for diatomic gases in the 2D case, and $\zeta^2 = \zeta_i \zeta_i$.

Because of the conservations of mass, momentum, and energy in the particle collision process, the following compatibility condition is satisfied

$$\int \frac{g - f}{\tau} \psi d\Xi = 0 \qquad (5)$$

where ψ is a vector of the collision invariants, defined as

$$\psi = \left[1, \xi_x, \xi_y, \frac{1}{2}(\xi_x^2 + \xi_y^2 + \zeta^2)\right]^T \qquad (6)$$

with the notation $d\Xi = d\xi_x d\xi_y d\zeta_1 d\zeta_2 \cdots d\zeta_k$ used.

From the definition of the gas distribution function, the macroscopic mass, momentum, and energy densities of the gas flow can be written as

$$W = \begin{bmatrix} \rho \\ \rho u \\ \rho v \\ \rho E \end{bmatrix} = \int f \psi d\Xi = \int f \begin{bmatrix} 1 \\ \xi_x \\ \xi_y \\ \frac{1}{2}(\xi_x^2 + \xi_y^2 + \zeta^2) \end{bmatrix} d\Xi \qquad (7)$$

3. Gas-Kinetic BGK Scheme

3.1. Solution of the BGK Equation

It can be proven from the Chapman–Enskog expansion that the above BGK model recovers the governing axisymmetric N-S equations, which serves as the theoretical basis for the present BGK scheme. By using the method of characteristics, the generalized solution of Equation (3) at any time t and any cell interface $x_{i+1/2}$ is

$$f(x_{i+1/2}, t, \xi, \zeta) = \frac{1}{\tau} \int_0^t e^{-(t-t')/\tau} g(x(t'), t', \xi, \zeta) dt' + e^{-t/\tau} f_0(x(0), 0, \xi, \zeta) \qquad (8)$$

where $x(t') = x_{i+1/2} - (t - t')\xi$ describes a particle motion trajectory with $t' \in [0, t]$ and $\xi = [\xi_x, \xi_y]^T$. The solution f describes the gas evolution process, which starts with an initial state f_0 and approaches its equilibrium state g. In the following, we show how to determine these two unknowns. For simplicity, the x-direction and y-direction are assumed as the normal and tangential directions to the local cell interface, respectively, and $x_{i+1/2} = [0,0]^T$ is assumed. Note the difference between this local coordinate system and the previous global axial–radial system.

First, we construct the initial state f_0. To account for the flow discontinuities, which are common in hypersonic flows, both equilibrium and non-equilibrium distribution functions should be considered. The second-order accuracy is constructed as

$$f_0(x(0), \xi, \zeta) = \begin{cases} g^l[1 - (\mathbf{a}^l \cdot \xi)t - \tau(A^l + \mathbf{a}^l \cdot \xi)], & \xi_x > 0 \Leftrightarrow x < 0 \\ g^r[1 - (\mathbf{a}^r \cdot \xi)t - \tau(A^r + \mathbf{a}^r \cdot \xi)], & \xi_x \leq 0 \Leftrightarrow x \geq 0 \end{cases} \qquad (9)$$

where g^l and g^r denote the local Maxwellians defined at the left and right sides of the cell interface, respectively, and the corresponding slopes $\mathbf{a}^{l(r)} = [a^{l(r)}, b^{l(r)}]^T$ and $A^{l(r)}$ are related to the spatial and temporal derivatives of $g^{l(r)}$, respectively

$$\begin{aligned} a^{l(r)} g^{l(r)} &= \frac{\partial g^{l(r)}}{\partial x} \\ b^{l(r)} g^{l(r)} &= \frac{\partial g^{l(r)}}{\partial y} \\ A^{l(r)} g^{l(r)} &= \frac{\partial g^{l(r)}}{\partial t} \end{aligned} \qquad (10)$$

The derivatives of $g^{l(r)}$ can be directly derived from Equation (4), where the left and right macroscopic states are reconstructed using the second-order MUSCL scheme. The minmod limiter is used to prevent unphysical oscillation and spurious solutions in the shock regions. By using the chain rule for the derivatives in Equation (10) and rearranging the terms, the spatial and temporal slopes can be expressed as a linear combination of the collision invariants

$$\begin{aligned} a^{l(r)} &= a^{l(r)}_\alpha \psi_\alpha \\ b^{l(r)} &= b^{l(r)}_\alpha \psi_\alpha , \qquad \alpha = 1, 2, 3, 4 \\ A^{l(r)} &= A^{l(r)}_\alpha \psi_\alpha \end{aligned} \qquad (11)$$

where $a_\alpha^{l(r)}$, $b_\alpha^{l(r)}$, and $A_\alpha^{l(r)}$ are local constant coefficients and have explicit formulations. For example, the expressions for $a_\alpha^{l(r)}$ are given by (omit the superscripts)

$$\begin{aligned} a_1 &= \frac{\partial \rho}{\rho \partial x} - 2\lambda \left(u \frac{\partial u}{\partial x} + v \frac{\partial v}{\partial x} \right) + \left(\frac{K+2}{2\lambda} - u^2 - v^2 \right) \frac{\partial \lambda}{\partial x} \\ a_2 &= 2 \left(u \frac{\partial \lambda}{\partial x} + \lambda \frac{\partial u}{\partial x} \right) \\ a_3 &= 2 \left(v \frac{\partial \lambda}{\partial x} + \lambda \frac{\partial v}{\partial x} \right) \\ a_4 &= -2 \frac{\partial \lambda}{\partial x} \end{aligned} \quad (12)$$

The same holds for $b_\alpha^{l(r)}$, only by changing $\partial/\partial x$ to $\partial/\partial y$. The flow gradients in the above formulations are obtained by applying Green's theorem to the respective cells. As for $A_\alpha^{l(r)}$, because the non-equilibrium part of f_0 does not directly contribute to conservative variables, thus we have

$$A_\alpha^{l(r)} \int g^{l(r)} \psi_\alpha \psi d\Xi = -\int g^{l(r)} (a^{l(r)} \xi_x + b^{l(r)} \xi_y) \psi d\Xi \quad (13)$$

from which $A_\alpha^{l(r)}$ can be solved.

Next we construct the time-dependent equilibrium state g shown in Equation (8). Also to the second-order accuracy, it can be expressed as

$$g(x(t'), t', \xi, \zeta) = \begin{cases} g_0 \left[1 + \overline{A} t' - \overline{a}^l \xi_x (t-t') - \overline{b}^l \xi_y (t-t') \right], & \xi_x > 0 \Leftrightarrow x < 0 \\ g_0 \left[1 + \overline{A} t' - \overline{a}^r \xi_x (t-t') - \overline{b}^r \xi_y (t-t') \right], & \xi_x \leq 0 \Leftrightarrow x \geq 0 \end{cases} \quad (14)$$

where g_0 is an initial Maxwellian. The corresponding slopes $\overline{a}^{l(r)} = [\overline{a}^{l(r)}, \overline{b}^{l(r)}]^T$ and $\overline{A}$ are linked to the spatial and temporal derivatives of g_0, respectively

$$\begin{aligned} \overline{a}^{l(r)} g_0 &= \left(\frac{\partial g_0}{\partial x} \right)^{l(r)} \\ \overline{b}^{l(r)} g_0 &= \left(\frac{\partial g_0}{\partial y} \right)^{l(r)} \\ \overline{A} g_0 &= \frac{\partial g_0}{\partial t} \end{aligned} \quad (15)$$

The derivatives of g_0 are also derived from Equation (4), where the "average" macroscopic parameters $\overline{\rho}$, $\overline{\lambda}$, $\overline{u}$, $\overline{v}$ are obtained from Equations (8) and (9) with the limits $x \to (0,0)$ and $t' \to 0$ used. This gives

$$\overline{W} = \begin{bmatrix} \overline{\rho} \\ \overline{\rho u} \\ \overline{\rho v} \\ \overline{\rho E} \end{bmatrix} = \int [g^l H(\xi_x) + g^r (1 - H(\xi_x))] \begin{bmatrix} 1 \\ \xi_x \\ \xi_y \\ \frac{1}{2}(\xi_x^2 + \xi_y^2 + \zeta^2) \end{bmatrix} d\Xi \quad (16)$$

with $H(\xi_x)$ the Heaviside function.

Then $\overline{a}^{l(r)}$ and $\overline{b}^{l(r)}$ are determined similar to Equations (11) and (12), and the gradients of "average" flow variables are obtained by applying Green's theorem to both sides of the cell interface.

Substituting the expressions of f_0 and g into Equation (8), the generalized solution f of the BGK equation can be written as

$$\begin{aligned}
f(x_{i+1/2}, t, \boldsymbol{\xi}, \zeta) \\
= \gamma_1 g_0 + \gamma_2 g_0 \overline{A} + \gamma_3 g_0 \Big[&(\overline{a}^{-l} \cdot \boldsymbol{\xi}) H(\xi_x) + (\overline{a}^{-r} \cdot \boldsymbol{\xi})(1 - H(\xi_x)) \Big] \\
+ \gamma_4 \Big[g^l(1 - \tau A^l) H(\xi_x) &+ g^r(1 - \tau A^r)(1 - H(\xi_x)) \Big] \\
+ \gamma_5 \Big[g^l(a^l \cdot \boldsymbol{\xi}) H(\xi_x) &+ g^r(a^r \cdot \boldsymbol{\xi})(1 - H(\xi_x)) \Big]
\end{aligned} \quad (17)$$

with the definitions of

$$\begin{array}{ll}
\gamma_1 = 1 - e^{-t/\tau} & \gamma_2 = t - \tau(1 - e^{-t/\tau}) \\
\gamma_3 = t e^{-t/\tau} - \tau(1 - e^{-t/\tau}) & \gamma_4 = e^{-t/\tau} \\
\gamma_5 = -(t + \tau) e^{-t/\tau} &
\end{array} \quad (18)$$

For the remaining unknown $\overline{A}$ in Equation (17), we can solve it using time integration of the compatibility condition (Equation (5)) over a whole time step Δt, i.e.,

$$\int_0^{\Delta t} \int (f - g) \boldsymbol{\psi} d\Xi = 0 \quad (19)$$

For the simulation of viscous flows, the collision time τ is constructed as

$$\tau = \frac{\mu_L + \mu_T}{p} + c \Delta t \frac{|p_l - p_r|}{|p_l + p_r|} \quad (20)$$

where μ_L and μ_T denote the laminar viscosity and eddy viscosity at the cell interface, respectively. The laminar viscosity μ_L is calculated using the Sutherland formula, and the eddy viscosity μ_T is obtained by employing a turbulence model, such as the Spalart–Allmaras model [24] used here. The second term was designed for stability reasons, where c is a constant and can be chosen in the range of 1 to 5.

3.2. Evaluation of Numerical Fluxes

Once the time evolution of f has been obtained, the numerical fluxes at each cell interface can be evaluated according to the relations between the macroscopic variables and the microscopic distribution function, i.e.,

$$F(x_{i+1/2}, t) = \int \xi_x \boldsymbol{\psi} f(x_{i+1/2}, t, \boldsymbol{\xi}, \zeta) d\Xi \quad (21)$$

Because the original BGK model recovers the macroscopic equations with a Prandtl number of $Pr = 1$, in order to deal with arbitrary Pr, a Prandtl number fix is used based on the modification of the energy flux. According to the definition of q, we have

$$\begin{aligned}
q &= \tfrac{1}{2} \int (\xi_x - \overline{u})((\xi_x - \overline{u})^2 + (\xi_y - \overline{v})^2 + \zeta^2) f d\Xi \\
&= \int \xi_x \Big(\tfrac{1}{2}(\overline{u}^2 + \overline{v}^2)\psi_1 + \psi_4 - u\psi_2 - v\psi_3 \Big) f d\Xi - \overline{u} \int \Big(\tfrac{1}{2}(\overline{u}^2 + \overline{v}^2)\psi_1 + \psi_4 - \overline{u}\psi_2 - \overline{v}\psi_3 \Big) f d\Xi
\end{aligned} \quad (22)$$

By substituting the expression of f into the above equation, we obtain an accurate time-dependent q. It should be noted that all of the terms in Equation (22) were already obtained when solving the BGK equation, thus no extra moment computations are required. Then, the Prandtl number fix is achieved by modifying the energy flux as

$$F_4^{fix} = F_4 + \left(\frac{1}{Pr} - 1 \right) q \quad (23)$$

For the turbulent simulations, q is divided into the laminar heat flux q_L and turbulent heat flux q_T according to the respective viscosities, i.e.,

$$q_L = \frac{q\mu_L}{\mu_L + \mu_T}, \quad q_T = \frac{q\mu_T}{\mu_L + \mu_T} \tag{24}$$

and the modified energy flux becomes

$$F_4^{fix} = F_4 + \left(\frac{1}{Pr} - 1\right)q_L + \left(\frac{1}{Pr_T} - 1\right)q_T \tag{25}$$

with Pr_T being the turbulent Prandtl number.

In the present work, a perfect gas is assumed with Prandtl numbers of $Pr = 0.72$ and $Pr_T = 0.9$, and a specific heat ratio of $\gamma = 1.4$. The thermal conductivity coefficient k is calculated from the relationship $k = c_p(\mu_L/Pr + \mu_T/Pr_T)$, with c_p being the specific heat coefficient at a constant pressure.

3.3. Update of Flow Variables

It is seen from Equations (17) and (21) that both the solution f and the numerical fluxes F are time-dependent. To update the flow variables, a direct idea is to adopt explicit time integration methods such as the popular multistage schemes. However, to ensure correct flux balance throughout a cell, the computational time step Δt_c should be set to be identical in the whole flow field. Moreover, for numerical stability, this can be no greater than the minimum value among all of the local time steps, i.e., $\Delta t_c \leq \min(\Delta t)$. Accordingly, this may significantly decrease the computational efficiency for steady-state flow computations. Instead, we adopt a more efficient approach by using a separate discretization in space and time (i.e., the method of lines), and the time-averaged fluxes are introduced as follows

$$\overline{F}(x_{i+1/2}) = \frac{1}{\Delta t}\int_0^{\Delta t}\int \xi_x \psi f(x_{i+1/2}, t, \xi, \zeta)d\Xi \tag{26}$$

where Δt is called the flux time averaging step, so as to distinguish from the computational time step Δt_c. With this approach, local time stepping is used to accelerate the convergence, and a non-uniform Δt_c is allowed that can take a value much larger than in the original BGK scheme.

By using the cell-centered finite volume method in Equation (1) for spatial discretization, we obtain

$$\frac{\partial W}{\partial t} = -\frac{1}{\Omega}\sum_{m=1}^{N_F}(\overline{F}\Delta S)_m + Q = R \tag{27}$$

where $N_F = 4$ for structured grids, ΔS_m is the area of the face m, and R represents the residual vector.

To further improve the computational efficiency, the above equation is solved in an implicit way

$$\left(\frac{\Omega}{\Delta t_c}I + \frac{\partial R}{\partial W}\right)\Delta W^{(n)} = -R^{(n)} \tag{28}$$

where $\Delta W^{(n)} = W^{(n+1)} - W^{(n)}$ denotes the update of the solution in time and n and $n+1$ are the current and new time levels, respectively. The recently-developed JFNK–BGK method [25] was employed to solve the above linearized system so as to quickly obtain an update of the flow variables. As a result, the present implicit BGK scheme has a comparable computational efficiency to conventional CFD methods.

3.4. Code Validation

To ensure that the thermal protection analysis results obtained by the BGK scheme are reliable and accurate, validating the developed code through the simulation of "clean" hypersonic flow is essential. An example of a cylindrical leading-edge model in a Mach

6.47, Reynolds number 9.98×10^5 flow (based on the model diameter) was selected to be studied. The experimental investigation of this model was conducted in the NASA Langley's high temperature tunnel [26]. The free-stream pressure and temperature are 648.1 Pa and 241.5 K, respectively. The cylindrical surface is assumed to have a uniform temperature of T_{wall} = 294.4. For this planar model, the computational model and the grid used are shown in Figure 1.

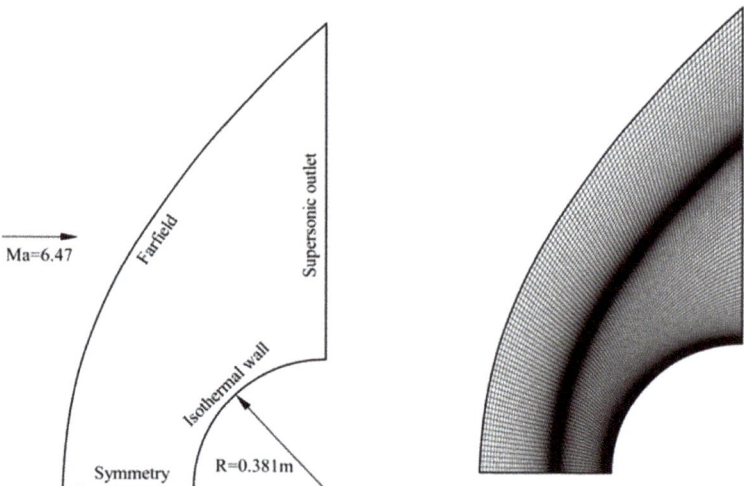

Figure 1. Computational model of the cylindrical leading-edge case and the grid used.

Different from our previous studies making assumptions about laminar flows, this work accounts for the turbulence effects. The first cell height to wall Δs is determined by the condition of $y^+ \leq 1$. A grid sensitivity study is performed in advance, and a 101 × 201 grid (in tangential and normal directions, respectively) with $\Delta s = 1 \times 10^{-6}$ m is selected to be used. This results in a grid-independent value of stagnation-point heat flux q_{stag} of 488.7 kW/m^2. This value agrees well with those from Zhang et al. [27] (485.5 kW/m^2), Dechaumphai et al. [28] (482.6 kW/m^2), and our previous laminar computation [23] (488.5 kW/m^2), although all of the experimental data are below (670.0 kW/m^2). This discrepancy can be attributed to neglecting the 3D effects, the uncertainty in turbulence modeling, and measurement errors.

Figure 2 shows the computed distribution of temperature along the symmetry line. A typical aerothermal phenomenon in hypersonic flows around a blunt body is observed. The free-stream temperature first undergoes a rapid increase across the shock, and then drops suddenly from over 2000 K to the fixed wall temperature within a thin thermal boundary layer. It is also found that the thicknesses of the shock and boundary layer are favorably thin, indicating a high accuracy of the BGK scheme for capturing discontinuities. The predicted shock location (−54.9 mm) shows good agreement with those from Guo et al. [29] (−54.6 mm) and Zhang et al. [27] (−55.0 mm).

The computed pressure and heat flux distributions along the cylinder wall are shown in Figure 3. The abscissa is defined as the angle from the stagnation point of the cylindrical body. Both the pressure and heat flux are normalized by their stagnation-point values, respectively, and those from the experiment are also presented. As shown in the figure, for both pressure and heat flux distributions, the present results agree very well with the experimental data.

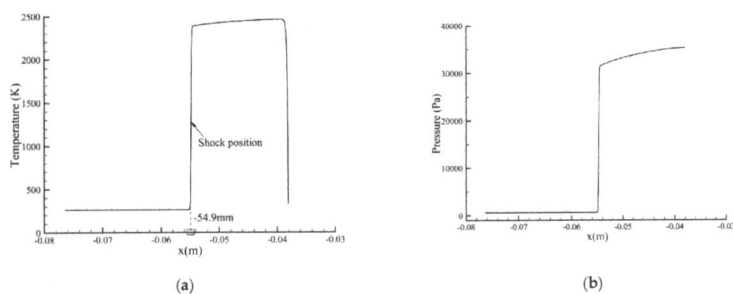

Figure 2. Computed distribution of (**a**) temperature and (**b**) pressure along the symmetry line.

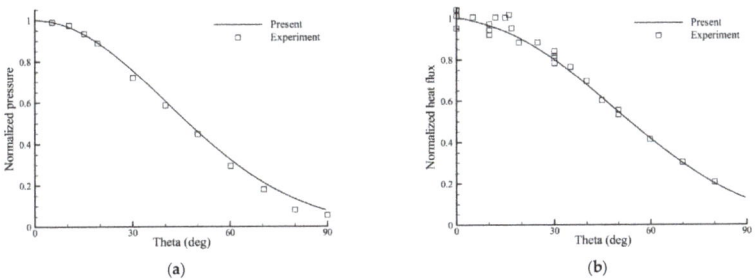

Figure 3. Distributions of (**a**) pressure and (**b**) heat flux along the cylinder wall.

Finally, the computed density contour is compared to that from the Schlieren photograph [26]. As shown in Figure 4, good agreements were observed in the captured shock. All of the above results validate the satisfactory accuracy of the present BGK scheme for hypersonic flows.

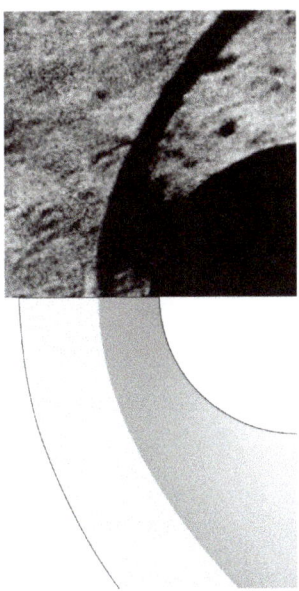

Figure 4. Computed density contour (**lower**) and Schlieren photograph (**upper**).

4. Numerical Results and Discussions

In this section, two widely used thermal protection systems are investigated using the developed method. One is using the spike and the other one is using the opposing jet. Both their performances and mechanisms to reduce heat flux are analyzed.

4.1. Thermal Protection System by Using Spike

The first case is a spiked blunt body experimentally investigated by Motoyama et al. [5]. The experiments are conducted in a 0.2 m radius Mach 7 hypersonic wind tunnel. The stagnation temperature is 860 K and the free-stream Reynolds number is 4×10^5 (based on the diameter of the hemispherical body). Various configurations are tested in the experiment, and three typical models are considered in this case. One is a conical spike, the second is a hemispherical spike, and the third uses a hemispherical disk on a spike nose. The first two are often referred to as an aerospike model, while the third belongs to the aerodisk model. Their configurations are given in Figure 5, together with the original hemispherical body without a spike.

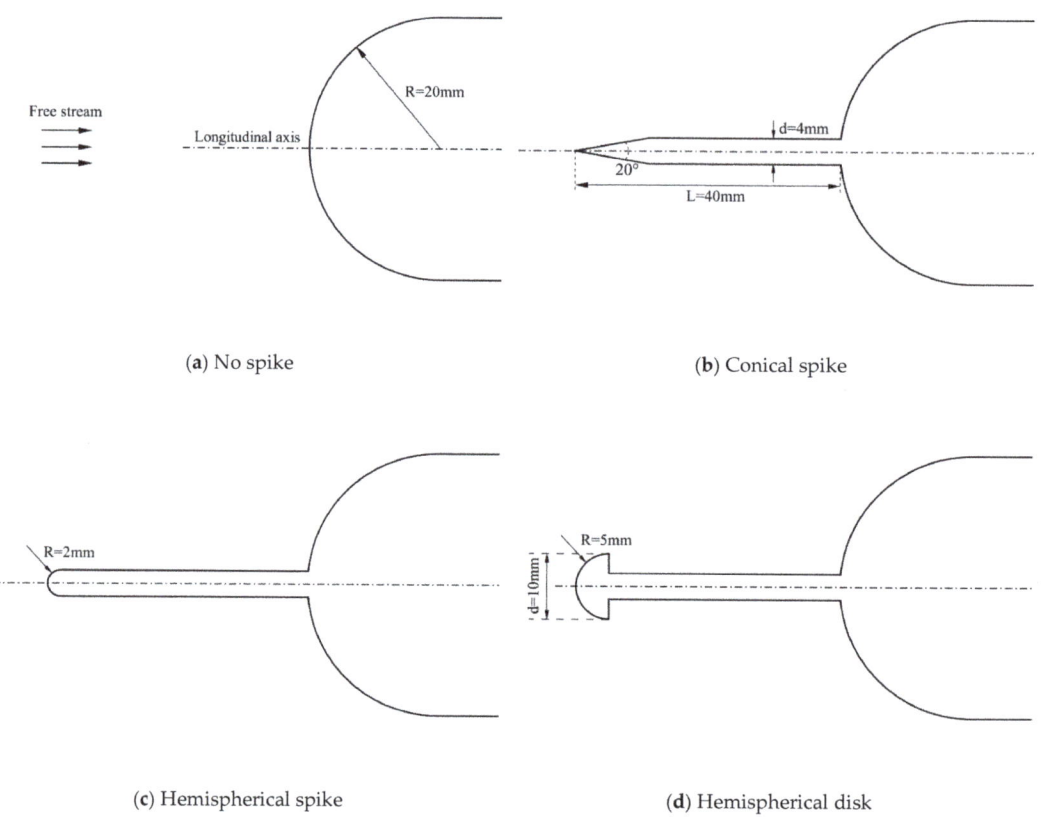

Figure 5. Different configurations of the spike attached to a hemispherical body.

Because of the axis symmetry of geometry and flow conditions, the computation is simplified using a 2D axisymmetric model. Multi-block structured grids are employed to discretize the computational domain. The total number of grid cells used for these four models is about 0.12 million, which has been shown to be fine enough through a previous grid independence study. The first cell height to wall is set to keep y^+ near 1.

Figure 6 presents the computed surface pressure distributions of the hemispherical body from the present method and a conventional N-S solver using the AUSM+ scheme. The abscissa represents the angle from the stagnation point of the hemisphere body, and the pressure data are normalized by the specific heat ratio and free-stream pressure. The experimental and theoretical results are also presented for comparison, if available. For all of the cases, both methods predict very similar pressure distributions. The numerical results of the no-spike case agree better with the experimental data than the inviscid theory [30]. This verifies the reliability of the BGK scheme for axisymmetric hypersonic flows. In the aerospike cases (conical spike and hemispherical spike), the predicted variations of pressure are, in general, consistent with the experimental data, despite the discrepancy in the shoulder location of the sharp pressure peak. As can be seen later, this region corresponds with the high heat flux region where reattachment of the shear layer occurs. In contrast, the change in pressure on the hemispherical body with the aerodisk (hemispherical disk) is relatively smooth, and, meanwhile, better agreements are found between the computed and experimental results.

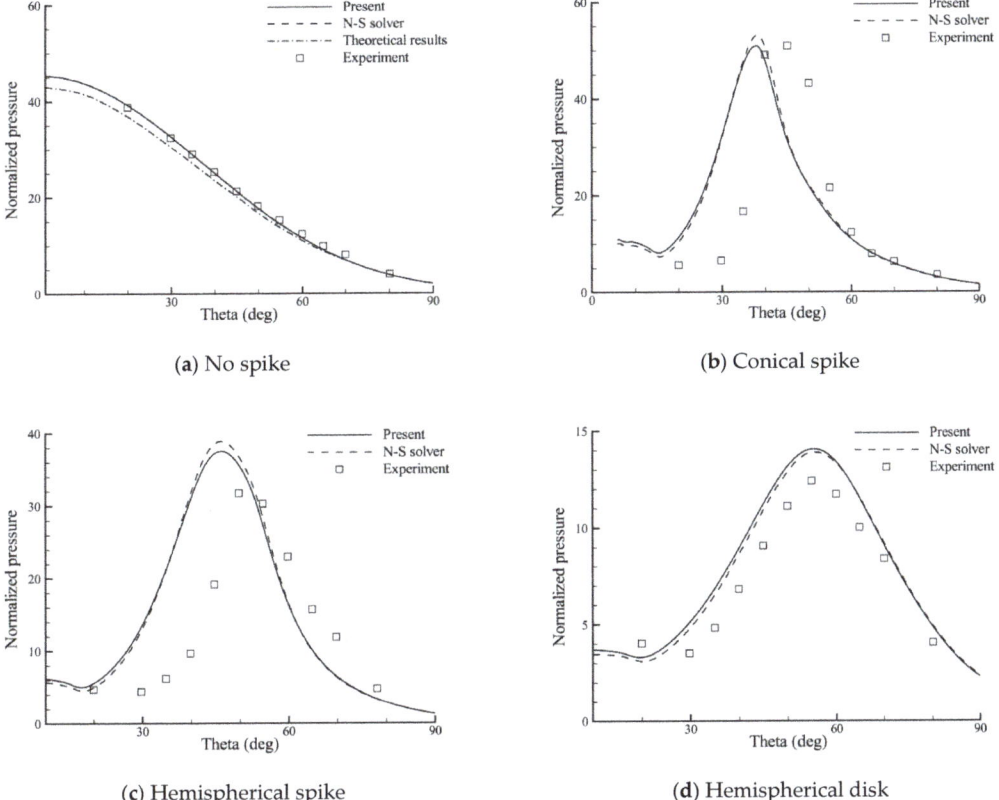

Figure 6. Surface pressure distributions of the hemispherical body with the use of different spikes.

As a result of the lack of instantaneous surface temperature data in the original report, a uniform and constant wall temperature is assumed. Figure 7 shows the comparisons of the heat flux distributions for the same four cases, where the theoretical heat flux is obtained from the laminar flow theory [31]. Overall, the computed results are in line with the experimental trends, but the comparisons are less satisfactory. Particularly, in the aerospike cases, the predicted heat flux peaks appear earlier in the hemispherical body surface and seem higher and more sharp. A similar phenomena can also be found in references [32,33], and the deviations can be attributed to the assumption of a uniform wall temperature and experimental errors. In fact, it was argued in the original report [5] that "In the aerospike case, the heat flux distribution curve has a more-rounded peak than expected because of the estimated data around the peak in that case. For this reason, the actual heat flux at the shoulder of the body may be higher in the aerospike case". Despite this, good agreements between the two methods indicate the effectiveness of the BGK scheme in the thermal protection analysis of the spike. As shown in the figure, the use of each spike can reduce the heat flux near the stagnation point of the hemispherical body. However, the heat fluxes at the shoulder of the hemispherical body are higher than the no-spike case, and the values may even exceed the stagnation-point value of the no-spike case, except for the hemispherical disk. Therefore, aerodynamic heating is more effectively reduced with use of an aerodisk.

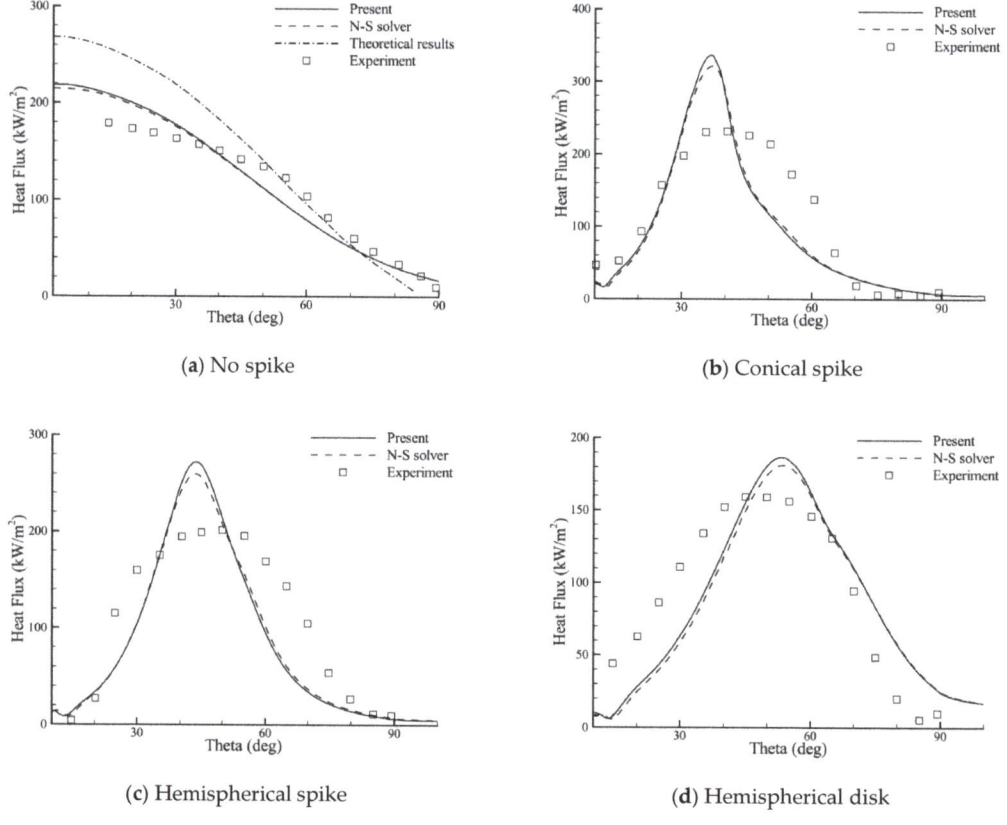

Figure 7. Surface heat flux distributions of the hemispherical body with the use of different spikes.

The above findings can be more intuitively seen in Figure 8. It is first observed that the computed density contours are close to the Schlieren photographs of the flowfield. In the aerospike cases, the thin shock wave from the spike nose, the shear layer from the near-wall separation, and the recompression shock from the reattachment point are clearly visible. However, the predicted location of the reattachment point is slightly ahead of the experimental measurement, which yields the errors in peak location shown in Figures 6 and 7. In addition, a high temperature region can be observed around the reattachment point of the shear layer (which is not shown here). Then, in the aerodisk case, a bow shock is generated far from the hemispherical body. The body is mostly enveloped within the large recirculation region, which is separated from the inviscid flow within the bow shock by the flow separation that caused a shear layer. The captured reattachment shock agrees well with the Schlieren photograph in terms of both the location and structure. Furthermore, as the oblique shock does not directly impinge on the body surface, the temperature rise is not as significant as that in the aerospike cases.

(a) Conical spike

(b) Hemispherical spike

(c) Hemispherical disk

Figure 8. Density contours (**lower**) and Schlieren photographs (**upper**) for different spikes.

4.2. Thermal Protection System by Using Opposing Jet

The second case is a blunt body experimentally studied by Hayashi et al. [34] in a blowdown-type supersonic wind tunnel. The blunt body has a diameter of 50 mm and the nozzle exit has a diameter of 4 mm. The free-stream conditions include Mach number $M_\infty = 3.98$, total pressure $p_0 = 1.37$ MPa, and total temperature $T_0 = 397$ K. A uniform wall temperature $T_w = 295$ K is assumed. An opposing jet is blown with a coolant gas at a total temperature $T_{0j} = 300$ K and specified total pressure ratio PR. The jet Mach number is 1.0, and the Reynolds number is 2.1×10^6 (based on the diameter of the blunt body). The total pressure ratio PR is defined as the ratio of the total pressure of jet p_{0j} to the total pressure of the free stream $p_{0\infty}$, i.e.,

$$PR = \frac{p_{0j}}{p_{0\infty}}$$

Four stable jet conditions of $PR = 0, 0.4, 0.6, 0.8$ are studied, where $PR = 0$ represents no jet. The computational model for this case is shown in Figure 9. The computational grid used has a size of 401×301 and the first cell height to wall is $\Delta s = 1 \times 10^{-6}$ m. The grid is tangentially clustered near the nozzle exit. The physical properties at the nozzle exit are determined by using the isentropic relations together with the prescribed total pressure ratio and total temperature.

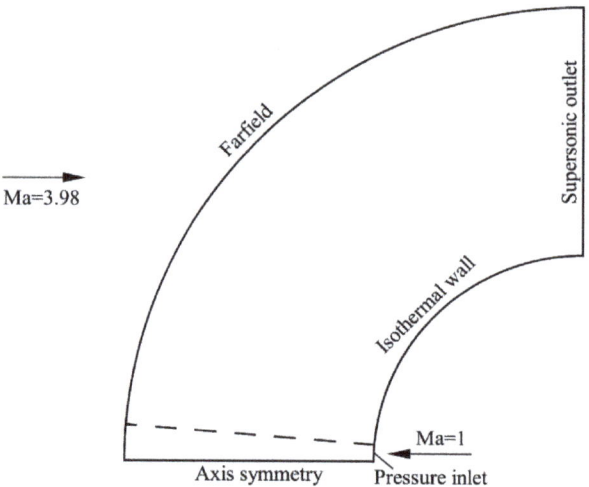

Figure 9. Computational model for the hypersonic flow past a blunt body with an opposing jet.

Before showing the computed results, it is worth mentioning that a slight self-induced oscillation phenomenon is found in the flow fields of the opposing jet. Fortunately, these oscillations are small and become weakened with the increase in the total pressure ratio, and thus the results are evaluated by some averaging.

Figure 10 compares the computed surface pressure distributions with the numerical results of Hayashi et al. [35]. The horizontal axis is the angle from the stagnation point of the blunt body. For the no-jet case, both methods predict almost the same results. For the cases where the opposing jet blows, the overall pressure significantly decreases due to the presence of flow recirculation. In these cases, good agreements are observed over the majority of the curves, although the present results predict higher peaks and lower valleys near the recirculation region for $PR = 0.4$ and 0.6. It is also found that as PR increases, the pressure in the recirculation region gradually decreases.

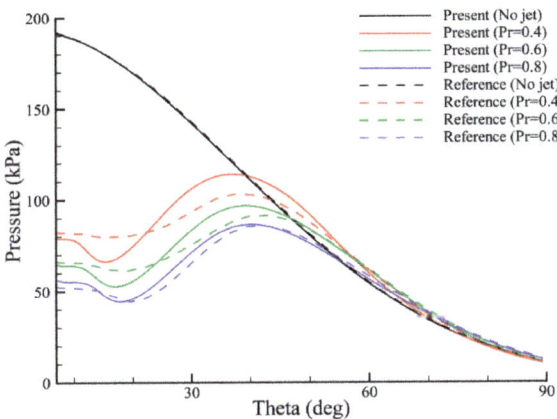

Figure 10. Surface pressure distributions for different total pressure ratios.

The comparisons of the heat flux distributions for different total pressure ratios are shown in Figure 11. As in the experiments, the Stanton number St is used to compare each heat flux distribution, which is defined as

$$St = \frac{q_w}{c_p(T_{aw}-T_w)\rho_\infty V_\infty}$$

$$T_{aw} = T_\infty\left[1 + \frac{\sqrt[3]{Pr}(\gamma-1)M_\infty^2}{2}\right]$$

where q_w is the heat flux, T_{aw} is the adiabatic wall temperature, and T_w is the wall temperature.

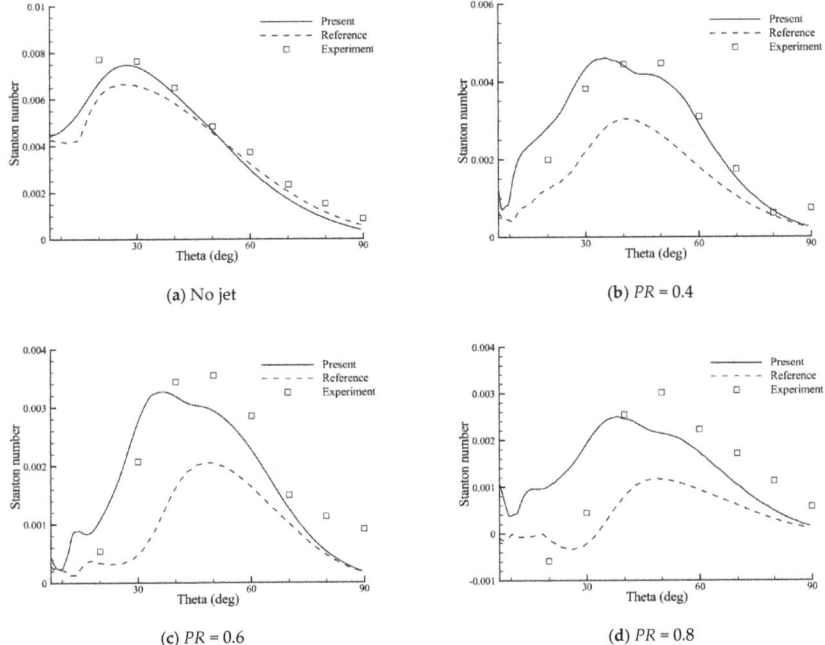

(a) No jet

(b) $PR = 0.4$

(c) $PR = 0.6$

(d) $PR = 0.8$

Figure 11. Surface heat flux distributions for different total pressure ratios.

As shown in the figures, the heat flux in the no-jet case can be reduced using the opposing jet. With the increase in PR, this heat reduction is more effective. In the no-jet case, good agreements with experiment are obtained. In the cases of blowing the opposing jet, the values of heat flux are higher than the reference [35], but the peaks appear ahead. This is directly caused by the difference in the predicted recirculation regions. The discrepancy between the computed and experimental results is probably as a result of the surface roughness of the experimental model and the turbulence modeling error. Nevertheless, the present results show overall better agreements with the experiment, indicating the effectiveness of the BGK scheme in the thermal protection analysis of the opposing jet.

Figure 12 further shows the computed density contours and Schlieren photographs. In the no-jet case, the predicted bow shock agrees very well with that of the experiment, while in other cases, the position of the bow shock is located slightly upstream. This discrepancy is also seen in [35]. At each non-zero PR, a lot of unique characteristics are clearly and accurately captured by the present method, including Mach disk, contact surface, barrel shock wave, recompression shock wave, and the triple point. Particularly, the predicted Mach disk and barrel shock agree well with the experimental results.

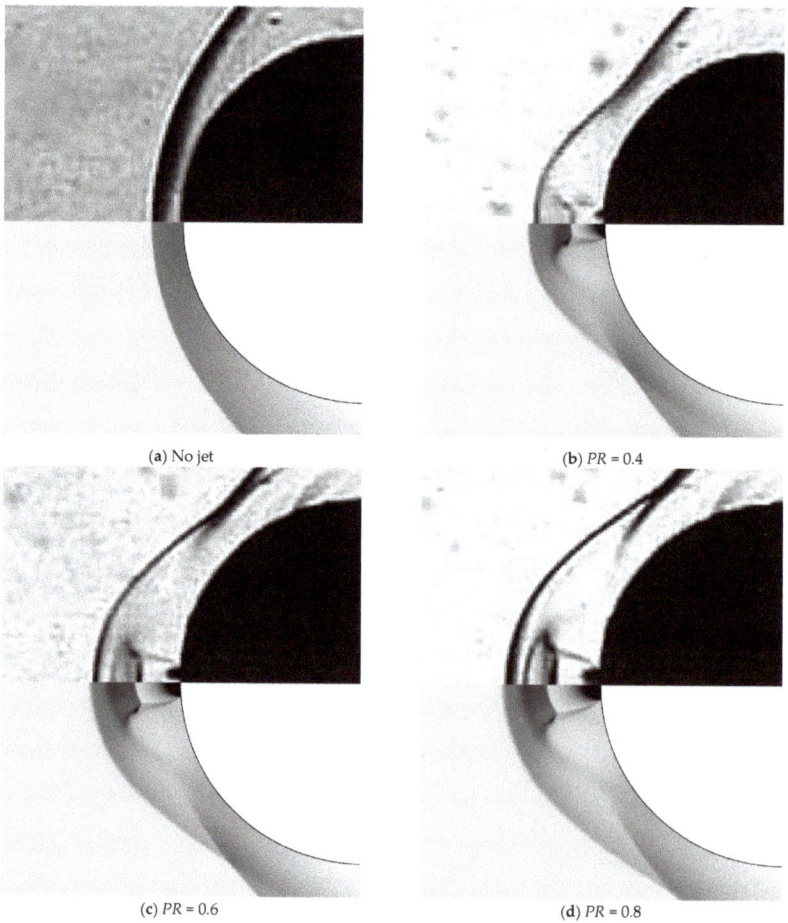

Figure 12. Density contours (**lower**) and Schlieren photographs (**upper**) for different total pressure ratios.

Finally, the computed temperature contours and streamlines are shown in Figure 13. From the visualizations of the flow fields and the curves of the heat flux distributions, it is found that the opposing jet reduces the heat flux mainly through two mechanisms: one is to prevent the hot flow downstream of the bow shock from reaching the body surface, and the other one is to form the recirculation region to protect the body surface. For the former one, the jet flow acts similarly to a mechanical spike. When it passes through the Mach disk and meets the free stream, the contact surface is formed. The contact surface moves upstream with an increase in the total pressure ratio. For the latter one, the recirculation region is formed around the nozzle exit and the recompression shock starts from the reattachment point. The jet flow passing through the barrel shock has a relatively low temperature, covering the recirculation region with cool gas. When the total pressure ratio increases, this cool flow region becomes larger and the temperature of the recirculation region decreases, resulting in a stronger cooling effect. This tendency is shown in Figure 12.

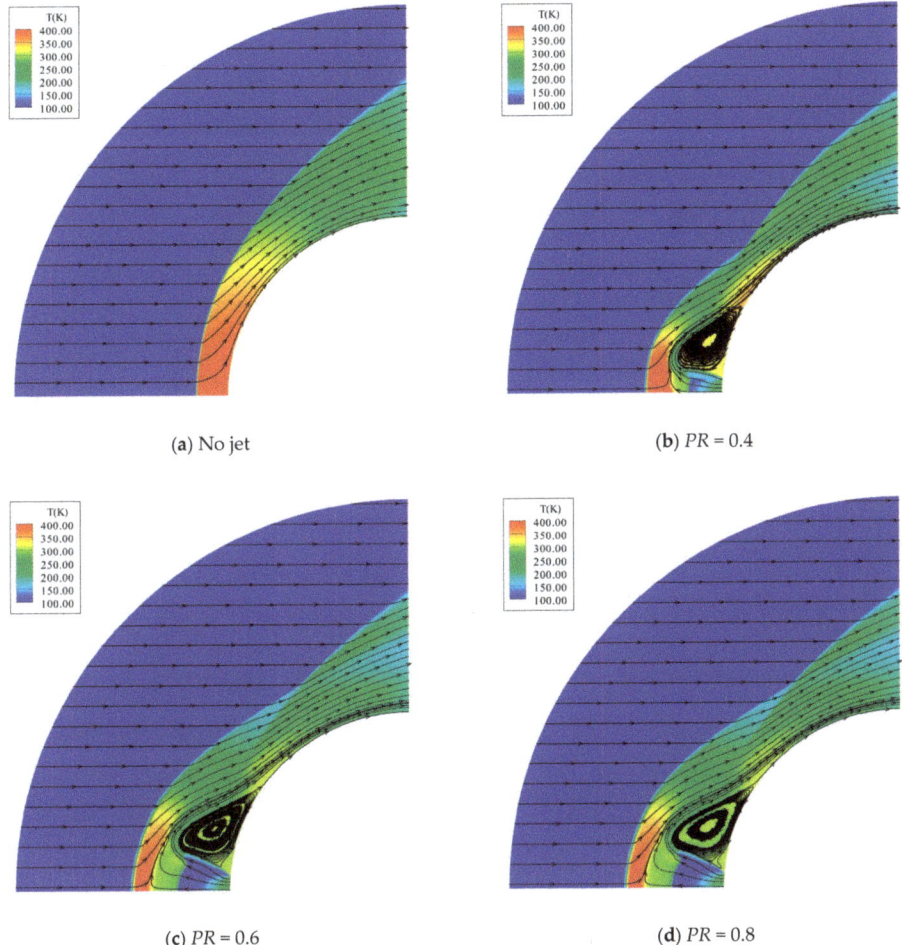

Figure 13. Temperature contours and streamlines for different total pressure ratios.

5. Conclusions

In recent years, the gas-kinetic BGK scheme has shown to be very promising in the simulation of hypersonic flows because of its advantages of having a delicate dissipation mechanism, automatic satisfaction of entropy condition, and positivity preserving. Motivated by this, it is herein extended to thermal protection system analysis, which is essential to vehicles at a hypersonic flight speed. Within a finite volume framework, the present BGK scheme is designed for the evaluation of the total fluxes across the cell interface by reconstructing the solution of the Boltzmann equation. A benchmark hypersonic flow past a cylindrical leading-edge model is first used to validate the developed code. Then, two representative thermal protection systems using spikes and opposing jets are investigated. In addition to predict the reduction of aerodynamic heating, different shapes of spikes and their effectiveness are analyzed in the former TPS and the effects of total pressure ratio of the jet are studied in the latter TPS. The computed results are compared with experimental, theoretical, or other numerical results. The mechanisms to reduce aerodynamic heating using two TPSs are also discussed. It is concluded that the BGK scheme shows good reliability and accuracy in thermal protection system analysis and has bright prospects in engineering applications.

Author Contributions: Conceptualization, T.G.; investigation, D.Z. and Q.L.; methodology, D.Z. and B.D.; validation, B.D. and Q.L.; writing—original draft, D.Z.; writing—review and editing, Z.L. All authors have read and agreed to the published version of the manuscript.

Funding: This research was funded by the National Natural Science Foundation of China (grant nos. 12102187 and 11872212), the Natural Science Foundation of Jiangsu Province (grant no. BK20190386), and a project funded by the Priority Academic Program Development of Jiangsu Higher Education Institutions.

Conflicts of Interest: The authors declare no conflict of interest.

References

1. Bertin, J.J.; Cummings, R.M. Critical hypersonic aerothermodynamic phenomena. *Annu. Rev. Fluid Mech.* **2005**, *38*, 129–157. [CrossRef]
2. Kubota, H.; Uchida, S. Thermal Protection System with Use of Porous Media for a Hypersonic Reentry Vehicle. *J. Porous Media* **1999**, *2*, 71–85. [CrossRef]
3. Aso, S.; Miyamoto, Y.; Kurotaki, T.; Isomura, Y.; Kurosaki, R.; Katayama, M.; Aso, S.; Miyamoto, Y.; Kurotaki, T.; Isomura, Y.; et al. Experimental and computational study on reduction of aerodynamic heating load by film cooling in hypersonic flows. In Proceedings of the 35th Aerospace Sciences Meeting and Exhibit, Reno, NV, USA, 6–9 January 1997; American Institute of Aeronautics and Astronautics: Reston, VA, USA, 1997. [CrossRef]
4. Warren, C.H.E. An experimental investigation of the effect of ejecting a coolant gas at the nose of a bluff body. *J. Fluid Mech.* **2006**, *8*, 400–417. [CrossRef]
5. Motoyama, N.; Mihara, K.; Miyajima, R.; Watanuki, T.; Kubota, H. Thermal protection and drag reduction with use of spike in hypersonic flow. In Proceedings of the 10th AIAA/NAL-NASDA-ISAS International Space Planes and Hypersonic Systems and Technologies Conference, Kyoto, Japan, 24–27 April 2001; American Institute of Aeronautics and Astronautics: Reston, VA, USA, 2001. [CrossRef]
6. Takaki, R. Numerical Simulation of Heating Rate Reduction by Directed Energy Air Spike. *Jpn. Soc. Aeronaut. Space Sci.* **2003**, *50*, 123. [CrossRef]
7. Usui, H.; Matsumoto, H.; Yamashita, F.; Yamane, M.; Takenaka, S. Computer experiments on Radio Blackout of a Reentry Vehicle. In Proceedings of the 6th Spacecraft Charging Technology, Middlesex County, MA, USA, 2–6 November 1998; pp. 107–110.
8. Keenan, J.; Candler, G. Simulation of ablation in Earth atmospheric entry. In Proceedings of the 28th Thermophysics Conference, Orlando, FL, USA, 6–9 July 1993; American Institute of Aeronautics and Astronautics: Reston, VA, USA, 1993. [CrossRef]
9. Sziroczak, D.; Smith, H. A review of design issues specific to hypersonic flight vehicles. *Prog. Aerosp. Sci.* **2016**, *84*, 1–28. [CrossRef]
10. Blazek, J.Z. *Computational Fluid Dynamics: Principles and Applications*, 3rd ed.; Elsevier: Amsterdam, The Netherlands, 2015. [CrossRef]
11. Toro, E.F. *Riemann Solvers and Numerical Methods for Fluid Dynamics: A Practical Introduction*; Springer Science & Business Media: Berlin, Germany, 2013.
12. Liou, M.-S. A sequel to AUSM, Part II: AUSM+-up for all speeds. *J. Comput. Phys.* **2006**, *214*, 137–170. [CrossRef]
13. Xu, K. Gas-kinetic schemes for unsteady compressible flow simulations. *Lect. Ser. Van Kareman Inst. Fluid Dyn.* **1998**, *3*, 153–155.

14. Xu, K.; Martinelli, L.; Jameson, A. Gas-Kinetic Finite Volume Methods, Flux-Vector Splitting, and Artificial Diffusion. *J. Comput. Phys.* **1995**, *120*, 48–65. [CrossRef]
15. Xu, K. A Gas-Kinetic BGK Scheme for the Navier–Stokes Equations and Its Connection with Artificial Dissipation and Godunov Method. *J. Comput. Phys.* **2001**, *171*, 289–335. [CrossRef]
16. Xu, K.; Mao, M.L.; Tang, L. A multidimensional gas-kinetic BGK scheme for hypersonic viscous flow. *J. Comput. Phys.* **2005**, *203*, 405–421. [CrossRef]
17. Li, Q.B.; Fu, S.; Xu, K. Application of Gas-Kinetic Scheme with Kinetic Boundary Conditions in Hypersonic Flow. *AIAA J.* **2005**, *43*, 2170–2176. [CrossRef]
18. Tan, S.; Li, Q.; Xiao, Z.; Fu, S. Gas kinetic scheme for turbulence simulation. *Aerosp. Sci. Technol.* **2018**, *78*, 214–227. [CrossRef]
19. Li, Q.; Fu, S. Application of Gas-Kinetic BGK Scheme in Three-Dimensional Flow. In Proceedings of the 49th AIAA Aerospace Sciences Meeting including the New Horizons Forum and Aerospace Exposition, Orlando, FL, USA, 4–7 January 2011; American Institute of Aeronautics and Astronautics: Reston, VA, USA, 2011. [CrossRef]
20. Li, Z.-H.; Zhang, H.-X. Gas-kinetic numerical studies of three-dimensional complex flows on spacecraft re-entry. *J. Comput. Phys.* **2009**, *228*, 1116–1138. [CrossRef]
21. Yang, L.M.; Shu, C.; Wu, J. A three-dimensional explicit sphere function-based gas-kinetic flux solver for simulation of inviscid compressible flows. *J. Comput. Phys.* **2015**, *295*, 322–339. [CrossRef]
22. Liu, Y.Y.; Yang, L.M.; Shu, C.; Zhang, H.W. Three-dimensional high-order least square-based finite difference-finite volume method on unstructured grids. *Phys. Fluids* **2020**, *32*, 123604. [CrossRef]
23. Zhou, D.; Lu, Z.L.; Guo, T.Q.; Chen, G.P. A loosely-coupled gas-kinetic bgk scheme for conjugate heat transfer in hypersonic flows. *Int. J. Heat Mass Transf.* **2019**, *147*, 119016. [CrossRef]
24. Spalart, P.; Allmaras, S. A one-equation turbulence model for aerodynamic flows. In Proceedings of the 30th Aerospace Sciences Meeting and Exhibit, Reno, NV, USA, 6–9 January 1992; American Institute of Aeronautics and Astronautics: Reston, VA, USA, 1992. [CrossRef]
25. Zhou, D.; Lu, Z.L.; Guo, T.Q. Improvement of Computational Efficiency of Circular Function-based Gas Kinetic Scheme by Using Jacobian-free Newton-Krylov Method. *Comput. Fluids* **2018**, *161*, 121–135. [CrossRef]
26. Wieting, A.R. Experimental Study of Shock Wave Interference Heating on a Cylindrical Leading Edge. NASA TM-100484. 1987. Available online: https://ntrs.nasa.gov/citations/19870017721 (accessed on 12 August 2022).
27. Zhang, S.; Chen, F.; Liu, H. Time-Adaptive, Loosely Coupled Strategy for Conjugate Heat Transfer Problems in Hypersonic Flows. *J. Thermophys. Heat Transf.* **2014**, *28*, 635–646. [CrossRef]
28. Dechaumphai, P.; Wieting, A.R.; Thornton, E.A. Flow-thermal-structural study of aerodynamically heated leading edges. *J. Spacecr. Rocket.* **1989**, *26*, 201–209. [CrossRef]
29. Guo, S.; Xu, J.; Qin, Q.; Gu, R. Fluid–Thermal Interaction Investigation of Spiked Blunt Bodies at Hypersonic Flight Condition. *J. Spacecr. Rocket.* **2016**, *53*, 629–643. [CrossRef]
30. Hayes, W.D.; Probstein, R.F.; Probstein, R.R. *Hypersonic Inviscid Flow*; Courier Corporation: Chelmsford, MA, USA, 2004.
31. Lees, L. Laminar Heat Transfer Over Blunt-Nosed Bodies at Hypersonic Flight Speeds. *J. Jet Propuls.* **1956**, *26*, 259–269. [CrossRef]
32. Zhu, L.; Tian, X.; Li, W.; Yan, M.; Tang, X.; Huang, M. Nonablative Dual-Jet Strategy for Drag and Heat Reduction of Hypersonic Blunt Vehicles. *J. Aerosp. Eng.* **2021**, *34*, 04021052. [CrossRef]
33. Wang, Z.-Y.; Fang, S.-Z.; Guo, J.; Ni, Z.-J.; Xu, Y. Research on drag reduction and heat prevention performance of spike with the channel concept for hypersonic blunt body. In Proceedings of the 2022 International Symposium on Aerospace Engineering and Systems, Toronto, ON, Canada, 6–8 July 2022; p. 012004.
34. Hayashi, K.; Aso, S. Effect of Pressure Ratio on Aerodynamic Heating Reduction due to Opposing Jet. In Proceedings of the 36th AIAA Thermophysics Conference, Orlando, FL, USA, 23–26 June 2003; American Institute of Aeronautics and Astronautics: Reston, VA, USA, 2003. [CrossRef]
35. Hayashi, K.; Aso, S.; Tani, Y. Numerical Study of Thermal Protection System by Opposing Jet. In Proceedings of the 43rd AIAA Aerospace Sciences Meeting and Exhibit, Reno, NE, USA, 10–13 January 2005; American Institute of Aeronautics and Astronautics: Reston, VA, USA, 2005. [CrossRef]

Article

Study of the Imbibition Phenomenon in Porous Media by the Smoothed Particle Hydrodynamic (SPH) Method

Jie Liu, Tao Zhang * and Shuyu Sun *

Computational Transport Phenomena Laboratory, Physical Science and Engineering Division (PSE),
King Abdullah University of Science and Technology, Thuwal 23955-6900, Saudi Arabia
* Correspondence: tao.zhang.1@kaust.edu.sa (T.Z.); shuyu.sun@kaust.edu.sa (S.S.)

Abstract: Over recent decades, studies in porous media have focused on many fields, typically in the development of oil and gas reservoirs. The imbibition phenomenon, a common mechanism affecting multi-phase flows in porous media, has shown more significant impacts on unconventional reservoir development, where the effect of the pore space increases with decreased pore sizes. In this paper, a comprehensive SPH method is applied, considering the binary interactions among the particles to study the imbibition phenomenon in porous media. The model is validated with physically meaningful results showing the effects of surface tension, contact angle, and pore structures. A heterogeneous porous medium is also constructed to study the effect of heterogeneity on the imbibition phenomenon; it can be referred from the results that the smaller pore throats and wetting surfaces are more preferred for the imbibition. The results show that the SPH method can be applied to solve the imbibition problems, but the unstable problem is still a sore point for the SPH method.

Keywords: SPH method; two-phase; porous media

1. Introduction

The two-phase problem is common in the academic and engineering fields [1,2]. For example, the flooding processes in the development of petroleum, which include liquid flooding and gas flooding [3,4], are usually accompanied by multi-phase problems. In the oil and gas reservoir, porous media are occupied by the liquid and gas phases with the states of liquid bridges and clusters, and the pore size ranges from nanometers to micrometers [5]; accordingly, the two-phase problem is the key point in the development of reservoirs. Furthermore, the cohesion and the contact angle are always the main research points academically [6].

A number of methods have been used to handle the two-phase problem due to their applicability [7–11]. The non-linear partial differential equation of the two-phase and incompressible fluid was proposed and applied in a porous media [12]. The finite volume method was applied to the two-phase flow in a fractured porous media with fully implicit discretization [13]. The finite element method was also developed for the two-phase immiscible flow problems [14,15].

Apart from the mesh method, the particle method, such as the molecular dynamics, was also applied to the multi-phase problems, revealing the mechanism of phase behaviors at the atomic scale [16–19]. The smoothed particle hydrodynamics (SPHs) method, a mesh-free method, is fully particle discretized [20], which is good at dealing with the free surface and large deformation problems [6,21]. If the gas phase is taken into consideration based on the free surface problem, it turns into a two-phase problem [22,23].

The SPH method is applied for multi-phase problems using several computational fluid dynamics techniques [10,24–26]. For example, the technique of interface tracking between different fluid phases is usually carried out by the color function, and the relation between the surface tension and curvature is controlled by the Young–Laplace equation [27,28]. In the unconventional reservoir, such as the shale reservoir, the pore

size is extremely small; as a result, the effects of the micro-confined space cannot be ignored [29–31]. Abdolahzadeh et al. [32] studied the mixing processes for the two-phase flow in a single channel with various structures by the meshless SPH method. Tartakovsky et al. [33] studied the mineral precipitation and reaction flow in porous media using the SPH method. They found that the SPH method was good at studying the flow and transport behaviors in pore-scale space. Bui et al. [34] developed the SPH method by coupling the behaviors of the fluid and solid phases in porous media, and the results show that the two-phase SPH method is promising for coupled problems. Kazemi et al. [35] used the spatial averaging method to obtain the mass and momentum conservation equations for comparative research of previous studies. In this case, the pairwise force SPH method has been proposed [36,37], but further studies of its application and validation are still needed.

In this work, the SPH method, which considers the effect of the interaction force between particles, is applied to imbibition problems of the gas and liquid phases innovatively. The homogeneous and inhomogeneous porous media are built, where the particles of the gas and liquid phases are filled as the shapes of bridges and clusters. The sensitivity of the porous media's structure, the pore size, and the contact angle are also examined.

2. Methodology

2.1. The Governing Equations

In this work, the weakly compressible fluid is adopted, and the non-linear term in the momentum equation is not taken into consideration [38,39]. The equation of state is needed to calculate the pressures as follows [40]:

$$\frac{d\rho}{dt} = -\rho \nabla \cdot \mathbf{u} \tag{1}$$

$$\rho \frac{d\mathbf{u}}{dt} = -\nabla p + \nabla \cdot \left(\mu\left(\nabla \mathbf{u} + \nabla \mathbf{u}^{\mathrm{T}}\right)\right) + \mathbf{g} + \mathbf{F}^S \tag{2}$$

$$p = p_{eq}\frac{n}{n_{eq}}, \tag{3}$$

where the ρ denotes the density of the fluid, the $\mathbf{u}$ denotes the fluid velocity, the $\mathbf{g}$ denotes the gravity acceleration, the $\mathbf{F}^S$ denotes the surface tension term, the p_{eq} denotes the pressure in the equilibrium state, the n_{eq} denotes the number density in the equilibrium state, the p denotes the pressure of the fluid, and the n denotes the number density of the fluid. The Young–Laplace equation is adopted to build the sharp interface model as follows [27,40,41]:

$$(p_l - p_g)\mathbf{n} = (\boldsymbol{\tau}_l - \boldsymbol{\tau}_g)\cdot\mathbf{n} + k\sigma\mathbf{n} \tag{4}$$

$$\sigma_{lg}\cos\theta_e + \sigma_{sl} = \sigma_{sg}, \tag{5}$$

where the p_l and p_g denote the pressures of the liquid and gas phases, respectively; the $\boldsymbol{\tau}_l$ and the $\boldsymbol{\tau}_g$ denote the viscous stress tensors of the liquid and gas phases, respectively; the $\mathbf{n}$ denotes the normal unit vector perpendicular to the interface; the σ denotes the surface tension coefficient; and the θ_e denotes the equilibrium contact angle.

2.2. The SPH Model

The SPH method, which is meshless, is carried out by the kernel function approximation and particle approximation as follows:

$$A(\mathbf{r}) \approx \int A(\mathbf{r}')W(\mathbf{r}-\mathbf{r}',h)d\mathbf{r}' \tag{6}$$

$$A(\mathbf{r}) \approx \sum_b m_b \frac{A_b}{\rho_b} A(\mathbf{r}')W(\mathbf{r}-\mathbf{r}_b,h), \tag{7}$$

where the $A(\mathbf{r})$ denotes the field function; the W denotes the kernel function; the $\mathbf{r}$ denotes the distance between particles; the h denotes the smooth length; the m_b, ρ_b, and A_b denote the mass, density, and field function of particle b, respectively. According to Equations (6) and (7), the differential operators can be discretized in the SPH forms as follows:

$$\nabla A_a \approx \sum_b m_b \frac{A_b}{\rho_b} A_a \nabla W_{ab} \tag{8}$$

$$\nabla \cdot A_a \approx \sum_b m_b \frac{A_b}{\rho_b} A_a \cdot \nabla W_{ab} \tag{9}$$

$$\nabla \times A_a \approx \sum_b m_b \frac{A_b}{\rho_b} A_a \times \nabla W_{ab}, \tag{10}$$

where $W_{ab} = W_a - W_b$. By balancing the coding complexity and computational efficiency, the cubic spline kernel function is adopted as follows [20]:

$$W(\mathbf{r}, h) = \sigma_d \begin{cases} 6(q^3 - q^2) + 1, & 0 \leq q \leq 0.5 \\ 2(1-q)^3, & 0.5 < q \leq 1 \\ 0, & q > 1 \end{cases} \tag{11}$$

where $q = \|\mathbf{r}\|/h$, the σ_d denotes the normalization factor of the kernel function, $\sigma_{1D} = 4/(3h)$, $\sigma_{2D} = 40/(7\pi h^2)$, and $\sigma_{3D} = 8/(\pi h^3)$. Therefore, the continuity equation of weakly compressible fluid can be written in the form of SPH discretization as follows [41]:

$$\frac{d\rho_a}{dt} = \sum_b m_b \mathbf{u}_{ab} \cdot \nabla_a W_{ab}, \tag{12}$$

where $\mathbf{u}_{ab} = \mathbf{u}_a - \mathbf{u}_b$ and $\nabla_a W_{ab} = -\nabla_b W_{ab}$. However, in the momentum equation, it is not a good choice to use the direct discretization form of the pressure gradient since the symmetric form is more stable for the multi-phase problem [6,42], as written in Equation (13).

$$\left(\frac{1}{\rho}\nabla p\right)_a = \sum_b m_b \left(\frac{p_a + p_b}{\rho_a \rho_b}\right) \nabla_a W_{ab}. \tag{13}$$

By using the divergence operator and the discretization of the SPH method, the viscosity term can be written as follows [43,44]:

$$\left(\frac{\mu}{\rho}\nabla^2 \mathbf{u}\right)_a = \sum_b m_b \frac{(\mu_a + \mu_b)\mathbf{r}_{ab} \cdot \nabla_a W_{ab}}{\rho_a \rho_b (\mathbf{r}_{ab}^2 + 0.01h^2)} \mathbf{u}_{ab}, \tag{14}$$

where the term $0.01h^2$ is used to avoid the singularities [45]. To handle the problem of the gas and liquid phases, the pairwise force is calculated in the surface tension term, where the attractive and repulsive forces can be addressed as follows [46]:

$$\mathbf{F}_{ab}^s = \begin{cases} -s_{\alpha\beta} r_{ab} [A \Psi_{\varepsilon_0}(r_{ab}) + \Psi_{\varepsilon}(r_{ab})] & r_{ab} \leq h \\ 0 & r_{ab} > h \end{cases}, \tag{15}$$

where the $\mathbf{F}_{ab}^s$ denotes the interfacial tension force between particles a and b and the $s_{\alpha\beta}$ denotes the strength coefficient of the interaction. For the two-dimensional cases, $\varepsilon = \frac{h}{3.5}$, $\varepsilon_0 = \frac{\varepsilon}{2}$, $\Psi_{\varepsilon}(r_{ab}) = e^{\frac{r_{ab}^2}{2\varepsilon^2}}$, and $A = \left(\frac{\varepsilon}{\varepsilon_0}\right)^3$. The two-phase problem in this study is immiscible; thus, the particles in the same phase need a larger interaction force, and the strength coefficients can be calculated as follows [46,47]:

$$\begin{cases} s_{\alpha\alpha} = s_{\beta\beta} = 0.5n^{-2}\left(\frac{h}{3}\right)^{-5}\frac{\sigma}{\lambda} \\ s_{s\alpha} = 0.5n^{-2}\left(\frac{h}{3}\right)^{-5}\frac{\sigma}{\lambda}(1 + 0.5\cos\theta) \\ s_{s\beta} = 0.5n^{-2}\left(\frac{h}{3}\right)^{-5}\frac{\sigma}{\lambda}(1 - 0.5\cos\theta) \end{cases} \tag{16}$$

where the n denotes the average number density of the fluid, the σ denotes the surface tension coefficient, and $\lambda = \frac{3}{4\pi^2}(2^7 - 3^2 \times 2^4 \pi^2 + 3^3 \pi^4)$. Therefore, $s_{\alpha\alpha} = s_{\beta\beta} = s_{s\alpha} = s_{s\beta}$ if the contact angle is 90°, which suggests that the neutral wetting condition can be obtained. The boundary conditions are as follows [21]:

$$\mathbf{F}_i^{bound} = \sum_{j=1}^{N_{bound}} \mathbf{f}_{ij}^{bound} \tag{17}$$

$$\mathbf{f}_{ij}^{bound} = \begin{cases} -\left[U_{max}^2 \frac{\min\left((\mathbf{u}_i - \mathbf{u}_j)\cdot\hat{\mathbf{n}}_j, -1\right) W_{ij} H_{ij} \hat{\mathbf{n}}_j}{|\mathbf{r}_{ij}\cdot\mathbf{n}_j|} \right], & (\mathbf{u}_i - \mathbf{u}_j)\cdot\hat{\mathbf{n}}_j < 0 \\ 0, & (\mathbf{u}_i - \mathbf{u}_j)\cdot\hat{\mathbf{n}}_j > 0 \end{cases} \tag{18}$$

where the i denotes the index of the fluid particle, the j denotes the index of the solid particle, the $\mathbf{u}_i$ denotes the fluid velocity, the $\mathbf{u}_j$ denotes the solid velocity, and the $\hat{\mathbf{n}}_j$ denotes the normal vector for the solid particle j. The solid particles' velocity and pressure are obtained as follows:

$$\mathbf{u}_j = -\frac{\sum_i^{N_f} \mathbf{u}_i W_{ij}}{\sum_i^{N_f} W_{ij}} \tag{19}$$

$$p_j = \frac{\sum_i^{N_f} p_i W_{ij} + (\mathbf{g} - \mathbf{b}_j)\cdot \sum_i^{N_f} \rho_i \mathbf{r}_{ij} W_{ij}}{\sum_i^{N_f} W_{ij}} \tag{20}$$

where the N_f denotes the number of fluid particles, the N_{bound} denotes the number of solid particles, and the $\mathbf{b}_j$ denotes the prescribed acceleration for solid particles.

2.3. The Relaxation of the Solid Boundary

The arrangement of the particles affects the interaction between the fluid and solid particles, and the relaxation of the solid phase can make the results more accurate. The solid particles are filled within the specific region randomly. After that, the particles are relaxed, and the particles that move out of the region will be pushed back manually using the level-set method [48,49]. Finally, the relaxed solid particles can be obtained, and the result is shown in Section 3.1.

3. Results and Discussion

In Section 3.1, the validation of the SPH method is verified on the two-phase problems. The sensitivity of the porous media's structure is tested in Section 3.2. Section 3.3 presents the phase behaviors of the gas and liquid phases in heterogeneous porous media.

3.1. The Validation of the Scheme

In order to verify the method for the two-phase problem of the gas and liquid, two simple cases are studied without gravity. The realistic three-dimensional porous media model is not adopted because the computational resources are huge for the three-dimensional cases. Although the realistic porous media model can present realistic results, the regular model can show the validation of the method more clearly. As shown in Figure 1, the solid particles are adopted to build a box for the simulation, and the gas and liquid particles are filled within the box. The size of the box is 2 cm × 1 cm. The initial distribution of the liquid particles is rectangular. With the effect of the surface tension between the two phases, the liquid phase tends to form the shape of a droplet, and the particles show a good arrangement on the interface, presenting a good match with previous studies [50,51]. The properties of the gas and liquid phases are shown in Table 1.

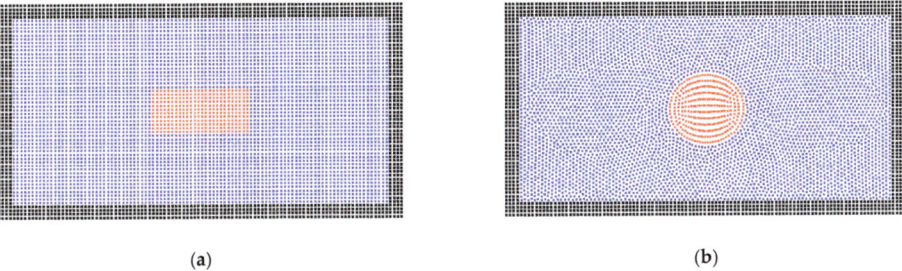

(a)   (b)

Figure 1. The (**a**) initial state and (**b**) equilibrium state for the gas–liquid phases in the center of the system. The red particles represent the liquid phase, the blue particles represent the gas phase, and the black particles are solid wall particles. The size of the box is 2 cm × 1 cm.

Table 1. The parameters of the gas and liquid phases.

Phase	Density/(kg·m^{-3})	Viscosity/(mPa·s)
Gas	1.225	0.019
Liquid	1000	0.925

The contact angle between the liquid droplet and solid wall is also verified in the same condition, as seen in Figure 2. The liquid particles are filled at the bottom of the box with a rectangular shape. After the equilibrium simulation, the liquid phase formed a wetting droplet on the wall's surface with the contact angle of 50°, which has a good match with the preset value. Figure 2c presents a non-wetting case with a contact angle of 130°. These two basic cases show the good validation of the SPH method on the two-phase problem.

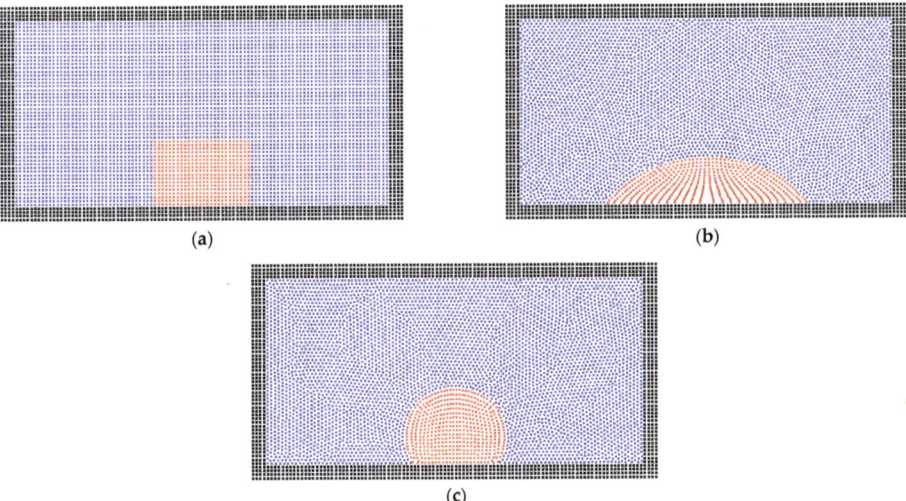

Figure 2. The (**a**) initial state and equilibrium states with (**b**) the contact angle of 50° and (**c**) 130° for the gas–liquid phases on the wall's surface.

In addition, the solid phase is relaxed using the level-set method [49] because the arrangement of solid particles affects the fluid–solid interactions, such as the solid structure in Figure 3a. As shown in Figure 3b, the solid particles are packed randomly, and the solid particles are relaxed within the solid region [52,53]. Finally, the relaxed solid structure can be obtained in Figure 3c.

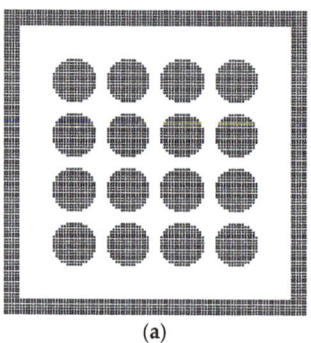 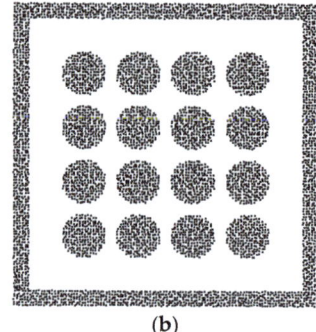 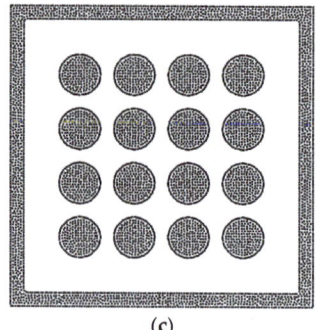

(a) (b) (c)

Figure 3. (a) The regular arrangement of solid particles. (b) The initial state before relaxing and (c) the relaxed state.

3.2. The Sensitivity of the Porous Media's Structure for the Two-Phase Behavior

As shown in Figure 3, a simple porous media model is built with a number of solid spheres to represent the rock matrixes. The common states for the liquid in the rock pores are the liquid bridge and the liquid cluster. Therefore, in order to examine the effects of porous media on the imbibition problem, different initial liquid states are adopted in this study. Figure 4a presents an initial stripe state for the liquid phase, and the equilibrium state is shown in Figure 4b. In the wetting condition, the phenomenon of liquid bridge states can be observed [54]. In porous media, the liquid phase, with the effect of the surface tension, tends to move into the pore throat between the solid matrixes. Due to the homogeneity of the porous media, the liquid phase is in a balanced condition and cannot transport across the pore throat. The curvature of the matrix is also a reason why transportation is inhibited. Because the smallest pore size is in the center of the pore channel, the pore size tends to be larger if the liquid particles move out from the center position.

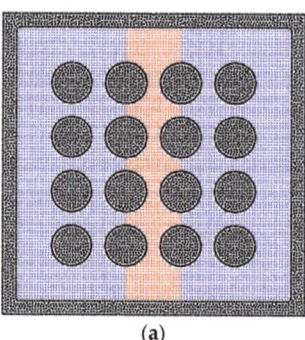 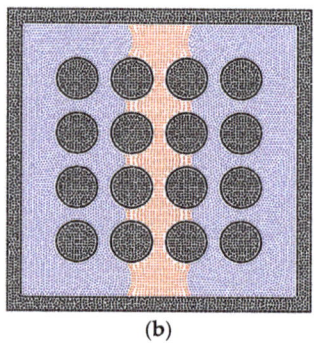

(a) (b)

Figure 4. The phase distributions of the gas and liquid phases in the homogeneous porous media (contact angle = 50°). The (**a**) initial state and (**b**) equilibrium state for a liquid bridge are depicted in the system.

Apart from the liquid bridge state, the cluster state is also common in porous media. In order to judge the effect of solid matrixes accurately, the edges of the initial region are defined at the centers between different solid matrixes, as shown in Figure 5a. According to the results in Section 3.1, the liquid phase tends to be a sphere droplet in the center of the domain. However, because of the effects of the porous media and surface tension, the liquid phase still shows a smoothed square shape. Furthermore, the particles on the solid matrix's surface tend to be taken apart by the surface tension, but the sphere shape of the solid matrix maintains the stability of the liquid film relatively.

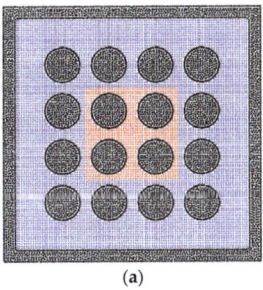 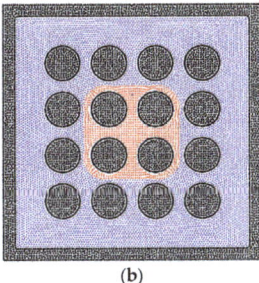

(a)   (b)

Figure 5. The phase distributions of the gas and liquid phases in the homogeneous porous media (contact angle = 50°). The (**a**) initial state and (**b**) equilibrium state for a liquid cluster are depicted in the system.

There are various structures of rock matrixes in the reservoir. To test the effects of the solid structures clearly, the square shape of the matrix is studied in this section. The bridge and cluster liquid states are constructed initially, which are the same as that in the sphere matrix system. Figure 6b depicts the equilibrium state of the liquid bridge, which corresponds to the state in Figure 4b, but the liquid phase can go further into the square pore throat than the throat with the curvature because the throat size is constant. In Figure 6d, the wider liquid bridge is also tested, and the trapezoidal shape of the liquid bridge can be observed due to the edge effect of the square solid matrix [55]. In addition, the results of liquid cluster distributions are presented in Figure 7. The main difference is that the liquid cluster is separated at the positions of sharp corners, which is caused by the surface tension. As exhibited in Figure 7c, the separated liquid particles can move into the pore throat. Therefore, the pore throat with the curvature can block the fluid flow more easily than the square pore throat. In addition, as shown in Figure 8, the larger initial liquid cluster tends to invade the pore throats as a result of the wetting boundary condition. The particle resolution independence test is also presented in Figure 9, and the results show that the imbibition phenomenon addressed by the SPH method is relatively independent of resolutions. Figure 9a,c exhibit the imbibition trends toward the smaller pore space.

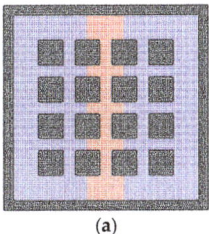 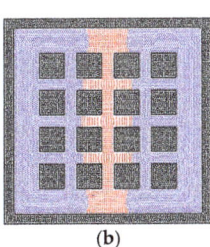 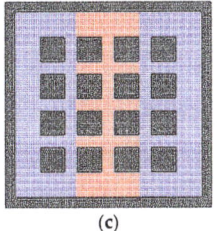 

(a)   (b)   (c)   (d)

Figure 6. The phase distributions of the gas and liquid phases in the homogeneous porous media (contact angle = 50°), where the solid matrixes are represented by square solid particles. The (**a**) initial state and (**b**) equilibrium state for a liquid bridge are depicted in the system. The (**c**) initial state and (**d**) equilibrium state for the wider liquid bridge are also depicted in the system.

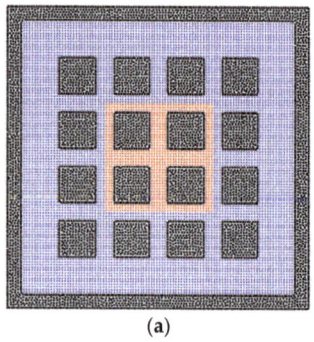  

(a) (b) (c)

Figure 7. The phase distributions of the gas and liquid phases in the homogeneous porous media (contact angle = 50°), where the solid matrixes are represented by square solid particles. The (**a**) initial state, (**b**) transition state, and (**c**) equilibrium state for a liquid cluster are depicted in the system.

(a) (b)

Figure 8. The phase distributions of the gas and liquid phases in the homogeneous porous media (contact angle = 50°), where the solid matrixes are represented by square solid particles. The (**a**) initial state and (**b**) equilibrium state for a larger liquid cluster are depicted in the system.

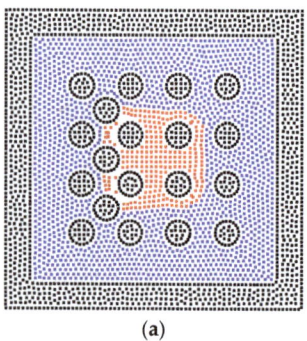 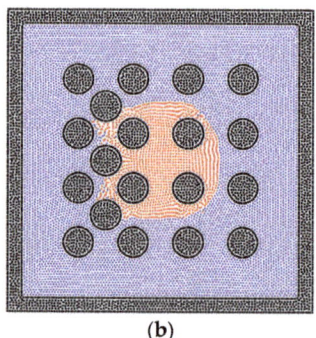 

(a) (b) (c)

Figure 9. The phase distributions of the gas and liquid phases in the homogeneous porous media (contact angle = 50°) with various resolutions, (**a**) 50 × 50, (**b**) 100 × 100, and (**c**) 200 × 200.

3.3. The Two-Phase Behavior in the Heterogeneous Porous Media

The pore network in porous media is usually heterogeneous, especially in the unconventional reservoir [56], and the heterogeneity of porous media is performed by the solid matrix with different sizes, inducing the different phase distributions of fluid particles. As depicted in Figure 10, the radii of solid matrixes do not change the phase distributions much in the homogeneous porous media. Therefore, the solid matrixes with different radii are inserted in the bulk of pores, as shown in Figure 11, in order to test the results in heterogeneous porous media. The imbibition effect is stronger in the results in Figure 11a,b, where the liquid phase particles already move around the inserted solid matrixes. However, in Figure 11c, the liquid phase is stopped at the position of the inserted solid matrixes because the smaller radius induces the larger pore size, which weakens the effect of interfacial tension of the liquid phase. The quantitative results are also presented in Figure 12.

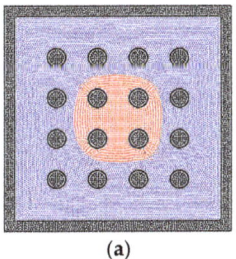  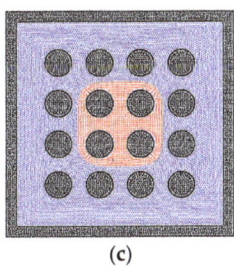 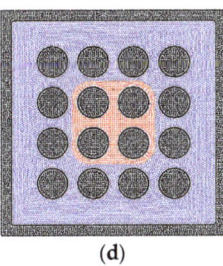

(a) (b) (c) (d)

Figure 10. The equilibrium state for the liquid cluster in the homogeneous porous media (contact angle = 50°), and (**a**) R = 0.5 mm, (**b**) R = 0.6 mm, (**c**) R = 0.7 mm, (**d**) R = 0.8 mm, where R is the radius of each sphere wall.

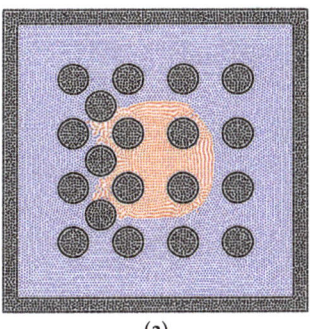 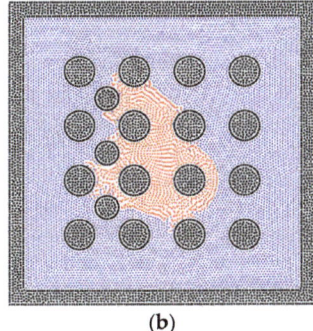 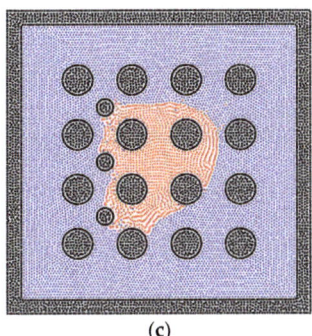

(a) (b) (c)

Figure 11. The phase distributions of the gas and liquid phases in the heterogeneous porous media (R = 0.6 mm, contact angle = 50°), where the solid matrixes with different sizes are filled in the bulk pores on the left side, and (**a**) r = 0.6 mm, (**b**) r = 0.48 mm, (**c**) r = 0.36 mm, where r is the radius of each inserted sphere wall.

Apart from the size of the solid matrix, the contact angle is also a key point in studying the phase distribution in heterogeneous porous media. Hence, different contact angles between the liquid and solid phases are adopted and tested, which correspond to the condition of wetting, neutral, and non-wetting boundaries. As shown in Figure 13a, the liquid phase can easily perform the phenomenon of imbibition within the wetting system. In the neutral system, the imbibition of the liquid phase happens with the effect of the surface tension, but the preference of the pore size cannot be judged. Figure 13c shows the distribution of the liquid and gas phases in the non-wetting system; the liquid phase is excluded from the dense part of porous media, as shown in Figure 14. This also corresponds to previous studies because the liquid phase turns into the non-wetting phase in this condition [57–59].

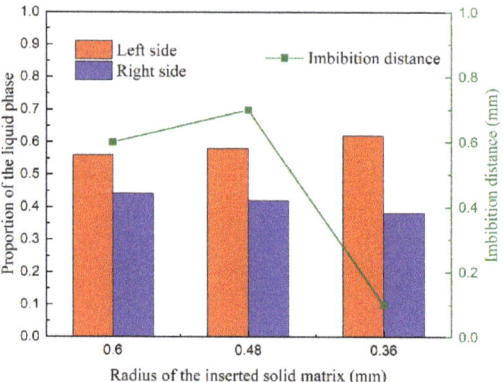

Figure 12. The proportion of the liquid phase distribution at the left and right sides and the imbibition distance of the liquid phase in the cases with different inserted solid matrix radii.

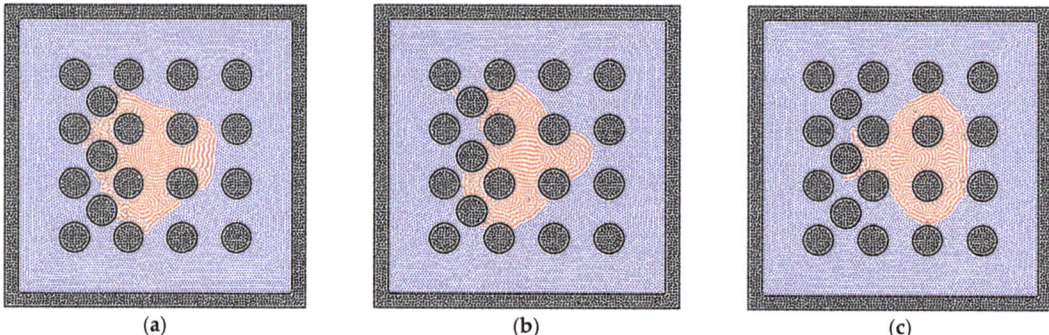

Figure 13. The phase distributions of the gas and liquid phases in the heterogeneous porous media (R = 0.6 mm), where the different contact angles are examined, and (**a**) contact angle = 30°, (**b**) contact angle = 90°, (**c**) contact angle = 150°.

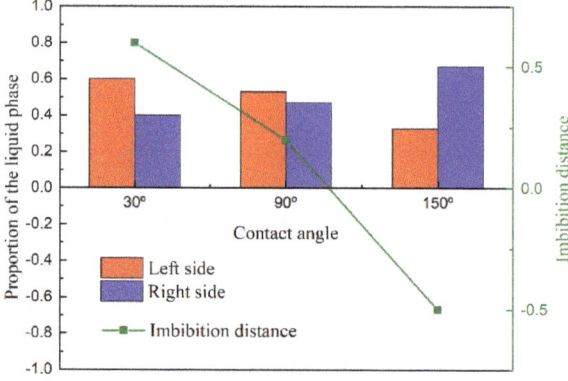

Figure 14. The proportion of the liquid phase distribution at the left and right sides and the imbibition distance of the liquid phase in the cases with different contact angles.

4. Conclusions

In this work, the SPH method is adopted to study the gas–liquid imbibition problem in porous media. Firstly, the porous media model is built by solid particles, and the liquid and gas particles are filled in the model regularly. The SPH algorithm is verified by the basic gas–liquid models in the wetting and non-wetting systems, and the validation of the surface tension is also confirmed with a droplet model. Due to the complexity of reservoirs, the sensitivity of the porous media's structure is examined, and the solid boundary with the curvature tends to inhibit the imbibition of the liquid phase. To mimic the heterogeneity of reservoirs, the heterogeneous porous media model is built, and the effects of the solid matrix's size and contact angle are also tested. The smaller pore size facilitates the imbibition of the liquid phase, and the wetting solid boundary for the liquid phase contributes to the imbibition process. In contrast, the non-wetting solid boundary makes the gas the wetting phase, and the process is inversed accordingly. The imbibition behavior simulated by the SPH method is meaningful for understanding the development of oil and gas reservoirs. In this study, the applications of the SPH method in the multi-phase cases still have some problems, such as volume expansion and interface tracking, which are the points to address in our future research.

Author Contributions: Conceptualization, J.L. and S.S.; methodology, J.L.; software, J.L.; validation, J.L., T.Z. and S.S.; formal analysis, J.L.; investigation, J.L.; resources, T.Z.; data curation, T.Z.; writing—original draft preparation, J.L.; writing—review and editing, T.Z.; visualization, J.L.; supervision, S.S.; project administration, S.S.; funding acquisition, S.S. All authors have read and agreed to the published version of the manuscript.

Funding: This research was funded by the National Natural Scientific Foundation of China (Grants No. 51874262 and 51936001) and the King Abdullah University of Science and Technology (KAUST) through the grants BAS/1/1351-01, URF/1/4074-01, and URF/1/3769-01.

Institutional Review Board Statement: Not applicable.

Informed Consent Statement: Not applicable.

Data Availability Statement: Not applicable.

Acknowledgments: We would like to express appreciation to the colleagues in our research group.

Conflicts of Interest: The authors declare no conflict of interest.

References

1. Stewart, H.B.; Wendroff, B. Two-phase flow: Models and methods. *J. Comput. Phys.* **1984**, *56*, 363–409. [CrossRef]
2. Drew, D.A. Mathematical modeling of two-phase flow. *Annu. Rev. Fluid Mech.* **1983**, *15*, 261–291. [CrossRef]
3. Yang, Y.; Li, Y.; Yao, J.; Iglauer, S.; Luquot, L.; Zhang, K.; Sun, H.; Zhang, L.; Song, W.; Wang, Z. Dynamic pore-scale dissolution by CO_2-saturated brine in carbonates: Impact of homogeneous versus fractured versus vuggy pore structure. *Water Resour. Res.* **2020**, *56*, e2019WR026112. [CrossRef]
4. Wang, X.; Yin, H.; Zhao, X.; Li, B.; Yang, Y. Microscopic remaining oil distribution and quantitative analysis of polymer flooding based on CT scanning. *Adv. Geo-Energy Res.* **2019**, *3*, 448–456. [CrossRef]
5. Liu, J.; Yang, Y.; Sun, S.; Yao, J.; Kou, J. Flow Behaviors of Shale Oil in Kerogen Slit by Molecular Dynamics Simulation. *Chem. Eng. J.* **2022**, *434*, 134682. [CrossRef]
6. Monaghan, J.J. Smoothed particle hydrodynamics. *Annu. Rev. Astron. Astrophys.* **1992**, *30*, 543–574. [CrossRef]
7. Qiao, Z.; Sun, S. Two-phase fluid simulation using a diffuse interface model with Peng–Robinson equation of state. *SIAM J. Sci. Comput.* **2014**, *36*, B708–B728. [CrossRef]
8. Zhu, G.; Kou, J.; Yao, B.; Wu, Y.-s.; Yao, J.; Sun, S. Thermodynamically consistent modelling of two-phase flows with moving contact line and soluble surfactants. *J. Fluid Mech.* **2019**, *879*, 327–359. [CrossRef]
9. Kou, J.; Sun, S. A new treatment of capillarity to improve the stability of IMPES two-phase flow formulation. *Comput. Fluids* **2010**, *39*, 1923–1931. [CrossRef]
10. Zhang, T.; Li, Y.; Li, Y.; Sun, S.; Gao, X. A self-adaptive deep learning algorithm for accelerating multi-component flash calculation. *Comput. Methods Appl. Mech. Eng.* **2020**, *369*, 113207. [CrossRef]
11. Zhang, T.; Sun, S. A coupled Lattice Boltzmann approach to simulate gas flow and transport in shale reservoirs with dynamic sorption. *Fuel* **2019**, *246*, 196–203. [CrossRef]

12. Douglas, J., Jr. Finite difference methods for two-phase incompressible flow in porous media. *SIAM J. Numer. Anal.* **1983**, *20*, 681–696. [CrossRef]
13. Reichenberger, V.; Jakobs, H.; Bastian, P.; Helmig, R. A mixed-dimensional finite volume method for two-phase flow in fractured porous media. *Adv. Water Resour.* **2006**, *29*, 1020–1036. [CrossRef]
14. Chessa, J.; Belytschko, T. An extended finite element method for two-phase fluids. *J. Appl. Mech.* **2003**, *70*, 10–17. [CrossRef]
15. Durlofsky, L.J. A triangle based mixed finite element—finite volume technique for modeling two phase flow through porous media. *J. Comput. Phys.* **1993**, *105*, 252–266. [CrossRef]
16. Liu, J.; Zhao, Y.; Yang, Y.; Mei, Q.; Yang, S.; Wang, C. Multicomponent Shale Oil Flow in Real Kerogen Structures via Molecular Dynamic Simulation. *Energies* **2020**, *13*, 3815. [CrossRef]
17. Yang, Y.; Liu, J.; Yao, J.; Kou, J.; Li, Z.; Wu, T.; Zhang, K.; Zhang, L.; Sun, H. Adsorption behaviors of shale oil in kerogen slit by molecular simulation. *Chem. Eng. J.* **2020**, *387*, 124054. [CrossRef]
18. Feng, Q.; Xu, S.; Xing, X.; Zhang, W.; Wang, S. Advances and challenges in shale oil development: A critical review. *Adv. Geo-Energy Res.* **2020**, *4*, 406–418. [CrossRef]
19. Liu, J.; Tang, Q.; Kou, J.; Xu, D.; Zhang, T.; Sun, S. A quantitative study on the approximation error and speed-up of the multi-scale MCMC (Monte Carlo Markov chain) method for molecular dynamics. *J. Comput. Phys.* **2022**, 111491. [CrossRef]
20. Liu, M.; Liu, G. Smoothed particle hydrodynamics (SPH): An overview and recent developments. *Arch. Comput. Methods Eng.* **2010**, *17*, 25–76. [CrossRef]
21. Liu, J.; Xie, X.; Meng, Q.; Sun, S. Effects of Membrane Structure on Oil–Water Separation by Smoothed Particle Hydrodynamics. *Membranes* **2022**, *12*, 387. [CrossRef]
22. Monaghan, J.J. Simulating free surface flows with SPH. *J. Comput. Phys.* **1994**, *110*, 399–406. [CrossRef]
23. Liu, Y.; Iglauer, S.; Cai, J.; Amooie, M.A.; Qin, C. Local instabilities during capillary-dominated immiscible displacement in porous media. *Capillarity* **2019**, *2*, 1–7. [CrossRef]
24. Sivanesapillai, R.; Falkner, N.; Hartmaier, A.; Steeb, H. A CSF-SPH method for simulating drainage and imbibition at pore-scale resolution while tracking interfacial areas. *Adv. Water Resour.* **2016**, *95*, 212–234. [CrossRef]
25. Yang, H.; Yang, C.; Sun, S. Active-set reduced-space methods with nonlinear elimination for two-phase flow problems in porous media. *SIAM J. Sci. Comput.* **2016**, *38*, B593–B618. [CrossRef]
26. Feng, X.; Chen, M.-H.; Wu, Y.; Sun, S. A fully explicit and unconditionally energy-stable scheme for Peng-Robinson VT flash calculation based on dynamic modeling. *J. Comput. Phys.* **2022**, *463*, 111275. [CrossRef]
27. McCamy, C.S. Correlated color temperature as an explicit function of chromaticity coordinates. *Color Res. Appl.* **1992**, *17*, 142–144. [CrossRef]
28. Chen, T.; Chiu, M.-S.; Weng, C.-N. Derivation of the generalized Young-Laplace equation of curved interfaces in nanoscaled solids. *J. Appl. Phys.* **2006**, *100*, 074308. [CrossRef]
29. Yang, Y.; Che Ruslan, M.F.A.; Narayanan Nair, A.K.; Sun, S. Effect of ion valency on the properties of the carbon dioxide–methane–brine system. *J. Phys. Chem. B* **2019**, *123*, 2719–2727. [CrossRef]
30. El-Amin, M.; Salama, A.; Sun, S. Numerical and dimensional analysis of nanoparticles transport with two-phase flow in porous media. *J. Pet. Sci. Eng.* **2015**, *128*, 53–64. [CrossRef]
31. Li, Y.; Yang, H.; Sun, S. Fully implicit two-phase VT-flash compositional flow simulation enhanced by multilayer nonlinear elimination. *J. Comput. Phys.* **2022**, *449*, 110790. [CrossRef]
32. Abdolahzadeh, M.; Tayebi, A.; Mansouri Mehryan, M. Numerical Simulation of Mixing in Active Micromixers Using SPH. *Transp. Porous Media* **2022**, 1–18. [CrossRef]
33. Tartakovsky, A.M.; Meakin, P.; Scheibe, T.D.; Wood, B.D. A smoothed particle hydrodynamics model for reactive transport and mineral precipitation in porous and fractured porous media. *Water Resour. Res.* **2007**, *43*. [CrossRef]
34. Bui, H.H.; Nguyen, G.D. A coupled fluid-solid SPH approach to modelling flow through deformable porous media. *Int. J. Solids Struct.* **2017**, *125*, 244–264. [CrossRef]
35. Kazemi, E.; Luo, M. A comparative study on the accuracy and conservation properties of the SPH method for fluid flow interaction with porous media. *Adv. Water Resour.* **2022**, *165*, 104220. [CrossRef]
36. Viccione, G.; Bovolin, V.; Carratelli, E.P. Defining and optimizing algorithms for neighbouring particle identification in SPH fluid simulations. *Int. J. Numer. Methods Fluids* **2008**, *58*, 625–638. [CrossRef]
37. Yang, T.; Lin, M.; Martin, R.R.; Chang, J.; Hu, S. Versatile interactions at interfaces for SPH-based simulations. In Proceedings of the Eurographics/ACM SIGGRAPH Symposium on Computer Animation, Zurich, Switzerland, 11–13 July 2016; Association for Computing Machinery: New York, NY, USA, 2016; pp. 57–66.
38. He, X.; Luo, L.-S. Lattice Boltzmann model for the incompressible Navier–Stokes equation. *J. Stat. Phys.* **1997**, *88*, 927–944. [CrossRef]
39. Mohd-Yusof, J. Combined immersed-boundary/B-spline methods for simulations of flow in complex geometries. *Cent. Turbul. Res. Annu. Res. Briefs* **1997**, *161*, 317–327.
40. Tartakovsky, A.M.; Meakin, P. Pore scale modeling of immiscible and miscible fluid flows using smoothed particle hydrodynamics. *Adv. Water Resour.* **2006**, *29*, 1464–1478. [CrossRef]
41. Zhu, Y.; Fox, P.J. Simulation of pore-scale dispersion in periodic porous media using smoothed particle hydrodynamics. *J. Comput. Phys.* **2002**, *182*, 622–645. [CrossRef]

42. Price, D.J. Smoothed particle hydrodynamics and magnetohydrodynamics. *J. Comput. Phys.* **2012**, *231*, 759–794. [CrossRef]
43. Morris, J.P.; Fox, P.J.; Zhu, Y. Modeling low Reynolds number incompressible flows using SPH. *J. Comput. Phys.* **1997**, *136*, 214–226. [CrossRef]
44. Zhu, Y.; Fox, P.J.; Morris, J.P. A pore-scale numerical model for flow through porous media. *Int. J. Numer. Anal. Methods Geomech.* **1999**, *23*, 881–904. [CrossRef]
45. Koschier, D.; Bender, J.; Solenthaler, B.; Teschner, M. Smoothed particle hydrodynamics techniques for the physics based simulation of fluids and solids. *arXiv* **2020**, arXiv:2009.06944.
46. Tartakovsky, A.M.; Trask, N.; Pan, K.; Jones, B.; Pan, W.; Williams, J.R. Smoothed particle hydrodynamics and its applications for multiphase flow and reactive transport in porous media. *Comput. Geosci.* **2016**, *20*, 807–834. [CrossRef]
47. Tartakovsky, A.M.; Panchenko, A. Pairwise force smoothed particle hydrodynamics model for multiphase flow: Surface tension and contact line dynamics. *J. Comput. Phys.* **2016**, *305*, 1119–1146. [CrossRef]
48. Osher, S.; Fedkiw, R.; Piechor, K. Level set methods and dynamic implicit surfaces. *Appl. Mech. Rev.* **2004**, *57*, B15–B16. [CrossRef]
49. Osher, S.; Fedkiw, R.P. Level set methods: An overview and some recent results. *J. Comput. Phys.* **2001**, *169*, 463–502. [CrossRef]
50. Yang, Q.; Yao, J.; Huang, Z., Asif, M. A comprehensive SPH model for three-dimensional multiphase interface simulation. *Comput. Fluids* **2019**, *187*, 98–106. [CrossRef]
51. Yang, Q.; Yao, J.; Huang, Z.; Zhu, G.; Liu, L.; Song, W. Pore-scale investigation of petro-physical fluid behaviours based on multiphase SPH method. *J. Pet. Sci. Eng.* **2020**, *192*, 107238. [CrossRef]
52. Zhang, C.; Rezavand, M.; Zhu, Y.; Yu, Y.; Wu, D.; Zhang, W.; Zhang, S.; Wang, J.; Hu, X. SPHinXsys: An open-source meshless, multi-resolution and multi-physics library. *Softw. Impacts* **2020**, *6*, 100033. [CrossRef]
53. Zhang, C.; Rezavand, M.; Zhu, Y.; Yu, Y.; Wu, D.; Zhang, W.; Wang, J.; Hu, X. SPHinXsys: An open-source multi-physics and multi-resolution library based on smoothed particle hydrodynamics. *Comput. Phys. Commun.* **2021**, *267*, 108066. [CrossRef]
54. He, M.; Szuchmacher Blum, A.; Aston, D.E.; Buenviaje, C.; Overney, R.M.; Luginbühl, R. Critical phenomena of water bridges in nanoasperity contacts. *J. Chem. Phys.* **2001**, *114*, 1355–1360. [CrossRef]
55. Fang, G.; Amirfazli, A. Understanding the edge effect in wetting: A thermodynamic approach. *Langmuir* **2012**, *28*, 9421–9430. [CrossRef] [PubMed]
56. Yang, Y.; Wang, K.; Zhang, L.; Sun, H.; Zhang, K.; Ma, J. Pore-scale simulation of shale oil flow based on pore network model. *Fuel* **2019**, *251*, 683–692. [CrossRef]
57. Meng, Q.; Cai, J. Recent advances in spontaneous imbibition with different boundary conditions. *Capillarity* **2018**, *1*, 19–26. [CrossRef]
58. Cai, J.; Sun, S. Fractal analysis of fracture increasing spontaneous imbibition in porous media with gas-saturated. *Int. J. Mod. Phys. C* **2013**, *24*, 1350056. [CrossRef]
59. Zhang, T.; Zhang, Y.; Katterbauer, K.; Al Shehri, A.; Sun, S.; Hoteit, I. Phase equilibrium in the hydrogen energy chain. *Fuel* **2022**, *328*, 125324. [CrossRef]

Article

Free-Energy-Based Discrete Unified Gas Kinetic Scheme for van der Waals Fluid

Zeren Yang [1], Sha Liu [1,2], Congshan Zhuo [1,2] and Chengwen Zhong [1,2,*]

[1] School of Aeronautics, Northwestern Polytechnical University, Xi'an 710072, China; zeren@mail.nwpu.edu.cn (Z.Y.); shaliu@nwpu.edu.cn (S.L.); zhuocs@nwpu.edu.cn (C.Z.)
[2] National Key Laboratory of Science and Technology on Aerodynamic Design and Research, Northwestern Polytechnical University, Xi'an 710072, China
* Correspondence: zhongcw@nwpu.edu.cn

Abstract: The multiphase model based on free-energy theory has been experiencing long-term prosperity for its solid foundation and succinct implementation. To identify the main hindrance to developing a free-energy-based discrete unified gas-kinetic scheme (DUGKS), we introduced the classical lattice Boltzmann free-energy model into the DUGKS implemented with different flux reconstruction schemes. It is found that the force imbalance amplified by the reconstruction errors prevents the direct application of the free-energy model to the DUGKS. By coupling the well-balanced free-energy model with the DUGKS, the influences of the amplified force imbalance are entirely removed. Comparative results demonstrated a consistent performance of the well-balanced DUGKS despite the reconstruction schemes utilized. The capability of the DUGKS coupled with the well-balanced free-energy model was quantitatively validated by the coexisting density curves and Laplace's law. In the quiescent droplet test, the magnitude of spurious currents is reduced to a machine accuracy of 10^{-15}. Aside from the excellent performance of the well-balanced DUGKS in predicting steady-state multiphase flows, the spinodal decomposition test and the droplet coalescence test revealed its stability problems in dealing with transient flows. Further improvements are required on this point.

Keywords: free-energy model; discrete unified gas-kinetic scheme; multiphase flow; flux reconstruction

1. Introduction

Multiphase fluid flow characterized by the concurrent presence of multiple thermodynamic phases is frequently encountered in industrial processes and engineering applications. Insightful understanding of the multiphase flow behavior could facilitate improvements in manufacturing technology and production efficiency. Due to the restriction on measurement technology and the experimental platform, it is particularly challenging to reveal the flow details by experimental methods. Benefiting from the substantial improvements in computing power, numerical simulation technology has been developed into a powerful tool for the study of complicated behaviors arising in multiphase fluid flow. By numerically solving the set of interface capturing and hydrodynamic equations, a multitude of research studies [1–4] vividly detail the interface dynamics and flow structures from a macroscopic perspective. Essentially, the interfacial phenomenon represents the macroscopic manifestation of the microscopic interactions among fluid molecules [5]. Numerical methods based on realistic microscopic physics could offer in-depth findings regarding multiphase phenomena, but the heavy computational requirement of such methods for industry-scale multiphase problems is far beyond affordable. In recent years, numerical schemes constructed with the mesoscopic theory [6] have been emerging as a compelling methodology for resolving multiphase flow patterns as this bridges the gap between the macroscopic descriptions of multiphase dynamics and microscopic intermolecular interactions and, thus, generates insightful understandings at an affordable cost.

Among various previously proposed mesoscopic approaches [7–9], the lattice Boltzmann (LB) method [7] has received particular attention for its concise and intuitive way of representing intermolecular interactions. Generally, the lattice Boltzmann multiphase models developed in the past few decades can be categorized into four classifications: the color-gradient model [10], the phase-field model [11,12], the pseudopotential model [13], and the free-energy model [14]. The phase-field model employs independent sets of distribution functions to separately transfer mass and momentum, which could cause mass non-conservation problems near the interface region [15]. The pseudopotential model and the free-energy model employ a single set of distribution functions to ensure a coherent transport of mass and momentum, which conforms to the physical reality that mass and momentum are simultaneously transferred by the unique molecules. Compared to the pseudopotential model, where interactions are built heuristically, the free-energy model is constructed upon the stationary-action principle, which possesses a firm physical background. Over the last couple of decades, the free-energy lattice Boltzmann method has been successfully applied to numerically tackle a variety of flow issues including the contact line movement [16,17], multicomponent fluids' flow [18,19], wetting boundaries [20,21], and large-density-ratio fluid flow [22,23]. The primitive free-energy multiphase model proposed by Swift et al. [14] reflects the interaction effects via a modified equilibrium distribution function, whose second-order moment incorporates a nonideal thermodynamic pressure tensor. However, this primitive model suffers from a lack of Galilean invariance due to the superfluous terms recovered in the momentum equation. Later, Swift et al. [24] tried to remedy this defect by introducing additional terms to the pressure tensor, but an analysis through the Chapman–Enskog expansion demonstrated that the lack of Galilean invariance cannot be entirely eliminated. Based on Swift et al.'s work, Inamuro et al. [25] proposed a Galilean-invariant free-energy model with the guidance of asymptotic theory. Kalarakis et al. [26] restored the Galilean invariance of the free-energy model to second-order accuracy by modifying the zero-order momentum flux tensor. Wagner and Li [27] replaced the contribution of the nonideal pressure tensor with a corrected force term and improved the Galilean invariance of the model in large velocity situations. Meanwhile, Lee and Fischer [28] reformulated the pressure form of the interaction force into a potential form and reduced the magnitude of the spurious velocity to a machine level, at the cost of including the information in next-nearest-neighbor cells. Subsequently, Guo et al. [5] spotted that the spurious velocity originates from the force imbalance at the discrete level. Based on this finding, Lou and Guo [29] applied the Lax–Wendroff scheme to the lattice Boltzmann free-energy model and successfully mitigated the effects of the force imbalance. Very recently, Guo [30] proposed a well-balanced lattice Boltzmann scheme with which the spurious velocity can be ultimately minimized to the machine accuracy. The previously mentioned improvements were carried out within the framework of the lattice Boltzmann method, which inherits its advantages such as great simplicity and high efficiency. However, the uniformity requirement on the grid types posed by the LB method prevents its application in industrial cases.

Developed in the framework of the finite volume method, the discrete unified gas-kinetic scheme (DUGKS) [31] suffers no restriction in terms of the grid types. With the information of the Knudsen number incorporated in the construction of the interface flux, the DUGKS exhibits the capability of properly modeling a wide range of fluid flows ranging from the continuum regime to the free-molecule regime [32]. Over the past decade, the DUGKS has proven its excellent performance in predicting microscale gas flows [33,34], multicomponent gas flows [35,36], turbulent flows [37–39], compressible flows [40–42], radiative heat transfer [43,44], and so forth [45]. A comparative study [46] has demonstrated the stability superiority of the DUGKS over that of the LB method in terms of nearly incompressible flows. However, the DUGKS studies centered on multiphase fluid flows remain limited [47,48] and the multiphase DUGKS has been primarily confined to the phase-field model [49]. Although Yang et al. [50] developed a pseudopotential-based DUGKS for binary fluid flow, a free parameter is needed to guarantee the isotropic property of the fluid interface. Inspired by the well-balanced LB scheme [30], Zeng et al. [51] proposed a well-balanced DUGKS for two-phase fluid flows using the free-energy model. Comparative results demonstrated the superior performance of the DUGKS over that of the LB method. Nevertheless, there is still a lack of an insightful comprehension as to the isotropic property of free-energy-based DUGKS. In this research, we elucidate the mechanism for the nonisotropic phenomena produced by the free-energy-based DUGKS using different reconstruction approaches. Then, we couple the well-balanced free-energy model with the DUGKS implemented with different reconstruction schemes to investigate practical van der Waals (vdW) fluid flows. The rest of this paper is organized as follows. In Section 2, the primitive and the well-balanced free-energy models are introduced, followed by the detailed explanation of the Strang-splitting DUGKS. The comparative numerical results, as well as brief discussions are presented in Section 3. Finally, a summary is given in Section 4.

2. Numerical Methodology

In this section, the first part theoretically introduces the free-energy model based on the vdW chemical potential and the second part exhaustively explains the Strang-splitting DUGKS implemented with different reconstruction schemes.

2.1. Free-Energy Model

Considering a multiphase system, the free-energy functional in terms of the fluid density ρ can be expressed as [14,24]

$$\mathcal{F} = \int \phi(\rho, \nabla \rho) d\Omega_V = \int \left(E_f(\rho) + \frac{\kappa}{2} |\nabla \rho|^2 \right) d\Omega_V, \quad (1)$$

where Ω_V is the spatial region occupied by the system, $\phi(\rho, \nabla \rho)$ denotes the total free-energy density, in which $E_f(\rho)$ represents the bulk free-energy density, and $\frac{\kappa}{2}|\nabla \rho|^2$ signifies the interface free-energy density. The parameter κ is a positive constant determined by the interface thickness and the surface tension coefficient. Minimization of the free-energy $\mathcal{F}$ that is subject to the constraint of a constant mass $\mathcal{M}$ evolves the system towards the equilibrium condition, where

$$\mathcal{M} = \int \rho d\Omega_v. \quad (2)$$

To impose the mass constraint, a transformed free-energy functional $\mathcal{L}$ is constructed using the method of Lagrange multipliers:

$$\mathcal{L} = \mathcal{F} - \lambda \mathcal{M}, \quad (3)$$

where λ is the Lagrange multiplier. Minimization of the constrained free-energy demands the corresponding first variation to be zero:

$$\delta \mathcal{L} = 0, \quad (4)$$

which yields the following Euler–Lagrange equation:

$$\frac{\partial \psi}{\partial \rho} - \nabla \cdot \left(\frac{\partial \psi}{\partial (\nabla \rho)} \right) = \frac{dE_f}{d\rho} - \kappa \nabla^2 \rho - \lambda = 0, \quad (5)$$

where

$$\psi(\rho, \nabla \rho) = \phi(\rho, \nabla \rho) - \lambda \rho. \quad (6)$$

The chemical potential μ_c is defined as the variation of the free-energy $\mathcal{F}$ with respect to the density [52]:

$$\mu_c = \frac{\delta \mathcal{F}}{\delta \rho} = \frac{dE_f}{d\rho} - \kappa \nabla^2 \rho. \quad (7)$$

As the integrand of transformed free-energy $\mathcal{L}$ does not explicitly contain any spatial coordinates, it remains invariant regardless of the spatial translations [3]. Noether's theorem [53] says that the invariance of the free-energy with respect to spatial translations corresponds to a conserved tensorial current J satisfying [54]:

$$\nabla \cdot J = 0, \tag{8}$$

where J is a second-rank tensor given by

$$J = -\psi I + \nabla \rho \otimes \frac{\partial \psi(\rho, \nabla \rho)}{\partial (\nabla \rho)}, \tag{9}$$

in which I is the identity matrix. Substituting Equations (5) and (6) into Equation (9) leads to

$$J = \left(\rho \mu_c - E_f - \frac{\kappa}{2}|\nabla \rho|^2\right) I + \kappa \nabla \rho \nabla \rho. \tag{10}$$

The bulk pressure p_b is connected to the bulk free-energy density E_f via the Legendre transform [54]:

$$p_b(\rho) = \rho \frac{dE_f}{d\rho} - E_f(\rho), \tag{11}$$

with which the conserved current tenor J can be identified as the thermodynamic pressure tensor P in such a way that

$$P \equiv J = \left(p_b - \kappa \rho \nabla^2 \rho - \frac{\kappa}{2}|\nabla \rho|^2\right) I + \kappa \nabla \rho \nabla \rho. \tag{12}$$

With some basic algebraic manipulations, the divergence of the pressure tensor can be simplified as

$$\nabla \cdot P = \rho \nabla \mu_c. \tag{13}$$

In the traditional free-energy model [28], the total effects of excess pressure accounting for the phase interactions can be represented by the following interaction force

$$F = \nabla \cdot P_0 - \nabla \cdot P = \nabla p_0 - \rho \nabla \mu_c, \tag{14}$$

where $P_0 = p_0 I$ denotes the pressure tensor of an ideal gas. In the well-balanced free-energy model [30], the interaction force is defined as

$$F = -\rho \nabla \mu_c \tag{15}$$

in order to eliminate the force imbalance at the discrete level.

The only remaining task is to determine the bulk free-energy density E_f. In the work of Zeng et al. [51], E_f takes a double-well form, which relates to no specific equation of state (EOS). In the current research, the bulk pressure is evaluated by the nonideal van der Waals EOS [55] expressed as

$$p_b = \frac{\rho RT}{1 - b\rho} - a\rho^2, \tag{16}$$

where parameter a denotes the intermolecular interaction strength, parameter b indicates the volume correction, R stands for the gas constant, and T represents the temperature. The corresponding bulk free-energy density can be obtained by solving Equation (11):

$$E_f(\rho) = \rho RT \ln\left(\frac{\rho}{1 - b\rho}\right) - a\rho^2. \tag{17}$$

The chemical potential can then be obtained according to Equation (7):

$$\mu_c = RT\left[\ln\left(\frac{\rho}{1-b\rho} + \frac{1}{1-b\rho}\right)\right] - 2a\rho - \kappa\nabla^2\rho, \tag{18}$$

with which the interaction force $\boldsymbol{F}$ can be evaluated. In the current research, the parameters in the vdW-EOS were set as [56] $a = 9/392, b = 2/21, R = 1$. κ was fixed at 0.02 if not otherwise specified. The critical density and temperature are given as $\rho_c = 3.5$ and $T_c = 1/14$.

2.2. Strang-Splitting DUGKS

In this subsection, the evolution process of the discrete unified gas-kinetic scheme is exhaustively clarified. Then, the Strang splitting scheme for the incorporation of the interaction force is introduced.

2.2.1. Discrete Unified Gas-Kinetic Scheme

The investigation of multiphase flow problems in the current research was conducted by numerically solving the Boltzmann-BGK equation:

$$\frac{\partial f}{\partial t} + \boldsymbol{\xi}\cdot\nabla_x f = \Omega \equiv -\frac{f - f^E}{\tau}, \tag{19}$$

where $f = f(\boldsymbol{x}, \boldsymbol{\xi}, t)$ denotes the distribution function (DF), referring to a cluster of particles residing at position $\boldsymbol{x}$ with a velocity of $\boldsymbol{\xi}$ at time t, τ indicates the relaxation time, and f^E represents the Maxwellian distribution function approached by f within each collision. The nondimensionalization of Equation (19) is presented in the Appendix A. The moments of distribution functions correspond to the conservative flow variables via

$$\rho = \int f d\boldsymbol{\xi} = \int f^E d\boldsymbol{\xi}, \quad \rho\boldsymbol{u} = \int \boldsymbol{\xi} f d\boldsymbol{\xi} = \int \boldsymbol{\xi} f^E d\boldsymbol{\xi}, \tag{20}$$

where $\boldsymbol{u}$ denotes the velocity of the flow field. To numerically solve Equation (19), discretization of the physical and velocity space is a prerequisite. To determine the discrete velocity points along each single dimension, the three-point Gauss–Hermite quadrature is employed. The two-dimensional discrete velocity points can be derived from the tensor product of the single-dimensional velocities, which turns out to be the D2V9 velocity model commonly used in the LB community:

$$\boldsymbol{\xi}_i = \sqrt{3c_s^2}\begin{bmatrix} 0 & 1 & 0 & -1 & 0 & 1 & -1 & -1 & 1 \\ 0 & 0 & 1 & 0 & -1 & 1 & 1 & -1 & -1 \end{bmatrix},$$

where $\boldsymbol{\xi}_i$ is the ith discrete velocity and $c_s = 1/\sqrt{3}$ is the model speed of sound. The ideal gas pressure p_0 shown in Equation (14) relates to the density ρ through $p_0 = \rho c_s^2$.

With the discretization of the velocity space, the Boltzmann-BGK equation turns into

$$\frac{\partial f_i}{\partial t} + \boldsymbol{\xi}_i\cdot\nabla_x f_i = \Omega_i \equiv -\frac{f_i - f_i^E}{\tau}, \tag{21}$$

where the subscript i indicates the distribution function for particles possessing a velocity of $\boldsymbol{\xi}_i$. Subdividing the physical space into a set of grid cells and integrating Equation (21) over a certain cell lead to

$$\frac{d}{dt}\int_{V_c} f_i(\boldsymbol{x}, t)d\boldsymbol{x} + \int_{\partial V_c}(\boldsymbol{\xi}\cdot\boldsymbol{n})f_i(\boldsymbol{x}, t)dS = \int_{V_c}\Omega_i(\boldsymbol{x}, t)d\boldsymbol{x}, \tag{22}$$

where V_c denotes the integral cell centered at position x_c, ∂V_c denotes the surface boundary of the cell, dS is the surface element, and n is the unit vector normal to the surface element. Integrating Equation (22) over a time step of length $\Delta t = t_{n+1} - t_n$ yields

$$f_i^{n+1} - f_i^n + \frac{\Delta t}{|V_c|} F_i^{n+1/2} = \frac{\Delta t}{2} \left[\Omega_i^{n+1} + \Omega_i^n \right], \tag{23}$$

where $|V_c|$ measures the volume of cell V_c and f_i^n and Ω_i^n approximate the cell averages of V_c in such a way that

$$f_i^n = \frac{1}{|V_c|} \int_{V_c} f_i(x, t_n) dx, \tag{24a}$$

$$\Omega_i^n = \frac{1}{|V_c|} \int_{V_c} \Omega_i(x, t_n) dx. \tag{24b}$$

$F_i^{n+1/2}$ measures the kinetic flux at the mid-time $t_n + \Delta t / 2$ by

$$F_i^{n+1/2} = \int_{\partial V_c} (\xi_i \cdot n) f_i(x, t_n + \Delta t / 2) dS. \tag{25}$$

Note that the midpoint rule is applied to compute the time integral of the kinetic flux and the trapezoidal rule is applied to evaluate the time integral of the collision term in Equation (23). To remove the implicit treatment of the collision term, two auxiliary distribution functions are introduced:

$$\tilde{f}_i = f_i - \frac{\Delta t}{2} \Omega_i, \tilde{f}_i^+ = f_i + \frac{\Delta t}{2} \Omega_i. \tag{26}$$

Substituting Equation (26) into Equation (23), we obtain a fully explicit evolution equation:

$$\tilde{f}_i^{n+1} = \tilde{f}_i^{+,n} + \frac{\Delta t}{2} F_i^{n+1/2}. \tag{27}$$

To obtain the kinetic flux $F_i^{n+1/2}$, the primitive distribution function $f_i(x_f, t_{n+1/2})$ on the cell surface needs to be first evaluated. To this end, we integrate Equation (21) along the characteristic line over a time step length of $\delta t = \Delta t / 2$:

$$f_i(x_f, t_{n+1/2}) - f_i(x_f - \xi_i \delta t, t_n) = \frac{\delta t}{2} \left[\Omega_i(x_f, t_{n+1/2}) + \Omega_i(x_f - \xi_i \delta t, t_n) \right]. \tag{28}$$

Note that the trapezoidal rule is once again applied for the time integral of the collision term. Similar to the treatment of Equation (23), the implicitness of Equation (28) is eliminated with the help of the following auxiliary distribution functions:

$$\tilde{f} = f - \frac{\delta t}{2} \Omega, \tilde{f}^+ = f + \frac{\delta t}{2} \Omega. \tag{29}$$

Equation (28) can then be rearranged as

$$\tilde{f}_i(x_f, t_{n+1/2}) = \tilde{f}_i^+(x_f - \xi_i \delta t, t_n). \tag{30}$$

The auxiliary distribution function $\tilde{f}_i^+(x_f - \xi_i \delta t, t_n)$ on the right-hand side of Equation (30) can be interpolated from the cell-centered $\tilde{f}_i^+(x_c, t_n)$, which could be directly constructed via Equation (29). Based on the expansion point of the Taylor series [57], the reconstruction schemes can be classified into the face-based reconstruction scheme (FRS) or the cell-based reconstruction scheme (CRS). The FRS takes the form of

$$\tilde{f}_i^+(x_f - \xi_i \delta t, t_n) = \tilde{f}_i^+(x_f, t_n) - \xi_i \delta t \cdot \nabla \tilde{f}_i^+(x_f, t_n), \tag{31}$$

in which the face-centered $f_i^+(x_f, t_n)$ can be reconstructed from the cell-centered $f_i^+(x_c, t_n)$ via the central difference (CD) scheme [31] or the weighted essentially non-oscillatory (WENO) scheme [58]. The upwind CRS takes the form of

$$\tilde{f}_i^+(x_f - \xi_i \delta t) = \begin{cases} \tilde{f}_i^+(x_l) + (\delta x_l - \xi_i \delta t) \cdot \nabla \tilde{f}_i^+(x_l) + (\delta x_l - \xi_i \delta t)^2 : \nabla^2 \tilde{f}_i^+(x_l)/2, & \xi_i \cdot n \leq 0, \\ \tilde{f}_i^+(x_r) + (\delta x_r - \xi_i \delta t) \cdot \nabla \tilde{f}_i^+(x_r) + (\delta x_r - \xi_i \delta t)^2 : \nabla^2 \tilde{f}_i^+(x_r)/2, & \xi_i \cdot n > 0, \end{cases} \quad (32)$$

where $\delta x_l = x_f - x_l$ measures the distance from the face center x_f to the adjacent cell center x_l on one side, while $\delta x_r = x_f - x_r$ measures the distance from the face center x_f to the adjacent cell center x_r on the other side. An average value is used if $\xi_i \cdot n = 0$. After finishing the reconstruction of $\tilde{f}_i^+(x_f - \xi_i \delta t, t_n)$, the face-centered auxiliary distribution function $\tilde{f}_i(x_f, t_{n+1/2})$ can be directly obtained via Equation (30). With a straightforward transformation of Equation (29), the primitive distribution function $f_i(x_f, t_{n+1/2})$ can be calculated by

$$f = \frac{2\tau}{2\tau + \delta t} \tilde{f} + \frac{\delta t}{2\tau + \delta t} f^E. \quad (33)$$

The kinetic flux $F_i^{n+1/2}$ can then be evaluated by its definition. After that, the auxiliary distribution function $\tilde{f}_i(x_c, t_{n+1})$ at the next time step can be updated by Equation (27). Similarly, with a transformation of Equation (26), the primitive distribution function can be calculated by

$$f = \frac{2\tau}{2\tau + \Delta t} \tilde{f} + \frac{\Delta t}{2\tau + \Delta t} f^E. \quad (34)$$

The equilibrium distribution function f_i^E for the primitive free-energy model is expressed as

$$f_i^E = \omega_i \rho \left[1 + \frac{\xi_i \cdot u}{c_s^2} + \frac{uu : (\xi_i \xi_i - c_s^2 I)}{2 c_s^4} \right], \quad (35)$$

where $\omega_i = 4/9$ for $i = 0$, $\omega_i = 1/9$ for $i = \{1, 2, 3, 4\}$, and $\omega_i = 1/36$ for $i = \{5, 6, 7, 8\}$. The equilibrium distribution function f_i^E for the well-balanced free-energy model is defined as

$$f_i^E = \begin{cases} \rho + \omega_0 \rho s_0(u), & i = 0, \\ \omega_i \rho s_i(u), & i \neq 0, \end{cases} \quad (36)$$

where

$$s_i(u) = \left[\frac{\xi_i \cdot u}{c_s^2} + \frac{uu : (\xi_i \xi_i - c_s^2 I)}{2 c_s^4} \right]. \quad (37)$$

Obviously, the information of macroscopic conservative variables should be first evaluated for the updating of the equilibrium distribution function. Considering the relationship between the auxiliary DF and the primitive DF presented in Equations (26) and (29), the cell-centered conservative variables are updated by

$$\rho = \sum_i f_i = \sum_i \tilde{f}_i, \quad \rho u = \sum_i \xi_i f_i = \sum_i \xi_i \tilde{f}_i, \quad (38)$$

and the face-centered conservative variables are updated by

$$\rho = \sum_i f_i = \sum_i \tilde{f}_i, \quad \rho u = \sum_i \xi_i f_i = \sum_i \xi_i \tilde{f}_i. \quad (39)$$

The time step length Δt is determined by the Courant–Friedrichs–Lewy (CFL) condition:

$$\Delta t = C \frac{\Delta x}{\sqrt{3 c_s^2}}, \quad (40)$$

where C denotes the CFL number and Δx measures the grid spacing.

2.2.2. Strang-Splitting Scheme

To date, the evolution process of DUGKS without considering force terms has been exhaustively clarified. To incorporate the interaction effects between different phases, a source distribution function f_i^S accounting for the force effects is introduced. To correctly recover the macroscopic hydrodynamic equation, the expression of f_i^S for the primitive free-energy model is defined as

$$f_i^S = \omega_i \left[\frac{\xi_i \cdot F}{c_s^2} + \frac{uF : (\xi_i \xi_i - c_s^2 I)}{c_s^4} \right], \tag{41}$$

where F is the interaction force defined in Equation (14). The expression of f_i^S for the well-balanced free-energy model is defined as

$$f_i^S = \omega_i \left[\frac{\xi_i \cdot F}{c_s^2} + \frac{u(F + c_s^2 \nabla \rho) : (\xi_i \xi_i - c_s^2 I)}{c_s^4} + \frac{1}{2} \left(\frac{\xi_i^2}{c_s^2} - D \right) (u \cdot \nabla \rho) \right], \tag{42}$$

where $D = 2$ is the spatial dimension. To circumvent the calculation of the interaction force on the cell interface, the Strang-splitting scheme is employed [59]. With such a treatment, the force effects are considered before and after the evolution process of the DUGKS:

$$\frac{\partial f_i}{\partial t} = \frac{1}{2} f_i^S, \tag{43a}$$

$$\frac{\partial f_i}{\partial t} + \xi_i \cdot \nabla_x f_i = \Omega_i \equiv -\frac{f_i - f_i^E}{\tau}, \tag{43b}$$

$$\frac{\partial f_i}{\partial t} = \frac{1}{2} f_i^S, \tag{43c}$$

As Equation (43b) remains identical to Equation (21), it can be solved by the DUGKS procedure addressed previously. Equations (43a) and (43c) can be numerically solved by the forward Euler method:

$$f_i^* = f_i^n + \frac{\Delta t}{2} f_i^{S,n}. \tag{44}$$

The conservative variables should be accordingly updated via

$$\rho^* = \rho^n, u^* = u^n + \frac{\Delta t}{2} \frac{F^n}{\rho^n}. \tag{45}$$

The gradient operator and Laplacian operator appearing in Equations (7), (14) and (15) are implemented via the isotropic difference scheme [60].

3. Numerical Results

In this section, several numerical tests are conducted by the Strang-splitting DUGKS to compare the performance of the primitive free-energy model and that of the well-balanced free-energy model. The nonisotropic property caused by the reconstruction procedure in the DUGKS is especially discussed. For steady tests, the iteration terminates once the L_2-norm error satisfies

$$E(Q) = \sqrt{\frac{\sum_x |Q(x, t_n) - Q(x, t_{n-1000})|^2}{\sum_x |Q(x, t_n)|^2}} < e, \tag{46}$$

where Q is either the flow density ρ or the flow velocity u, t_{n-1000} denotes the moment 1000 time steps ahead of t_n, and e is the error threshold.

3.1. Flat Interface

As a benchmark test, the flat interface has been widely applied to validate the performance of newly proposed models [30,55,56]. The computational domain is a $L_0 \times 16L_0$ rectangular region with $L_0 = 16$. A uniform Cartesian mesh with a grid spacing of unity is employed to subdivide this domain. Initially, the region bounded by $y_L = 4L_0$ and $y_H = 12L_0$ is filled up with the liquid fluid, while the rest is occupied by the gas fluid. The periodic boundary condition is applied to all the sides. The relaxation time τ was fixed at 0.3. The CFL number was set as 0.5. The reduced temperature $T_r = T/T_c$ ranged from 0.55 to 0.95. The density field is initialized by

$$\rho(x,y) = \rho_g + \frac{\rho_l - \rho_g}{2}\left[\tanh\frac{2(y-y_L)}{W} - \tanh\frac{2(y-y_H)}{W}\right], \qquad (47)$$

where W measures the interface thickness and ρ_l and ρ_g represent the liquid density and the gas density, respectively. Three reconstruction schemes were utilized to explore the influences of varying reconstruction errors on the performance of the DUGKS coupled with different free-energy models. Figure 1a illustrates the coexisting curves predicted by the DUGKS coupled with the primitive free-energy model. It can be observed that varying the reconstruction schemes offers different coexisting results. The central difference face-based reconstruction scheme (CD-FRS) provides satisfactory results in conditions of a high reduced temperature T_r. As T_r decreases, the results deviate apparently from the theoretical results generated by the Maxwell equal-area law [61]. The WENO-Z face-based reconstruction scheme (WENO-Z-FRS) and the upwind cell-based reconstruction scheme (CRS) produce inconsistent results in conditions of high T_r. As T_r decreases, both of them suffer from the stability problem. The fact that different reconstruction schemes generate divergent outcomes results from the force imbalance in the primitive free-energy model [30]. As the standard LB method involves no reconstruction process, the influences of the force imbalance on the numerical results remain limited. When it is coupled with numerical methods containing a reconstruction process, the effect of the force imbalance becomes amplified by the reconstruction errors. Figure 1b illustrates the results produced by the DUGKS coupled with the well-balanced free-energy model, in which the force imbalance was entirely eliminated. It can be identified that the coexisting densities predicted by different reconstruction schemes coincide exactly with the theoretical results. Moreover, the DUGKS implemented with different reconstruction schemes performs equally well in conditions of a low reduced temperature T_r, which demonstrates the fundamental accuracy and stability of this method. Figure 2 illustrates the comparative chemical potential profiles produced by the DUGKS coupled with different free-energy models at $T_r = 0.75$, $\tau = 0.3$, $C = 0.5$. Regardless of the reconstruction schemes utilized, the well-balanced free-energy-based DUGKS provides a nearly constant chemical potential profile, while the primitive free-energy-based DUGKS offers a varied chemical potential profile across the interfaces. Taking a closer look at the comparative profiles, we can identify that the chemical potential value produced by the DUGKS coupled with the primitive model varies along with the reconstruction schemes used, which should be attributed to the differences in the reconstruction errors. The chemical potential produced by the DUGKS coupled with the well-balanced model holds a nearly constant value of 0.006126, which demonstrates the excellent performance of the well-balanced DUGKS in predicting steady two-phase systems governed by free-energy theory.

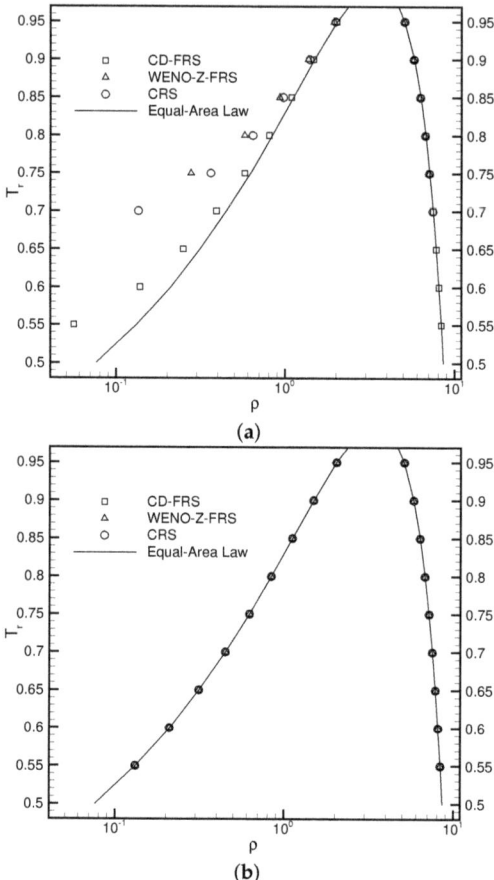

Figure 1. Coexisting curves produced by the DUGKS coupled with (**a**) primitive model and (**b**) well-balanced model, $\tau = 0.3$, $C = 0.5$.

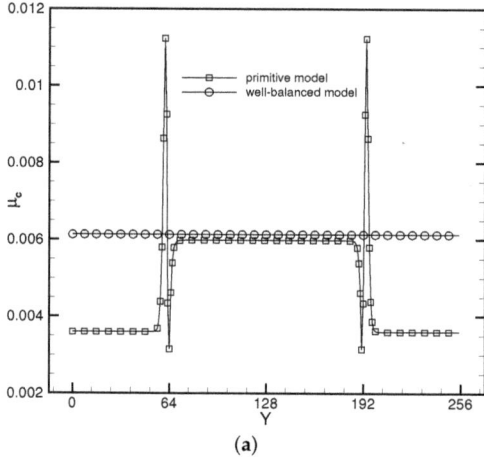

Figure 2. *Cont.*

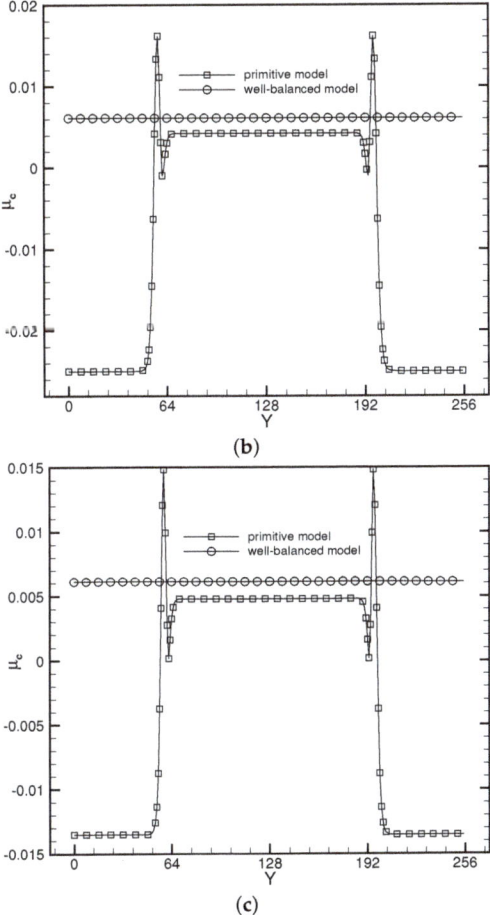

Figure 2. Profiles of chemical potential μ_c produced by the DUGKS with (**a**) CD-FRS, (**b**) WENO-Z-FRS, and (**c**) CRS, $T_r = 0.75, \tau = 0.3, C = 0.5$.

3.2. Quiescent Droplet

The quiescent droplet test serves as one of the fundamental benchmarks for validating the basic capability of the newly proposed multiphase methods. A circular droplet is initially placed at the center of an $L_0 \times L_0$ square domain, with $L_0 = 256$. A uniform Cartesian mesh is used to discretize the physical domain, with the grid spacing Δx fixed at unity. The density field is initialized according to

$$\rho(x,y) = \frac{\rho_l + \rho_g}{2} - \frac{\rho_l - \rho_g}{2}\tanh\left[\frac{2\left(\sqrt{|x-x_c|^2 + |y-y_c|^2} - R_d\right)}{W}\right], \tag{48}$$

where ρ_l and ρ_g correspond, respectively, to the coexisting liquid and gas densities, (x_c, y_c) indicates the center location of the square domain, R_d denotes the droplet radius, and W measures the interface thickness. The computing process terminates once the L_2-norm error of density evaluated by Equation (46) is below 10^{-10}. Figures 3–5 illustrate the density contours produced by the DUGKS coupled with different free-energy models and implemented by various reconstruction schemes at $T_r = 0.9, \tau = 0.6, C = 0.5$. The interfaces produced with the primitive free-energy model suffer from the nonisotropic problem regardless of the reconstruction scheme utilized, which is caused by the force imbalance addressed previously. The second-order central-difference face-based reconstruction scheme (CD-FRS) evolves the initially circular interface into a roughly square interface, which should be attributed to the relatively large reconstruction errors. With a long time evolution, the fifth-order WENO-Z face-based reconstruction scheme (WENO-Z-FRS) shifts the quiescent droplet away from the center position. The interface profile deforms less than that produced by the CD-FRS, which might be attributed to the low level of reconstruction errors of WENO-Z. The interface profile generated by the third-order cell-based reconstruction scheme (CRS) is rather close to circular, which is due to the less nonisotropic reconstruction errors. A similar phenomenon can be observed in the results produced by the pseudopotential-based DUGKS. The interface profiles produced with the well-balanced free-energy model preserve a universal isotropic property across all reconstruction schemes, which demonstrates the elimination of the force imbalance. Figure 6 illustrates the contour of the velocity field produced by the DUGKS implemented with the CRS at $T_r = 0.9, \tau = 0.6, C = 0.5$. When the steady-state is reached, the velocity field produced by the primitive model exhibits a typical patten of large spurious currents, while the velocity field obtained with the well-balanced model provides spurious currents of machine accuracy. The excellent performance of the well-balanced DUGKS is thus verified by the comparative results.

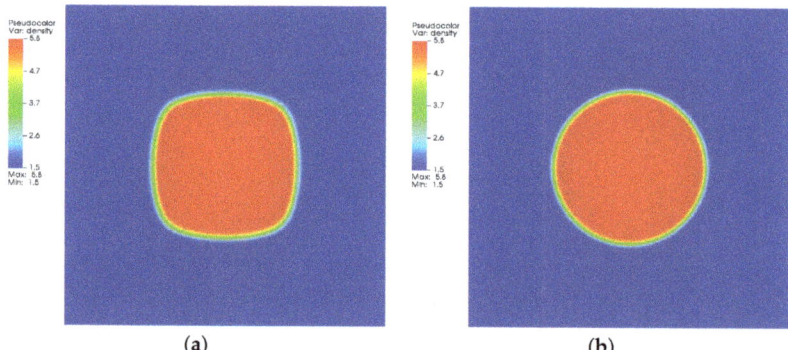

Figure 3. Density contours produced by DUGKS implemented with CD-FRS coupled with (**a**) primitive model and (**b**) well-balanced model, $T_r = 0.9, \tau = 0.6, C = 0.5$.

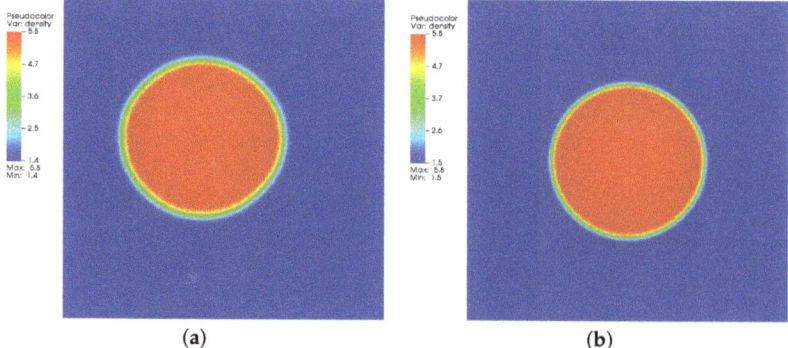

Figure 4. Density contours produced by DUGKS implemented with WENO-Z-FRS coupled with (**a**) primitive model and (**b**) well-balanced model, $T_r = 0.9, \tau = 0.6, C = 0.5$.

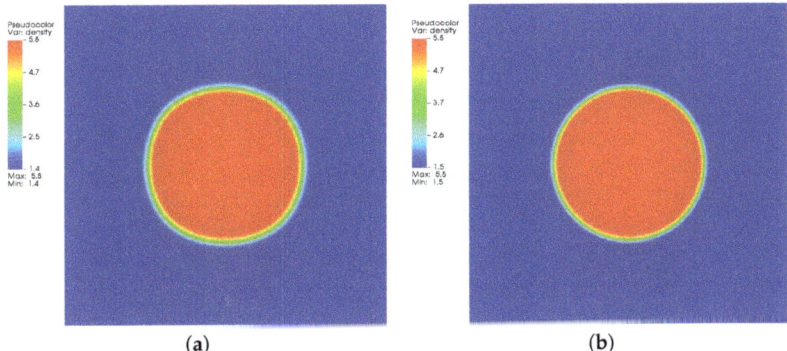

Figure 5. Density contours produced by DUGKS implemented with CRS coupled with (**a**) primitive model and (**b**) well-balanced model, $T_r = 0.9$, $\tau = 0.6$, $C = 0.5$.

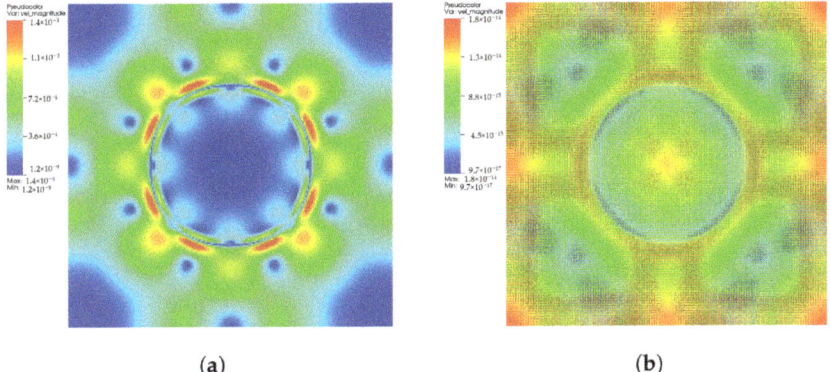

Figure 6. Velocity contours produced by DUGKS implemented with CRS coupled with (**a**) primitive model and (**b**) well-balanced model, $T_r = 0.9$, $\tau = 0.6$, $C = 0.5$.

To quantitatively assess its capability, Laplace's law is validated by the well-balanced DUGKS implemented with the CRS. Figure 7 illustrates the relations between the pressure jump ΔP and the reciprocal of radius R_d obtained at $\tau = 0.3$, $C = 0.8$. The linear relation can be clearly identified from the results, which conforms to Laplace's law: $\Delta P = \sigma / R_d$. The chemical potential varies along with the reduced temperature T_r, which results in the alteration of the surface tension coefficient σ. The CFL number was set as 0.8, at which the FRS fails to operate properly. The stability superiority of the CRS over that of the FRS in the condition of a large time step size makes it more appealing for multiphase flow simulations.

3.3. Spinodal Decomposition

Previous benchmark tests were limited to steady-state problems. Here, the spinodal decomposition test was adopted to assess the capability of DUGKS in dealing with transient problems. The computational domain is an $L_0 \times L_0$ square region subdivided by the uniform Cartesian mesh. The grid spacing $\Delta x = 1$, and the characteristic length $L_0 = 512$. The periodic boundary condition was applied to all the sides. The density field is initialized by

$$\rho(x, y) = (\rho_l + \rho_g)/3 + \text{random}(0, 1)/100, \tag{49}$$

where ρ_l and ρ_g represent the liquid density and the gas density and $\text{random}(0, 1)$ creates density fluctuations that induce the spinodal decomposition process. Figures 8–12 illustrate the snapshots of the density distribution produced by the DUGKS coupled with the well-balanced free-energy model at $T_r = 0.9$, $\tau = 0.6$, $C = 0.5$. In the early stages, the tiny fluctuations generate local inhomogeneities, which initialize the phase separation. As the system evolves, the inhomogeneities drive the material of the heavy fluid into small droplets and interfaces separating different phases begin to emerge. With the continual evolution of the whole system, some of these droplets gradually coalesce into large ones. Eventually, a complete quiescent droplet is formed. It can be identified that the results produced by the central difference face-based reconstruction scheme (CD-FRS) are nearly identical to those generated by the third-order cell-based reconstruction scheme (CRS), which demonstrates the consistent behaviors of the well-balanced DUGKS. The WENO-Z face-based reconstruction scheme (WENO-Z-FRS) fails to provide a converged solution in such a condition. Moreover, the well-balanced DUGKS fails to predict the evolution process of the spinodal decomposition when the reduced temperature is below 0.8. To investigate the multiphase flow dynamics by the well-balanced DUGKS, further improvements are required.

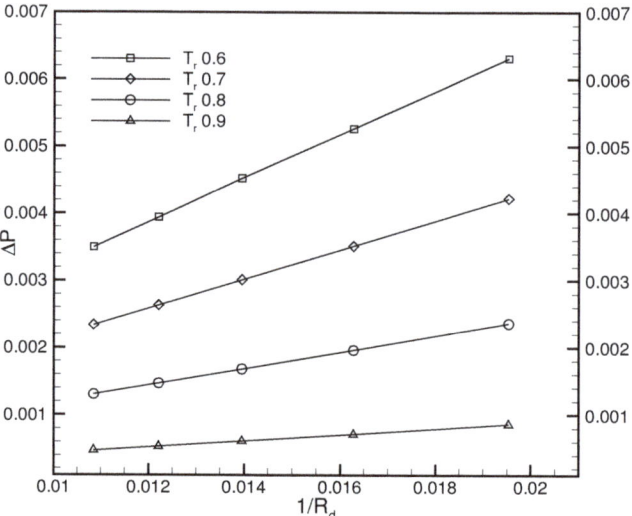

Figure 7. Validation of Laplace's law, $\tau = 0.3$, $C = 0.8$.

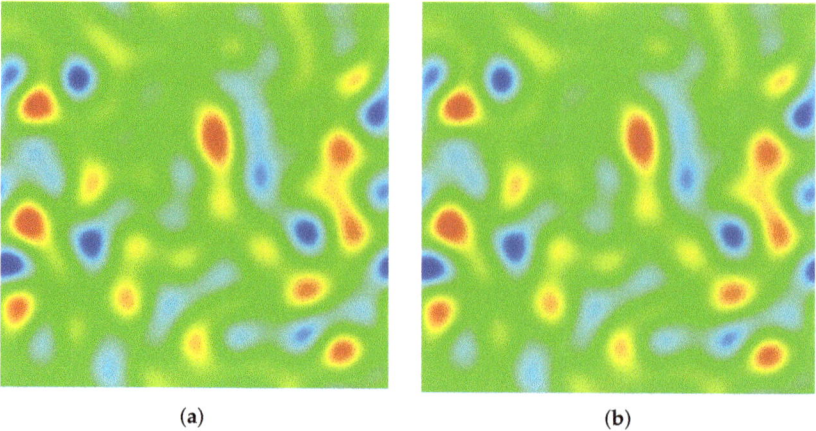

Figure 8. Snapshots of the density distribution produced by the DUGKS implemented with (**a**) CD-FRS and (**b**) CRS, $T_r = 0.9$, $\tau = 0.6$, $C = 0.5$, $t = 2500$.

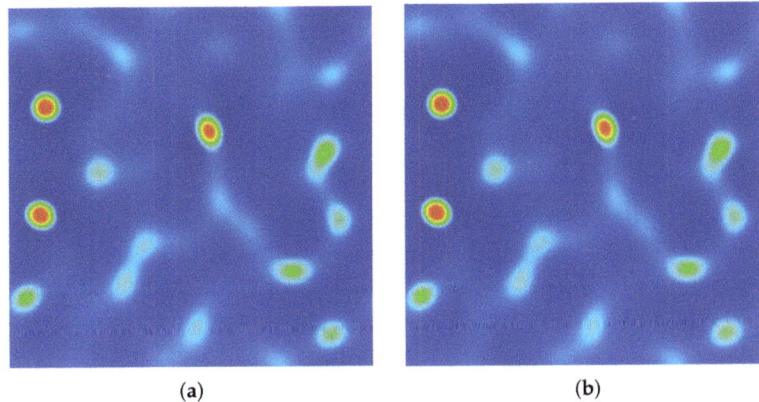

Figure 9. Snapshots of the density distribution produced by the DUGKS implemented with (**a**) CD-FRS and (**b**) CRS, $T_r = 0.9$, $\tau = 0.6$, $C = 0.5$, $t = 6000$.

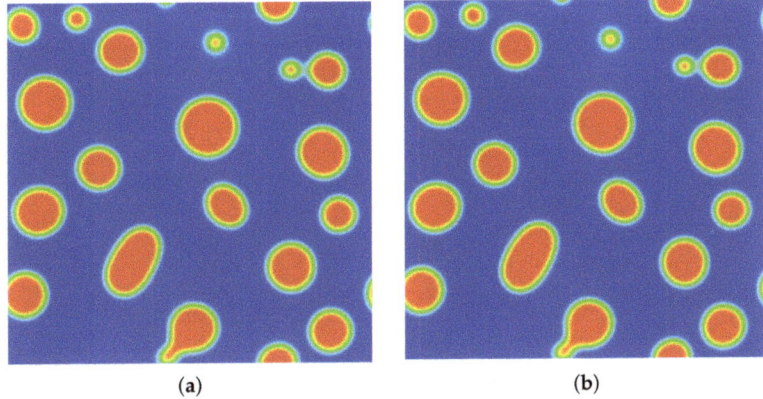

Figure 10. Snapshots of the density distribution produced by the DUGKS implemented with (**a**) CD-FRS and (**b**) CRS, $T_r = 0.9$, $\tau = 0.6$, $C = 0.5$, $t = 7500$.

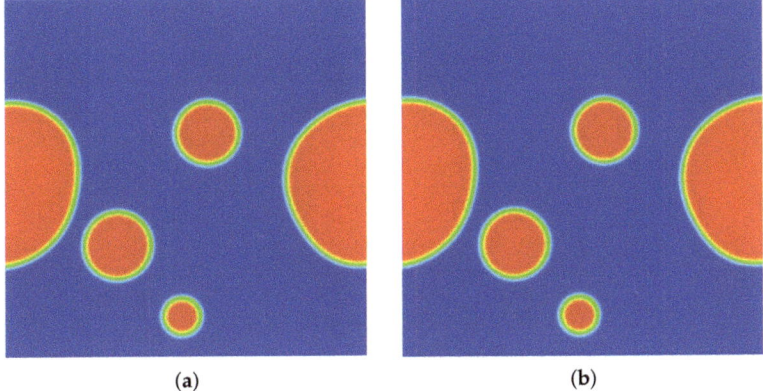

Figure 11. Snapshots of the density distribution produced by the DUGKS implemented with (**a**) CD-FRS and (**b**) CRS, $T_r = 0.9$, $\tau = 0.6$, $C = 0.5$, $t = 25{,}000$.

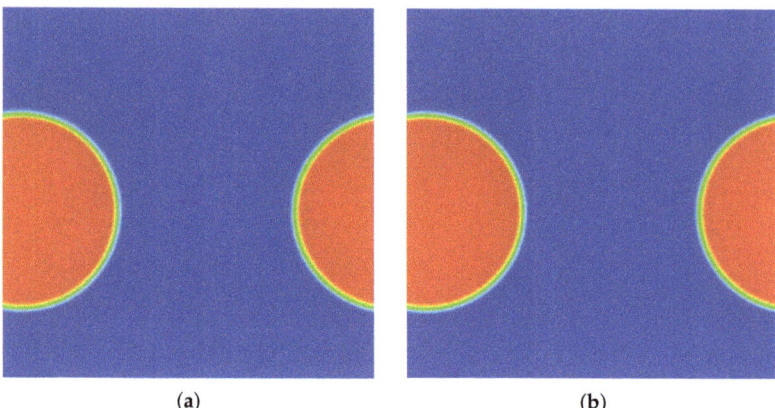

Figure 12. Snapshots of the density distribution produced by the DUGKS implemented with (**a**) CD-FRS and (**b**) CRS, $T_r = 0.9$, $\tau = 0.6$, $C = 0.5$, $t = 250{,}000$.

3.4. Droplet Coalescence

Simulations of the droplet coalescence phenomenon were used to further investigate the capacity of the well-balanced DUGKS for transient problems. The computational domain is a rectangle $2L_0 \times L_0$ domain with $L_0 = 256$. The domain was subdivided into finite grid cells by a uniform Cartesian mesh with a grid spacing of unity. To avoid wall boundary influence, a periodic boundary condition was used in all directions. Initially, two circular droplets were arranged in accordance with [51]

$$\rho(x,y) = \frac{\rho_l + \rho_g}{2} + \frac{\rho_l - \rho_g}{2}\left[1 - \tanh\left(\frac{2d_A}{W}\right) - \tanh\left(\frac{2d_B}{W}\right)\right], \quad (50)$$

where ρ_l and ρ_g correspond separately to the liquid and gas densities, W measures the interface thickness, and d_A and d_B are defined as

$$d_A = \sqrt{(x-x_A)^2 + (y-y_A)^2} - R_0, \quad d_B = \sqrt{(x-x_B)^2 + (y-y_B)^2} - R_0, \quad (51)$$

in which R_0 denotes the droplet radius and $(x_A, y_A) = (L_0 - R_0 - W/2, L_0/2)$ and $(x_B, y_B) = (L_0 + R_0 + W/2, L_0/2)$ represent the central position of droplets A and B, respectively. Other parameters were set as $\kappa = 0.02$, $R_0 = 0.2L_0$, $W = 5$, and $\tau = 0.3$. The initial profile of two droplets is illustrated in Figure 13. The coalescence process starts when the droplets come in contact with each other. As the process continues, a liquid bridge of radius r_b that connects the two droplets is formed [51]. Previous research [62] identified the linear relation between the scaled radius r^* and the dimensionless time t^*, with

$$r^* = r_b/R_0, \quad t^* = t/\sqrt{\rho_l R_0^3 \sigma}, \quad (52)$$

where σ is the surface tension coefficient. According to the validation of Laplace's law illustrated in Figure 7, the surface tension coefficient is 0.1203 for $T_r = 0.8$ and 0.0435 for $T_r = 0.9$. Figure 14 presents the radius variation of the liquid bridge with regard to the dimensionless time t^*. The linear coefficient for the fitting result provided by the DUGKS using the primitive model is 1.4, while the linear coefficient for the fitting result produced with the well-balanced model is 1.03, which is in good agreement with the result predicted by Zeng et al. [51]. The evolution of the L_2-norm of the velocity field produced by the DUGKS using the well-balanced model at $T_r = 0.8$ and $T_r = 0.9$ is shown in Figure 15. It can be identified that the L_2-norm of the velocity field reaches a magnitude of 10^{-14}, which is consistent with the results predicted at the steady-state. Figure 16 illustrates the density and velocity contours produced by the well-balanced DUGKS at $t = 6 \times 10^6$, $T_r = 0.8$,

$\tau = 0.3$, $C = 0.8$. It can be observed that the interface maintains excellent isotropy and the velocity field holds a maximum magnitude of 10^{-16}, which demonstrates the excellent ability of the well-balanced DUGKS. However, it is important to note that when the lowered temperature T_r is less than 0.7, the DUGKS is unable to predict the coalescence process. More efforts are required to increase the stability of the well-balanced DUGKS.

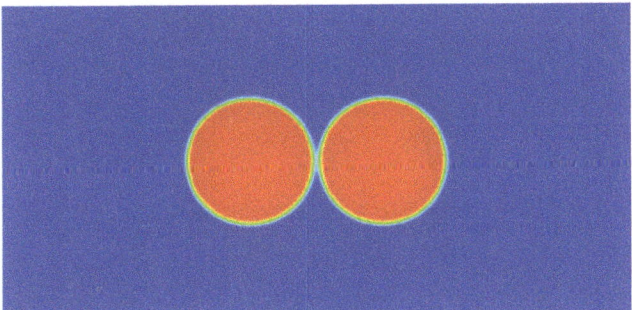

Figure 13. Initial distribution of the density field.

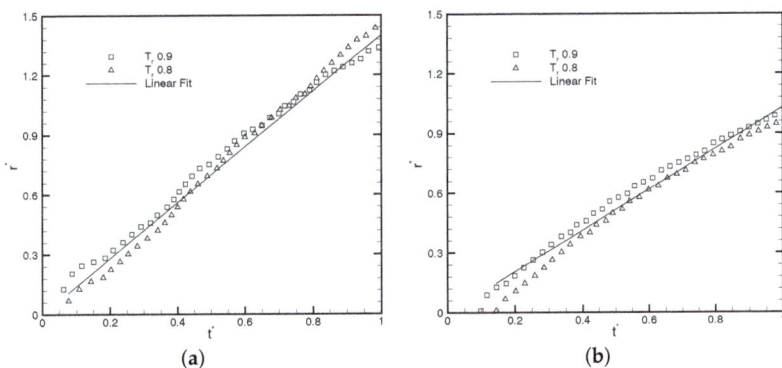

Figure 14. Radius variation of the liquid bridge with regard to the dimensionless time produced by DUGKS coupled with (**a**) primitive model and (**b**) well-balanced model, $\tau = 0.3$, $C = 0.8$.

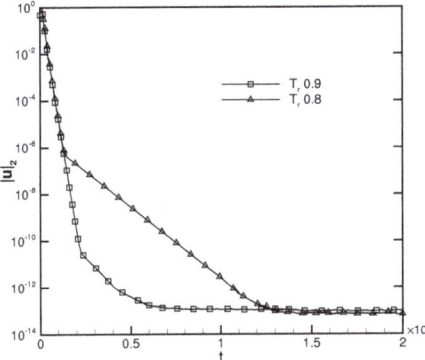

Figure 15. L_2-norm of the velocity field produced by the well-balanced DUGKS with the evolution of time, $\tau = 0.3$, $C = 0.8$.

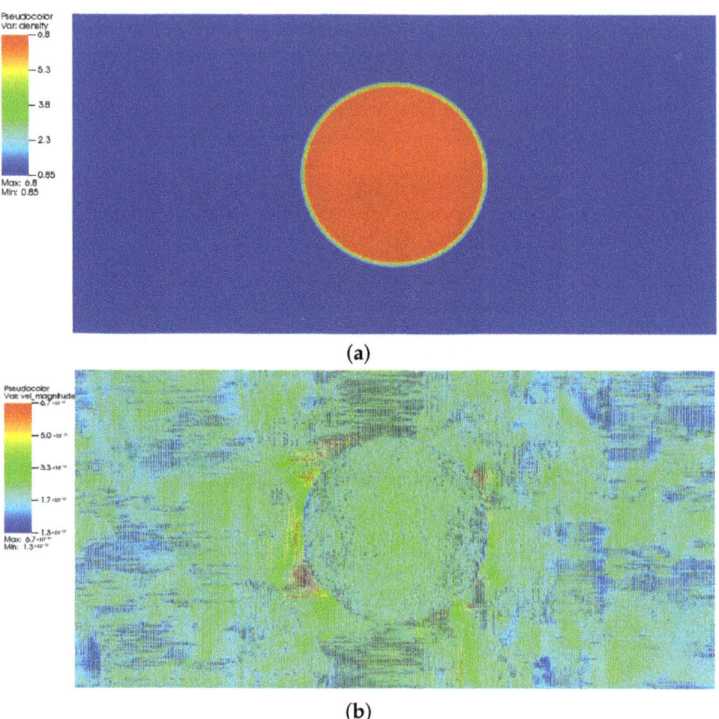

Figure 16. Contours of (**a**) density field and (**b**) velocity field produced by the well-balanced DUGKS at $t = 6 \times 10^6$, $T_r = 0.8$, $\tau = 0.3$, $C = 0.8$.

4. Conclusions

A free-energy-based discrete unified gas-kinetic scheme (DUGKS) was developed by coupling the well-balanced free-energy model with the DUGKS to investigate the van der Waals fluid. The performance of this well-balanced scheme was compared against the counterpart of the DUGKS coupled with the primitive free-energy model. Comparative results produced with different reconstruction schemes demonstrated the force imbalance in the primitive free-energy model, which prevents its direct application to the DUGKS. By coupling the well-balanced free-energy model with the DUGKS, the amplified effects of the force imbalance are entirely eliminated and the influences of nonisotropic reconstruction errors on the fluid interfaces are totally removed. Numerical tests of a flat interface, quiescent droplet, spinodal decomposition, and droplet coalescence were adopted to assess the performance of the DUGKS coupled with the well-balanced free-energy model. Coexisting density curves and Laplace's law were utilized to evaluate its capability quantitatively. It was proven that the well-balanced DUGKS could always produce consistent results despite the reconstruction schemes utilized in steady cases. When dealing with transient problems, the reconstruction scheme employing WENO-Z to evaluate face unknowns tends to be more unstable. When the reduced temperature is below 0.7, the DUGKS coupled with the well-balanced free-energy model suffers from stability problems. Further improvements are required to apply this scheme to predict transient multiphase fluid flows.

Author Contributions: Z.Y.: methodology, software, validation, formal analysis, data curation, writing—original draft preparation. S.L.: funding acquisition, methodology, writing—review and editing. C.Z. (Congshan Zhuo): supervision, funding acquisition, resources, investigation, writing–review and editing. C.Z. (Chengwen Zhong): project administration, funding acquisition, conceptualization, writing—reviewing and editing. All authors have read and agreed to the published version of the manuscript.

Funding: This study is sponsored by the National Numerical Wind Tunnel Project, the National Natural Science Foundation of China (Nos. 11902266, 11902264, 12072283), and the 111 Project of China (B17037).

Institutional Review Board Statement: Not applicable.

Informed Consent Statement: Not applicable.

Data Availability Statement: The data that support the findings of this study are available from the corresponding author upon reasonable request.

Acknowledgments: This work was supported by the high-performance computing power and technical support provided by Xi'an Future Artificial Intelligence Computing Center.

Conflicts of Interest: The authors declare no conflict of interest.

Appendix A. Nondimensionalization of the Boltzmann-BGK Equation

The nondimensionalization process of the Boltzmann-BGK equation is analyzed in this part. The dimensional Boltzmann-BGK equation with a source term reads

$$\frac{\partial f}{\partial t} + \xi \cdot \nabla_x f = -\frac{1}{\tau}\left(f - f^E\right) + f^S, \tag{A1}$$

where f represents the distribution function, t is the time, x is the position, ξ is the particle velocity, τ is the relaxation time, f^E indicates the equilibrium distribution function, and f^S accounts for the source distribution function. Introducing the characteristic length l_c, the characteristic velocity u_c, the characteristic density ρ_c, and multiplying Equation (A1) by $l_c/(\rho_c u_c)$ on both sides, we have

$$\frac{\partial f^*}{\partial t^*} + \xi^* \cdot \nabla_{x^*} f^* = -\frac{l_c}{u_c \tau}\left(f^* - f^{E,*}\right) + f^{S,*}, \tag{A2}$$

where

$$t^* = \frac{tu_c}{l_c}, \xi^* = \frac{\xi}{u_c}, x^* = \frac{x}{l_c}, f^* = \frac{f}{\rho_c}, f^{E,*} = \frac{f^E}{\rho_c}, f^{S,*} = \frac{f^S l_c}{\rho_c u_c}. \tag{A3}$$

As the relaxation time τ is evaluated by $\tau = \mu/\rho_c c_s^2$, where μ is the dynamic viscosity, the multiplier $l_c/(u_c \tau)$ becomes

$$\frac{l_c}{u_c \tau} = \frac{l_c \rho_c c_s^2}{u_c \mu} = \frac{\text{Re}}{\text{Ma}}, \tag{A4}$$

where

$$\text{Ma} = \frac{u_c}{c_s}, \text{Re} = \frac{\rho_c l_c c_s}{\mu}. \tag{A5}$$

Equation (A2) turns into

$$\frac{\partial f^*}{\partial t^*} + \xi^* \cdot \nabla_{x^*} f^* = -\frac{\text{Re}}{\text{Ma}}\left(f^* - f^{E,*}\right) + f^{S,*}, \tag{A6}$$

which is the dimensionless Boltzmann-BGK equation. In multiphase simulation involving droplet dynamics, the Reynolds number is generally defined as

$$\text{Re}_d = \frac{\rho_c u_c l_c}{\mu}. \tag{A7}$$

With this definition, the dimensionless Boltzmann-BGK equation becomes

$$\frac{\partial f^*}{\partial t^*} + \xi^* \cdot \nabla_{x^*} f^* = -\frac{\text{Re}_d}{\text{Ma}^2}\left(f^* - f^{E,*}\right) + f^{S,*}. \tag{A8}$$

References

1. Hirt, C.; Nichols, B. Volume of fluid (VOF) method for the dynamics of free boundaries. *J. Comput. Phys.* **1981**, *39*, 201–225. [CrossRef]
2. Unverdi, S.O.; Tryggvason, G. A front-tracking method for viscous, incompressible, multi-fluid flows. *J. Comput. Phys.* **1992**, *100*, 25–37. [CrossRef]
3. Anderson, D.M.; McFadden, G.B.; Wheeler, A.A. Diffuse-interface methods in fluid mechanics. *Annu. Rev. Fluid Mech.* **1998**, *30*, 139–165. [CrossRef]
4. Sethian, J.A.; Smereka, P. Level set methods for fluid interfaces. *Annu. Rev. Fluid Mech.* **2003**, *35*, 341–372. [CrossRef]
5. Guo, Z.; Zheng, C.; Shi, B. Force imbalance in lattice Boltzmann equation for two-phase flows. *Phys. Rev. E* **2011**, *83*, 036707. [CrossRef]
6. Fox, R.O. Large-eddy-simulation tools for multiphase flows. *Annu. Rev. Fluid Mech.* **2012**, *44*, 47–76. [CrossRef]
7. Aidun, C.K.; Clausen, J.R. Lattice-Boltzmann method for complex flows. *Annu. Rev. Fluid Mech.* **2010**, *42*, 439–472. [CrossRef]
8. Gan, Y.; Xu, A.; Zhang, G.; Succi, S. Discrete Boltzmann modeling of multiphase flows: hydrodynamic and thermodynamic non-equilibrium effects. *Soft Matter* **2015**, *11*, 5336–5345. [CrossRef]
9. Wang, Y.; Shu, C.; Shao, J.; Wu, J.; Niu, X. A mass-conserved diffuse interface method and its application for incompressible multiphase flows with large density ratio. *J. Comput. Phys.* **2015**, *290*, 336–351. [CrossRef]
10. Gunstensen, A.K.; Rothman, D.H.; Zaleski, S.; Zanetti, G. Lattice Boltzmann model of immiscible fluids. *Phys. Rev. A* **1991**, *43*, 4320–4327. [CrossRef]
11. He, X.; Chen, S.; Zhang, R. A lattice Boltzmann scheme for incompressible multiphase flow and its application in simulation of Rayleigh-Taylor instability. *J. Comput. Phys.* **1999**, *152*, 642–663. [CrossRef]
12. Geier, M.; Fakhari, A.; Lee, T. Conservative phase-field lattice Boltzmann model for interface tracking equation. *Phys. Rev. E* **2015**, *91*, 063309. [CrossRef] [PubMed]
13. Shan, X.; Chen, H. Lattice Boltzmann model for simulating flows with multiple phases and components. *Phys. Rev. E* **1993**, *47*, 1815–1819. [CrossRef] [PubMed]
14. Swift, M.R.; Osborn, W.R.; Yeomans, J.M. Lattice Boltzmann simulation of nonideal fluids. *Phys. Rev. Lett.* **1995**, *75*, 830–833. [CrossRef]
15. Yang, K.; Guo, Z. Lattice Boltzmann method for binary fluids based on mass-conserving quasi-incompressible phase-field theory. *Phys. Rev. E* **2016**, *93*, 043303. [CrossRef]
16. Briant, A.J.; Wagner, A.J.; Yeomans, J.M. Lattice Boltzmann simulations of contact line motion. I. Liquid-gas systems. *Phys. Rev. E* **2004**, *69*, 031602. [CrossRef]
17. Briant, A.J.; Yeomans, J.M. Lattice Boltzmann simulations of contact line motion. II. Binary fluids. *Phys. Rev. E* **2004**, *69*, 031603. [CrossRef] [PubMed]
18. Li, Q.; Wagner, A.J. Symmetric free-energy-based multicomponent lattice Boltzmann method. *Phys. Rev. E* **2007**, *76*, 036701. [CrossRef]
19. Zhang, J.; Kwok, D.Y. A mean-field free energy lattice Boltzmann model for multicomponent fluids. *Eur. Phys. J. Spec. Top.* **2009**, *171*, 45–53. [CrossRef]
20. Wiklund, H.; Lindström, S.; Uesaka, T. Boundary condition considerations in lattice Boltzmann formulations of wetting binary fluids. *Comput. Phys. Commun.* **2011**, *182*, 2192–2200. [CrossRef]
21. Wen, B.; Huang, B.; Qin, Z.; Wang, C.; Zhang, C. Contact angle measurement in lattice Boltzmann method. *Comput. Math. Appl.* **2018**, *76*, 1686–1698. [CrossRef]
22. Yan, Y.; Zu, Y. A lattice Boltzmann method for incompressible two-phase flows on partial wetting surface with large density ratio. *J. Comput. Phys.* **2007**, *227*, 763–775. [CrossRef]
23. Wen, B.; Zhao, L.; Qiu, W.; Ye, Y.; Shan, X. Chemical-potential multiphase lattice Boltzmann method with superlarge density ratios. *Phys. Rev. E* **2020**, *102*, 013303. [CrossRef] [PubMed]
24. Swift, M.R.; Orlandini, E.; Osborn, W.R.; Yeomans, J.M. Lattice Boltzmann simulations of liquid-gas and binary fluid systems. *Phys. Rev. E* **1996**, *54*, 5041–5052. [CrossRef]
25. Inamuro, T.; Konishi, N.; Ogino, F. A Galilean invariant model of the lattice Boltzmann method for multiphase fluid flows using free-energy approach. *Comput. Phys. Commun.* **2000**, *129*, 32–45. [CrossRef]
26. Kalarakis, A.N.; Burganos, V.N.; Payatakes, A.C. Galilean-invariant lattice-Boltzmann simulation of liquid-vapor interface dynamics. *Phys. Rev. E* **2002**, *65*, 056702. [CrossRef]
27. Wagner, A.; Li, Q. Investigation of Galilean invariance of multi-phase lattice Boltzmann methods. *Phys. A Stat. Mech. Appl.* **2006**, *362*, 105–110. [CrossRef]
28. Lee, T.; Fischer, P.F. Eliminating parasitic currents in the lattice Boltzmann equation method for nonideal gases. *Phys. Rev. E* **2006**, *74*, 046709. [CrossRef]
29. Lou, Q.; Guo, Z. Interface-capturing lattice Boltzmann equation model for two-phase flows. *Phys. Rev. E* **2015**, *91*, 013302. [CrossRef]
30. Guo, Z. Well-balanced lattice Boltzmann model for two-phase systems. *Phys. Fluids* **2021**, *33*, 031709. [CrossRef]

31. Guo, Z.; Xu, K.; Wang, R. Discrete unified gas kinetic scheme for all Knudsen number flows: Low-speed isothermal case. *Phys. Rev. E* **2013**, *88*, 033305. [CrossRef] [PubMed]
32. Guo, Z.; Wang, R.; Xu, K. Discrete unified gas kinetic scheme for all Knudsen number flows. II. Thermal compressible case. *Phys. Rev. E* **2015**, *91*, 033313. [CrossRef] [PubMed]
33. Zhu, L.; Guo, Z. Numerical study of nonequilibrium gas flow in a microchannel with a ratchet surface. *Phys. Rev. E* **2017**, *95*, 023113. [CrossRef] [PubMed]
34. Liu, H.; Cao, Y.; Chen, Q.; Kong, M.; Zheng, L. A conserved discrete unified gas kinetic scheme for microchannel gas flows in all flow regimes. *Comput. Fluids* **2018**, *167*, 313–323. [CrossRef]
35. Zhang, Y.; Zhu, L.; Wang, R.; Guo, Z. Discrete unified gas kinetic scheme for all Knudsen number flows. III. Binary gas mixtures of Maxwell molecules. *Phys. Rev. E* **2018**, *97*, 053306. [CrossRef] [PubMed]
36. Zhang, Y.; Zhu, L.; Wang, P.; Guo, Z. Discrete unified gas kinetic scheme for flows of binary gas mixture based on the McCormack model. *Phys. Fluids* **2019**, *31*, 017101. [CrossRef]
37. Wang, P.; Wang, L.P.; Guo, Z. Comparison of the lattice Boltzmann equation and discrete unified gas-kinetic scheme methods for direct numerical simulation of decaying turbulent flows. *Phys. Rev. E* **2016**, *94*, 043304. [CrossRef]
38. Bo, Y.; Wang, P.; Guo, Z.; Wang, L.P. DUGKS simulations of three-dimensional Taylor–Green vortex flow and turbulent channel flow. *Comput. Fluids* **2017**, *155*, 9–21. [CrossRef]
39. Zhang, R.; Zhong, C.; Liu, S.; Zhuo, C. Large-eddy simulation of wall-bounded turbulent flow with high-order discrete unified gas-kinetic scheme. *Adv. Aerodyn.* **2020**, *2*, 26. [CrossRef]
40. Chen, J.; Liu, S.; Wang, Y.; Zhong, C. Conserved discrete unified gas-kinetic scheme with unstructured discrete velocity space. *Phys. Rev. E* **2019**, *100*, 043305. [CrossRef]
41. Zhong, M.; Zou, S.; Pan, D.; Zhuo, C.; Zhong, C. A simplified discrete unified gas–kinetic scheme for compressible flow. *Phys. Fluids* **2021**, *33*, 036103. [CrossRef]
42. Wen, X.; Wang, L.P.; Guo, Z.; Shen, J. An improved discrete unified gas kinetic scheme for simulating compressible natural convection flows. *J. Comput. Phys. X* **2021**, *11*, 100088. [CrossRef]
43. Guo, Z.; Xu, K. Discrete unified gas kinetic scheme for multiscale heat transfer based on the phonon Boltzmann transport equation. *Int. J. Heat Mass Transf.* **2016**, *102*, 944–958. [CrossRef]
44. Luo, X.P.; Wang, C.H.; Zhang, Y.; Yi, H.L.; Tan, H.P. Multiscale solutions of radiative heat transfer by the discrete unified gas kinetic scheme. *Phys. Rev. E* **2018**, *97*, 063302. [CrossRef]
45. Guo, Z.; Xu, K. Progress of discrete unified gas-kinetic scheme for multiscale flows. *Adv. Aerodyn.* **2021**, *3*, 6. [CrossRef]
46. Wang, P.; Zhu, L.; Guo, Z.; Xu, K. A comparative study of LBE and DUGKS methods for nearly incompressible flows. *Commun. Comput. Phys.* **2015**, *17*, 657–681. [CrossRef]
47. Zhang, C.; Yang, K.; Guo, Z. A discrete unified gas-kinetic scheme for immiscible two-phase flows. *Int. J. Heat Mass Transf.* **2018**, *126*, 1326–1336. [CrossRef]
48. Yang, Z.; Zhong, C.; Zhuo, C. Phase-field method based on discrete unified gas-kinetic scheme for large-density-ratio two-phase flows. *Phys. Rev. E* **2019**, *99*, 043302. [CrossRef]
49. Yang, Z.; Liu, S.; Zhuo, C.; Zhong, C. Conservative multilevel discrete unified gas kinetic scheme for modeling multiphase flows with large density ratios. *Phys. Fluids* **2022**, *34*, 043316. [CrossRef]
50. Yang, Z.; Liu, S.; Zhuo, C.; Zhong, C. Pseudopotential-based discrete unified gas kinetic scheme for modeling multiphase fluid flows. *Res. Sq.* **2022**. [CrossRef]
51. Zeng, W.; Zhang, C.; Guo, Z. Well-balanced discrete unified gas-kinetic scheme for two-phase systems. *Phys. Fluids* **2022**, *34*, 052111. [CrossRef]
52. Jacqmin, D. Calculation of two-phase Navier-Stokes flows using phase-field modeling. *J. Comput. Phys.* **1999**, *155*, 96–127. [CrossRef]
53. Goldstein, H.; Poole, C.; Safko, J. *Classical Mechanics*, 3rd ed.; Pearson: London, UK, 2001.
54. Sbragaglia, M.; Chen, H.; Shan, X.; Succi, S. Continuum free-energy formulation for a class of lattice Boltzmann multiphase models. *Europhys. Lett.* **2009**, *86*, 24005. [CrossRef]
55. Wen, B.; Zhou, X.; He, B.; Zhang, C.; Fang, H. Chemical-potential-based lattice Boltzmann method for nonideal fluids. *Phys. Rev. E* **2017**, *95*, 063305. [CrossRef]
56. Li, Q.; Yu, Y.; Huang, R.Z. Achieving thermodynamic consistency in a class of free-energy multiphase lattice Boltzmann models. *Phys. Rev. E* **2021**, *103*, 013304. [CrossRef]
57. Yang, Z.; Zhong, C.; Zhuo, C.; Liu, S. Spatio-temporal error coupling and competition in meso-flux construction of discrete unified gas-kinetic scheme. *Comput. Fluids* **2022**, *244*, 105537. [CrossRef]
58. Borges, R.; Carmona, M.; Costa, B.; Don, W.S. An improved weighted essentially non-oscillatory scheme for hyperbolic conservation laws. *J. Comput. Phys.* **2008**, *227*, 3191–3211. [CrossRef]
59. Tao, S.; Zhang, H.; Guo, Z.; Wang, L.P. A combined immersed boundary and discrete unified gas kinetic scheme for particle–fluid flows. *J. Comput. Phys.* **2018**, *375*, 498–518. [CrossRef]
60. Kumar, A. Isotropic finite-differences. *J. Comput. Phys.* **2004**, *201*, 109–118. [CrossRef]

61. Chen, L.; Kang, Q.; Mu, Y.; He, Y.L.; Tao, W.Q. A critical review of the pseudopotential multiphase lattice Boltzmann model: Methods and applications. *Int. J. Heat Mass Transf.* **2014**, *76*, 210–236. [CrossRef]
62. Wu, M.; Cubaud, T.; Ho, C.M. Scaling law in liquid drop coalescence driven by surface tension. *Phys. Fluids* **2004**, *16*, L51–L54. [CrossRef]

Article

A Well-Balanced Unified Gas-Kinetic Scheme for Multicomponent Flows under External Force Field

Tianbai Xiao

Department of Mathematics, Karlsruhe Institute of Technology, 76131 Karlsruhe, Germany; tianbai.xiao@kit.edu

Abstract: The study of the evolution of the atmosphere requires careful consideration of multicomponent gaseous flows under gravity. The gas dynamics under an external force field is usually associated with an intrinsic multiscale nature due to large particle density variation along the direction of force. A wonderfully diverse set of behaviors of fluids can be observed in different flow regimes. This poses a great challenge for numerical algorithms to accurately and efficiently capture the scale-dependent flow physics. In this paper, a well-balanced unified gas-kinetic scheme (UGKS) for a gas mixture is developed, which can be used for the study of cross-scale multicomponent flows under an external force field. The well-balanced scheme here indicates the capability of a numerical method to evolve a gravitational system under any initial condition to the hydrostatic equilibrium and to keep such a solution. Such a property is crucial for an accurate description of multicomponent gas evolution under an external force field, especially for long-term evolving systems such as galaxy formation. Based on the Boltzmann model equation for gas mixtures, the UGKS leverages the space–time integral solution to construct numerical flux functions and, thus, provides a self-conditioned mechanism to recover typical flow dynamics in various flow regimes. We prove the well-balanced property of the current scheme formally through theoretical analysis and numerical validations. New physical phenomena, including the decoupled transport of different gas components in the transition regime, are presented and studied.

Keywords: fluid mechanics; kinetic theory; rarefied gas dynamics; multicomponent flows; well-balanced schemes

Citation: Xiao, T. A Well-Balanced Unified Gas-Kinetic Scheme for Multicomponent Flows under External Force Field. *Entropy* **2022**, *24*, 1110. https://doi.org/10.3390/e24081110

Academic Editors: Zhen Chen, Liming Yang and Liangqi Zhang

Received: 4 July 2022
Accepted: 9 August 2022
Published: 12 August 2022

Publisher's Note: MDPI stays neutral with regard to jurisdictional claims in published maps and institutional affiliations.

Copyright: © 2022 by the authors. Licensee MDPI, Basel, Switzerland. This article is an open access article distributed under the terms and conditions of the Creative Commons Attribution (CC BY) license (https://creativecommons.org/licenses/by/4.0/).

1. Introduction

The challenge of modeling and simulating real gas evolution in engineering and environmental applications has attracted continuous attention from the CFD community. To be precise, the Earth's atmosphere needs to be considered, at least as a binary mixture of nitrogen and oxygen under a gravitational field. Compared with the classical fluid dynamics of pure gas, theoretical and numerical studies on multicomponent gas systems under an external force field are very limited. The goal of this paper is to advance the cutting-edge research in this direction, with a particular focus on multiscale and non-equilibrium flows.

The characteristic scale and flow regime is usually categorized by the Knudsen number Kn. When Kn is large, the Boltzmann equation is established at the molecular mean free path and traveling time between successive intermolecular collisions. Such spatiotemporal scales can be referred to as the kinetic scale. Based on the first physical principle, it is natural to extend the Boltzmann equation to gas mixtures by tracking the evolution of each component. With a different molecular mass and gas constant R, different gas components transport with different velocity $u \sim \sqrt{RT}$, where T is temperature, leading to strong non-equilibrium transport phenomena. Such an effect occurs dramatically when the mass ratio is large, such as the rounding motion of ions and electrons in plasma physics.

On the other hand, when Kn is small, the characteristic scale of flow structures is basically much larger than the mean free path, and a macroscopic model is favored to describe the flow evolution collectively. In the hydrodynamic limit, the Euler and Navier–Stokes equations are routinely used, where different gas components present consistent collective behavior. Additional constitutive equations are required to track the evolution of different components. Such additional equations can be the equations for the volume fraction, mass fraction, or ratio of specific heats of a mixture [1,2]. It is a nontrivial task since the information of particle interactions among different components at the kinetic scale is lost during the coarse-grained process and should be modeled back to the macroscopic system in a consistent fashion.

Different equations and the corresponding numerical algorithms are scale-dependent methods to describe flows at a certain level. However, in real-world gaseous flows, there may not exist a clear scale separation between different flow regimes. For example, under the gravitational field, the density varies significantly along the direction of force, as does the mean free path and local Knudsen number. As a result, the atmosphere can thus be divided into several layers, and a continuous variation of flow physics will emerge from the kinetic physics in the upper atmospheric layer to the hydrodynamics in the lower high-density region. Due to such an intrinsic multiscale nature, the corresponding numerical algorithm should have the capability of capturing the cross-scale flow physics effectively.

For a gas dynamic system under a steady external force field from an arbitrary initial condition, the entropy-increasing process leads to a hydrostatic equilibrium state. Such a static solution is achieved and preserved due to the balance between the external force and inhomogeneous fluxes. The capacity to capture such an equilibrium solution along a physically accurate path is the so-called well-balanced property, which is important for a numerical algorithm to solve long-term fluid dynamics under an external force field. For the equilibrium flow when Kn approaches zero, such as the gravitational Euler system, many efforts have been devoted to the construction of well-balanced schemes for single-component flow [3–5]. For more general gas dynamic equations with the inclusion of viscosity and heat conductivity, a few works have been performed based on the gas-kinetic scheme [6–8]. However, to the best of the author's knowledge, the study of the cross-scale modeling and computation of multicomponent gas dynamics under an external force field is very limited.

In recent years, the unified gas-kinetic scheme (UGKS) has been developed for the simulation of multiscale gaseous flow [9,10]. Based on the Boltzmann model equation, the UGKS uses an analytical integral solution in the construction of numerical flux functions. The coupled modeling of particle transport and the collision of the evolution solution guarantees the multiscale nature of the method. For the gas dynamic system related to an external force, in order to develop a well-balanced gas-kinetic scheme, it is important to take the external force effect into the flux transport across a cell interface accurately. Based on this idea, a well-balanced unified gas-kinetic scheme for single-component flow [11] has been proposed. In this paper, a similar methodology is used in the flux function for the further development of the unified gas-kinetic scheme for a gas mixture. It is worth mentioning that, due to the versatility of kinetic theory, it is natural to develop kinetic schemes for other multi-particle systems, including shallow water equations [12], radiative transfer [13], weakly coupled plasma physics [14], etc.

This paper is organized as follows. Section 2 is a brief introduction of the kinetic theory of multicomponent gases and the asymptotic analysis of the current Boltzmann model. Section 3 presents the construction of the well-balanced unified gas-kinetic scheme for a gas mixture under an external force field. Section 4 includes numerical examples to demonstrate the performance of the scheme. The last section is the conclusion.

2. Kinetic Theory

2.1. Boltzmann Equation and Relaxation Model

The kinetic theory describes the evolution of gases in a statistical fashion. The Boltzmann equation for single-component flows is written as

$$\frac{\partial f}{\partial t} + u_i \frac{\partial f}{\partial x_i} + \phi_i \frac{\partial f}{\partial u_i} = Q(f,f),$$

where $u_i = (u,v,w)$ is the particle velocity, ϕ_i is the external forcing term, and $Q(f,f)$ denotes the two-body collision term. Here, Einstein's summation convention is adopted for tensor operations. The above equation can be extended to a gas mixture, where the evolution equation for the distribution function of each species s is written as

$$\frac{\partial f_s}{\partial t} + u_i \frac{\partial f_s}{\partial x_i} + \phi_i \frac{\partial f_s}{\partial u_i} = Q_s(f,f). \tag{1}$$

The collision term can be written as

$$Q_s(f,f) = \sum_{r=1}^{N} Q_{sr}(f_s, f_r) = \sum_{r=1}^{N} \int_{\mathbb{R}^3} \int_{\mathbb{S}^2} (f'_s f'_r - f_s f_r) g_{sr} \sigma_{sr} d\Omega du_{ri}, \tag{2}$$

where f' is the post-collision distribution and r is the index of different gas species. The term g_{sr} is the relative speed of two molecular classes, and $\sigma_{sr}d\Omega$ is the differential cross-section for the collision specified. Here, $Q_{ss}(f_s, f_s)$ is called the self-collision term and $Q_{sr}(f_s, f_r)$ is the cross-collision term.

Due to the complexity of the collision integral in Equation (2), simplified kinetic models have been proposed for single-component gas evolution [15]. Such a model is expected to satisfy some key structures of the original Boltzmann equation, such as positivity, correct exchange coefficients, entropy inequality, and indifferentiability. Here, we introduce a BGK-type model proposed by Andries, Aoki, and Perthame (AAP) [16], which could satisfy all the properties required above. In the AAP model, a single collision operator for species s is defined as

$$Q_s(f) = \frac{f_s^+ - f_s}{\tau_s}. \tag{3}$$

Here, the equilibrium state is defined based on modified macroscopic variables, i.e.,

$$f_s^+ = n_s \left(\frac{m_s}{2\pi k_B T'_s}\right)^{3/2} \exp\left(-\frac{m_s}{2k_B T'_s}(u_s - U'_s)^2\right), \tag{4}$$

where $\{U'_s, T'_s\}$ is the modified bulk velocity and temperature, n_s is the number density, m_s is the molecular mass, and k_B is the Boltzmann constant. The determination of modified temperature T'_s and velocity U'_s can be found in [17] to take into account the interaction among different gas species:

$$\begin{aligned}
U'_{si} &= U_{si} + \tau_s \sum_{r \neq s} 2\frac{\rho_r}{m_s + m_r} \theta_{sr}(U_{ri} - U_{si}), \\
\frac{3}{2}k_B T'_s &= \frac{3}{2}k_B T_s - \frac{m_s}{2}(U'_s - U_s)^2 \\
&\quad + \tau_s \sum_{r \neq s} 4 m_s \frac{\rho_r}{(m_s + m_r)^2} \theta_{sr} \left(\frac{3}{2}k_B T_r - \frac{3}{2}k_B T_s + \frac{m_r}{2}(U_r - U_s)^2\right),
\end{aligned} \tag{5}$$

where $\rho = mn$ is the mass density.

The collision frequency is determined by

$$\frac{1}{\tau_s} = \beta \sum_r \theta_{sr} n_r, \tag{6}$$

where β can be chosen as either the unit for simplicity or to coincide with the collision time of the single-component gas when all components are the same species. The parameter θ_{sr} is defined as

$$\theta_{sr} = \frac{4\sqrt{\pi}}{3}\left(\frac{2k_B T_s}{m_s} + \frac{2k_B T_r}{m_r}\right)^{1/2}\left(\frac{d_s + d_r}{2}\right)^2, \qquad (7)$$

for the hard sphere model and

$$\theta_{sr} = 0.422\pi\left(\frac{a_{sr}(m_s + m_r)}{m_s m_r}\right), \qquad (8)$$

for the Maxwell molecule, where d_s, d_r are the molecular diameters and a_{sr} is the proportionality of the intermolecular force.

With the defined collision operator, the BGK-type kinetic model equation can be written as

$$\frac{\partial f_s}{\partial t} + u_i \frac{\partial f_s}{\partial x_i} + \phi_i \frac{\partial f_s}{\partial u_i} = \frac{f_s^+ - f_s}{\tau_s}. \qquad (9)$$

2.2. Asymptotic Analysis

The macroscopic conservative flow variables can be obtained from the moments of the particle distribution function, i.e.,

$$\mathbf{W}_s = \begin{pmatrix} \rho_s \\ \rho_s U_{si} \\ \rho_s E_s \end{pmatrix} = \int_{\mathbb{R}^3} f_s \psi d\Xi,$$

where $\psi = \left(m_s, m_s u_i, \frac{1}{2}m_s u_i u_i\right)^T$ is a vector of moments for collision invariants and $d\Xi = dudvdw$. Taking the moments of Equation (9) yields the balance laws of density, momentum, and energy in each species s, i.e.,

$$\begin{aligned}
\frac{\partial \rho_s}{\partial t} + \frac{\partial \rho_s U_{si}}{\partial x_i} &= 0, \\
\frac{\partial \rho_s U_{si}}{\partial t} + \frac{\partial \rho_s U_{si} U_{sj}}{\partial x_j} + \frac{\partial T_{sij}}{\partial x_j} &= \rho_s \phi_i + \int_{\mathbb{R}^3} u_i Q_s(f) d\Xi, \\
\frac{\partial \rho_s E_s}{\partial t} + \frac{\partial \rho_s E_s U_{si}}{\partial x_i} + \frac{\partial (T_{sij} U_{sj} + q_{si})}{\partial x_i} &= \rho_s U_{si} \phi_i + \int_{\mathbb{R}^3} \frac{1}{2} u_i u_i Q_s(f) d\Xi.
\end{aligned} \qquad (10)$$

The term T_{ij} is the stress tensor, and q_i is the heat flux. It is noticeable that, due to the momentum and energy exchanges among different species in the mixture, the collision integrals $\int u_i Q_s(f,f)d\Xi$ and $\int \frac{1}{2}u_i u_i Q_s(f,f)d\Xi$ are no longer equal to zero, while the total density, momentum, and energy are still conserved in the flow evolution. Therefore, summing up the above equations, we can obtain

$$\begin{aligned}
\frac{\partial \rho_s}{\partial t} + \frac{\partial \rho_s U_i}{\partial x_i} &= -\frac{\partial J_{si}}{\partial x_i}, \\
\frac{\partial \rho U_i}{\partial t} + \frac{\partial \rho U_i U_j}{\partial x_j} + \frac{\partial T_{ij}}{\partial x_j} &= \rho \phi_i, \\
\frac{\partial \rho E}{\partial t} + \frac{\partial \rho E U_i}{\partial x_i} + \frac{\partial (T_{ij} U_j + q_i)}{\partial x_i} &= \rho U_i \phi_i.
\end{aligned} \qquad (11)$$

where $J_{si} = \int (u_i - U_i) f_s d\Xi$. As shown in [16], by inserting the Chapman–Enskog expansion, e.g., the zeroth-order approximation:

$$f_s \simeq f_s^+ + O(\tau_s),$$

and the first-order approximation:

$$f_s \simeq f_s^+ - \tau_s(\partial_t f_s^+ + u_i \partial_{x_i} f_s^+) + O(\tau_s^2),$$

into the determination of the stress tensor and heat flux, one can derive the Euler and Navier–Stokes equations, respectively.

For multicomponent flows, the mass transfer is another important topic. Here, we used diffusive scaling to illustrate the mechanism of mass transfer and diffusion in the current model. We introduce dimensionless variables denoted with asterisks:

$$t = t^* t_0, \quad x = x^* x_0, \quad u_i = u_i^* u_0, \quad f = f^* f_0,$$

where t_0 is the reference time scale, x_0 is the reference length scale, and so on. With the dimensionless terms plugged into Equation (9), we obtain (after immediately dropping the asterisks)

$$\text{St}\frac{\partial f_s}{\partial t} + u_i \frac{\partial f_s}{\partial x_i} + \phi_i \frac{\partial f_s}{\partial u_i} = \frac{1}{\text{Kn}} Q_s(f),$$

where $\text{St} = x_0/u_0 t_0$ is the Strouhal number and Kn is the Knudsen number. In the diffusive limit, we assume $\text{St} \simeq \text{Kn} = \epsilon$. The stiff term $1/\epsilon$ on the right-hand side implies that the limiting solution $\lim_{\epsilon \to 0} f_s^\epsilon$ is close to the local equilibrium. We make this assumption and compute the moment system in the same way as Equations (10) and (11), which yields

$$\epsilon \frac{\partial n_s^\epsilon}{\partial t} + \epsilon \frac{\partial (n_s^\epsilon U_{si}^\epsilon)}{\partial x_i} = 0,$$

$$\epsilon^2 \frac{\partial \rho_s^\epsilon U_{si}^\epsilon}{\partial t} + \epsilon^2 \frac{\partial (\rho_s^\epsilon U_{si}^\epsilon U_{sj}^\epsilon)}{\partial x_j} + \frac{\partial (n_s^\epsilon k_B T^\epsilon)}{\partial x_i} = \frac{1}{\epsilon} \int m_s u_i Q_s(f^\epsilon) d\Xi + \epsilon^2 \rho_s^\epsilon \phi_i.$$

For simplicity, here, we adopt the number density in the continuity equation. Truncating the above equations at the leading order in ϵ leads to

$$\frac{\partial n^\epsilon}{\partial t} + \frac{\partial n^\epsilon U_i^\epsilon}{\partial x_i} = 0,$$

$$\frac{\partial n_s^\epsilon k_B T^\epsilon}{\partial x_i} = \frac{1}{\epsilon} \int m_s u_i Q_s(f^\epsilon) d\Xi.$$

If the isothermal assumption is made, the second equation with $\epsilon \to 0$ reduces to

$$\frac{\partial n_s^\epsilon}{\partial x_i} = \frac{1}{\epsilon k_B T^\epsilon} \int m_s u_i Q_s(f^\epsilon) d\Xi = \frac{U_{si}' - U_{si}}{\epsilon k_B T}$$
$$= \sum_{r \neq s} \frac{(U_{ri} - U_{si})}{D_{ij}}, \quad (12)$$

where the coefficients D_{ij} are determined by the collision time in Equation (6) and the interaction model in Equation (5). Equation (12) is exactly the Maxwell–Stefan diffusion law [18]. As analyzed, even though the Maxwell–Stefan theory is basically understood as a more generalized law than Fick's law to describe mass transfer, its applicability is mainly limited to the continuum limit and thermodynamic equilibrium. To study the mass and heat transfer in multiscale and non-equilibrium fluids, we must resort to reliable numerical methods, which is the core task in the next section.

3. Numerical Algorithm

3.1. Construction of Interface Distribution Function

The key ingredient in the UGKS is the integral solution constructed from the BGK-type relaxation model. Here, we used the one-dimensional case to illustrate the construction of the numerical algorithm first. Without loss of generality, we assumed the interface between two neighbor cells $x_{i+1/2} = 0$ and $t^n = 0$. Given a local constant collision time τ_s, the integral solution of Equation (9) along the characteristic line is written as

$$f_s(0, t, u_k) = \frac{1}{\tau_s} \int_0^t f_s^+(x', t', u_k') e^{-(t-t')/\tau} dt' + e^{-t/\tau} (f_s)_0(x^0, 0, u_k^0), \tag{13}$$

where $x_i' = x_i - u_i'(t - t') - \frac{1}{2}\phi_i(t - t')^2$ denotes the particle trajectories in physical space, $u_i' = u_i - \phi_i(t - t')$ is the particle velocities under acceleration, (x^0, u^0) is the initial location in the phase space for the particle that passes through the cell interface at time t, and $(f_s)_0$ is the particle distribution function of species s at the beginning of the n-th time step.

In the numerical algorithm, the initial gas distribution function $(f_s)_0$ of each gas component s around the cell interface $x_{i+1/2}$ is reconstructed as follows:

$$(f_s)_0(x, 0, u_k) = \begin{cases} (f_s)_{i+1/2,k}^L + (\sigma_s)_{i,k} x, & x \leq 0, \\ (f_s)_{i+1/2,k}^R + (\sigma_s)_{i+1,k} x, & x > 0, \end{cases} \tag{14}$$

where $(f_s)_{i+1/2,k}^{L,R}$ are the reconstructed values of the initial distribution functions from both sides of the cell interface. Based on the reconstructed distribution functions, the macroscopic conservative variables at a cell interface can be evaluated through

$$\mathbf{W}_s = \sum_{u_k>0} f_{i+1/2,k}^L \psi d\Xi + \sum_{u_k<0} f_{i+1/2,k}^R \psi d\Xi,$$

which can be used to determine the modified macroscopic variables $\mathbf{W}_s'$ in Equation (5) and the equilibrium distribution $(f_s)_0^+$ in Equation (4).

For the second part of the integral solution, the equilibrium distribution is expanded in space and time around a cell interface as

$$f_s^+ = (f_s)_0^+ \left[1 + (1 - H[x]) a^L x + H[x] a^R x + At \right], \tag{15}$$

where $H[x]$ is the Heaviside step function. Here, a_s^L, a_s^R, and A_s are from the Taylor expansion of a Maxwellian:

$$a_s^{L,R} = a_1^{L,R} + a_2^{L,R} u + a_3^{L,R} \frac{1}{2} u^2 = a_\alpha^{L,R} \psi_\alpha,$$

$$A_s = A_1 + A_2 u + A_3 \frac{1}{2} u^2 = A_\alpha \psi_\alpha.$$

The spatial slopes a_s^L, a_s^R can be obtained from the slopes of modified conservative variables on both sides of a cell interface:

$$\left(\frac{\partial \mathbf{W}_s'}{\partial x} \right)^L = \int a_s^L (f_s)_0^+ \psi d\Xi, \quad \left(\frac{\partial \mathbf{W}_s'}{\partial x} \right)^R = \int a_s^R (f_s)_0^+ \psi d\Xi.$$

The time derivative A_s of f_s^+ is related to the temporal variation of conservative flow variables:

$$\frac{\partial \mathbf{W}_s'}{\partial t} = \int A_s (f_s)_0^+ \psi d\Xi,$$

and it can be calculated via the time derivative of the overall compatibility condition for the gas mixture:

$$\frac{d}{dt} \int \sum_{r=1}^s (f_r^+ - f_r) \psi d\Xi \Big|_{x=0, t=0} = 0.$$

Once we determine all the coefficients, the integral solution can be rewritten as

$$\begin{aligned}
f_s(0, t, u_k) =& \left(1 - e^{-t/\tau}\right)(f_s)_0^+ \\
&+ \left(\tau(-1 + e^{-t/\tau}) + te^{-t/\tau}\right) a_s^{L,R} u_k (f_s)_0^+ \\
&- \left[\tau\left(\tau(-1 + e^{-t/\tau}) + te^{-t/\tau}\right) + \frac{1}{2}t^2 e^{-t/\tau}\right] a_s^{L,R} \phi_x (f_s)_0^+ \\
&+ \tau\left(t/\tau - 1 + e^{-t/\tau}\right) A_s (f_s)_0^+ \\
&+ e^{-t/\tau}\left[\left((f_s)_{i+1/2,k^0}^L + \left(-(u_k - \phi_x t)t - \frac{1}{2}\phi_x t^2\right)(\sigma_s)_{i,k^0}\right) H[u_k - \frac{1}{2}\phi_x t] \right.\\
&\left. + \left((f_s)_{i+1/2,k^0}^R + \left(-(u_k - \phi_x t)t - \frac{1}{2}\phi_x t^2\right)(\sigma_s)_{i+1,k^0}\right)(1 - H[u_k - \frac{1}{2}\phi_x t])\right],
\end{aligned} \tag{16}$$

from which we can evaluate the numerical fluxes for both the particle distribution function and macroscopic conservative variables.

3.2. Two-Dimensional Case

Following the integral solution of the relaxation model, it is natural to extended the UGKS to the multidimensional case. Under the force $\phi = (\phi_x, \phi_y)$, the integral solution of the AAP kinetic model in the two-dimensional Cartesian coordinate system is written as

$$\begin{aligned}
f_s(x, y, t, u, v) =& \frac{1}{\tau} \int_{t^n}^{t} f_s^+(x', y', t', u', v') e^{-(t-t')/\tau} dt' \\
&+ e^{-(t-t^n)/\tau} (f_s)_0^n (x^n, y^n, t^n, u^n, v^n),
\end{aligned} \tag{17}$$

where $x' = x - u'(t - t') - \frac{1}{2}\phi_x(t - t')^2$, $y' = y - v'(t - t') - \frac{1}{2}\phi_y(t - t')^2$, $u' = u - \phi_x(t - t')$, and $v' = v - \phi_y(t - t')$. For simplicity, we will drop the subscript s to denote a single gas species.

In the unified scheme, at the center of a cell interface $(x_{i+1/2}, y_j)$, the solution $f_{i+1/2,j,k,l}$ is constructed from the integral solution Equation (17). With the notations $x_{i+1/2} = 0, y_j = 0$ at $t^n = 0$, the time-dependent interface distribution function for species s goes to

$$\begin{aligned}
f(0, 0, t, u_k, v_l) =& \frac{1}{\tau} \int_0^t f^+(x', y', t', u'_k, v'_l) e^{-(t-t')/\tau} dt' \\
&+ e^{-t/\tau} f_0(-u_k t + \frac{1}{2}\phi_x t^2, -v_l t + \frac{1}{2}\phi_y t^2, 0, u_k - \phi_x t, v_l - \phi_y t).
\end{aligned}$$

To second-order accuracy, the initial gas distribution function f_0 is reconstructed as

$$f_0(x, y, 0, u_k, v_l) = \begin{cases} f_{i+1/2,j,k,l}^L + \sigma_{i,j,k,l} x + \theta_{i,j,k,l} y, & x \leq 0, \\ f_{i+1/2,j,k,l}^R + \sigma_{i+1,j,k,l} x + \theta_{i+1,j,k,l} y, & x > 0, \end{cases} \tag{18}$$

where $f_{i+1/2,j,k,l}^L$ and $f_{i+1/2,j,k,l}^R$ are the reconstructed initial distribution functions on the left- and right-hand sides of a cell interface. The slope of f at the (i, j)-thcell and the (k, l)-thdiscretized velocity point in the x-direction and y-direction are denoted by $\sigma_{i,j,k,l}$ and $\theta_{i,j,k,l}$.

The modified equilibrium distribution function around a cell interface is constructed as

$$f^+ = f_0^+ \left[1 + (1 - H[x])a^L x + H[x]a^R x + by + At\right],$$

where f_0^+ is the equilibrium distribution at $(x = 0, t = 0)$. The coefficients above can be determined in the same way as the one-dimensional case.

The time-dependent interface distribution function is written as

$$
\begin{aligned}
f(0,0,t,u_k,v_l) =& \left(1 - e^{-t/\tau}\right) f_0^+ \\
&+ \left(\tau(-1+e^{-t/\tau}) + te^{-t/\tau}\right) a^{L,R} u_k f_0^+ \\
&- \left[\tau\left(\tau(-1+e^{-t/\tau}) + te^{-t/\tau}\right) + \frac{1}{2}t^2 e^{-t/\tau}\right] a^{L,R} \phi_x f_0^+ \\
&+ \left(\tau(-1+e^{-t/\tau}) + te^{-t/\tau}\right) b v_l f_0^+ \\
&- \left[\tau\left(\tau(-1+e^{-t/\tau}) + te^{-t/\tau}\right) + \frac{1}{2}t^2 e^{-t/\tau}\right] b \phi_y f_0^+ \\
&+ \tau\left(t/\tau - 1 + e^{-t/\tau}\right) A f_0^+ \\
&+ e^{-t/\tau} \left[\left(f_{i+1/2,k^0,l^0}^L + \left(-(u_k - \phi_x t)t - \frac{1}{2}\phi_x t^2\right) \sigma_{i,k^0,l^0}\right.\right. \\
&+ \left(-(v_l - \phi_y t)t - \frac{1}{2}\phi_y t^2\right) \theta_{i,k^0,l^0} \bigg) H[u_k - \frac{1}{2}\phi_x t] \\
&+ \left(f_{i+1/2,k^0,l^0}^R + \left(-(u_k - \phi_x t)t - \frac{1}{2}\phi_x t^2\right) \sigma_{i+1,k^0,l^0}\right. \\
&+ \left.\left.\left(-(v_l - \phi_y t)t - \frac{1}{2}\phi_y t^2\right) \theta_{i+1,k^0,l^0} \right)(1 - H[u_k - \frac{1}{2}\phi_x t])\right].
\end{aligned}
\tag{19}
$$

The extension of the above method to the three-dimensional case is straightforward.

3.3. Update Algorithm

With the cell-averaged distribution function for species s in the gas mixture:

$$
f_{x_i,y_j,t^n,u_k,v_l} = f_{i,j,k,l}^n = \frac{1}{\Omega_{i,j}(x,y)\Omega_{k,l}(u,v)} \int_{\Omega_{i,j}} \int_{\Omega_{k,l}} f(x,y,t^n,u,v)dxdydudv,
$$

the direct modeling for its evolution gives the conservation laws of macroscopic variables and the particle distribution function in a discretized space:

$$
\begin{aligned}
\mathbf{W}_{i,j}^{n+1} =& \mathbf{W}_{i,j}^n + \frac{1}{\Omega_{i,j}} \int_{t^n}^{t^{n+1}} \sum_{i=1} \Delta \mathbf{L}_i \cdot \mathbf{F}_i dt \\
&+ \frac{1}{\Omega_{i,j}} \int_{t^n}^{t^{n+1}} \int_{\Omega_{i,j}} \mathbf{Q}_{i,j} dxdydt + \frac{1}{\Omega_{i,j}} \int_{t^n}^{t^{n+1}} \int_{\Omega_{i,j}} \mathbf{G}_{i,j} dxdydt,
\end{aligned}
\tag{20}
$$

$$
\begin{aligned}
f_{i,j,k,l}^{n+1} =& f_{i,j,k,l}^n + \frac{1}{\Omega_{i,j}} \int_{t^n}^{t^{n+1}} \sum_{i=1} u_i \hat{f}_i(t) \Delta L_i dt \\
&+ \frac{1}{\Omega_{i,j}} \int_{t^n}^{t^{n+1}} \int_{\Omega_{i,j}} Q(f) dxdydt + \frac{1}{\Omega_{i,j}} \int_{t^n}^{t^{n+1}} \int_{\Omega_{i,j}} G(f) dxdydt,
\end{aligned}
\tag{21}
$$

where $\mathbf{F}_i$ is the flux of conservative variables across the cell interface $\Delta \mathbf{L}_i = \Delta L_i \mathbf{n}_i$, $\hat{f}_i$ is the time-dependent gas distribution function at the cell interface, and ΔL_i is the cell interface length. $\mathbf{Q}_{i,j}$, $Q(f)$ are the source terms from intermolecular collisions, and $\mathbf{G}_{i,j}$, $G(f)$ are the external forcing terms:

$$
\begin{aligned}
Q(f) &= \frac{f_{i,j,k,l}^+ - f_{i,j,k,l}^{n+1/2}}{\tau}, \\
\mathbf{Q}_{i,j} &= \int_{\Omega_{k,l}} \frac{f_{i,j,k,l}^+ - f_{i,j,k,l}^{n+1/2}}{\tau} \psi dudv,
\end{aligned}
\tag{22}
$$

$$G(f) = -\phi_x \frac{\partial}{\partial u} f_{i,j,k,l}^{n+1/2} - \phi_y \frac{\partial}{\partial v} f_{i,j,k,l}^{n+1/2},$$
$$\mathbf{G}_{i,j} = \int_{\Omega_{k,l}} \left(-\phi_x \frac{\partial}{\partial u} f_{i,j,k,l}^{n+1/2} - \phi_y \frac{\partial}{\partial v} f_{i,j,k,l}^{n+1/2} \right) \psi du dv.$$
(23)

In the UGKS, we use the semi-implicit method to model the collision term and the fully implicit one for the external forcing term:

$$\begin{aligned} f_{i,j,k,l}^{n+1} = & f_{i,j,k,l}^n + \frac{1}{\Omega_{i,j}} \left(F_{i-1/2,j,k,l} - F_{i+1/2,j,k,l} \right) + \frac{1}{\Omega_{i,j}} \left(F_{i,j-1/2,k,l} - F_{i,j+1/2,k,l} \right) \\ & + \frac{\Delta t}{2} \left(\frac{f_{i,j,k,l}^{+(n+1)} - f_{i,j,k,l}^{n+1}}{\tau^{n+1}} + \frac{f_{i,j,k,l}^{+(n)} - f_{i,j,k,l}^n}{\tau^n} \right) - \Delta t \left(\phi_x \frac{\partial}{\partial u} f_{i,j,k,l}^{n+1} + \phi_y \frac{\partial}{\partial v} f_{i,j,k,l}^{n+1} \right). \end{aligned}$$
(24)

In order to update the gas distribution function implicitly, we solve Equation (20) first, and its solution can be used for the construction of the equilibrium state in Equation (24) at t^{n+1}. In the current scheme, the collision term for macroscopic variables is treated as

$$\frac{1}{\Omega_{i,j}} \int_{t^n}^{t^{n+1}} \int_{\Omega_{i,j}} \mathbf{Q}_{i,j} dx dy dt = \frac{\Delta t}{\tau} [(\mathbf{W}')^n - \mathbf{W}^n],$$
(25)

where $(\mathbf{W}')^n$ is the modified macroscopic conservative variable. For the external forcing source, we adopted the numerical methodology proposed by Slyz and Prendergast [19], where the energy source term from the external force can be absorbed into the energy flux as $\Phi \mathbf{F}^\rho$, where $\mathbf{F}^\rho$ is the mass flux, to ensure the accurate conservation of energy. A similar implicit upwind update as [11] was adopted to update the particle distribution function.

With the help of the implicit update algorithm, the time step is not restricted by the collision time and is fully determined by the CFL condition:

$$\Delta t = \text{CFL} \min \left\{ \frac{\Delta x \Delta y}{u_{max} \Delta y + v_{max} \Delta x}, \frac{\Delta u \Delta v}{|\phi_x| \Delta v + |\phi_y| \Delta u} \right\},$$
(26)

where CFL is the CFL number, $\{u_{max} = \max(|u_k|), v_{max} = \max(|v_l|)\}$ is the largest discretized particle velocity of all gas components in the x- and y-directions, and $\{\Delta u, \Delta v\}$ is the distance between two neighboring velocity points.

3.4. Analysis on the Well-Balanced Property

In this part, we prove the well-balanced property of the current scheme theoretically. In the continuum regime with intensive intermolecular collisions, the fluid element picture can be used to describe the bulk property of flow transport. We adopted the one-dimensional Euler equations for multicomponent flow under force field Φ, i.e.,

$$\begin{aligned} (\rho_1)_t + (\rho_1 U)_x &= 0, \\ (\rho_2)_t + (\rho_2 U)_x &= 0, \\ (\rho U)_t + (\rho U^2 + p)_x &= \rho \phi_x, \\ (\rho E)_t + ((\rho E + p) U)_x &= \rho U \phi_x. \end{aligned}$$

where $\rho, \rho U, \rho E, p$ are the total density, momentum, energy, and pressure. It is clear that the equations above allow a simply hydrostatic solution where the macroscopic flow is absent and the pressure gradient is balanced by the density stratification:

$$\rho = \rho(x) = \rho_1(x) + \rho_2(x), U = 0, p_x = (p_1)_x + (p_2)_x = (\rho_1 + \rho_2)\phi_x.$$

Given a constant force field ϕ_x, the above solution can be rewritten as

$$\rho = \rho_1 + \rho_2 = \rho_0 \exp\left(\frac{\phi_x x}{RT}\right), U = 0, p = p_1 + p_2 = p_0 \exp\left(\frac{\phi_x x}{RT}\right), \tag{27}$$

where R is the gas constant. Such a steady-state solution needs to be maintained due to the exact balance between the gravitational source term and the inhomogeneous flux function for each gas component in the mixture, i.e.,

$$\frac{1}{\Delta x}\int_{t^n}^{t^{n+1}} (F_{i-1/2} - F_{i+1/2})dt + \frac{1}{\Delta x}\int_{t^n}^{t^{n+1}}\int_{x_{1-1/2}}^{x_{i+1/2}} G_i dt = 0. \tag{28}$$

In the hydrodynamic scale where $\Delta t \gg \tau$, under hydrostatic balance, the intensive particle collision will converge the interface distribution function in Equation (16) to

$$f_{i+1/2} = f_0^+ - \tau a u f_0^+ - \tau^2 a \phi_x f_0^+. \tag{29}$$

The velocity moments $\int u^\alpha f_0^+ du = \rho \langle u^\alpha \rangle$ of the above solution can be evaluated analytically. The coefficient a in Equation (29) can be determined by the slopes of conservative variables:

$$a_3 = \frac{4(\lambda_0')^2}{(K+1)\rho_0}\left[2(\rho E')_x + \left((U_0')^2 - \frac{K+1}{2\lambda_0'}\right)\rho_x - 2\bar{U}_0(\rho U')_x\right],$$

$$a_2 = \frac{2\lambda_0'}{\rho_0}[(\rho U')_x - U_0'\rho_x] - U_0' a_3,$$

$$a_1 = \frac{1}{\rho_0}\rho_x - U_0' a_2 - \frac{1}{2}\left((U_0')^2 + \frac{K+1}{2\lambda_0'}\right)a_3,$$

where (U_0', λ_0') are the modified primitive variables in Equation (5). In the isothermal and static case, the above equation can be further reduced to

$$a_1 = \frac{1}{\rho_0}\frac{\partial \rho}{\partial x}, a_2 = a_3 = 0.$$

Therefore, the fluxes of density, momentum, and energy can be obtained via $F_{i+1/2} = \int u f_{i+1/2}\psi du$, i.e.,

$$F_{i+1/2}^\rho = 0,$$
$$F_{i+1/2}^{\rho U} = \frac{\rho_{i+1/2}}{2\lambda'},$$
$$F_{i+1/2}^{\rho E} = 0.$$

At the same time, the source term in Equation (28) is

$$\mathbf{G}_i = \int -\phi_x f_u \psi du.$$

The source term from the external force can be integrated as

$$G^\rho = 0,$$
$$G^{\rho U} = \rho\phi_x,$$
$$G^{\rho E} = \rho U \phi_x = 0.$$

For the momentum balance equation, we can use the exponential density distribution in Equation (27) to check the well-balanced relationship in Equation (28). As the temperature is uniform in the flow domain, the modified λ' is equivalent to each component's λ, and the balance relationship is

$$\int_{x_{i-1/2}}^{x_{i+1/2}} G_i^{\rho u} dx = \int_{x_{i-1/2}}^{x_{i+1/2}} \rho \phi_x dx = RT(\rho_{i+1/2} - \rho_{i-1/2}) = -(F_{i-1/2} - F_{i+1/2}),$$

from which we can see that the well-balanced property is precisely satisfied in the current scheme.

In another limit of the Knudsen regime, where $\tau \gg \Delta t$, the current method recovers a purely upwind method:

$$f_{i+1/2,k} = \begin{cases} f_{i+1/2,k^0}^L + \left(-u_k t + \frac{1}{2}\phi_x t^2\right)\sigma_{i,k^0}, & u_k - \frac{1}{2}\phi_x t \geq 0, \\ f_{i+1/2,k^0}^R + \left(-u_k t + \frac{1}{2}\phi_x t^2\right)\sigma_{i+1,k^0}, & u_k - \frac{1}{2}\phi_x t < 0. \end{cases}$$

With the forcing effect on each particle, the particle distribution function will become distorted in the velocity space, and the deviation from the equilibrium state is restricted with the particle collision time τ. There is no more isothermal equilibrium due to the non-equilibrium heat transfer induced by the force field, as analyzed in [20]. In this case, the good hydrostatic balance is only a coarse-grained concept based on statistical averaging.

3.5. Summary of the Algorithm

A detailed numerical solution algorithm for the current well-balanced UGKS is provided in Figure 1, and its implementation is available at the GitHub repository [21].

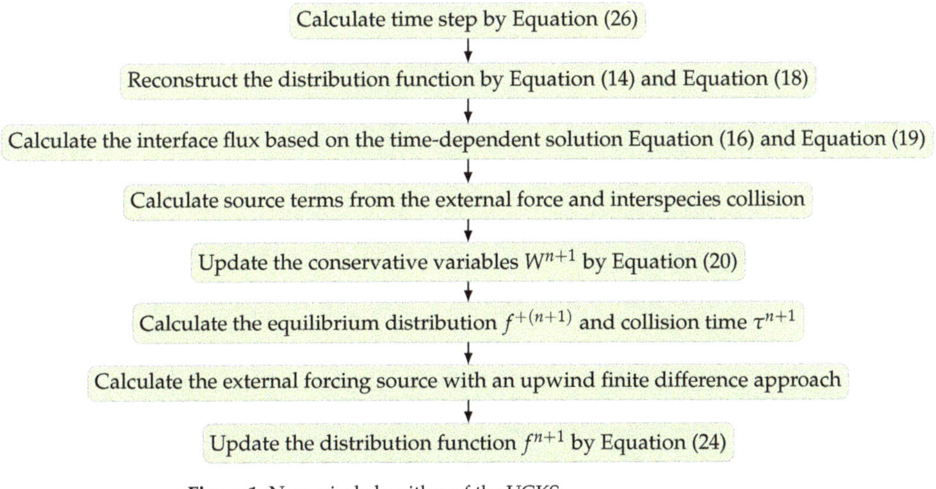

```
Calculate time step by Equation (26)
            ↓
Reconstruct the distribution function by Equation (14) and Equation (18)
            ↓
Calculate the interface flux based on the time-dependent solution Equation (16) and Equation (19)
            ↓
Calculate source terms from the external force and interspecies collision
            ↓
Update the conservative variables W^{n+1} by Equation (20)
            ↓
Calculate the equilibrium distribution f^{+(n+1)} and collision time τ^{n+1}
            ↓
Calculate the external forcing source with an upwind finite difference approach
            ↓
Update the distribution function f^{n+1} by Equation (24)
```

Figure 1. Numerical algorithm of the UGKS.

4. Numerical Experiments

In this section, we present numerical examples of a binary gas mixture to validate the well-balanced UGKS for multiscale and multicomponent flow. Multiscale simulations from free molecule flow to continuum two-species Euler solutions under a external force field are presented to demonstrate the capability of the unified scheme. The flow features in different regimes can be well captured by the unified scheme. Some interesting non-equilibrium phenomena, such as the characteristic behavior of different gas components in different flow regimes, are discussed. The hard sphere (HS) monatomic gas was employed in all test cases. With the overall number density $n = n_1 + n_2$ and molecular diameter $d = (d_1 + d_2)/2$, the Knudsen number can be defined as

$$\mathrm{Kn} = \frac{1}{\sqrt{2}\pi d^2 n},$$

and the parameter θ_{12} in Equation (7) becomes

$$\theta_{12} = \frac{4\sqrt{\pi}}{3}\left(\frac{1}{\lambda_1} + \frac{1}{\lambda_2}\right)^{1/2}\frac{1}{\sqrt{2}\pi\mathrm{Kn}(n_1 + n_2)},$$

with which we can determine the modified macroscopic variables and collision frequency in Equations (5) and (6). The parameter β in Equation (6) was chosen to be the unit.

In the current calculations, we considered a binary gas mixture with $\gamma = 5/3$ only. With the defined reference molecular mass and number density:

$$m_{ref} = \frac{m_1 n_{1ref} + m_2 n_{2ref}}{n_{1ref} + n_{2ref}}, \rho_0 = m_{ref}n_{ref} = m_{ref}(n_{1ref} + n_{2ref}),$$

the dimensionless variables are introduced as

$$\hat{x} = \frac{x}{L_0}, \hat{y} = \frac{y}{L_0}, \hat{\rho} = \frac{\rho}{\rho_0}, \hat{T} = \frac{T}{T_0},$$

$$\hat{u}_i = \frac{u_i}{(2kT_0/m_{ref})^{1/2}}, \hat{U}_i = \frac{U_i}{(2kT_0/m_{ref})^{1/2}}, \hat{f} = \frac{f}{n_0(2kT_0/m_{ref})^{3/2}},$$

$$\hat{P}_{ij} = \frac{P_{ij}}{\rho_0(2kT_0/m_{ref})}, \hat{q}_i = \frac{q_i}{(\rho_0/2)(2kT_0/m_{ref})^{3/2}}, \hat{\phi}_i = \frac{\phi_i}{2kT_0/(L_0 m_{ref})},$$

where u_i is the particle velocity, U_i is the macroscopic flow velocity, P_{ij} is the stress tensor, q_i is the heat flux, and ϕ_i is the external force acceleration. We drop the hat notation to denote dimensionless variables for simplicity henceforth.

4.1. Validation

In this part, we provide benchmark test cases to validate the current method. Both convection-dominated and diffusion-dominated flow problems are considered.

4.1.1. Normal Shock Structure

The first case is the normal shock structure for a binary gas mixture [22]. The two components A and B are assumed to have a molecular diameter and different masses $m_A/m_B = 2$. The upstream and downstream statuses are coupled by the Rankine–Hugoniot relationship, and the initial distribution functions are set as Maxwellian.

In the simulation, 100 uniform physical meshes were employed in physical domain $x \in [-25, 25]$ and 101 quadrature points were used in velocity space $u \in [-10, 10]$. The upstream Mach number was Ma = 1.5, and the Knudsen number was Kn = 1.0. The CFL number was set to be 0.7. Different number density fractions $n_A/(n_A + n_B) = 0.1, 0.5$, and 0.9 were considered.

Figures 2–4 present the normalized numerical solutions under different density concentrations. The benchmark solutions from the full Boltzmann equation computed by the fast spectral method [23,24] are provided as a reference. As can be seen, the results from the UGKS and the Boltzmann equation exhibit good agreement under different number density fractions. This test case validates the UGKS in convection-dominated non-equilibrium flows.

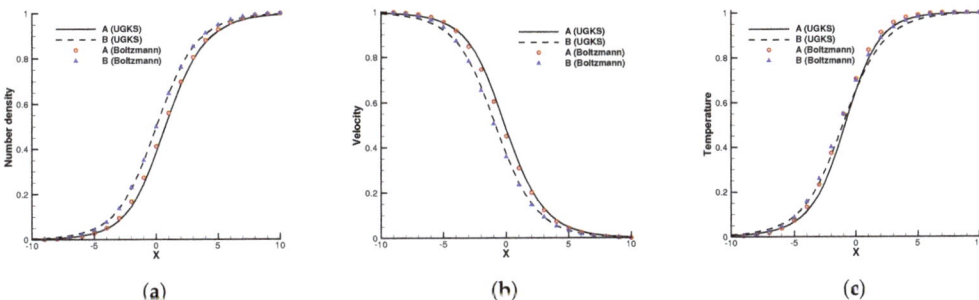

Figure 2. Normal shock profiles at $n_A/(n_A + n_B) = 0.1$. (**a**) Number density. (**b**) Velocity. (**c**) Temperature.

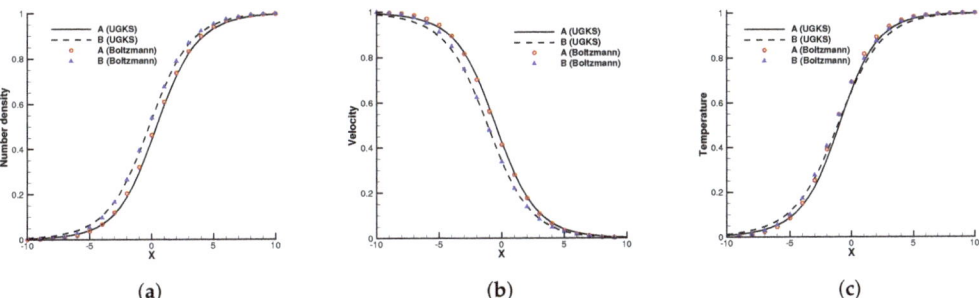

Figure 3. Normal shock profiles at $n_A/(n_A + n_B) = 0.5$. (**a**) Number density. (**b**) Velocity. (**c**) Temperature.

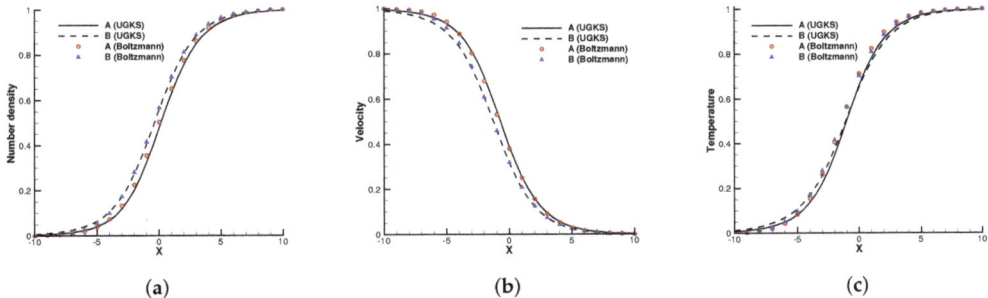

Figure 4. Normal shock profiles at $n_A/(n_A + n_B) = 0.9$. (**a**) Number density. (**b**) Velocity. (**c**) Temperature.

4.1.2. Fourier Flow

The second case is the Fourier flow. The two gas components were set in the same way as Section 4.1.1. The heat transfer problem was considered between two walls with different temperatures, i.e., $T_L = 1$ and $T_R = 0.5$. Maxwell's diffusive boundary condition was considered at both ends. The initial gas was stationary and had a uniform density and temperature.

In the simulation, 100 uniform physical meshes were employed in physical domain $x \in [0, 1]$ and 72 quadrature points were used in velocity space $u \in [-8, 8]$. The CFL number was set to be 0.7. Different Knudsen numbers were considered, i.e., Kn = 1 and 0.1.

Figures 5 and 6 present the temperature and density profiles. The benchmark full Boltzmann solutions are provided as a reference. It is clear that good agreement between the UGKS and reference solutions was achieved. In the rarefied regime, the number density profiles of two components deviate. Due to the different average molecular speeds, light molecules B tend to move towards hot regions, while heavy molecules to cold regions. This is a typical non-equilibrium flow phenomenon, which corresponds to the Soret effect [25]. In addition, the conservation of the system was checked. After 50 dimensionless time units when the convergent solution was obtained, the absolute error of the total mass was below 0.004‰. This test case validates the UGKS in diffusion-dominated non-equilibrium flows.

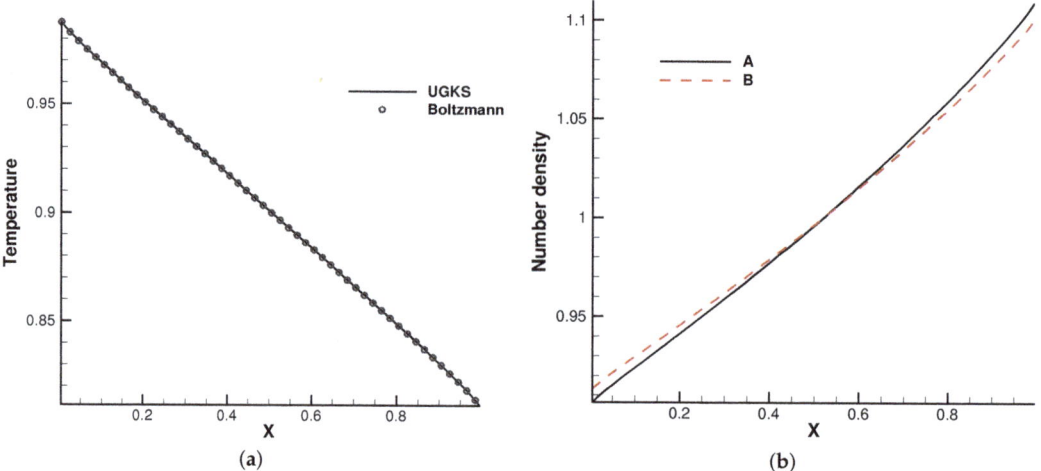

Figure 5. Kn = 0.1. (**a**) Temperature. (**b**) Number density.

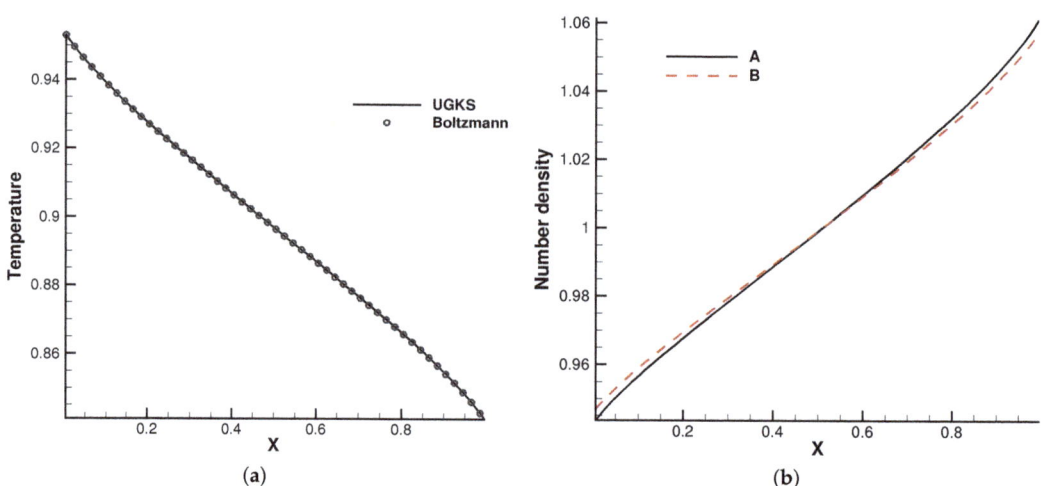

Figure 6. Kn = 1. (**a**) Temperature. (**b**) Number density.

4.2. Perturbed Hydrostatic Equilibrium Solution

In the first test case, we studied the one-dimensional wave propagation from the hydrostatic equilibrium flow field [3]. The binary gas mixture was stillinitially at the hydrostatic equilibrium solution, and the domain $x \in [0, 1]$ was under the external force field $\phi_x = -1.0$, which points towards the negative x-direction, i.e.,

$$\rho_0(x) = p_0(x) = \exp(\phi_x x), u_0(x) = 0.$$

The equilibrium solution was perturbed by the following pressure perturbation:

$$p(x, t = 0) = p_0(x) + 0.01 \exp(-100(x - 0.5)^2).$$

Here, ρ_0 and p_0 are the total density and pressure. In the gas mixture, the molecular mass ratio m_2/m_1 and number density ratio n_2/n_1 need to be specified to distribute the partition of density and pressure for each gas component.

In the simulation, 100 uniform physical meshes were employed in the physical domain and 101 quadrature points were used in the velocity space. The continuum flow regime was considered, and the Knudsen number was set as 10^{-5}. Two cases were simulated with different molecular mass and number density ratios. The first case was set up with $m_2/m_1 = 0.8$, $n_2/n_1 = 1$, while in the second case, $m_2/m_1 = 0.5$, $n_2/n_1 = 0.25$. Figure 7 shows the pressure profiles at $t = 0.18$ in the two cases. It can be seen that the small perturbation was well captured by the current well-balanced scheme without destroying the equilibrium solution in the bulk region. Such a capability is due to the unified treatment of particle transports and collisions under an external force field, as analyzed in [3,6]. Due to frequent intermolecular collisions in the continuum regime, different gas components behave coincidentally as a simple gas.

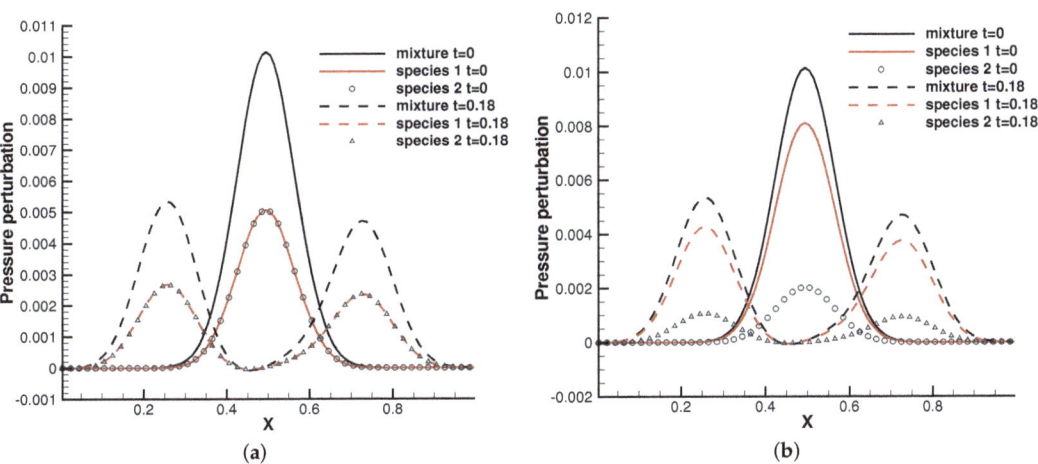

Figure 7. Pressure perturbation from a hydrostatic equilibrium solution. (a) $m_2/m_1 = 0.8$, $n_2/n_1 = 1$. (b) $m_2/m_1 = 0.5$, $n_2/n_1 = 0.25$.

4.3. Riemann Problem under an External Force Field

Next, we considered the discontinuous solutions developed in the hyperbolic system. The Sod shock tube problem was employed as the test case [7]. Similarly, two cases were considered with different molecular mass and number density ratios. In the first case, it was set up with $m_2/m_1 = 0.5$, $n_2/n_1 = 1$, and $m_2/m_1 = 0.5$, $n_2/n_1 = 0.25$ in the second case. The initial condition was set as

$$\rho = 1.0, U = 0.0, p = 1.0, x \leq 0.5,$$

$$\rho = 0.125, U = 0.0, p = 0.1, x > 0.5.$$

In the simulation, the external force $\phi_x = -1.0$ that points leftwards was considered. Different Knudsen numbers in the reference state were considered, Kn = 0.0001, Kn = 0.01, and Kn = 1.0, with respect to different flow regimes. The computational domain $x \in [0, 1]$ was divided into 100 cells, and 101 quadrature points were used in the velocity space. The specular reflection boundary condition was employed at both ends.

The profiles of macroscopic variables at $t = 0.2$ are presented in Figures 8 and 9. Under an external force field, the particles were driven towards the negative x-direction, resulting in the appearance of negative flow velocity near the left tube end. In comparison with the case without gravity, the thermodynamic quantities such as density, temperature, and pressure in the left side of the tube increase all together.

This numerical experiment validates the capability of the current method to simulate discontinuous cross-scale flow physics under an external force field. In the continuum limit with Kn = 0.0001, the limited resolution in space and time results in the two-species Euler solution, and the current scheme plays the role of a shock-capturing algorithm. The frequent collisions prevent the particle penetration between fluid elements, and different gas components show consistent behaviors, just like a single gas. With the increment of the Knudsen number and the collision time, the degree of freedom for the free transport of individual gas components increases and the flow physics changes significantly. There is a smooth transition from the Euler solution of the Riemann problem to a collisionless Boltzmann solution. As different gas components have a specific molecular mass, the light gas transports much faster than the heavier one in the tube, which is shown in Figures 8b and 9b.

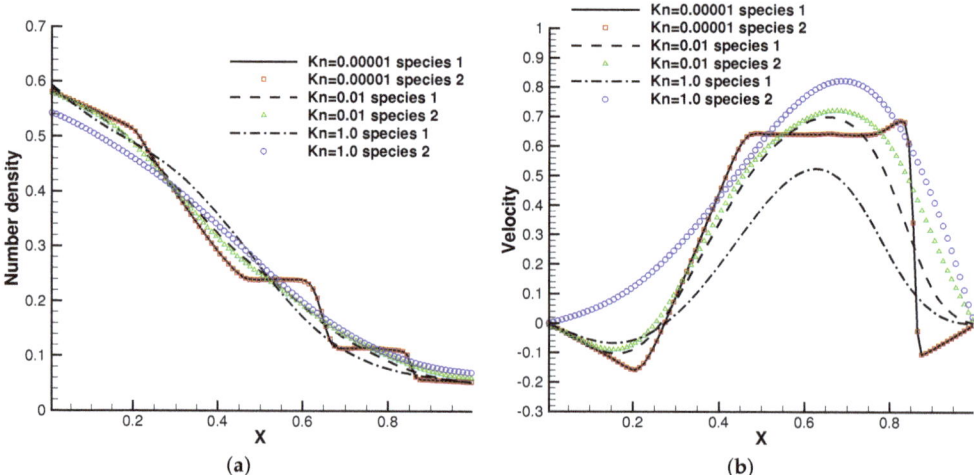

Figure 8. *Cont.*

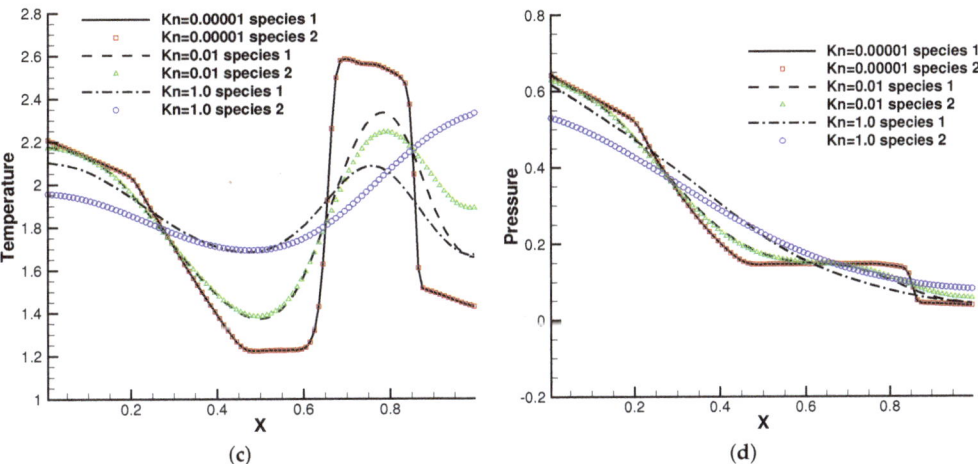

Figure 8. Sod test under an external force field with $m_2/m_1 = 0.5$, $n_2/n_1 = 1$. (**a**) Number density. (**b**) Velocity. (**c**) Temperature. (**d**) Pressure.

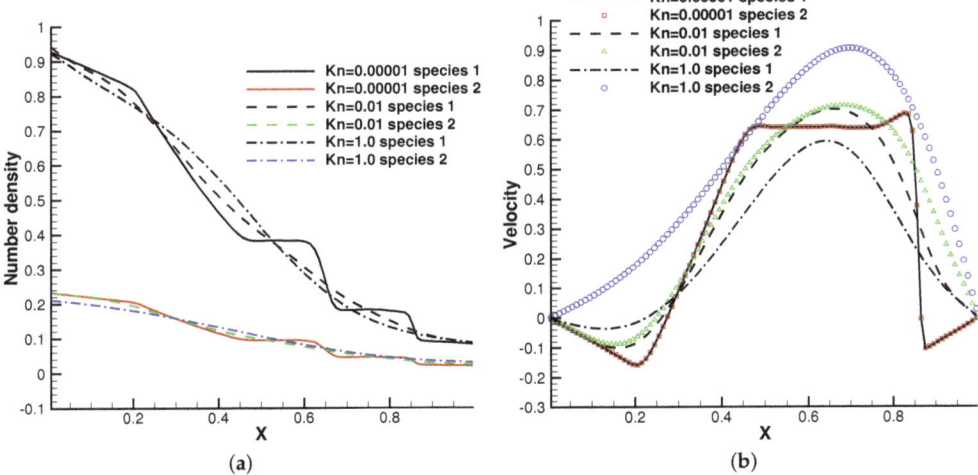

Figure 9. *Cont.*

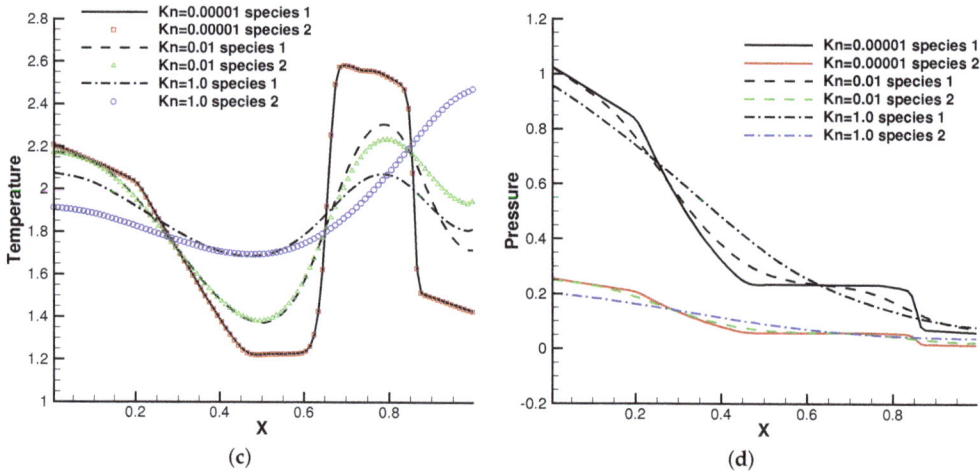

Figure 9. Sod test under an external force field with $m_2/m_1 = 0.5$, $n_2/n_1 = 0.25$. (**a**) Number density. (**b**) Velocity. (**c**) Temperature. (**d**) Pressure.

4.4. Rayleigh–Taylor Instability

We turn to the two-dimensional case and consider the Rayleigh–Taylor instability [3]. The initial condition of the gas dynamic system in a polar coordinate (r, θ) was set as

$$\rho_0(r) = e^{-\alpha(r+r_0)}, p_0(r) = \frac{1.5}{\alpha} e^{-\alpha(r+r_0)}, U_0 = 0,$$

where

$$\begin{cases} \alpha = 2.68, r_0 = 0.258, \ r \leq r_1, \\ \alpha = 5.53, r_0 = -0.308, \ r > r_1, \end{cases} \text{and} \begin{cases} r_1 = 0.6(1 + 0.02\cos(20\theta)), \text{ for density}, \\ r_1 = 0.62324965, \text{ for pressure}. \end{cases}$$

The molecular mass and number density ratio in the gas mixture was set up with $m_2/m_1 = 0.8$, $n_2/n_1 = 1$, and $m_2/m_1 = 0.25$, $n_2/n_1 = 1$. The external force potential satisfies $d\Phi/dr = 1.5$, and the force points towards the origin of the polar coordinates. Different Knudsen numbers in the reference state were considered as Kn = 0.0001, 0.01, and 1.0, The computational domain was divided into 60×60 uniform cells, and 29×29 quadrature points were used in the velocity space. The specular reflection condition was considered at all boundaries. Due to the density inversion contained in the initial flow field, the Rayleigh–Taylor instability will occur naturally as time evolves. A well-balanced method is expected to capture the flow motions around the unstable interface, while keeping the hydrostatic equilibrium solution in the bulk region.

Figures 10 and 11 plot the density contours and cross-sections of densities in all cells versus the radius with $m_2/m_1 = 0.8$ at different output times under different Knudsen numbers Figures 12 and 13 present the same results with $m_2/m_1 = 0.25$. As can be seen, in different flow regimes, different flow physics emerge around the Rayleigh–Taylor interface. In the continuum regime, the frequent intermolecular interactions provide the effective mechanism to quickly initiate and strengthen the flow mixing. As the Kn increases, the particle transport phenomena dominate the flow evolution, and thus, the particles have a greater chance of penetrating directly through the mixing layer into the inner zone. Therefore, the strength of the Rayleigh–Taylor instability is greatly reduced. Due to the fact that different gas components have different molecular masses, the profiles of different species can be different, corresponding to different Knudsen numbers. Figure 14 presents the density profiles of the two components at $t = 0.08$ and $Kn = 0.01$. It is clear that, while the lighter components have already completed the density inversion, the heavy components are still in the mixing process. This is due to the fact that molecules with smaller masses have a faster mean speed. In all cases, it is clear that the hydrostatic solution is well preserved by the current well-balanced scheme, and the mixing of fluids occurs locally.

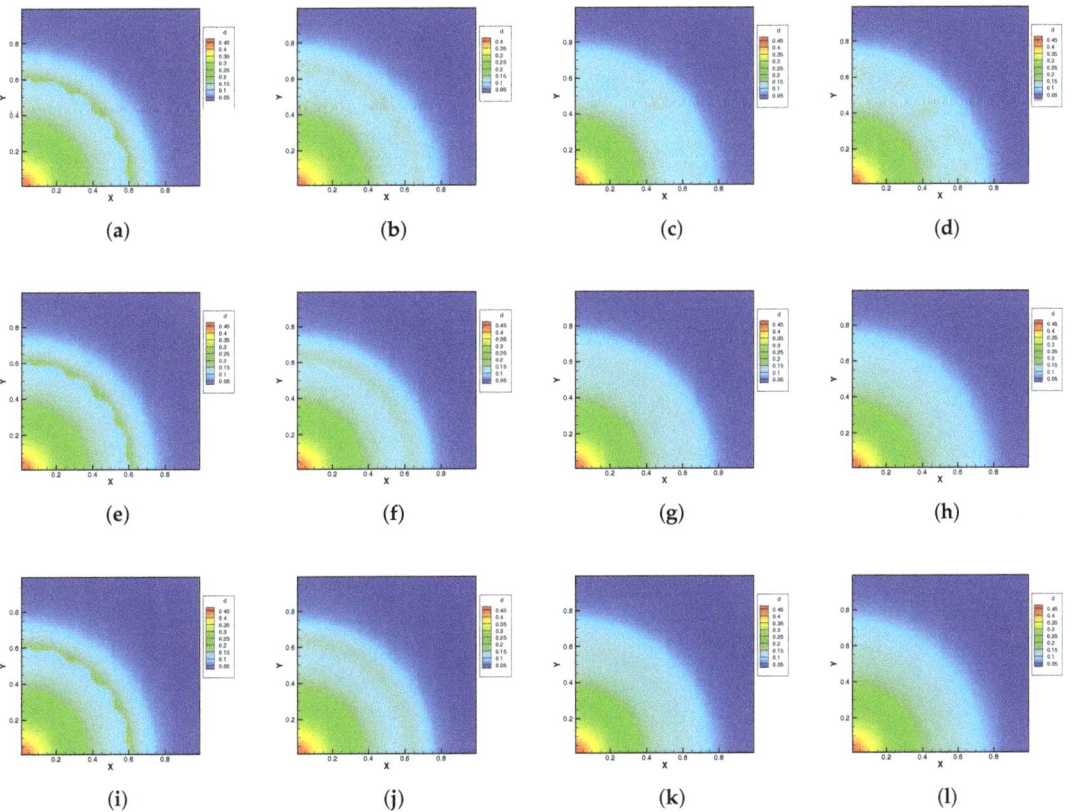

Figure 10. Density evolution under gravity at $m_2/m_1 = 0.8$ and reference Knudsen numbers 0.0001 (1st row), 0.01 (2nd row), and 1 (3rd row). (**a**) t = 0. (**b**) t = 0.8. (**c**) t = 1.4. (**d**) t = 2.0. (**e**) t = 0. (**f**) t = 0.08. (**g**) t = 0.16. (**h**) t = 0.24. (**i**) t = 0. (**j**) t = 0.08. (**k**) t = 0.16. (**l**) t = 0.24.

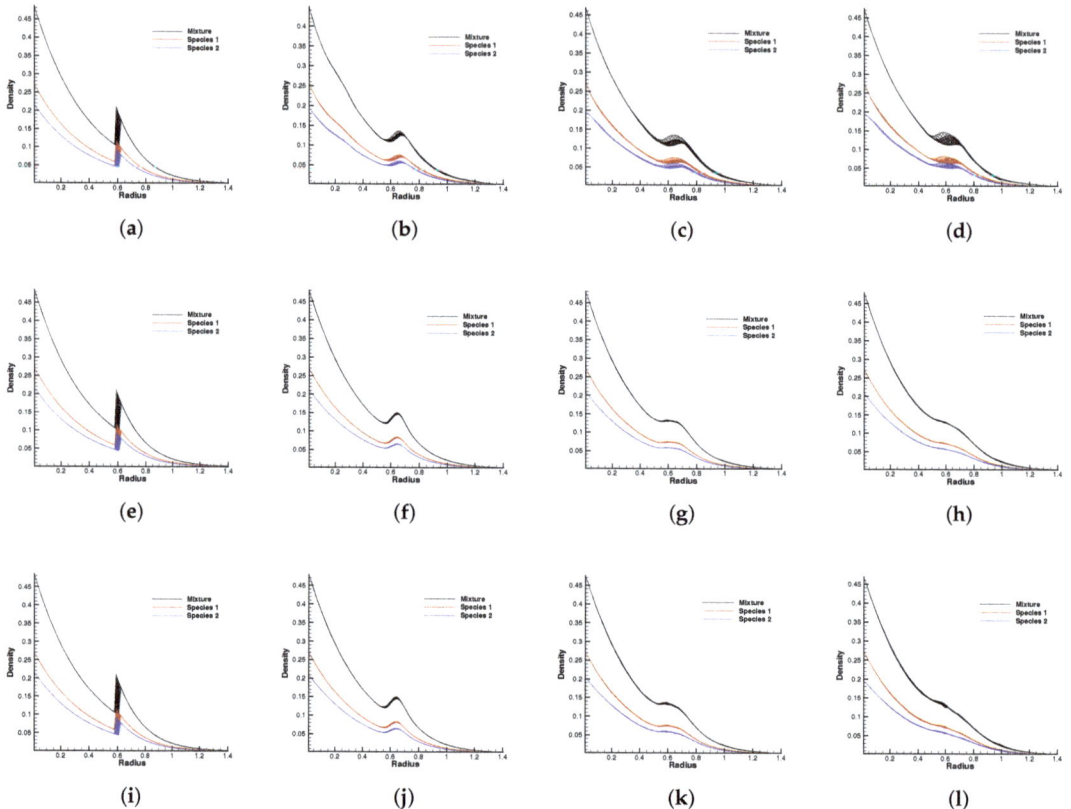

Figure 11. Density distribution along the radial direction at $m_2/m_1 = 0.8$ and reference Knudsen numbers 0.0001 (1st row), 0.01 (2nd row), and 1 (3rd row). (**a**) t = 0. (**b**) t = 0.8. (**c**) t = 1.4. (**d**) t = 2.0. (**e**) t = 0. (**f**) t = 0.08. (**g**) t = 0.16. (**h**) t = 0.24. (**i**) t = 0. (**j**) t = 0.08. (**k**) t = 0.16. (**l**) t = 0.24.

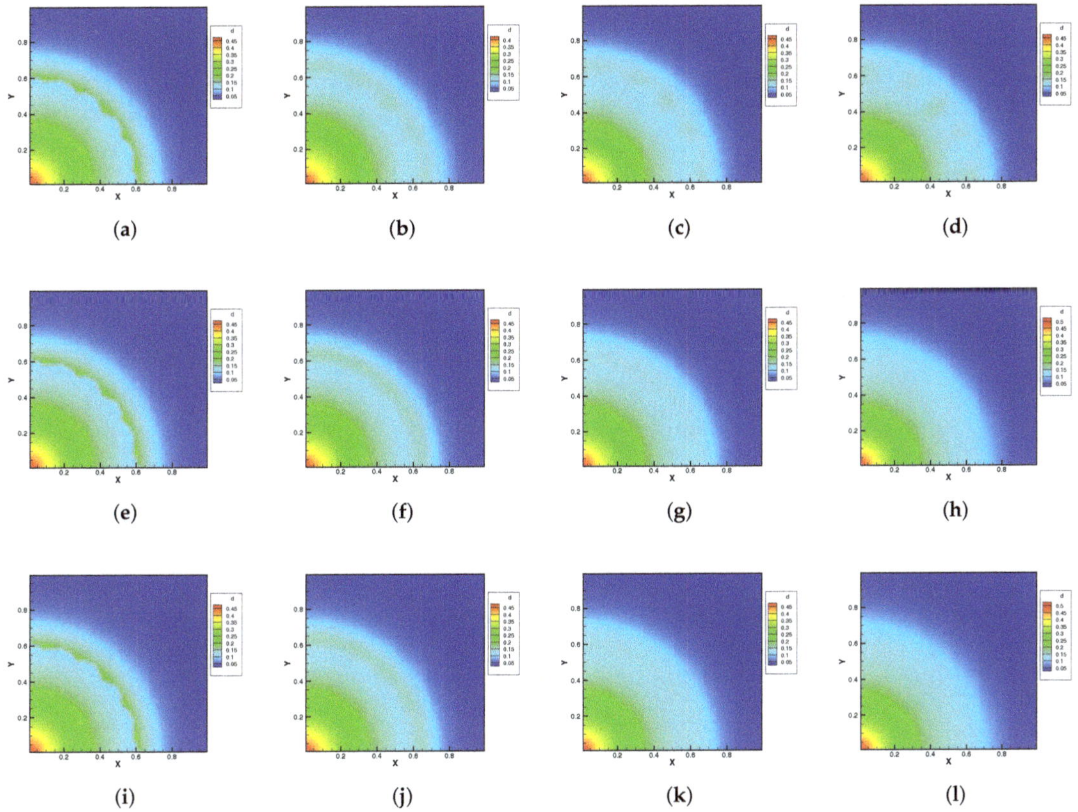

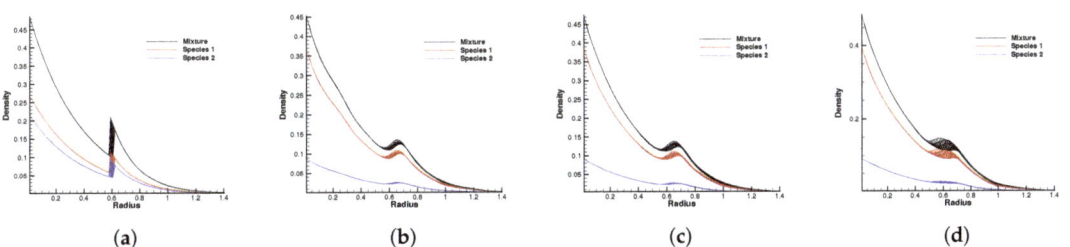

Figure 12. Density evolution under gravity at $m_2/m_1 = 0.25$ and reference Knudsen numbers 0.0001 (1st row), 0.01 (2nd row), and 1 (3rd row). (**a**) t = 0. (**b**) t = 0.8. (**c**) t = 1.4. (**d**) t = 2.0. (**e**) t = 0. (**f**) t = 0.08. (**g**) t = 0.16. (**h**) t = 0.24. (**i**) t = 0. (**j**) t = 0.08. (**k**) t = 0.16. (**l**) t = 0.24.

Figure 13. *Cont.*

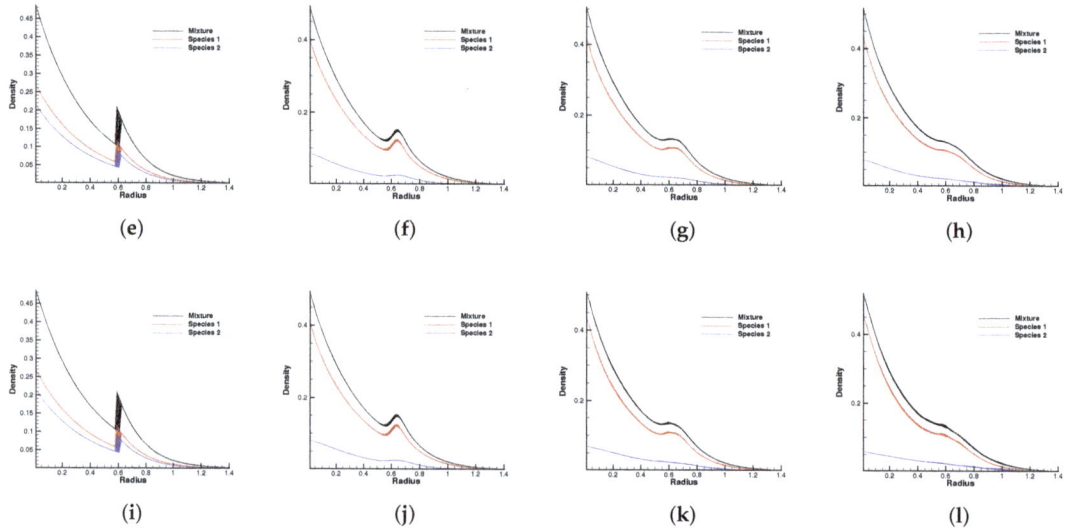

Figure 13. Density distribution along the radial direction at $m_2/m_1 = 0.25$ and reference Knudsen numbers 0.0001 (1st row), 0.01 (2nd row), and 1 (3rd row). (**a**) t = 0. (**b**) t = 0.8. (**c**) t = 1.4. (**d**) t = 2.0. (**e**) t = 0. (**f**) t = 0.08. (**g**) t = 0.16. (**h**) t = 0.24. (**i**) t = 0. (**j**) t = 0.08. (**k**) t = 0.16. (**l**) t = 0.24.

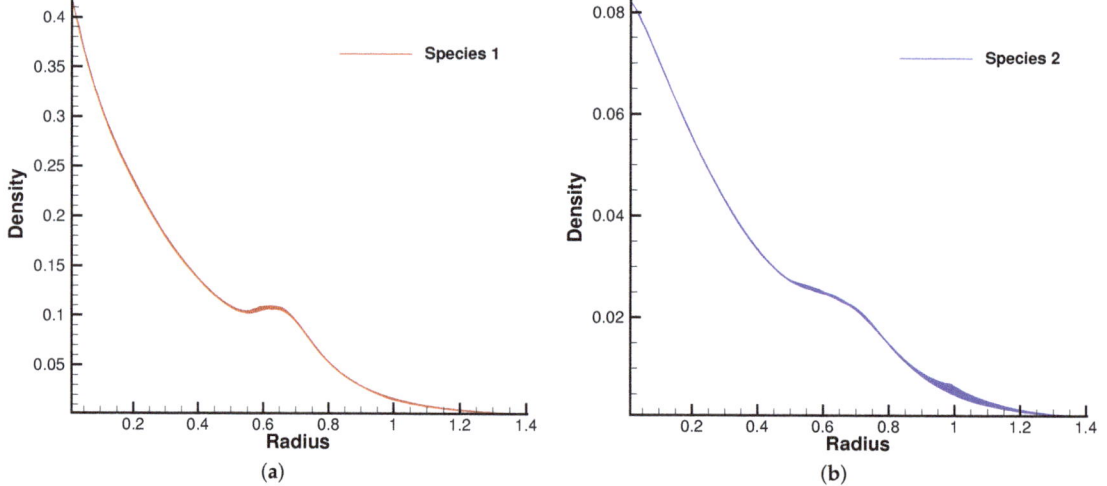

Figure 14. Density distribution for two gas components along the radial direction at $t = 0.08$ with reference Knudsen number 0.01. (**a**) Species 1. (**b**) Species 2.

4.5. Lid-Driven Cavity under Gravity

The lid-driven cavity problem is a standard test case for both hydrodynamic and kinetic solvers, which contains complex flow physics related to compressibility, shearing structure, heat transfer, the boundary effect, non-equilibrium effects, etc. In this case, we calculated a lid-driven cavity problem under an external force, which serves as a typical case for the multiscale algorithms.

A binary gas mixture is enclosed by four walls with $L = 1$. The upper wall moves in a tangential direction with a velocity $U_w = 0.15$. The external force was set to be $\phi_y = 0.0, -0.5, -1.0$, respectively, in the negative y-direction. The magnitude of gravity ϕ_y is denoted by g. The initial density and pressure were set up with

$$\rho(x, y, t = 0) = 2 \exp(\phi_y y), p(x, y, t = 0) = \exp(\phi_y y).$$

The molecular mass and number density ratio in the gas mixture was set up with $m_2/m_1 = 0.5, n_2/n_1 = 1$.

The Knudsen number in the reference state was set as Kn = 0.05. There were 45 × 45 uniform cells used in the physical space and 41 × 41 quadrature points used in the velocity space. Maxwell's diffusive boundary condition was used throughout the computation, and the wall temperature was $T_w = 1$.

Figures 15–17 present the numerical solutions related to different magnitudes of the external force. Due to the existence of a force field, along the forcing direction, the gas density changes significantly along the vertical direction of the cavity, as does the local Knudsen number. As as result, the gas inside the cavity, depending on the position of the y-axis, can stay in different flow regimes. Similar to the results of a single-component gas [26], the temperature of the gas around the upper surface of the cavity decreases in spite of the viscous heating effect. Such a phenomenon happens during the energy exchange among gravitational and kinetic energy and can be explained as a result of the non-equilibrium heat transfer driven by an external force. Different from the equilibrium thermodynamics, the shift and distortion of the gas distribution function due to the external forcing term provide the dominant mechanism for particle transports, especially in the rarefied regions. The density and velocity distributions at the central lines of the cavity, as well as the local Knudsen number are presented in Figures 18 and 19. As plotted, the increased external force results in the stabilizing effect, i.e., to reduce the rotating speed of the main vortex. With the increment of the force magnitude, the velocity profile is flattened, indicating a weaker vortex motion. This numerical results validates the current well-balanced method for the study of non-equilibrium flows under an external force field.

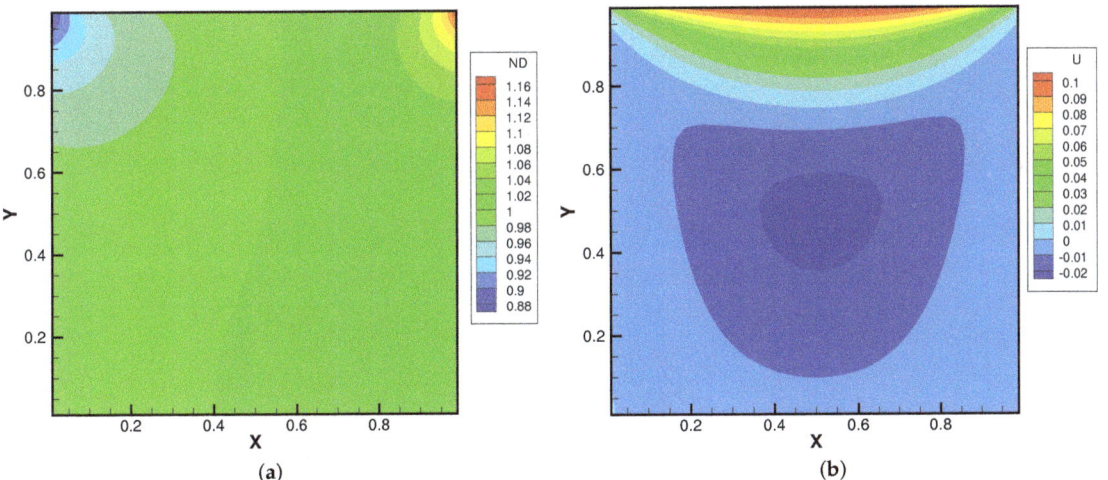

Figure 15. *Cont.*

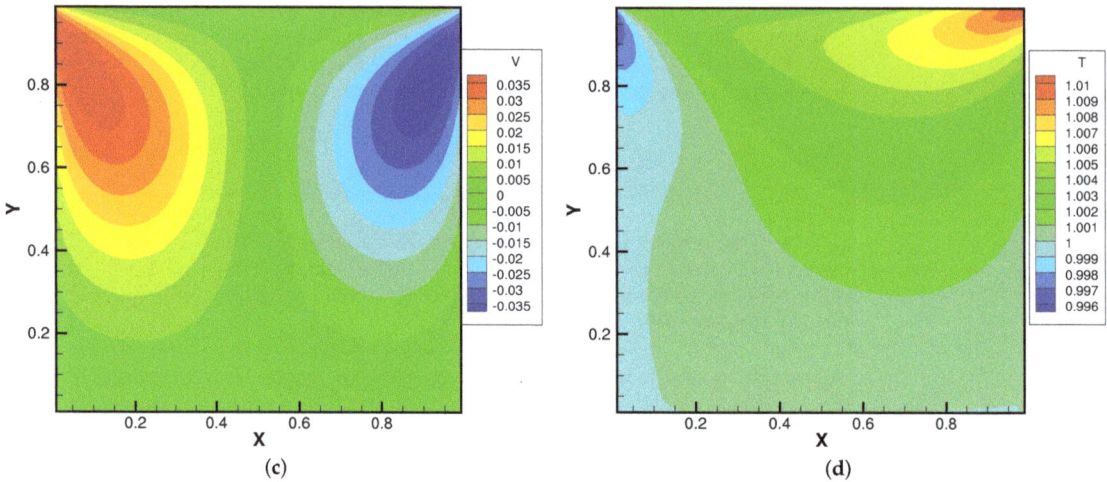

Figure 15. Lid-driven cavity solutions at $Kn_{ref} = 0.05$ and $\phi_y = 0$. (**a**) Number density. (**b**) U-velocity. (**c**) V-velocity. (**d**) Temperature.

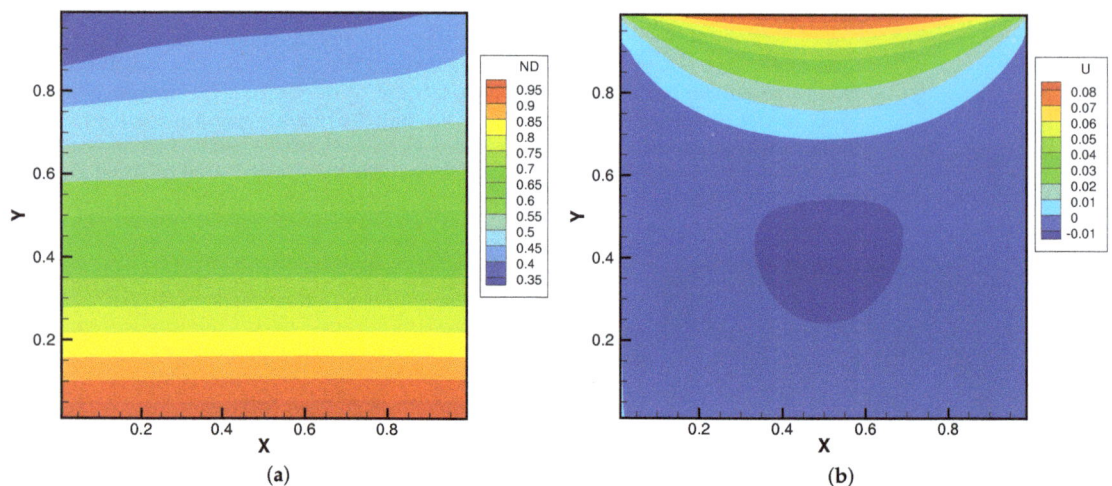

Figure 16. *Cont.*

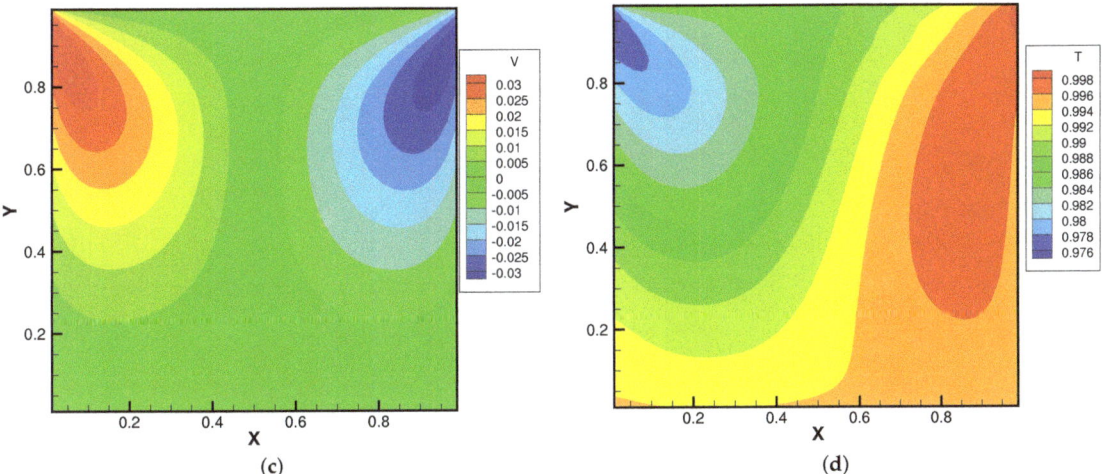

Figure 16. Lid-driven cavity solutions at $Kn_{ref} = 0.05$ and $\phi_y = -0.5$. (**a**) Number density. (**b**) U-velocity. (**c**) V-velocity. (**d**) Temperature.

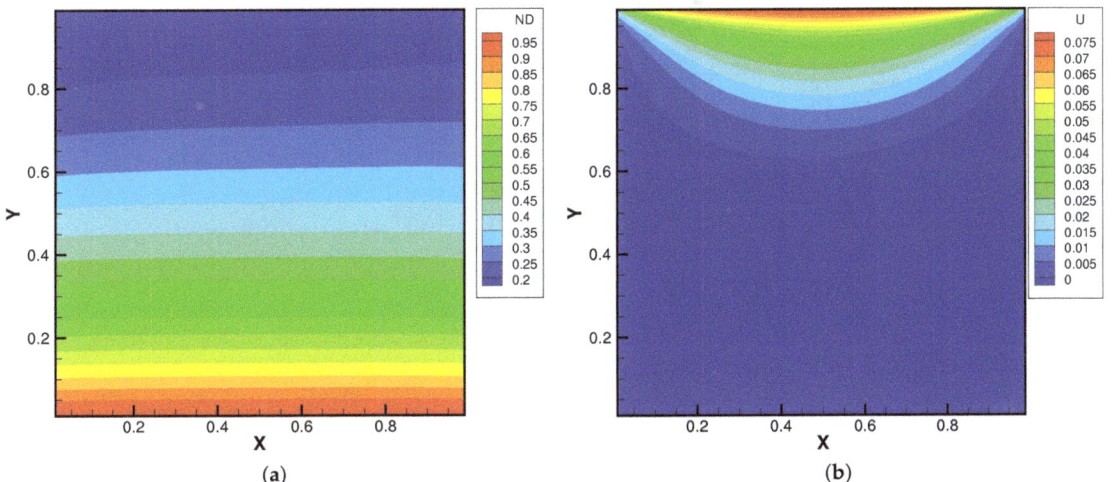

Figure 17. *Cont.*

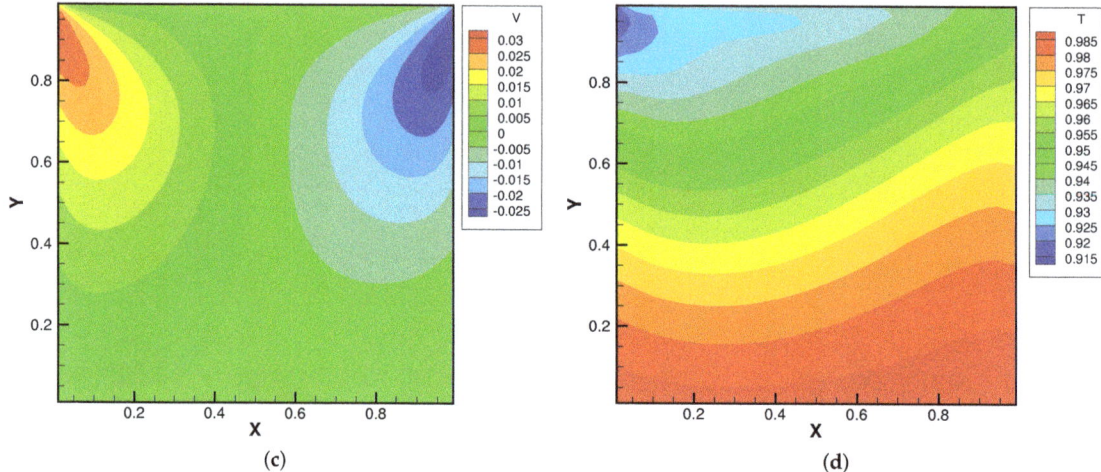

Figure 17. Lid-driven cavity solutions at $Kn_{ref} = 0.05$ and $\phi_y = -1.0$. (**a**) Number density. (**b**) U-velocity. (**c**) V-velocity. (**d**) Temperature.

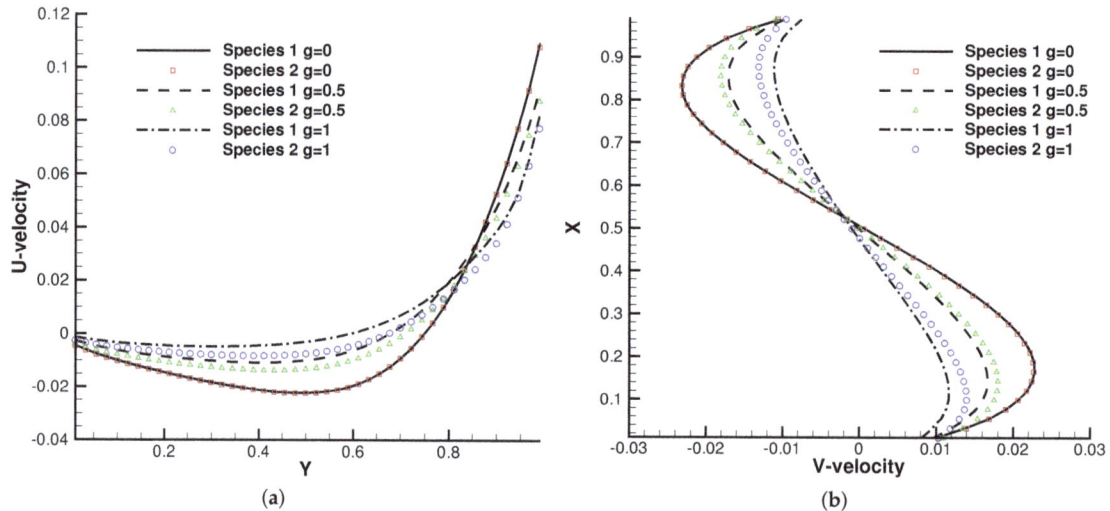

Figure 18. U,V velocity along the horizontal and vertical center lines of the cavity. (**a**) U-velocity. (**b**) V-velocity.

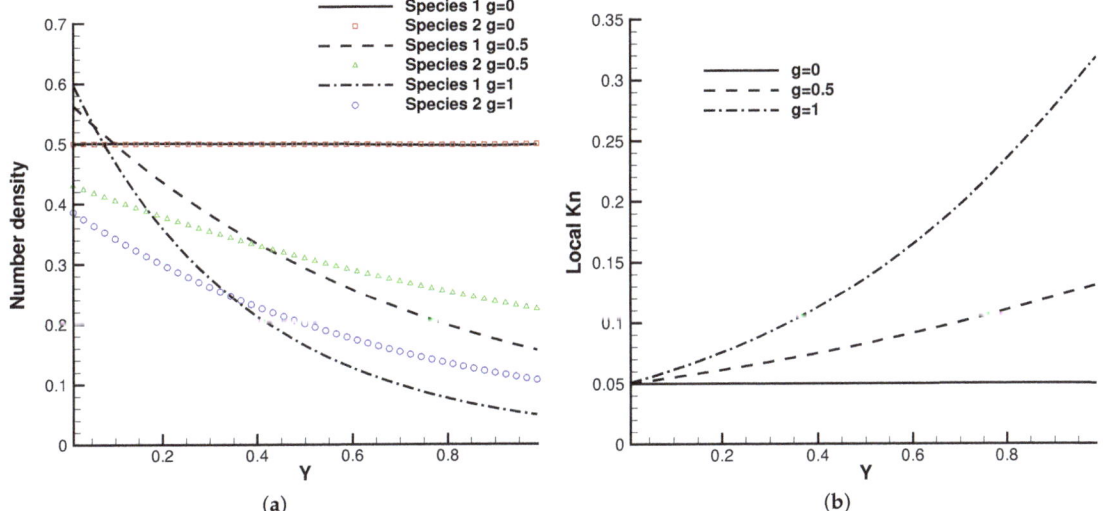

Figure 19. Number density and local Knudsen number along the vertical center line of the cavity. (**a**) Number density. (**b**) Local Knudsen number.

5. Conclusions

The atmosphere is composed of multicomponent flows under an external force. In this paper, a well-balanced unified gas-kinetic scheme for multicomponent flows has been developed. The well-balanced property of the unified scheme was validated through both theoretical demonstrations and numerical tests. The detailed strategy for the construction of the current algorithm was illustrated. Many numerical cases were provided to validate the scheme. New physical observations, such as the consistent transport in the hydrodynamic regime and the decoupled transport in the rarefied regime of different components, were clearly identified and discussed. The well-balanced UGKS provides an alternative choice for the study of real non-equilibrium gaseous flow on the Earth and beyond, which is useful in astronautical and astrophysical applications.

Funding: We acknowledge the support provided by the KIT-Publication Fund of the Karlsruhe Institute of Technology.

Institutional Review Board Statement: Not applicable.

Informed Consent Statement: Not applicable.

Data Availability Statement: The research data are available at https://github.com/vavrines/UGKS (11 August 2022).

Conflicts of Interest: The authors declare no conflict of interest.

References

1. Abgrall, R. How to Prevent Pressure Oscillations in Multicomponent Flow Calculations: A Quasi Conservative Approach. *J. Comput. Phys.* **1996**, *125*, 150–160. [CrossRef]
2. Fedkiw, R.P.; Aslam, T.; Merriman, B.; Osher, S. A Non-oscillatory Eulerian Approach to Interfaces in Multimaterial Flows (the Ghost Fluid Method). *J. Comput. Phys.* **1999**, *152*, 457–492. [CrossRef]
3. LeVeque, R.J.; Bale, D.S. Wave propagation methods for conservation laws with source terms. In *Hyperbolic Problems: Theory, Numerics, Applications*; Birkhäuser: Basel, Switzerland, 1999; pp. 609–618.
4. Botta, N.; Klein, R.; Langenberg, S.; Lützenkirchen, S. Well balanced finite volume methods for nearly hydrostatic flows. *J. Comput. Phys.* **2004**, *196*, 539–565. [CrossRef]
5. Xing, Y.; Shu, C.W. High order well-balanced WENO scheme for the gas dynamics equations under gravitational fields. *J. Sci. Comput.* **2013**, *54*, 645–662. [CrossRef]

6. Tian, C.; Xu, K.; Chan, K.; Deng, L. A three-dimensional multidimensional gas-kinetic scheme for the Navier–Stokes equations under gravitational fields. *J. Comput. Phys.* **2007**, *226*, 2003–2027. [CrossRef]
7. Luo, J.; Xu, K.; Liu, N. A well-balanced symplecticity-preserving gas-kinetic scheme for hydrodynamic equations under gravitational field. *SIAM J. Sci. Comput.* **2011**, *33*, 2356–2381. [CrossRef]
8. Chen, S.; Guo, Z.; Xu, K. A Well-Balanced Gas Kinetic Scheme for Navier–Stokes Equations with Gravitational Potential. *Commun. Comput. Phys.* **2020**, *28*, 902–926. [CrossRef]
9. Xu, K.; Huang, J.C. A unified gas-kinetic scheme for continuum and rarefied flows. *J. Comput. Phys.* **2010**, *229*, 7747–7764. [CrossRef]
10. Xu, K. *Direct Modeling for Computational Fluid Dynamics: Construction and Application of Unified Gas-Kinetic Schemes*; World Scientific: Singapore, 2015.
11. Xiao, T.; Cai, Q.; Xu, K. A well-balanced unified gas-kinetic scheme for multiscale flow transport under gravitational field. *J. Comput. Phys.* **2017**, *332*, 475–491. [CrossRef]
12. Prestininzi, P.; La Rocca, M.; Montessori, A.; Sciortino, G. A gas-kinetic model for 2D transcritical shallow water flows propagating over dry bed. *Comput. Math. Appl.* **2014**, *68*, 439–453. [CrossRef]
13. Schotthöfer, S.; Xiao, T.; Frank, M.; Hauck, C.D. Structure Preserving Neural Networks: A Case Study in the Entropy Closure of the Boltzmann Equation. In Proceedings of the International Conference on Machine Learning, PMLR, Baltimore, MD, USA, 17–23 July 2022; pp. 19406–19433.
14. Xiao, T.; Frank, M. A stochastic kinetic scheme for multi-scale plasma transport with uncertainty quantification. *J. Comput. Phys.* **2021**, *432*, 110139. [CrossRef]
15. Bhatnagar, P.L.; Gross, E.P.; Krook, M. A model for collision processes in gases. I. Small amplitude processes in charged and neutral one-component systems. *Phys. Rev.* **1954**, *94*, 511. [CrossRef]
16. Andries, P.; Aoki, K.; Perthame, B. A consistent BGK-type model for gas mixtures. *J. Stat. Phys.* **2002**, *106*, 993–1018. [CrossRef]
17. Morse, T. Energy and momentum exchange between nonequipartition gases. *Phys. Fluids* **1963**, *6*, 1420–1427. [CrossRef]
18. Bird, R.B. Transport phenomena. *Appl. Mech. Rev.* **2002**, *55*, R1–R4. [CrossRef]
19. Slyz, A.; Prendergast, K.H. Time-independent gravitational fields in the BGK scheme for hydrodynamics. *Astron. Astrophys. Suppl. Ser.* **1999**, *139*, 199–217. [CrossRef]
20. Xiao, T.; Xu, K.; Cai, Q.; Qian, T. An investigation of non-equilibrium heat transport in a gas system under an external force field. *Int. J. Heat Mass Transf.* **2018**, *126*, 362–379. [CrossRef]
21. Xiao, T. Kinetic. jl: A portable finite volume toolbox for scientific and neural computing. *J. Open Source Softw.* **2021**, *6*, 3060. [CrossRef]
22. Kosuge, S.; Aoki, K.; Takata, S. Shock-wave structure for a binary gas mixture: Finite-difference analysis of the Boltzmann equation for hard-sphere molecules. *Eur. J. -Mech.-B/Fluids* **2001**, *20*, 87–126. [CrossRef]
23. Wu, L.; White, C.; Scanlon, T.J.; Reese, J.M.; Zhang, Y. Deterministic numerical solutions of the Boltzmann equation using the fast spectral method. *J. Comput. Phys.* **2013**, *250*, 27–52. [CrossRef]
24. Xiao, T.; Xu, K.; Cai, Q. A unified gas-kinetic scheme for multiscale and multicomponent flow transport. *Appl. Math. Mech.* **2019**, *40*, 355–372. [CrossRef]
25. Rahman, M.; Saghir, M. Thermodiffusion or Soret effect: Historical review. *Int. J. Heat Mass Transf.* **2014**, *73*, 693–705. [CrossRef]
26. Xiao, T. A flux reconstruction kinetic scheme for the Boltzmann equation. *J. Comput. Phys.* **2021**, *447*, 110689. [CrossRef]

Article

Three-Dimensional Simulations of Anisotropic Slip Microflows Using the Discrete Unified Gas Kinetic Scheme

Wenqiang Guo and Guoxiang Hou *

School of Naval Architecture and Ocean Engineering, Huazhong University of Science and Technology, Wuhan 430074, China; gwq@hust.edu.cn
* Correspondence: houguoxiang@163.com

Citation: Guo, W.; Hou, G. Three-Dimensional Simulations of Anisotropic Slip Microflows Using the Discrete Unified Gas Kinetic Scheme. *Entropy* **2022**, *24*, 907. https://doi.org/10.3390/e24070907

Academic Editor: Andrés Santos

Received: 25 May 2022
Accepted: 28 June 2022
Published: 30 June 2022

Publisher's Note: MDPI stays neutral with regard to jurisdictional claims in published maps and institutional affiliations.

Copyright: © 2022 by the authors. Licensee MDPI, Basel, Switzerland. This article is an open access article distributed under the terms and conditions of the Creative Commons Attribution (CC BY) license (https://creativecommons.org/licenses/by/4.0/).

Abstract: The specific objective of the present work study is to propose an anisotropic slip boundary condition for three-dimensional (3D) simulations with adjustable streamwise and spanwise slip length by the discrete unified gas kinetic scheme (DUGKS). The present boundary condition is proposed based on the assumption of nonlinear velocity profiles near the wall instead of linear velocity profiles in a unidirectional steady flow. Moreover, a 3D corner boundary condition is introduced to the DUGKS to reduce the singularities. Numerical tests validate the effectiveness of the present method, which is more accurate than the bounce-back and specular reflection slip boundary condition in the lattice Boltzmann method. It is of significance to study the lid-driven cavity flow due to its applications and its capability in exhibiting important phenomena. Then, the present work explores, for the first time, the effects of anisotropic slip on the two-sided orthogonal oscillating micro-lid-driven cavity flow by adopting the present method. This work will generate fresh insight into the effects of anisotropic slip on the 3D flow in a two-sided orthogonal oscillating micro-lid-driven cavity. Some findings are obtained: The oscillating velocity of the wall has a weaker influence on the normal velocity component than on the tangential velocity component. In most cases, large slip length has a more significant influence on velocity profiles than small slip length. Compared with pure slip in both top and bottom walls, anisotropic slip on the top wall has a greater influence on flow, increasing the 3D mixing of flow. In short, the influence of slip on the flow field depends not only on slip length but also on the relative direction of the wall motion and the slip velocity. The findings can help in better understanding the anisotropic slip effect on the unsteady microflow and the design of microdevices.

Keywords: anisotropic slip; boundary condition; DUGKS; superhydrophobic surface; oscillating wall motion

1. Introduction

Surface characteristics play a critical role in designing and fabricating microfluidic devices. Superhydrophobicity is an important aspect of surface characteristics, which can significantly control flow and reduce drag [1–10]. Based on the knowledge of fluid mechanics, the no-slip boundary condition is valid at the solid–liquid interface. However, the liquid slip velocity is observed on the superhydrophobic surface. Unlike gas slip caused by Knudsen effects, liquid slip is modelled with two strategies [11]: introducing the force that repels water in the multiphase system; and modelling the slip boundary condition. For the former strategy, the forces are not well understood and determined. Existing research recognizes the critical role played by the latter strategy; therefore, it is emphasized in the present work.

The appropriate boundary condition is an important area in the simulation of fluid flows [12,13]. Recently, researchers have shown an increased interest in slip boundary conditions. For example, Min and Kim [14,15] directly modelled the hydrophobic wall with Navier's slip boundary condition by direct numerical simulation (DNS) based on the macroscopic Navier–Stokes equations. However, the Navier's slip boundary condition cannot be introduced to the lattice-Boltzmann-based methods, because the lattice-Boltzmann-based methods track the particle distribution function instead of the macroscopic variables. The lattice Boltzmann method (LBM) is appropriate for simulating mesoscopic physics that are hard to describe macroscopically. It has the advantages of simple algorithms, natural parallelization, and saving computing costs for simulating microflow [16], which proves to be a promising tool. Slip boundary conditions have been proposed and employed in the LBM, such as bounce-back and specular reflection (BSR) [11,17], discrete full diffusive and specular reflection (DSR) [18,19], discrete full diffusive and bounce-back (DBB) [20,21], and tangential momentum accommodation coefficient (TMAC) scheme [22]. Coupled with Navier's slip model [23], liquid slip can be characterized and adjusted by slip length. With assumption of the 2D unidirectional flow at a lower Reynolds number, the relation between the slip length and combination parameter of the coupled schemes [24–26] is determined. However, it is not valid in three-dimensional (3D) flows and turbulent flows. Moreover, the slip should be considered in streamwise and spanwise directions [1]. Existing studies about rice leaves have found that the anisotropic groove-like microstructures can lead to the anisotropic slip behavior of water droplets on the surfaces [27–29]. More recent studies have considered superhydrophobic surfaces with randomly distributed textures in streamwise and spanwise directions [8,30–35], indicating that the slip is anisotropic. For example, both spanwise and streamwise slip lengths have been measured on a randomly textured superhydrophobic surface [35]. Therefore, the present study considers the anisotropic slip in streamwise and spanwise directions for the 3D system based on the nonlinear velocity profiles near the wall, which is close to the actual situation.

Moreover, Guo et al. proposed a new finite-volume scheme named discrete unified gas kinetic scheme (DUGKS) based on the lattice Boltzmann equation [36]. The DUGKS has also been proved to be a promising numerical tool to simulate fluid flow [37–42], such as 3D turbulent channel flow. It is found that the DUGKS, even with a coarse nonuniform mesh, is overall better than the LBM [37]. So, the numerical simulation will be performed by the DUGKS in this work. Up to now, no attention has been paid to the 3D slip boundary condition in the DUGKS. Therefore, in the present study, the new slip boundary condition is proposed for the DUGKS instead of the LBM. The DUGKS is performed to simulate 3D flows with the proposed slip boundary condition. It is hoped that we provide a superior method to describe and characterize anisotropic slip on superhydrophobic surfaces.

To study the effect of anisotropic slip on flows in benchmark geometries, the present method is applied to the lid-driven cavity flow. It is an important problem in the field of fluid mechanics due to its applications, such as cooling of electronic gadgets, oil extraction, design of heat exchangers, solar ponds, acoustic liner, float glass productions, insulation materials, multiscreen gadgets for nuclear reactors, coating, food processing, crystal growth, etc. [43–49]. Moreover, it has capability in exhibiting important phenomena such as eddies, secondary flows, instabilities, transition, and turbulence [50]. The liquid slip flow in two-sided, orthogonal, oscillating, micro-lid-driven cavities has largely been oversighted. Recently, two-sided motion [51–54] and oscillatory flows in the cavity have also caught the necessary attention, except single-sided steady flows. The purposes of the literature cornering oscillatory flows in lid-driven cavities include:

1. To test and validate numerical solvers, such as least-squares finite element methods [55], Taylor-series-expansion- and least-squares-based lattice Boltzmann methods [56] and conservative level-set methods [57]. 2. To understand industrial applications, such as surface viscometer [58] and optimization of fluid mixing [59,60]. 3. To understand the flow characteristics, such as the single-sided oscillatory rarefied gas flows inside two- and three-dimensional cavities [61–63], and two-sided oscillating flows in two-dimensional lid-driven cavities [64].

The studies mentioned above have been solely restricted to the no-slip flow; the liquid slip flow in lid-driven cavities have largely been oversighted. Slip should be carefully considered in the design of micro-devices with moving parts. This work will generate fresh insight into the effects of anisotropic slip on the 3D flow in a two-sided oscillating micro-lid-driven cavity. In this work, for the first time, there are mainly two types of slip distribution: (1) pure streamwise slip emerges on both top and bottom wall surfaces; (2) both streamwise and spanwise slips emerge on the top wall surface. In a 3D global coordinate system, the unit velocity vector of the moving top and bottom walls is (1,0,0) and (0,1,0), respectively. The motion direction of the top and bottom walls is orthogonal. To the best of the authors' knowledge, no such study has been conducted before.

It is hoped that the present study will provide a superior method and contribute to a deeper understanding of the anisotropic slip. The paper is organized as follows. In Section 2, the D3Q19 lattice model and DUGKS are introduced, and the new slip boundary condition and corner boundary condition for the D3Q19 lattice model are derived theoretically. In Section 3, numerical validation is performed by simulating the 3D microchannel flow. Numerical results of 3D flow in a two-sided, oscillating, lid-driven cavity are discussed in Section 4. Section 5 gives the conclusions.

2. Numerical Methods

2.1. D3Q19 Lattice Model

D3Q19 lattice model [65] is adopted in this work. As shown in Figure 1, there are 19 discrete velocities in the D3Q19 lattice model, including one rest velocity ($\alpha = 0$) and 18 non-rest velocities ($\alpha = 1, ..., 18$).

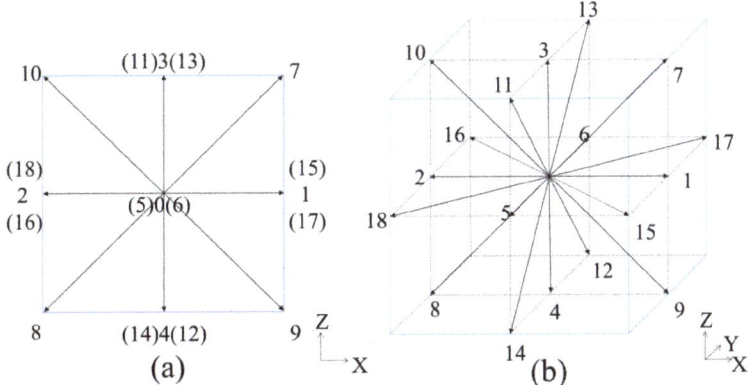

Figure 1. D3Q19 lattice model (**a**) 2D view; (**b**) 3D view.

As shown in Table 1, the velocity set includes the velocities $\{\xi_\alpha\}$ and the corresponding weights $\{W_\alpha\}$. The speed of the sound is $c = \sqrt{3RT} = 1$.

Table 1. The velocity set for the D3Q19 lattice model.

Velocities ξ_α	Number	Length $|\xi_\alpha|$	Weight W_α
$(0,0,0)c$	1	0	1/3
$(\pm 1, 0, 0)c, (0, \pm 1, 0)c, (0, 0, \pm 1)c$	6	1	1/18
$(\pm 1, \pm 1, 0)c, (\pm 1, 0, \pm 1)c, (0, \pm 1, \pm 1)c$	12	$\sqrt{2}$	1/36

2.2. Discrete Unified gas Kinetic Scheme

The discrete Boltzmann equation with the Bhatnagar–Gross–Krook (BGK) collision model [66] is the governing equation of the DUGKS:

$$\frac{\partial f_\alpha}{\partial t} + \xi_\alpha \cdot \nabla f_\alpha = \Omega \equiv \frac{f_\alpha^{eq} - f_\alpha}{\tau} \tag{1}$$

It is assumed that fluid particles move with the velocity ξ_α at position **x** and time t, so the velocity distribution function is $f_\alpha = f_\alpha(\mathbf{x}, \xi_\alpha, t)$. Ω and τ represent the collision term and relaxation time, respectively.

f_α^{eq} represents the Maxwellian equilibrium distribution function, which is approximated by Taylor expansion around zero particle velocity at low Mach number:

$$f_\alpha^{eq} = W_\alpha \rho \left[1 + \frac{\xi_\alpha \cdot \mathbf{u}}{c_s^2} + \frac{(\xi_\alpha \cdot \mathbf{u})^2}{2c_s^4} - \frac{|\mathbf{u}|^2}{2c_s^2} \right], c_s^2 = RT \quad (2)$$

The velocities $\{\xi_\alpha\}$ and the corresponding weights $\{W_\alpha\}$ are presented in Table 1.

The computational domain is divided into cuboid cells $V_{i,j,k} = \Delta x_i \Delta y_j \Delta z_k$ centered at $\mathbf{x}_{i,j,k} = (x_i, y_j, z_k)$ in the DUGKS. As a new finite volume scheme, the volumes-averaged values of the distribution function and collision term need to be computed. For example, the volumes-averaged value of the distribution function $f_\alpha^n(\mathbf{x}_{i,j,k})$ is computed as,

$$f_\alpha^n(\mathbf{x}_{i,j,k}) = \frac{1}{|V_{i,j,k}|} \int_{V_{i,j,k}} f_\alpha(\mathbf{x}, t^n) dV \quad (3)$$

In the DUGKS, the governing equation needs to be integrated on each cell, and the time step Δt is assumed to be constant. Equation (1) is integrated on a cell $V_{i,j,k}$ centered at $\mathbf{x}_{i,j,k}$ from time $t^n = n\Delta t$ to time $t^{n+1} = (n+1)\Delta t$, and the evolution of the distribution is advanced from t^n to t^{n+1} as,

$$f_\alpha^{n+1} - f_\alpha^n = -\frac{\Delta t}{|V_{i,j,k}|} \mathcal{F}_\alpha^{n+1/2} + \frac{\Delta t}{2} \left[\Omega_\alpha^n + \Omega_\alpha^{n+1} \right] \quad (4)$$

The scalar variable $\mathcal{F}_\alpha^{n+1/2}$ represents the flux across the cell interface,

$$\begin{aligned}\mathcal{F}_\alpha^{n+1/2}(\mathbf{x}_{i,j,k}) &= \int_{\partial V_{i,j,k}} (\xi_\alpha \cdot \mathbf{n}) f_\alpha^{n+1/2}(\mathbf{x}_b) dS = \\ &= [f_\alpha^{n+1/2}(\mathbf{x}_{i,j,k} + 0.5\Delta x_i \mathbf{e}_x) - f_\alpha^{n+1/2}(\mathbf{x}_{i,j,k} - 0.5\Delta x_i \mathbf{e}_x)] \xi_{\alpha,x} \Delta y_j \Delta z_k \\ &+ [f_\alpha^{n+1/2}(\mathbf{x}_{i,j,k} + 0.5\Delta y_j \mathbf{e}_y) - f_\alpha^{n+1/2}(\mathbf{x}_{i,j,k} - 0.5\Delta y_j \mathbf{e}_y)] \xi_{\alpha,y} \Delta x_i \Delta z_k \\ &+ [f_\alpha^{n+1/2}(\mathbf{x}_{i,j,k} + 0.5\Delta z_k \mathbf{e}_z) - f_\alpha^{n+1/2}(\mathbf{x}_{i,j,k} - 0.5\Delta z_k \mathbf{e}_z)] \xi_{\alpha,z} \Delta x_i \Delta y_j \end{aligned} \quad (5)$$

where $f_\alpha^{n+1/2}(\mathbf{x}_b)$ represents the distribution at the cell interface $\mathbf{x}_b$ at the time $t^{n+1/2} = t^n + h$ ($h = \Delta t/2$), and $\mathbf{e}_x$, $\mathbf{e}_y$, and $\mathbf{e}_z$ are unit vectors in x, y, and z directions, respectively.

For clarity, new distribution functions are introduced:

$$\tilde{f}_\alpha^n \equiv f_\alpha^n - \frac{\Delta t}{2}\Omega(f_\alpha^n), \tilde{f}_\alpha^{+,n} \equiv f_\alpha^n + \frac{\Delta t}{2}\Omega(f_\alpha^n) \quad (6)$$

The collision term can be expanded in the BGK collision model, and Equation (6) can be converted to the following equations:

$$f_{\alpha,j}^n = \frac{2\tau}{2\tau + \Delta t}\tilde{f}_{\alpha,j}^n + \frac{\Delta t}{2\tau + \Delta t}f_{\alpha,j}^{eq,n}, \tilde{f}_{\alpha,j}^{+,n} = \frac{2\tau - \Delta t}{2\tau + \Delta t}\tilde{f}_{\alpha,j}^n + \frac{2\Delta t}{2\tau + \Delta t}f_{\alpha,j}^{eq,n}. \quad (7)$$

The evolution equation of DUGKS from t^n to t^{n+1} is simplified as:

$$\tilde{f}_{\alpha,j}^{n+1} = \tilde{f}_{\alpha,j}^{+,n} - \frac{\Delta t}{|V_{i,j,k}|} \mathcal{F}_{\alpha,j}^{n+1/2} \quad (8)$$

Based on the conservation of mass, momentum, the density ρ, and velocity **u** can be computed from $\tilde{f}_\alpha$:

$$\rho^n = \sum_\alpha \tilde{f}_\alpha^n, \rho^n \mathbf{u}^n = \sum_\alpha \xi_\alpha \tilde{f}_\alpha^n \quad (9)$$

All other forms of the distribution function can be expressed in terms of $\tilde{f}_\alpha$ and f_α^{eq}. So, the distribution function $\tilde{f}_\alpha$ is mainly computed in the code.

The critical step is to evaluate the interface flux $\mathcal{F}_{\alpha,j}^{n+1/2}$. The midpoint integral formula is employed to evaluate $\mathcal{F}_{\alpha,j}^{n+1/2}$, due to its easy implementation and fast computation. For DUGKS with higher-order accuracy, more intermediate time steps need to be selected; for example, the flux at the cell interface at $t^* = t_n + \Delta t/6$ and $t^* = t_n + 3\Delta t/4$ need calculating.

In the present study, Equation (1) is integrated within a half time step ($h = \Delta t/2$) along the characteristic line with the endpoint ($\mathbf{x}_b$) located at the cell interface, and the following formula is obtained:

$$f_\alpha^{n+1/2}(\mathbf{x}_b) - f_\alpha^n(\mathbf{x}_b - h\boldsymbol{\xi}_\alpha) = \frac{h}{2}\left[\Omega\left(f_\alpha^{n+1/2}(\mathbf{x}_b)\right) + \Omega(f_\alpha^n(\mathbf{x}_b - h\boldsymbol{\xi}_\alpha))\right] \quad (10)$$

Similarly, new distribution functions are introduced and can be computed by expanding the collision term:

$$\overline{f}_\alpha^{n+1/2}(\mathbf{x}_b) \equiv f_\alpha^{n+1/2}(\mathbf{x}_b) - \frac{h}{2}\Omega\left(f_\alpha^{n+1/2}(\mathbf{x}_b)\right) = \frac{2\tau+h}{2\tau}f_\alpha^{n+1/2}(\mathbf{x}_b) - f_\alpha^{eq,n+1/2}(\mathbf{x}_b) \quad (11)$$

$$\overline{f}_\alpha^{+,n}(\mathbf{x}_b - h\boldsymbol{\xi}_\alpha) \equiv f_\alpha^n(\mathbf{x}_b - h\boldsymbol{\xi}_\alpha) + \frac{h}{2}\Omega(f_\alpha^n(\mathbf{x}_b - h\boldsymbol{\xi}_\alpha)),$$
$$\overline{f}_\alpha^{+,n} = \frac{2\tau-h}{2\tau+h}\overline{f}_\alpha^n + \frac{2h}{2\tau+h}f_\alpha^{eq,n}. \quad (12)$$

With new distribution functions, Equation (10) is converted to the following equation:

$$\overline{f}_\alpha^{n+1/2}(\mathbf{x}_b) = \overline{f}_\alpha^{+,n}(\mathbf{x}_b - h\boldsymbol{\xi}_\alpha) \quad (13)$$

With the Taylor expansion around the endpoint ($\mathbf{x}_b$) located at the cell interface, the right term of Equation (13) can be approximated as:

$$\overline{f}_\alpha^{+,n}(\mathbf{x}_b - h\boldsymbol{\xi}_\alpha) = \overline{f}_\alpha^{+,n}(\mathbf{x}_b) - h\boldsymbol{\xi}_\alpha \cdot \nabla\overline{f}_\alpha^{+,n}(\mathbf{x}_b) \quad (14)$$

where $\overline{f}_\alpha^{+,n}(\mathbf{x}_b)$ and its gradients $\nabla\overline{f}_\alpha^{+,n}(\mathbf{x}_b)$ can be approximated by the linear interpolations. In x-direction, e.g.,

$$\frac{\partial \overline{f}_\alpha^{+,n}(\mathbf{x}_{i,j,k}+0.5\Delta x_i \mathbf{e}_x)}{\partial x} \approx \frac{\overline{f}_\alpha^{+,n}(\mathbf{x}_{i+1,j,k}) - \overline{f}_\alpha^{+,n}(\mathbf{x}_{i,j,k})}{(\Delta x_i + \Delta x_{i+1})/2},$$
$$\overline{f}_\alpha^{+,n}(\mathbf{x}_{i,j,k}+0.5\Delta x_i \mathbf{e}_x) \approx \overline{f}_\alpha^{+,n}(\mathbf{x}_{i,j,k}) + \frac{\partial \overline{f}_\alpha^{+,n}(\mathbf{x}_{i,j,k}+0.5\Delta x_i \mathbf{e}_x)}{\partial x}\frac{\Delta x_i}{2}, \quad (15)$$

The distribution function $\overline{f}_\alpha^{+,n}$ can be computed from $\tilde{f}_\alpha$, as follows,

$$\overline{f}_\alpha^{+,n} = \frac{2\tau-h}{2\tau+\Delta t}\tilde{f}_\alpha^n + \frac{3h}{2\tau+\Delta t}f_\alpha^{eq,n} \quad (16)$$

Then, we obtain the function $\overline{f}_\alpha^{n+1/2}(\mathbf{x}_b)$. The density and velocity at the cell interface can also be evaluated, which can be used for the equilibrium distribution function $f_\alpha^{eq,n+1/2}(\mathbf{x}_b)$,

$$\rho^{n+1/2}\big|_{\mathbf{x}_b} = \sum_\alpha \overline{f}_\alpha^{n+1/2}(\mathbf{x}_b), \ (\rho\mathbf{u})^{n+1/2}\big|_{\mathbf{x}_b} = \sum_\alpha \boldsymbol{\xi}_\alpha \overline{f}_\alpha^{n+1/2}(\mathbf{x}_b) \quad (17)$$

Finally, the flux $\mathcal{F}_{\alpha,j}^{n+1/2}$ is evaluated according to Equation (5) after the distribution function $f_\alpha^{n+1/2}$ at the cell interface is determined by Equation (11). The tracked distribution function $\tilde{f}_\alpha$ can be updated to the next time step after the flux is obtained.

Particularly, the following equation will be used in the DUGKS,

$$\widetilde{f}_\alpha^{+,n} = \frac{4}{3}\overline{f}_\alpha^{+,n} - \frac{1}{3}\widetilde{f}_\alpha^n \tag{18}$$

For the present DUGKS, the relaxation time τ is computed from $\tau = \mu/p$, where μ is the dynamic viscosity coefficient. p ($p = \rho RT$) is the pressure, where R is the specific gas constant. In the following simulations, the temperature T is constant in the isothermal flow with $c_s^2 = RT = 1/3$. The time step Δt is determined by the Courant–Friedrichs–Lewy (CFL) condition [67], which is independent of the relaxation time τ for all flow regimes.

2.3. The Present Slip Boundary Condition

It can be seen intuitively that, considering the actual case with anisotropic slip, slip boundary conditions derived by adopting two-dimensional unidirectional flow are not valid. Therefore, a new anisotropic slip boundary condition is proposed in 3D flows. In this work, the anisotropic slip boundary condition is characterized and constructed by adjusting the relative magnitude of the streamwise and spanwise slip lengths. It is noted that x, y, and z denote the streamwise, spanwise, and wall-normal directions, respectively. It is noted that the DUGKS tracks the distribution function $\widetilde{f}_\alpha$, unlike the LBM.

Considering the impermeable wall boundary ($U_{Wz} = 0$), the unknown distributions are obtained by the specular reflection ($\widetilde{f}_\alpha^{sr}$) and the stress exerted by the wall ($\widetilde{f}_\alpha^{w}$).

$$\widetilde{f}_\alpha = \widetilde{f}_\alpha^{sr} + \widetilde{f}_\alpha^{w}(\boldsymbol{\xi}_\alpha \cdot \mathbf{n} > 0) \tag{19}$$

As shown in Figure 2, the unknown distributions are $\widetilde{f}_4, \widetilde{f}_8, \widetilde{f}_9, \widetilde{f}_{12}, \widetilde{f}_{14}$.

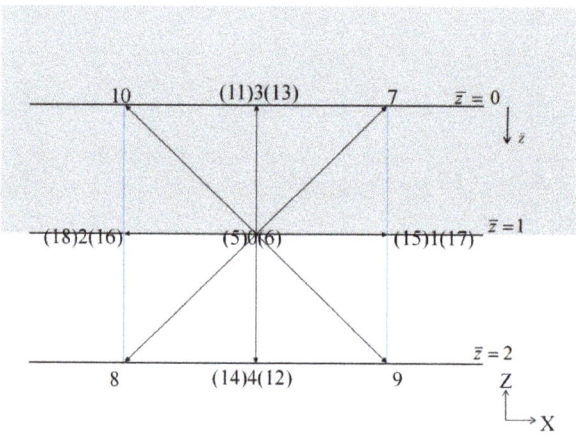

Figure 2. 2D sketch of the upper horizontal wall boundary in 3D.

The specular reflection $\widetilde{f}_\alpha^{sr}$ can be obtained by:

$$\widetilde{f}_4^{sr} = \widetilde{f}_3, \widetilde{f}_8^{sr} = \widetilde{f}_{10}, \widetilde{f}_9^{sr} = \widetilde{f}_7, \widetilde{f}_{12}^{sr} = \widetilde{f}_{13}, \widetilde{f}_{14}^{sr} = \widetilde{f}_{11} \tag{20}$$

With $\widetilde{f}_\alpha^{sr}$ determined, U_{SR} can be obtained by:

$$\rho = \sum_\alpha \widetilde{f}_\alpha \tag{21}$$

$$\rho U_{SR} = \sum_{\boldsymbol{\xi}_\alpha \cdot \mathbf{n} \leq 0} \left(\widetilde{f}_\alpha \boldsymbol{\xi}_\alpha \right)_\parallel + \sum_{\boldsymbol{\xi}_\alpha \cdot \mathbf{n} > 0} \left(\widetilde{f}_\alpha^{sr} \boldsymbol{\xi}_\alpha \right)_\parallel \tag{22}$$

The stress $\tilde{f}_\alpha^w$ contributes to the change in tangential momentum caused by the wall surface, as shown in the following equations:

$$\sigma' \rho (U_W - U_{SR}) = \sum_{\xi_\alpha \cdot n > 0} \left(\tilde{f}_\alpha^w \xi_\alpha \right)_\| \tag{23}$$

$$0 = \sum_{\xi_\alpha \cdot n > 0} \left(\tilde{f}_\alpha^w \xi_\alpha \right)_\perp \tag{24}$$

$$0 = \tilde{f}_\alpha^w \text{ (for normal direction)} \tag{25}$$

U_W and U_{SR} are the tangential velocity of the wall and the average tangential velocity under the specular reflection by the impermeable boundary, respectively. σ' represents a modified tangential momentum accommodation coefficient. $\mathbf{n}$ is the normal direction of the wall toward the fluid field. The subscripts "$\|$" and "$\perp$" represent the tangential and normal directions, respectively. The sum of normal parts is zero, ensuring that the function $\tilde{f}_\alpha^w$ only changes the tangential momentum. It is also shown that the calculation of density is not determined by $\sum \tilde{f}_\alpha^w$.

The following relations can be obtained for the case in Figure 2.

$$\text{x - direction}: \rho U_{SRx} = \tilde{f}_1 - \tilde{f}_2 + 2(\tilde{f}_7 - \tilde{f}_{10}) \tag{26}$$

$$\text{y - direction}: \rho U_{SRy} = \tilde{f}_8 - \tilde{f}_5 + 2(\tilde{f}_{13} - \tilde{f}_{11}) \tag{27}$$

The momentum can change due to the shear stress imposed on the wall:

$$\text{x - direction}: \sigma'_x \rho (U_{Wx} - U_{SRx}) = \sum_{\xi_\alpha \cdot n > 0} \left(\tilde{f}_\alpha^w \xi_\alpha \right)_x = \tilde{f}_9^w - \tilde{f}_8^w \tag{28}$$

$$\text{y - direction}: \sigma'_y \rho (U_{Wy} - U_{SRy}) = \sum_{\xi_\alpha \cdot n > 0} \left(\tilde{f}_\alpha^w \xi_\alpha \right)_y = \tilde{f}_{12}^w - \tilde{f}_{14}^w \tag{29}$$

For positive normal direction of the wall (i.e., +z direction):

$$0 = \sum_{\xi_\alpha \cdot n > 0} \left(\tilde{f}_\alpha^w \xi_\alpha \right)_z = \tilde{f}_4^w + \tilde{f}_8^w + \tilde{f}_9^w + \tilde{f}_{12}^w + \tilde{f}_{14}^w \tag{30}$$

$$0 = \tilde{f}_4^w \tag{31}$$

Based on the Maxwell equilibrium distribution function and Ref. [22], the density can be calculated,

$$\rho = \tilde{f}_0 + \tilde{f}_1 + \tilde{f}_2 + \tilde{f}_5 + \tilde{f}_6 + \tilde{f}_{15} + \tilde{f}_{16} + \tilde{f}_{17} + \tilde{f}_{18} + 2(\tilde{f}_3 + \tilde{f}_7 + \tilde{f}_{10} + \tilde{f}_{11} + \tilde{f}_{13}) \tag{32}$$

Then, $\tilde{f}_8^w, \tilde{f}_9^w, \tilde{f}_{12}^w, \tilde{f}_{14}^w$ and U_{SRx}, U_{SRy} are still unknown. σ'_x, σ'_y are the manually adjustable parameters, which are related to the streamwise and spanwise slip lengths, respectively.

There are five known equations in the system:

$$\begin{cases} \rho U_{SRx} = \tilde{f}_1 - \tilde{f}_2 + 2(\tilde{f}_7 - \tilde{f}_{10}) \\ \rho U_{SRy} = \tilde{f}_8 - \tilde{f}_5 + 2(\tilde{f}_{13} - \tilde{f}_{11}) \\ \sigma'_x \rho (U_{Wx} - U_{SRx}) = \sum_{\xi_\alpha \cdot n > 0} \left(\tilde{f}_i^w \xi_\alpha \right)_x = \tilde{f}_9^w - \tilde{f}_8^w \\ \sigma'_y \rho (U_{Wy} - U_{SRy}) = \sum_{\xi_\alpha \cdot n > 0} \left(\tilde{f}_i^w \xi_\alpha \right)_y = \tilde{f}_{12}^w - \tilde{f}_{14}^w \\ 0 = \tilde{f}_8^w + \tilde{f}_9^w + \tilde{f}_{12}^w + \tilde{f}_{14}^w \end{cases} \tag{33}$$

To make the system closed, the hypothesis is proposed:

$$\tilde{f}_8^w = -\tilde{f}_9^w \text{ or } \tilde{f}_{12}^w = -\tilde{f}_{14}^w \qquad (34)$$

In summary, a new slip boundary condition is proposed for the upper horizontal wall boundary in 3D:

$$\begin{aligned}
\tilde{f}_4 &= \tilde{f}_3 \\
\tilde{f}_8 &= \tilde{f}_{10} - \tfrac{1}{2}\sigma'_x\left\{\rho U_{Wx} - (\tilde{f}_1 - \tilde{f}_2 + 2(\tilde{f}_7 - \tilde{f}_{10}))\right\} \\
\tilde{f}_9 &= \tilde{f}_7 + \tfrac{1}{2}\sigma'_x\left\{\rho U_{Wx} - (\tilde{f}_1 - \tilde{f}_2 + 2(\tilde{f}_7 - \tilde{f}_{10}))\right\} \\
\tilde{f}_{12} &= \tilde{f}_{13} + \tfrac{1}{2}\sigma'_y\left\{\rho U_{Wy} - (\tilde{f}_6 - \tilde{f}_5 + 2(\tilde{f}_{13} - \tilde{f}_{11}))\right\} \\
\tilde{f}_{14} &= \tilde{f}_{11} - \tfrac{1}{2}\sigma'_y\left\{\rho U_{Wy} - (\tilde{f}_6 - \tilde{f}_5 + 2(\tilde{f}_{13} - \tilde{f}_{11}))\right\}
\end{aligned} \qquad (35)$$

With the external forcing term, the local velocities **u** are computed by,

$$\mathbf{u} = \frac{1}{\rho}\sum_i \xi_\alpha \tilde{f}_\alpha + \frac{\Delta t \cdot \vec{a}}{2} \qquad (36)$$

To eliminate the numerical slip due to force tangential to the wall, the external forcing term is introduced to the new slip boundary condition:

$$\begin{aligned}
\tilde{f}_4 &= \tilde{f}_3 \\
\tilde{f}_8 &= \tilde{f}_{10} - \tfrac{1}{2}\sigma'_x\left\{\rho(U_{Wx} - 0.5\Delta t a_x) - (\tilde{f}_1 - \tilde{f}_2 + 2(\tilde{f}_7 - \tilde{f}_{10}))\right\} \\
\tilde{f}_9 &= \tilde{f}_7 + \tfrac{1}{2}\sigma'_x\left\{\rho(U_{Wx} - 0.5\Delta t a_x) - (\tilde{f}_1 - \tilde{f}_2 + 2(\tilde{f}_7 - \tilde{f}_{10}))\right\} \\
\tilde{f}_{12} &= \tilde{f}_{13} + \tfrac{1}{2}\sigma'_y\left\{\rho(U_{Wy} - 0.5\Delta t a_y) - (\tilde{f}_6 - \tilde{f}_5 + 2(\tilde{f}_{13} - \tilde{f}_{11}))\right\} \\
\tilde{f}_{14} &= \tilde{f}_{11} - \tfrac{1}{2}\sigma'_y\left\{\rho(U_{Wy} - 0.5\Delta t a_y) - (\tilde{f}_6 - \tilde{f}_5 + 2(\tilde{f}_{13} - \tilde{f}_{11}))\right\}
\end{aligned} \qquad (37)$$

Similar manipulations can be applied to the lower wall and side walls boundary.

2.4. Relation between the Combination Parameters and Slip Lengths

Then, the relation between combination parameters (σ'_x, σ'_y) and slip lengths (b_x, b_y) is deduced to implement the new slip boundary condition. Previous research on the derivation of the relation is studied by taking the two-dimensional unidirectional steady flow as an example, which is expressed as [24–26]:

$$\rho = const, u_y = 0, a_y = 0, \frac{\partial \phi}{\partial x} = 0, \frac{\partial \phi}{\partial t} = 0 \qquad (38)$$

where ϕ denotes flow variable, such as the velocity or density.

In this work, it is assumed that the anisotropic slip includes two components in streamwise and spanwise directions. Take the liquid slip on a horizontal plane (perpendicular to the z-axis) as an example. The slip length includes two components, b_x, b_y in the x and y directions, respectively. With the assumption of anisotropic slip, the simulation and characterization of the slip effect on a superhydrophobic surface can match the actual situation.

The upper wall in 3D is employed to derive the relationship between the parameters σ'_x, σ'_y and the slip lengths b_x, b_y.

The flow near the wall satisfies the continuity equation:

$$\frac{\partial \rho}{\partial t} + \frac{\partial \rho u_x}{\partial x} + \frac{\partial \rho u_y}{\partial y} + \frac{\partial \rho u_z}{\partial z} = 0 \qquad (39)$$

With the assumption of no density change in the incompressible flow, the continuity equation can be written as,

$$\frac{\partial u_x}{\partial x} + \frac{\partial u_y}{\partial y} + \frac{\partial u_z}{\partial z} = 0 \tag{40}$$

In the 3D directional flows, the velocity distribution near the wall is assumed to be satisfied the following equations:

$$\frac{\partial u_x}{\partial y} = 0, \; \frac{\partial u_y}{\partial x} = 0, \; u_z = 0 \tag{41}$$

As shown in Figure 2, the local coordinate system $(\bar{x}, \bar{y}, \bar{z})$ in 3D is established in the lattice unit, where a node on the wall is served as the origin. The $\bar{x} - \bar{y}$ plane is located on the wall. The $\bar{z}$ direction is normal along the wall. In the local coordinate system, the boundary of the upper wall is located at the plane $\bar{z} = 1$, and the solid is located in the region ($\bar{z} < 1$), e.g., the plane $\bar{z} = 0$.

As shown in Ref. [68], the measured velocity profiles across the channel with a parabolic fit are observed and recorded. Therefore, in this work, it is assumed that the nonlinear velocity profiles near the wall are parabolic in the $\bar{z}$ direction, conforming to the quadratic term fitting. The velocity profiles can be linear when the quadratic coefficient is 0. Then, the function of velocity profiles near the wall will be simplified as follows:

$$u_x(\bar{x}, \bar{z}) = u_x(\bar{x}) + \alpha_1 \bar{z}^2 + \beta_1 \bar{z} + e_1 \tag{42}$$

$$u_y(\bar{y}, \bar{z}) = u_y(\bar{y}) + \alpha_2 \bar{z}^2 + \beta_2 \bar{z} + e_2 \tag{43}$$

The acceleration can be approximated by relations as follows [69]:

$$a_x \approx -\nu \frac{\partial^2 u_x(\bar{x}, \bar{z})}{\partial \bar{z}^2}, a_y \approx -\nu \frac{\partial^2 u_y(\bar{y}, \bar{z})}{\partial \bar{z}^2}. \tag{44}$$

Then, the coefficients can be obtained by the acceleration, $\alpha_1 = -0.5 \, a_x/\nu$, $\alpha_2 = -0.5 \, a_y/\nu$. The slip velocity can be expressed as:

$$u_{sx} = u_x(\bar{x}, \bar{z})|_{\bar{z}=1} - U_{Wx}, u_{sy} = u_y(\bar{y}, \bar{z})|_{\bar{z}=1} - U_{Wy}. \tag{45}$$

The slip velocity on a wall is characterized in the form of a Navier slip boundary condition in both the streamwise direction and the spanwise direction [35]:

$$u_{sx} = b_x \frac{\partial u_x}{\partial \bar{z}}|_{\text{wall}}, \; u_{sy} = b_y \frac{\partial u_y}{\partial \bar{z}}|_{\text{wall}} \tag{46}$$

Considering Equations (42) and (43), (46) can be written as:

$$u_{sx} = b_x \frac{\partial u_x}{\partial \bar{z}}|_{\bar{z}=0} = b_x \beta_1, u_{sy} = b_y \frac{\partial u_y}{\partial \bar{z}}|_{\bar{z}=0} = b_y \beta_2. \tag{47}$$

With the Taylor expansion around the $\bar{z} = 1$ in the local coordinate system, $u_x(\bar{z})$ and $u_y(\bar{z})$ can be approximated,

$$u_x(\bar{z})|_{\bar{z}=2} = u_x(\bar{z})|_{\bar{z}=1} + \Delta \bar{z} \frac{\partial u_x(\bar{z})}{\partial \bar{z}}|_{\bar{z}=1} + \frac{\Delta \bar{z}^2}{2}(\frac{\partial^2 u_x(\bar{z})}{\partial \bar{z}^2})|_{\bar{z}=1} + O(\Delta \bar{z}^3) \tag{48}$$

$$u_y(\bar{z})|_{\bar{z}=2} = u_y(\bar{z})|_{\bar{z}=1} + \Delta \bar{z} \frac{\partial u_y(\bar{z})}{\partial \bar{z}}|_{\bar{z}=1} + \frac{\Delta \bar{z}^2}{2}(\frac{\partial^2 u_y(\bar{z})}{\partial \bar{z}^2})|_{\bar{z}=1} + O(\Delta \bar{z}^3) \tag{49}$$

With the assumption of parabolic velocity profiles near the wall, substitute the above equations, and the following equations can be obtained,

$$u_x(\overline{x},\overline{z})|_{\overline{z}=2} - u_x(\overline{x},\overline{z})|_{\overline{z}=1} = (\Delta\overline{z}^2 + 2\Delta\overline{z})\alpha_1 + \Delta\overline{z}\beta_1,$$
$$u_y(\overline{y},\overline{z})|_{\overline{z}=2} - u_x(\overline{y},\overline{z})|_{\overline{z}=1} = (\Delta\overline{z}^2 + 2\Delta\overline{z})\alpha_2 + \Delta\overline{z}\beta_2. \tag{50}$$

Then, the relations between the coefficients are given as,

$$\beta_1 = \frac{(3 - \Delta\overline{z}^2 - 2\Delta\overline{z})}{\Delta\overline{z} - 1 + O(\Delta\overline{z})}\alpha_1 \tag{51}$$

$$\beta_2 = \frac{(3 - \Delta\overline{z}^2 - 2\Delta\overline{z})}{\Delta\overline{z} - 1 + O(\Delta\overline{z})}\alpha_2 \tag{52}$$

For D3Q19 lattice model, with $\rho\mathbf{u} = \sum_{\alpha=0}^{18}\boldsymbol{\xi}_\alpha f_\alpha$ known, the local velocities u_x, u_y at $\overline{z} = 1$ and 2 can be calculated as,

$$\rho u_x|_{\overline{z}=1} = \tilde{f}_1^1 - \tilde{f}_2^1 + \tilde{f}_7^1 - \tilde{f}_{10}^1 + \tilde{f}_9^1 - \tilde{f}_8^1,$$
$$\rho u_x|_{\overline{z}=2} = \tilde{f}_1^2 - \tilde{f}_2^2 + \tilde{f}_7^2 - \tilde{f}_{10}^2 + \tilde{f}_9^2 - \tilde{f}_8^2, \tag{53}$$

$$\rho u_y|_{\overline{z}=1} = \tilde{f}_6^1 - \tilde{f}_5^1 + \tilde{f}_{13}^1 - \tilde{f}_{11}^1 + \tilde{f}_{12}^1 - \tilde{f}_{14}^1,$$
$$\rho u_y|_{\overline{z}=2} = \tilde{f}_6^2 - \tilde{f}_5^2 + \tilde{f}_{13}^2 - \tilde{f}_{11}^2 + \tilde{f}_{12}^2 - \tilde{f}_{14}^2. \tag{54}$$

Combined with the proposed slip boundary condition, the following relations can be obtained:

$$\tilde{f}_9 - \tilde{f}_8 = \tilde{f}_7 - \tilde{f}_{10} + \sigma'_x\left\{\rho U_{Wx} - [\tilde{f}_1 - \tilde{f}_2 + 2(\tilde{f}_7 - \tilde{f}_{10})]\right\},$$
$$\tilde{f}_{12} - \tilde{f}_{14} = \tilde{f}_{13} - \tilde{f}_{11} + \sigma'_y\left\{\rho U_{Wy} - [\tilde{f}_6 - \tilde{f}_5 + 2(\tilde{f}_{13} - \tilde{f}_{11})]\right\}. \tag{55}$$

Then,

$$\rho u_x|_{\overline{z}=1} = (1 - \sigma'_x)[\tilde{f}_1^1 - \tilde{f}_2^1 + 2(\tilde{f}_7^1 - \tilde{f}_{10}^1)] + \sigma'_x\rho U_{Wx},$$
$$\rho u_x|_{\overline{z}=2} = (1 - \sigma'_x)[\tilde{f}_1^2 - \tilde{f}_2^2 + 2(\tilde{f}_7^2 - \tilde{f}_{10}^2)] + \sigma'_x\rho U_{Wx},$$
$$\rho u_y|_{\overline{z}=1} = (1 - \sigma'_y)[\tilde{f}_6^1 - \tilde{f}_5^1 + 2(\tilde{f}_{13}^1 - \tilde{f}_{11}^1)] + \sigma'_y\rho U_{Wy},$$
$$\rho u_y|_{\overline{z}=2} = (1 - \sigma'_y)[\tilde{f}_6^2 - \tilde{f}_5^2 + 2(\tilde{f}_{13}^2 - \tilde{f}_{11}^2)] + \sigma'_y\rho U_{Wy}. \tag{56}$$

The difference value between velocity at $\overline{z} = 1$ and $\overline{z} = 2$ can be written as:

$$u_x|_{\overline{z}=2} - u_x|_{\overline{z}=1} = \frac{1}{\rho}(1 - \sigma'_x)\{(\tilde{f}_1^2 - \tilde{f}_2^2) - (\tilde{f}_1^1 - \tilde{f}_2^1) + 2[(\tilde{f}_7^2 - \tilde{f}_{10}^2) - (\tilde{f}_7^1 - \tilde{f}_{10}^1)]\},$$
$$u_y|_{\overline{z}=2} - u_y|_{\overline{z}=1} = \frac{1}{\rho}(1 - \sigma'_y)\{(\tilde{f}_6^2 - \tilde{f}_5^2) - (\tilde{f}_6^1 - \tilde{f}_5^1) + 2[(\tilde{f}_{13}^2 - \tilde{f}_{11}^2) + (\tilde{f}_{13}^1 - \tilde{f}_{11}^1)]\}. \tag{57}$$

Inspired by Guo et al. [69], the collision and streaming rule in the LBM is adopted to establish the relationship between velocities near the wall. Considering the collision and streaming rule of LBE with BGK operator [70], the following relations can be obtained:

$$\text{x - direction}: \tilde{f}_7^1 - \tilde{f}_{10}^1 = \tilde{\tilde{f}}_7^2 - \tilde{\tilde{f}}_{10}^2, \tilde{f}_9^2 - \tilde{f}_8^2 = \tilde{\tilde{f}}_9^1 - \tilde{\tilde{f}}_8^1 \tag{58}$$

$$\text{y - direction}: \tilde{f}_{13}^1 - \tilde{f}_{11}^1 = \tilde{\tilde{f}}_{13}^2 - \tilde{\tilde{f}}_{11}^2, \tilde{f}_{12}^2 - \tilde{f}_{14}^2 = \tilde{\tilde{f}}_{12}^1 - \tilde{\tilde{f}}_{14}^1 \tag{59}$$

where $\tilde{\tilde{f}}$ denotes the tracked distribution function in the collision.

Then, Equation (57) can be simplified as follows:

$$u_x|_{\overline{z}=2} - u_x|_{\overline{z}=1} = \frac{3\sigma'_x}{\tau(1 - \sigma'_x)}(u_x|_{\overline{z}=1} - U_{Wx}) \tag{60}$$

$$u_y|_{\bar{z}=2} - u_y|_{\bar{z}=1} = \frac{3\sigma'_y}{\tau(1-\sigma'_y)}(u_y|_{\bar{z}=1} - U_{Wy}) \tag{61}$$

The slip velocity could be calculated as:

$$u_{sx} = b_x \frac{\partial u_x}{\partial \bar{z}}|_{\bar{z}=0} = b_x \beta_1 = u_x|_{\bar{z}=1} - U_{Wx} = \frac{\tau(1-\sigma'_x)}{3\sigma'_x}(u_x|_{\bar{z}=2} - u_x|_{\bar{z}=1}) \tag{62}$$

$$u_{sy} = b_x \frac{\partial u_y}{\partial \bar{z}}|_{\bar{z}=0} = b_y \beta_1 = u_y|_{\bar{z}=1} - U_{Wy} = \frac{\tau(1-\sigma'_y)}{3\sigma'_y}(u_y|_{\bar{z}=2} - u_y|_{\bar{z}=1}) \tag{63}$$

Finally, the relations between the slip lengths and parameters are obtained:

$$b_x = \frac{\tau(1-\sigma'_x)}{3\sigma'_x}(u_x|_{\bar{z}=2} - u_x|_{\bar{z}=1})/\beta_1 = (\Delta \bar{z}^2 + 2\Delta \bar{z})\frac{\alpha_1}{\beta_1} + \Delta \bar{z} \tag{64}$$

$$b_y = \frac{\tau(1-\sigma'_y)}{3\sigma'_y}(u_y|_{\bar{z}=2} - u_y|_{\bar{z}=1})/\beta_1 = (\Delta \bar{z}^2 + 2\Delta \bar{z})\frac{\alpha_2}{\beta_2} + \Delta \bar{z} \tag{65}$$

With the known values of $\alpha_1/\beta_1, \alpha_2/\beta_2$, Equations (64) and (65) can be simplified,

$$\sigma'_x = \frac{1}{1+\frac{3b_x}{A\tau}}, \sigma'_y = \frac{1}{1+\frac{3b_y}{A\tau}}. \tag{66}$$

where A denotes the correction coefficient and is determined by:

$$A = (\Delta \bar{z}^2 + \Delta \bar{z})\frac{\Delta \bar{z} - 1 + O(\Delta \bar{z}^3)}{3 - \Delta \bar{z}^2 - 2\Delta \bar{z}} + \Delta \bar{z} \tag{67}$$

where $\Delta \bar{z}$ is the lattice grid spacing.

For the upper horizontal wall boundary in 3D, a new slip boundary condition is significantly determined by Equations (35), (66), and (67). Similar derivation and operation can be applied to the lower wall and side walls.

2.5. Corner Boundary Condition

The above discussion on boundary conditions focuses on straight surfaces. Considering the singularity, the treatment of corners should not be ignored in numerical simulations of the flow, such as the lid-driven cavity flow. Although corners account for only a few nodes, these corners should not be underestimated because the particle can stream in the fluid domain, which has influences on the performance of the numerical simulation. One single point may contaminate the numerical solution everywhere [71]. One of the earliest systematic approaches to treating corners in DUGKS was proposed by Guo et al. [72]. However, this approach is limited to 2D implementations. In this work, to reduce the singularities and improve the performance of numerical simulation, an approach to treating the corner boundary condition is proposed for the DUGKS based on the D3Q19 model with 19 independent moments [73].

$$0^{\text{th}}: \rho = \sum_i f_i; \ 1^{\text{st}}: \rho u_\alpha = \sum_i f_i \xi_{i\alpha}; \ 2^{\text{nd}}: \Pi_{\alpha\beta} = \sum_i f_i \xi_{i\alpha} \xi_{i\beta};$$
$$3^{\text{rd}}: Q_{\alpha\beta\gamma} = \sum_i f_i \xi_{i\alpha} \xi_{i\beta} \xi_{i\gamma}; \ 4^{\text{th}}: S_{\alpha\beta\gamma\delta} = \sum_i f_i \xi_{i\alpha} \xi_{i\beta} \xi_{i\gamma} \xi_{i\delta}. \tag{68}$$

The 0th moment has 1 equation, the 1st moment has 3 equations, the 2nd moment has 6 equations, the 3rd moment has 6 equations, and the 4th moment has 3 equations. In the 3D domain, there are 12 unknowns at every corner. So, 12 linearly independent moments are required. For the D3Q19 model, as shown in Figure 1b, the unknown functions are $f_1, f_3, f_6, f_7, f_9, f_{10}, f_{11}, f_{12}, f_{13}, f_{15}, f_{16}, f_{17}$, considering the low-south-west corner. We select the momenta $\rho u_x, \rho u_y, \rho u_z$, the momentum fluxes and shear stresses

$\Pi_{xx}, \Pi_{yy}, \Pi_{zz}, \Pi_{xy}, \Pi_{xz}, \Pi_{yz}$, and three higher-order moments $Q_{xxy}, Q_{yyz}, Q_{xzz}$ as 12 linearly independent moments.

$$\text{rank}\begin{bmatrix} \widetilde{f}_1 + \widetilde{f}_9 - \widetilde{f}_{10} + \widetilde{f}_{15} - \widetilde{f}_{16} + \widetilde{f}_{17} & \rho u_x \\ \widetilde{f}_6 - \widetilde{f}_{11} + \widetilde{f}_{12} + \widetilde{f}_{13} - \widetilde{f}_{15} + \widetilde{f}_{16} + \widetilde{f}_{17} & \rho u_y \\ \widetilde{f}_3 + \widetilde{f}_7 - \widetilde{f}_9 + \widetilde{f}_{10} + \widetilde{f}_{11} - \widetilde{f}_{12} + \widetilde{f}_{13} & \rho u_z \\ \widetilde{f}_1 + \widetilde{f}_9 + \widetilde{f}_{10} + \widetilde{f}_{15} + \widetilde{f}_{16} + \widetilde{f}_{17} & \Pi_{xx} \\ \widetilde{f}_6 + \widetilde{f}_{11} + \widetilde{f}_{12} + \widetilde{f}_{13} + \widetilde{f}_{15} + \widetilde{f}_{16} + \widetilde{f}_{17} & \Pi_{yy} \\ \widetilde{f}_3 + \widetilde{f}_7 + \widetilde{f}_9 + \widetilde{f}_{10} + \widetilde{f}_{11} + \widetilde{f}_{12} + \widetilde{f}_{13} & \Pi_{zz} \\ \widetilde{f}_{17} - \widetilde{f}_{15} - \widetilde{f}_{16} & \Pi_{xy} \\ \widetilde{f}_7 - \widetilde{f}_9 - \widetilde{f}_{10} & \Pi_{xz} \\ \widetilde{f}_{13} - \widetilde{f}_{11} - \widetilde{f}_{12} & \Pi_{yz} \\ \widetilde{f}_{17} - \widetilde{f}_{15} + \widetilde{f}_{16} & Q_{xxy} \\ \widetilde{f}_7 + \widetilde{f}_9 - \widetilde{f}_{10} & Q_{xzz} \\ \widetilde{f}_{13} + \widetilde{f}_{11} - \widetilde{f}_{12} & Q_{yyz} \end{bmatrix} = 12 \quad (69)$$

The moments can be approximated by the Chapman–Enskog expansion as follows:

$$\Pi_{\alpha\beta} = \Pi_{\alpha\beta}^{(0)} + \varepsilon \Pi_{\alpha\beta}^{(1)} + O(\varepsilon^2) \approx \Pi_{\alpha\beta}^{(0)}, Q_{\alpha\beta} = Q_{\alpha\beta}^{(0)} + \varepsilon Q_{\alpha\beta}^{(1)} + O(\varepsilon^2) \approx Q_{\alpha\beta}^{(0)} \quad (70)$$

where the equilibrium part of the momentum flux tensor ($\Pi_{\alpha\beta}^{(0)}$) and the third-order moment ($Q_{\alpha\beta}^{(0)}$) can be expressed as:

$$\begin{aligned} \Pi_{\alpha\beta}^{(0)} &= \sum_i f_i^{(0)} \xi_{i\alpha} \xi_{i\beta} = \rho u_\alpha u_\beta + \rho c_s^2 \delta_{\alpha\beta}, \\ Q_{\alpha\beta\gamma}^{(0)} &= \sum_i f_i^{(0)} \xi_{i\alpha} \xi_{i\beta} \xi_{i\gamma} = \rho c_s^2 (u_\alpha \delta_{\beta\gamma} + u_\beta \delta_{\alpha\gamma} + u_\gamma \delta_{\alpha\beta}). \end{aligned} \quad (71)$$

The velocity is set to 0 at the corner, and some terms are assumed to be negligible. The momentum fluxes and shear stresses $\Pi_{xx}, \Pi_{yy}, \Pi_{zz}, \Pi_{xy}, \Pi_{xz}, \Pi_{yz}$, and three higher-order moments $Q_{xxy}, Q_{yyz}, Q_{xzz}$ are written as follows:

$$\begin{aligned} \Pi_{xx} &= \Pi_{yy} = \Pi_{zz} = \rho c_s^2 = \rho/3, \\ \Pi_{xy} &= \rho u_x u_y = 0, \Pi_{xz} = \rho u_x u_z = 0, \Pi_{yz} = \rho u_y u_z = 0, \\ Q_{xxy} &= \tfrac{\rho}{3}(u_x \delta_{xy} + u_x \delta_{xy} + u_y \delta_{xx}) = \tfrac{\rho}{3} u_y = 0, \\ Q_{yyz} &= \tfrac{\rho}{3}(u_y \delta_{yz} + u_y \delta_{yz} + u_z \delta_{yy}) = \tfrac{\rho}{3} u_z = 0, \\ Q_{xzz} &= \tfrac{\rho}{3}(u_x \delta_{zz} + u_x \delta_{xz} + u_z \delta_{xz}) = \tfrac{\rho}{3} u_x = 0. \end{aligned} \quad (72)$$

The unknown functions are calculated as:

$$\begin{aligned} \widetilde{f}_1 &= -\tfrac{\rho}{3} + \widetilde{f}_2 + 2\widetilde{f}_5 + 4\widetilde{f}_{14} + 4\widetilde{f}_{18} \\ \widetilde{f}_3 &= -\tfrac{\rho}{3} + \widetilde{f}_4 + 2\widetilde{f}_2 + 4\widetilde{f}_8 + 4\widetilde{f}_{18} \\ \widetilde{f}_6 &= -\tfrac{\rho}{3} + \widetilde{f}_5 + 2\widetilde{f}_4 + 4\widetilde{f}_8 + 4\widetilde{f}_{14} \\ \widetilde{f}_7 &= \tfrac{\rho}{6} - \widetilde{f}_2 - \widetilde{f}_8 - 2\widetilde{f}_{18} \\ \widetilde{f}_9 &= \widetilde{f}_8 \\ \widetilde{f}_{10} &= \tfrac{\rho}{6} - \widetilde{f}_2 - \widetilde{f}_8 - 2\widetilde{f}_{18} \\ \widetilde{f}_{11} &= \widetilde{f}_{14} \\ \widetilde{f}_{12} &= \tfrac{\rho}{6} - \widetilde{f}_4 - \widetilde{f}_{14} - 2\widetilde{f}_8 \\ \widetilde{f}_{13} &= \tfrac{\rho}{6} - \widetilde{f}_4 - \widetilde{f}_{14} - 2\widetilde{f}_8 \\ \widetilde{f}_{15} &= \tfrac{\rho}{6} - \widetilde{f}_5 - \widetilde{f}_{18} - 2\widetilde{f}_{14} \\ \widetilde{f}_{16} &= \widetilde{f}_{18} \\ \widetilde{f}_{17} &= \tfrac{\rho}{6} - \widetilde{f}_5 - \widetilde{f}_{18} - 2\widetilde{f}_{14} \end{aligned} \quad (73)$$

The density at the low-south-west corner is calculated as:

$$\rho = \tilde{f}_0 + 2(\tilde{f}_2 + \tilde{f}_4 + \tilde{f}_5) + 4(\tilde{f}_8 + \tilde{f}_{14} + \tilde{f}_{18}). \tag{74}$$

Similar manipulations can be applied to other corner nodes.

2.6. Algorithm

The updating of $\tilde{f}_\alpha$ from time $t^n = n\Delta t$ to time $t^{n+1} = (n+1)\Delta t$ in the DUGKS can be performed as the following brief algorithm.

1. Initialize the density, velocity, and viscosity. Obtain the values of $f_\alpha^{eq,n}$ and $\tilde{f}_\alpha^n$ at time $t = 0$.
2. Compute the distribution functions $\overline{f}_\alpha^{+,n}$ and $\tilde{f}_\alpha^{+,n}$ using Equations (16) and (18)
3. Compute the value of $\nabla \overline{f}_\alpha^{+,n}(x_b)$ and $\overline{f}_\alpha^{+,n}(x_b)$ using Equation (15).
4. Compute the distribution function $\overline{f}_\alpha^{n+1/2}(x_b)$ using Equations (14) and (13).
5. Get the macro values of density and velocity using Equation (17). Compute the equilibrium distribution function $f_\alpha^{eq,n+1/2}(x_b)$.
6. Compute the distribution function $f_\alpha^{n+1/2}(x_b)$ using Equation (13). Obtain the flux $\mathcal{F}_\alpha^{n+1/2}$ by Equation (5).
7. For the unknown distribution functions at the boundary or corner, the boundary conditions are employed, such as Equations (35) or (73).
8. Update the distribution function $\tilde{f}_\alpha^{n+1}$ using Equation (8). Obtain the macro values of density and velocity.
9. Repeat steps (2)–(8) until the convergence criterion is satisfied.

In C++ DUGKS computer code, the convergence criterion for attaining the steady-state solution is $\sum |u(t) - u(t - 1000\Delta t)| / \sum |u(t)| < 10^{-6}$, where $u(t)$ represents the velocity in the flow field.

3. Numerical Validation

The flow in a 3D channel is a fundamental case in science and engineering. Only a few references on the anisotropic slip boundary condition are available for comparison, so the flow in the 3D channel is selected as the case for numerical validation.

3.1. Comparison with Single-Component Lattice Boltzmann Simulation

In Ref. [11], the slip boundary condition is modelled by combining the bounce-back and specular reflection (BSR) scheme using the single-component lattice Boltzmann method. The relevant parameters in the present simulation remain the same as those in Ref. [11]. As shown in Figure 3, the microchannel's length, width, and height are 600 μm, 300 μm, and 30 μm, respectively. With the grid convergence study, the spatial discretization with resolution 400 × 200 × 20 (X, Y, and Z directions, respectively) is selected for the subsequent numerical simulations. The inlet and outlet along the X-direction adopt the periodic boundary condition. The remaining four walls adopt the no-slip/slip boundary conditions. For the no-slip case, the bounce-back scheme in LBM is used without treating the corner in Ref. [11], and the bounce-back scheme in DUGKS is used with the corner boundary condition in the present work. For the slip case, the BSR scheme is employed in Ref. [11], and the present method is employed in this work.

In the no-slip case, the present results agree well with the exact solution [74] and experimental result [9], as shown in Figure 4a. It is observed that the present results agree a little better with the exact solution than the BSR scheme in Ref. [11], which shows that the 3D corner boundary condition improves the accuracy.

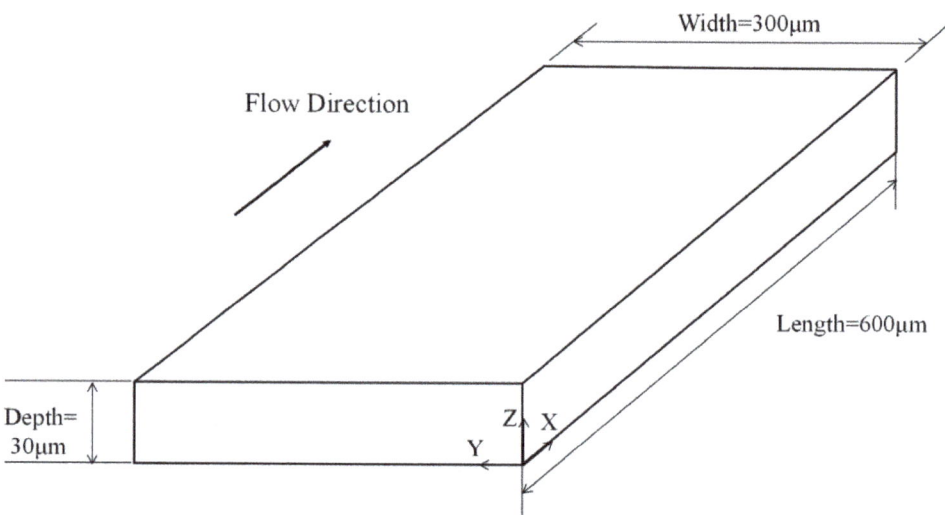

Figure 3. The diagram of a 3D microchannel.

In the slip case, the present results are closer to the experimental results [9] than those in Ref. [11], as shown in Figure 4b. The present method is more accurate than the BSR scheme in Ref. [11], which may be partly explained by the case that the BSR scheme can generate numerical slip, but the present method with the external force term can eliminate the numerical slip.

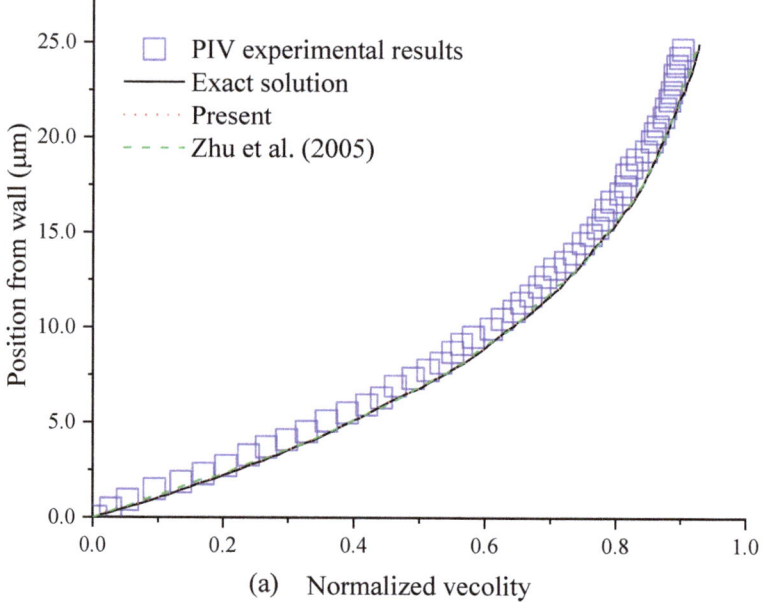

(a) Normalized vecolity

Figure 4. *Cont.*

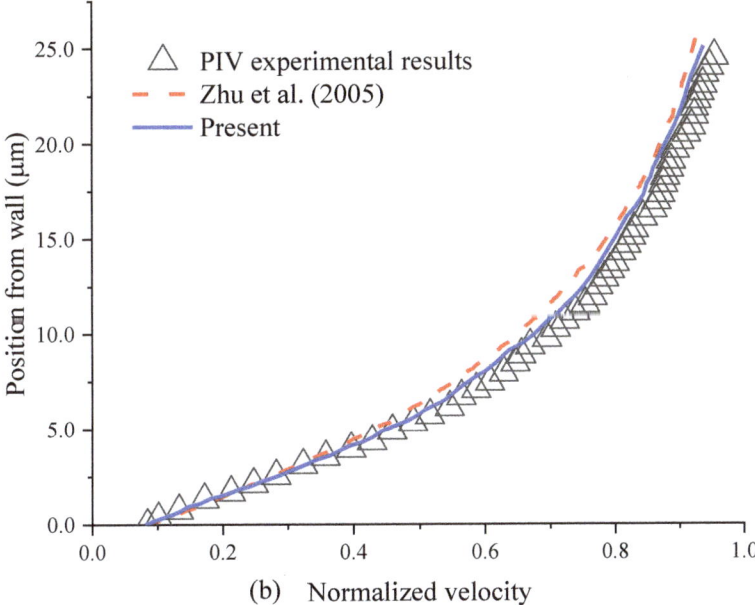

Figure 4. Velocity profiles in the no-slip case (**a**) and slip case (**b**). The data are obtained from the line (X = 300 μm, Z = 15 μm) normal to the right sidewall as a function of Y.

3.2. Comparison with Direct Numerical Simulation

In Ref. [14], the value of the streamwise slip length is set to equal the spanwise slip length. Furthermore, the case where the value of streamwise slip length is not equal to the spanwise slip length should be considered. With the different values of streamwise and spanwise slip lengths, the effect of anisotropic slip on velocity profiles and drag has been addressed using direct numerical simulations (DNS) of a turbulent channel flow [75]. In Ref. [75], the Navier slip length boundary condition adopts a linear slip length model. In this work, the present boundary condition is related to the second partial derivative of the velocity, with the assumption of nonlinear velocity profiles near the wall.

To test the accuracy of predicting the drag and velocity, the present method is performed in six different cases at $Re_\tau = u_{\tau 0}\delta/\nu = 180$: (1) Case 1: $b_x^{+0} = 0.1$, $b_y^{+0} = 1$; (2) Case 2: $b_x^{+0} = 0.316$, $b_y^{+0} = 1$; (3) Case 3: $b_x^{+0} = 3.16$, $b_y^{+0} = 1$; (4) Case 4: $b_x^{+0} = 10$, $b_y^{+0} = 1$; (5) Case 5: $b_x^{+0} = 0.631$, $b_y^{+0} = 1$; (6) Case 6: $b_x^{+0} = 2.51$, $b_y^{+0} = 10$. δ and ν denote the channel half-height and kinematic viscosity, respectively. $u_{\tau 0}$ denotes the wall shear (friction) velocity in channel flow with no-slip walls. It is noted that the superscript +0 indicates slip length scales given in units of the viscous length scale $\nu/u_{\tau 0}$ in the respective no-slip reference case [76].

The numerical results of the present method are compared to the data in Ref. [75]. The mean streamwise velocity profile is shown in Figure 5, and the root-mean-square (rms) velocity fluctuations are shown in Figure 6. As shown in Figures 5 and 6, the present method is also accurate in predicting the velocity profiles in a turbulent channel flow with an anisotropic slip wall. Similar conclusions to those reported by A. Busse and N. D. Sandham [75] are obtained: the streamwise slip length is mainly responsible for determining mean velocity profiles. Streamwise slip length always has a reducing effect on the intensity of the turbulent fluctuations, and the reducing effect will increase with increasing slip length. Finite streamwise slip length can limit the turbulence-intensifying effects of infinite spanwise slip, thereby limiting the adverse effects of spanwise slip.

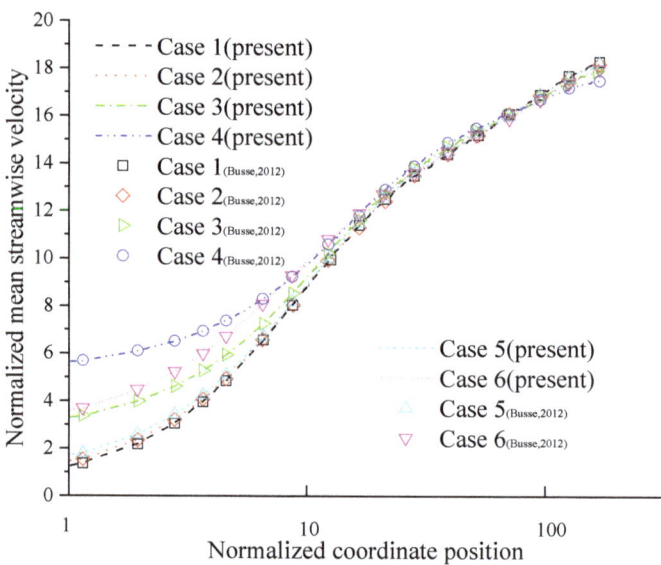

Figure 5. The mean streamwise velocity profiles.

To investigate the influence of an anisotropic slip on drag, the DUGKS simulations are conducted by adjusting the streamwise and spanwise slip lengths with the present slip boundary condition. The investigated slip length values are selected randomly. The present results are compared with those in Ref. [75].

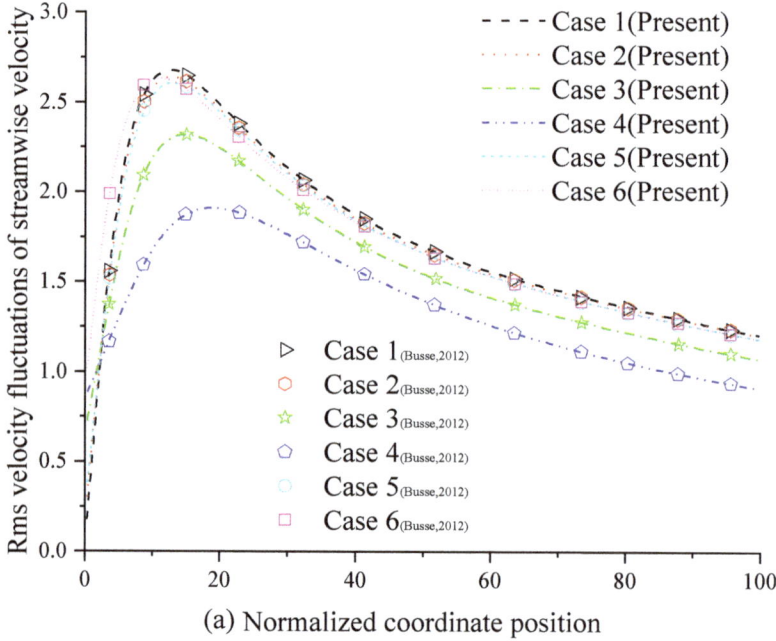

(a) Normalized coordinate position

Figure 6. *Cont.*

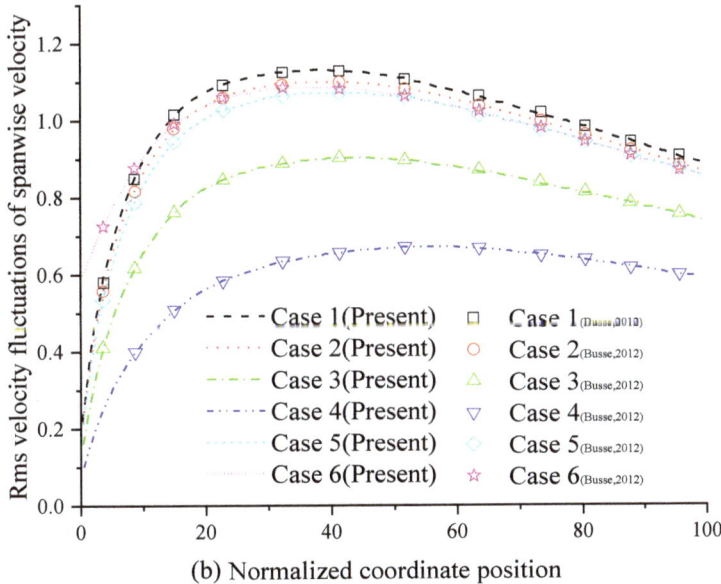

Figure 6. The rms velocity fluctuations of the streamwise velocity (**a**) and the spanwise velocity (**b**).

The percentage change in drag (DD) is defined by DD = $(dp/dx - dp/dx|_0)/(dp/dx|_0)$, where dp/dx and $dp/dx|_0$ represent the mean streamwise pressure gradient in the present and reference case, respectively. If DD < 0, the drag is reduced. The DD values are obtained from numerical results in the case of $Re_{\tau 0} = 180$ based on friction velocity $u_{\tau 0}$ in the reference case.

As shown in Figure 7, the dots match well with the lines, indicating that the present method is also accurate in predicting the change in drag. The same trends reported by Min and Kim [14] are recovered: drag is reduced in cases with pure streamwise slip and isotropic slip, but drag is increased in cases with pure spanwise slip.

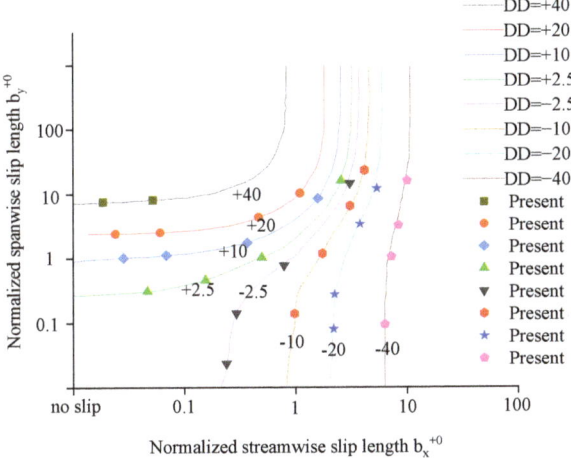

Figure 7. The percentage change in drag versus the streamwise and spanwise slip lengths. (Dots: present, Lines: DNS data [75]).

4. Application to the Two-Sided Orthogonal Oscillating Micro-Lid-Driven Cavity Flow

4.1. Problem Description

The problem is the micro-lid-driven cavity flow with two moving walls, as shown in Figure 8. For two-sided oscillating wall motion, the top and bottom walls move with oscillating velocity U = $U_0 \cos(\omega t)$, where U_0 = 1.0 m/s, oscillating frequency ω = 1875 π/s. The directions of the top and bottom walls are positive X-direction and Y-direction, respectively. The size of the cavity is 400 µm × 400 µm × 400 µm. The cavity is filled with water. The density and kinematic viscosity of water are $\rho = 1000$ kg/m^3 and $v = 1.0 \times 10^{-6}$ m^2/s, respectively. The Reynolds number is calculated as Re = $U_0 \times L/v$ = $1.0 \times 0.0004/10^{-6}$ = 400. For simplicity, ω has been dimensionalized as $\omega' = \omega L/U_0 = 0.75\pi$, and St = $\omega L^2/v = \omega'$Re = 300π.

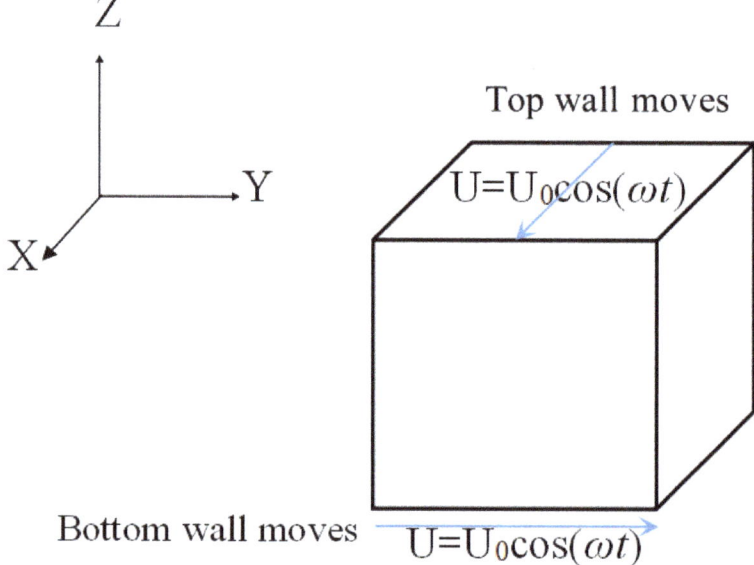

Figure 8. The two-sided orthogonal oscillating wall motion of the micro-lid-driven cavity.

4.2. Convergence Validation Study

To choose an optimal lattice size utilizing fewer computational resources, lattice size convergence is studied. Numerical simulations with two-sided uniformly moving wall motions are performed at Re = 400 using three lattice sizes: 80^3 (coarse), 120^3 (medium), and 160^3 (fine). Figure 9 shows the negligible improvement in the velocity profile on increasing the lattice size from 120^3 to 160^3.

So, the spatial discretization with resolution 120 × 120 × 120 is used for performing subsequent numerical simulations with two-sided orthogonal oscillating wall motions. To keep Re = 400, $U_{0\text{lattice}}$ = 1.0/15 and the kinematic viscosity is set to v_{lattice} = 0.02. The present slip boundary condition is applied to the top and bottom wall, and the corner boundary condition is applied to four corner nodes in the cavity. The four side walls remain at rest with the no-slip boundary condition.

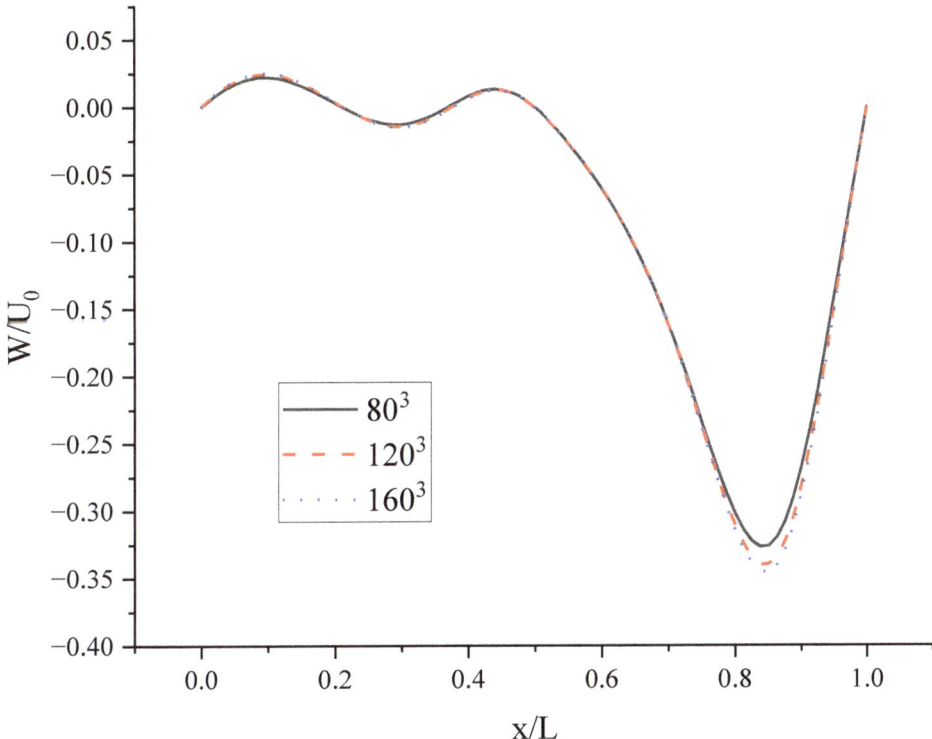

Figure 9. Velocity profiles for W on the horizontal centerlines of plane at y/L = 0.5.

4.3. Results and Discussion

There are mainly two types of slip distribution: pure streamwise slip emerges on both the top and bottom wall surfaces; and both streamwise and spanwise slips emerge on the top wall surface. For comparison, fourteen cases are considered: (a) both top and bottom walls: $b_x = b_y = 0$; (b) top wall: $b_x = 0.1$, $b_y = 0$, bottom wall: $b_x = b_y = 0$; (c) top wall: $b_x = b_y = 0$, bottom wall: $b_x = 0, b_y = 0.1$; (d) top wall: $b_x = 0, b_y = 0.1$, bottom wall: $b_x = b_y = 0$; (e) top wall: $b_x = 0.1$, $b_y = 0$, bottom wall: $b_x = 0$, $b_y = 0.1$; (f) top wall: $b_x = 0.1, b_y = 0.1$, bottom wall: $b_x = b_y = 0$; (g) top wall: $b_x = 0.1$, $b_y = 0$, bottom wall: $b_x = 0, b_y = 0.05$; (h) top wall: $b_x = 0.1$, $b_y = 0.05$, bottom wall: $b_x = b_y = 0$; (i) top wall: $b_x = 0.05$, $b_y = 0$, bottom wall: $b_x = 0$, $b_y = 0.1$; (j) top wall: $b_x = 0.05$, $b_y = 0.1$, bottom wall: $b_x = b_y = 0$; (k) top wall: $b_x = 0.1$, $b_y = 0$, bottom wall: $b_x = 0$, $b_y = 0.2$; (l) top wall: $b_x = 0.1$, $b_y = 0.2$, bottom wall: $b_x = b_y = 0$; (m) top wall: $b_x = 0.2$, $b_y = 0$, bottom wall: $b_x = 0$, $b_y = 0.1$; (n) top wall: $b_x = 0.2$, $b_y = 0.1$, bottom wall: $b_x = b_y = 0$. In Ref. [9], their work yields a slip length of approximately 1 μm at the wall coated with hydrophobic octadecyltrichlorosilane for water flow. In the present work, considering actual value of slip length, the values of 0.05, 0.1, and 0.2 in the lattice unit correspond to 0.25 μm, 0.5 μm, and 1 μm, respectively. The symbols b_x and b_y represent the slip length in the X and Y directions, respectively.

The velocity components and vorticity are important and common parameters to describe the flow. The present work performs a comprehensive parametric study discussing flow velocity components and vorticity. It is noted that U, V, and W are used to denote the velocity component in the X, Y, and Z directions, respectively. The vorticity magnitude is calculated as $\sqrt{\{(\partial W/\partial Y - \partial V/\partial Z)^2 + (\partial U/\partial Z - \partial W/\partial X)^2 + (\partial V/\partial X - \partial U/\partial Y)^2\}}$.

The contours for velocity U, V, and W and the vorticity magnitude of cases (a–n) at t = T, 0.25 T and 0.5 T are shown in Supplementary Material. It is found that nonphysical phenomena and numerical singularity do not exist, which shows that the present method is effective and the present results are credible. Furthermore, the centerline velocity profiles in the X, Y, and Z directions at t = T, 0.25 T and 0.5 T are shown in Figures 10–22.

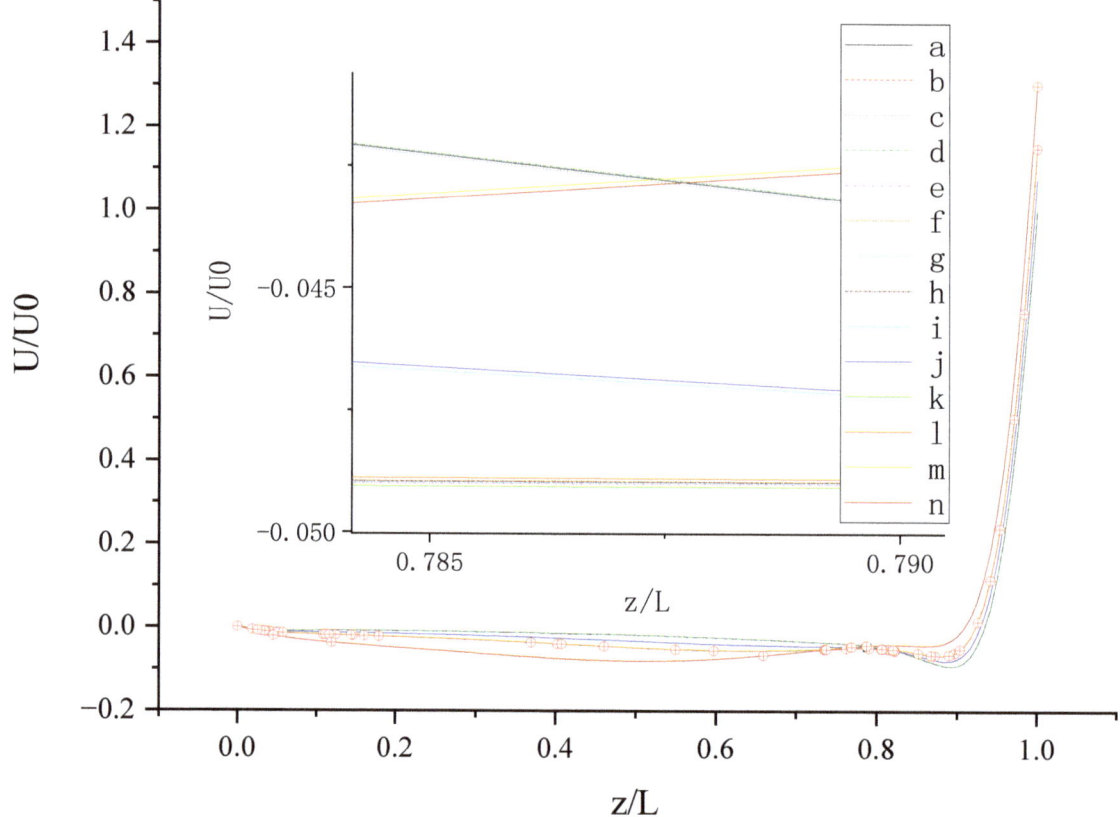

Figure 10. U along the centerline Z-axis at t = T. The red circles represent the points of intersection.

Figure 10 shows U (the velocity component in the X direction) along the centerline Z-axis at t = T and its magnified view. As shown in Figure 10, the 14 curves are divided into four groups according to the level of b_x (b_x = 0, 0.05, 0.1, and 0.2): group 1: cases (a, c, and d); group 2: cases (i and j); cases (b, e, f, g, h, k, and l); cases (m, and n). The slip length b_x has greater influence on U than b_y. It is found that velocity profiles in each group are very close. Therefore, for b_x at the same level, the existence of b_y on the top or bottom wall has almost no influence on the change in U along the centerline Z-axis. The greater b_x is, the greater the influence it has on the change in U along the centerline Z-axis for z/L < 0.9 (U < 0). For z/L > 0.9, U increases rapidly, and the closer the location is to the top wall, the faster U increases, and the greater the velocity gradient. When the curves intersect, the relative magnitude of the curves changes. The distribution of the intersection points is chaotic, as shown in the red circle in Figure 10. Therefore, when b_x = 0.1, the promotion effect of b_y on increasing U will change with the change in of z.

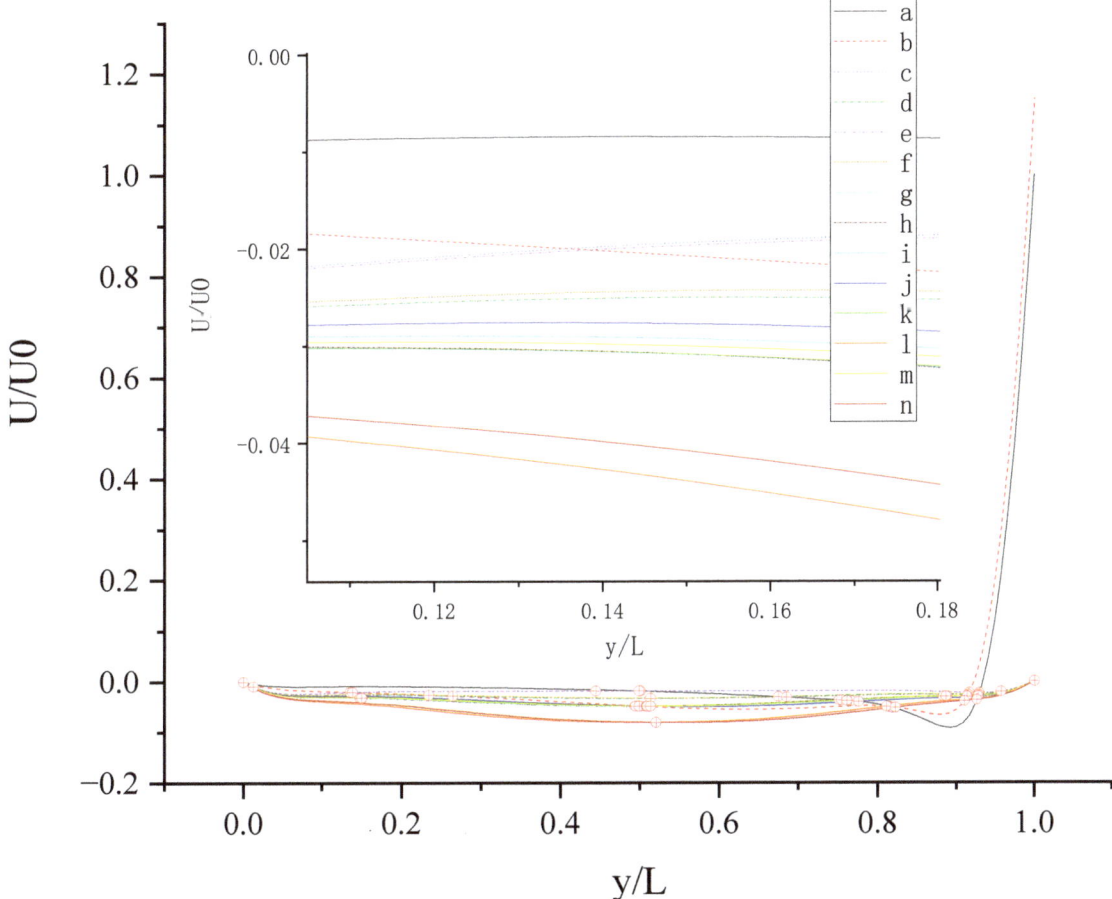

Figure 11. U along the centerline Y-axis at t = T. The red circles represent the points of intersection.

Figure 11 shows U (the velocity component in the X direction) along the centerline Y-axis at t = T and its magnified view. As shown in Figure 11, U is negative along the centerline Y-axis in cases (c-n), which indicates that the existence of b_y on the top wall or bottom wall results in the negative U along the centerline Y-axis. The anisotropic slip on the top wall with a larger slip length has a greater influence on the negative U along the centerline Y-axis, such as case (l) and case (n). For y/L < 0.52018, the absolute value of U in case (n) is less than that in case (l). For y/L > 0.52018, the absolute value of U in case (l) is less than that in case (n). Maybe there are more intersecting points near y/L = 0.5 and y/L = 0.915 because of the motion of the top and bottom walls and the interaction of the sidewalls and fluid.

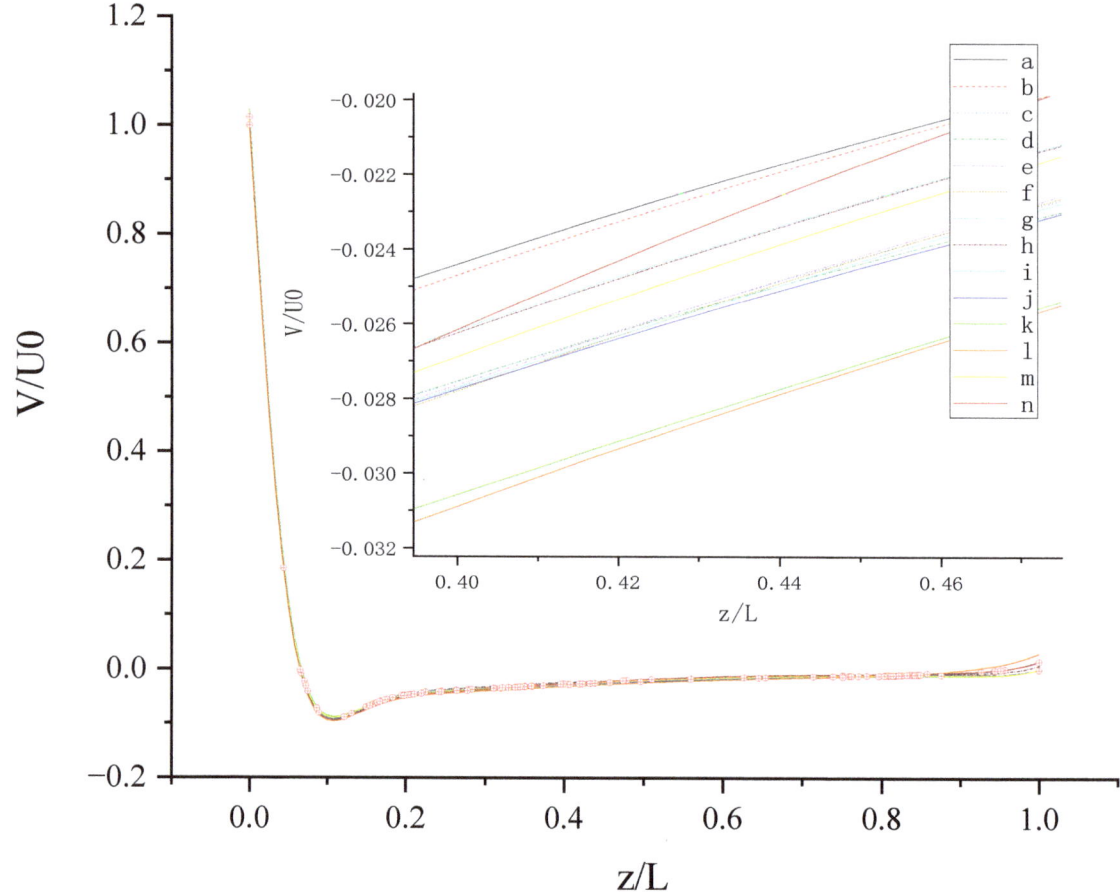

Figure 12. V along the centerline Z-axis at t = T. The red circles represent the points of intersection.

Figure 12 shows V (the velocity component in the Y direction) along the centerline Z-axis at t = T and its magnified view. As shown in Figure 12, the results of different slip combinations are relatively close with a slight difference, indicating that anisotropic slip has a minor influence on V along the centerline Z-axis. However, it can still be seen that the slip combination in case (l) has the greatest influence on V along the centerline Z-axis, where the absolute value of negative V is the largest, as shown in the magnified view. Near the top wall, the anisotropic slip in case (l) results in the maximum positive V. For z/L > 0.06554, the intersection points of the curves are mostly evenly distributed along the centerline Z-axis, indicating that the strong or weak influence of slip distribution on V will change at most positions along the centerline Z-axis. It may be caused by the time-dependent motion of both top and bottom walls. Maybe, in this condition, the velocity V is mainly influenced by the disordered flow driven by the walls, and the influence of slip on V is negligible. So, the effect of slip may be greatly reduced in the disordered flow.

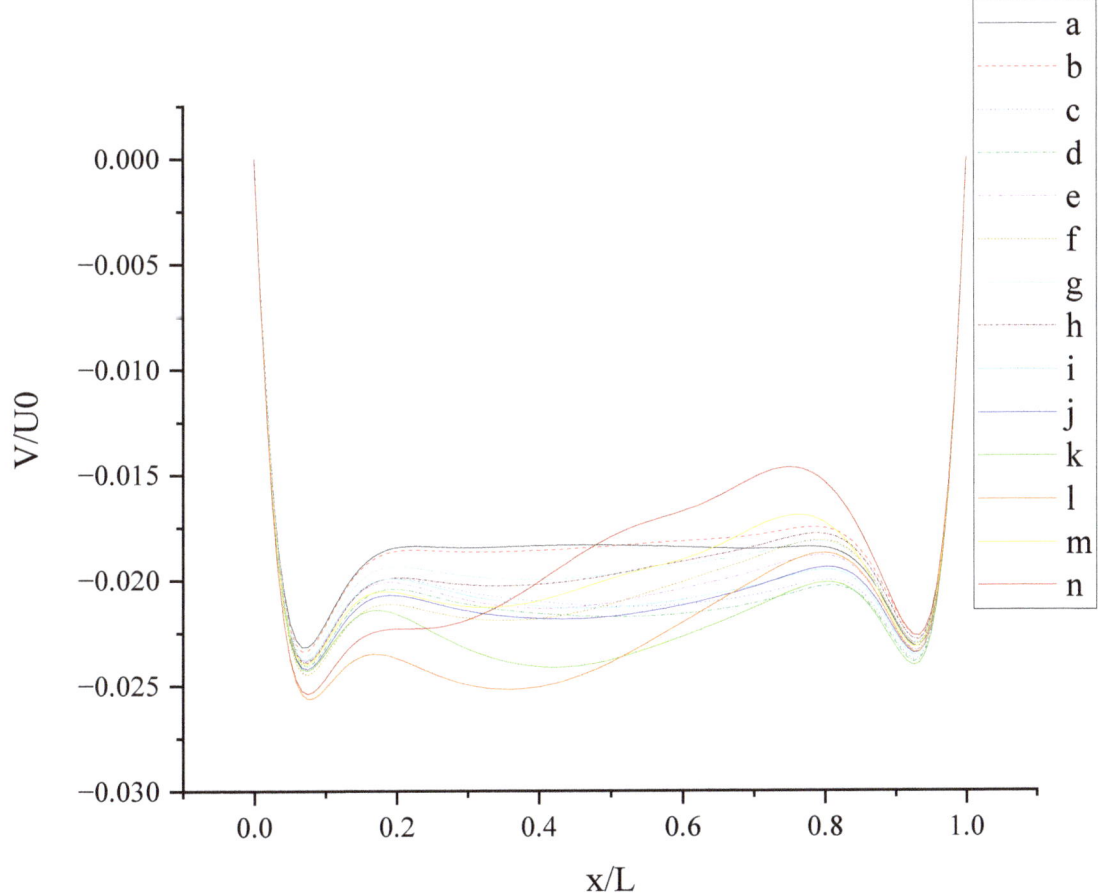

Figure 13. V along the centerline X-axis at t = T.

Figure 13 shows V (the velocity component in the Y direction) along the centerline X-axis at t = T. As shown in Figure 13, all curves have two troughs. For the no-slip condition, two troughs are located at $x/L \approx 0.07$ and $x/L \approx 0.93$. The slip condition makes the troughs closer to the center than the no-slip condition. Under the action of anisotropic slip, two peaks appear in the curve. The fluctuation range is large at large slip lengths, such as case (l) and case (n). Compared with pure slip in both top and bottom walls, anisotropic slip on the top wall results in stronger fluctuation disturbance and increases the 3D mixing of flow. The results of different slip combinations are similar near the side walls, and a great difference occurs in the cavity ($0.2 < x/L < 0.8$). The influence of slip on flow hardly propagates to the side walls, but mostly to the cavity.

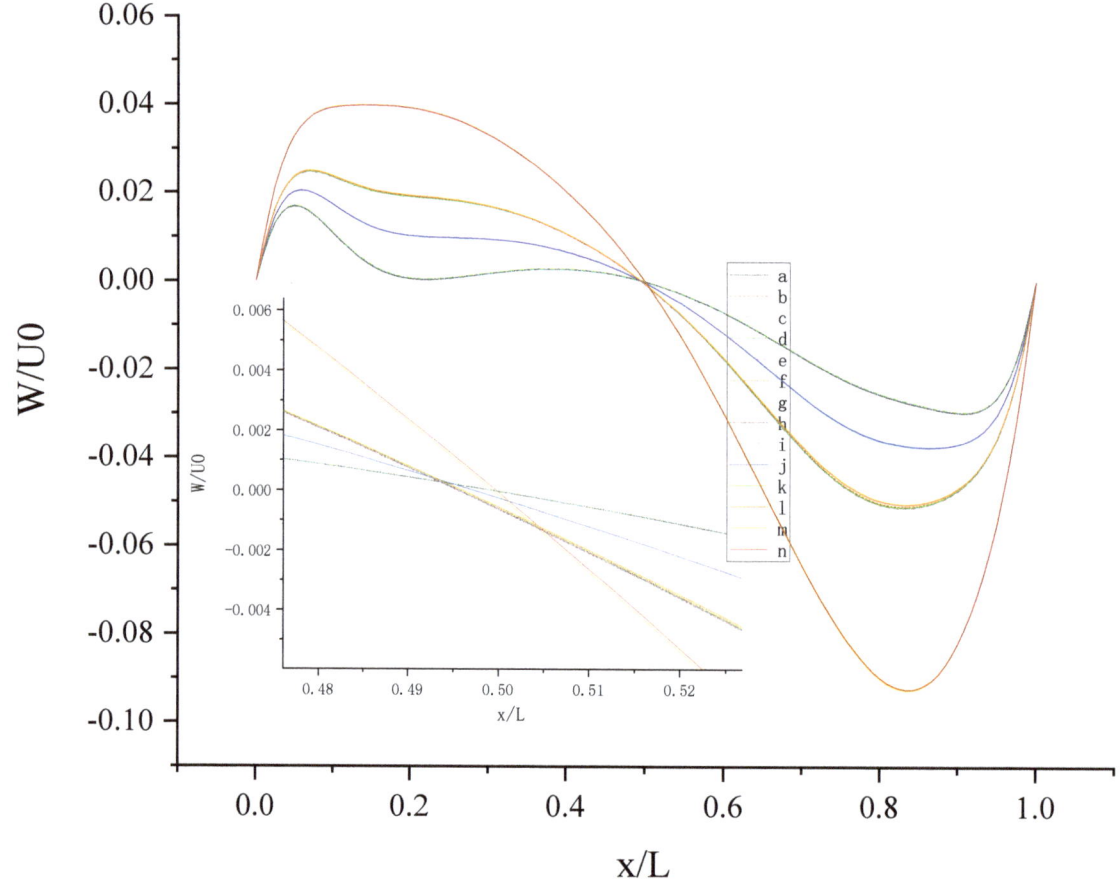

Figure 14. W along the centerline X-axis at t = T.

Figure 14 shows W (the velocity component in the Z direction) along the centerline X-axis at t = T and its magnified view. As shown in Figure 14, 14 curves were divided into four groups according to the level of b_x: b_x= 0,0.05, 0.1, 0.2. The larger b_x is, the greater the influence it has on the change in W along the centerline X-axis, and the larger the fluctuation range is, the closer the position of the peak or trough is to the center. For the same level of b_x, the existence of b_y on the top or bottom wall has little effect on the change in W along the centerline X-axis. For x/L ≈ 0.5, the direction of W reverses under the interaction of the top and bottom walls. This can be explained by the fact that the liquid inside the cavity flows clockwise.

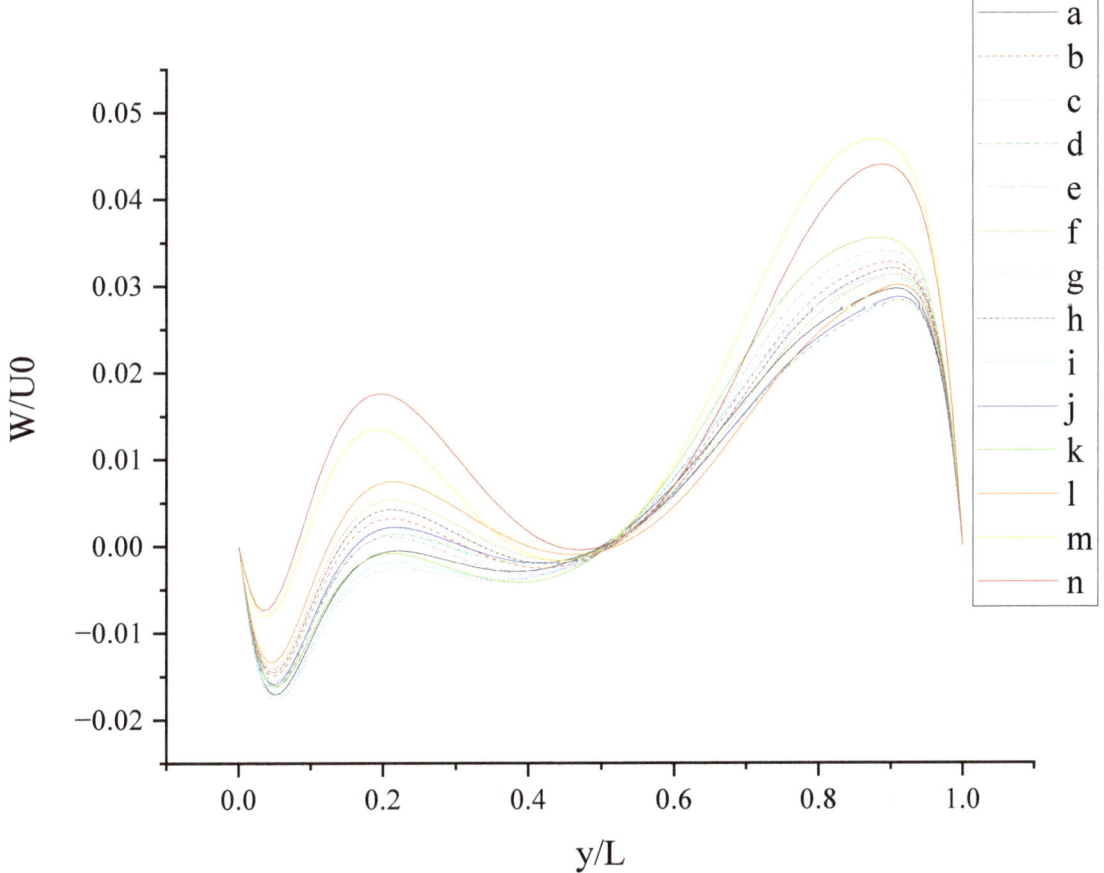

Figure 15. W along the centerline Y-axis at t = T.

Figure 15 shows W (the velocity component in the Z direction) along the centerline Y-axis at t = T. As shown in Figure 15, the large slip length will enhance the oscillation phenomenon of W along the centerline Y-axis and promote the increase in fluctuation amplitude, such as case (m) and case (n). This can be explained by the fact that the large slip length significantly increases the moving velocity of the wall. The existence of b_y on the top wall has a stronger effect on enhancing the amplitude of the left peak, and the existence of b_y on the bottom wall has a stronger effect on enhancing the amplitude of the right peak. The direction of b_y intersects with the motion direction of the top wall vertically, enhancing the disturbance of W near the left side wall; the direction of b_y is the same as the motion direction of the bottom wall, enhancing the disturbance of W near the right sidewall. So, the influence of slip on flow also depends on the slip direction and wall motion direction.

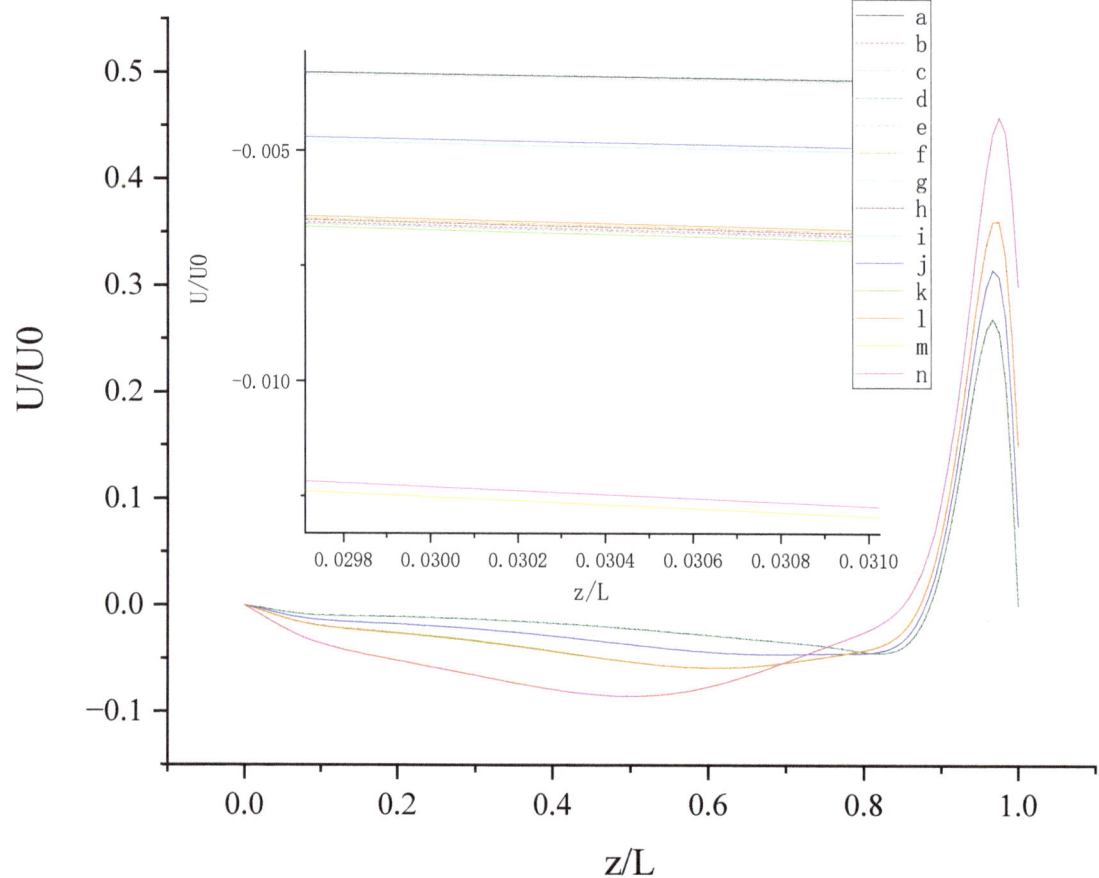

Figure 16. U along the centerline Z-axis at t = 0.25 T.

Figure 16 shows U (the velocity component in the X direction) along the centerline Z-axis at t = 0.25 T and its magnified view. As shown in Figure 16, the 14 curves are divided into four groups according to the level of b_x (b_x = 0, 0.05, 0.1, 0.2): group 1: cases (d, a, and c); group 2: cases (j and i); cases (l, f, h, b, g, e, and k); cases (n and m). It is found that velocity profiles for U in each group are very close. Therefore, for b_x at the same level, the existence of b_y on the top or bottom wall has almost no influence on the change in U along the centerline Z-axis. So, the direction of slip is also an important consideration. The larger b_x results in a larger peak near the top wall, which has a greater influence on the change in U along the centerline Z-axis. When b_x and b_y are fixed, the anisotropic slip on the top wall has a greater effect on the positive U than the pure slip on the top and bottom walls. This may be explained by the directional inconsistency. When U > 0, there is no intersection point in 14 curves, and with fixed b_x = 1, larger b_y on the top wall results in larger U. With the existence of b_y on the top wall, the increase in velocity is facilitated.

Figure 17 shows U (the velocity component in the X direction) along the centerline Y-axis at t = 0.25 T. As shown in Figure 17, the pure slip on the top and bottom walls makes the curve symmetrical, and the anisotropic slip on the top wall makes the trough closer to the right-side wall. The asymmetry can be caused by the direction of slip normal to the wall motion direction.

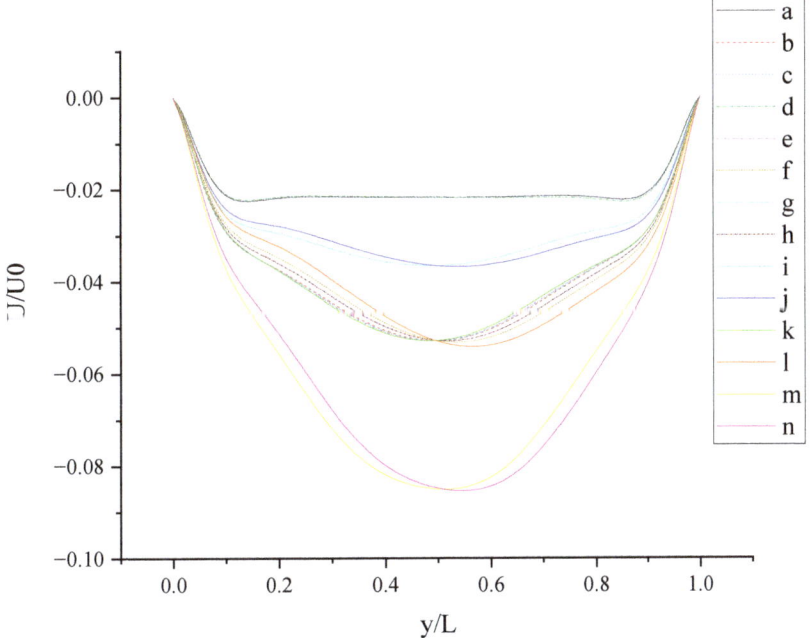

Figure 17. U along the centerline Y-axis at t = 0.25 T.

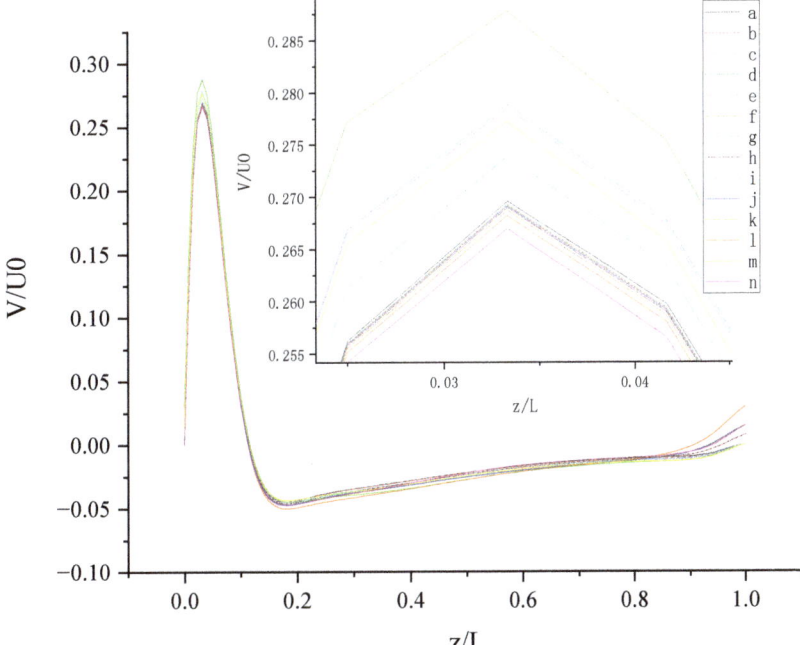

Figure 18. V along the centerline Z-axis at t = 0.25 T.

Figure 18 shows V (the velocity component in the Y direction) along the centerline Z-axis at t = 0.25 T and its magnified view. With the existence of b_y, the slip velocity component in the Y direction appears on the top wall, and the larger slip length makes the non-negative value of V larger, such as with the case (l). In the magnified view, the order of peak value is k, c, i, e, m, g, a, d, b, j, h, f, l, and n. With the existence of b_y on the bottom wall, the larger b_y results in a larger peak value. The existence of b_y can contribute to influencing the flow. With fixed $b_y = 0.1$, the larger b_x results in a smaller peak value.

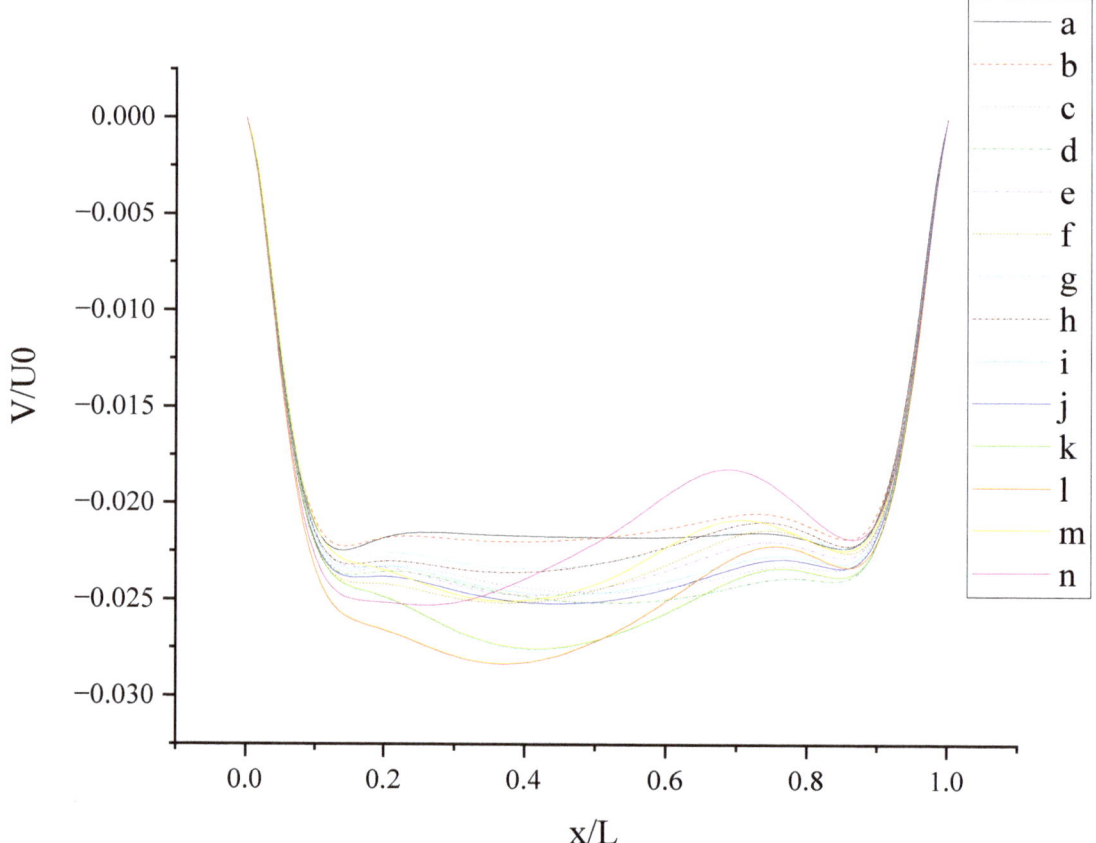

Figure 19. V along the centerline X-axis at t = 0.25 T.

At t = 0.25 T, the top and bottom walls move with oscillating velocity $U = U_0\cos(\omega t) = 0$, but the slip drives the flow in the cavity. The trough near the bottom wall is more obvious in Figure 19 than that in Figure 13, owing to the different oscillating velocity. The trend in curves in Figure 20 is similar to that in Figure 14. The order of peak value near the right side wall in Figure 21 is consistent with that in Figure 15, which shows that the oscillating velocity of the top and bottom wall has a weaker influence on W than on U and V. It is found that W is positive along the centerline Y-axis in case (n) at t = 0.25 T. Anisotropic slip with large slip length can result in the disruptive change. Maybe, in this condition, the flow is dominated by anisotropic slip.

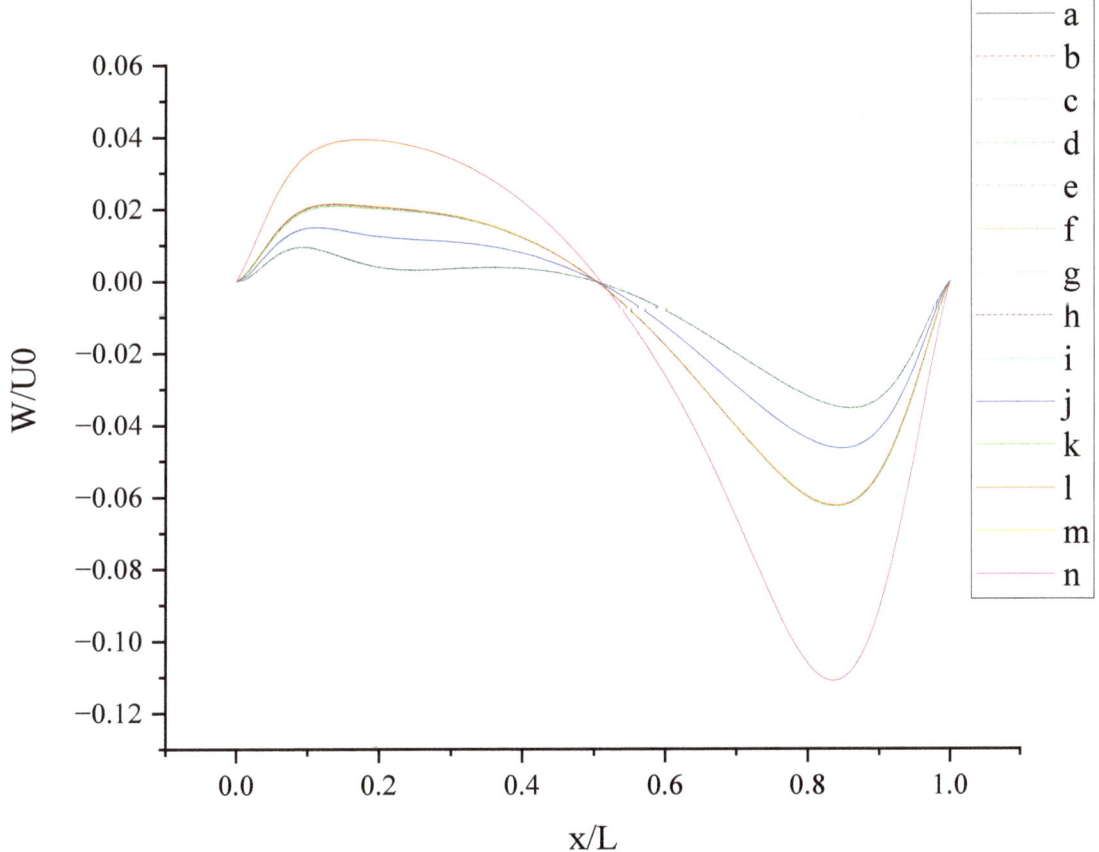

Figure 20. W along the centerline X-axis at t = 0.25 T.

As shown in Figure 22, the profiles of U along the centerline Y-axis at t = 0.5 T show no qualitative similarity with those at t = T and t = 0.25 T. The other five types of profiles at t = 0.5 T show some approximative mirror symmetry with those at t = T. Because the top and bottom walls move with oscillating velocity $U = U_0\cos(\omega t)$, the direction of velocity at t = 0.5 t is opposite to that at t = T.

As shown in Figures S1, S5, S6, S10, S11 and S15 in the Supplementary Materials, the contour of vorticity magnitude is concentrated on the top and bottom walls, owing to shear stress affected by the motion of the top and bottom walls. As shown in Table 2, the maximum vorticity magnitude at t = T and 0.5 T is about an order of magnitude larger than that at t = 0.25 T, owing to the time-dependent oscillating velocity of the top and bottom walls. Compared to the no-slip case, the maximum vorticity magnitude in slip cases changes very little at t = T and 0.5 T, and the maximum percentage change is 3% in case (k). Compared to the no-slip case, case (m) and case (n) obtain about a 120% increase in the percentage of the maximum vorticity magnitude at t = 0.25 T. It is found that the maximum vorticity magnitude makes no change at t = T and 0.5 T when the anisotropic slip exists on the top wall.

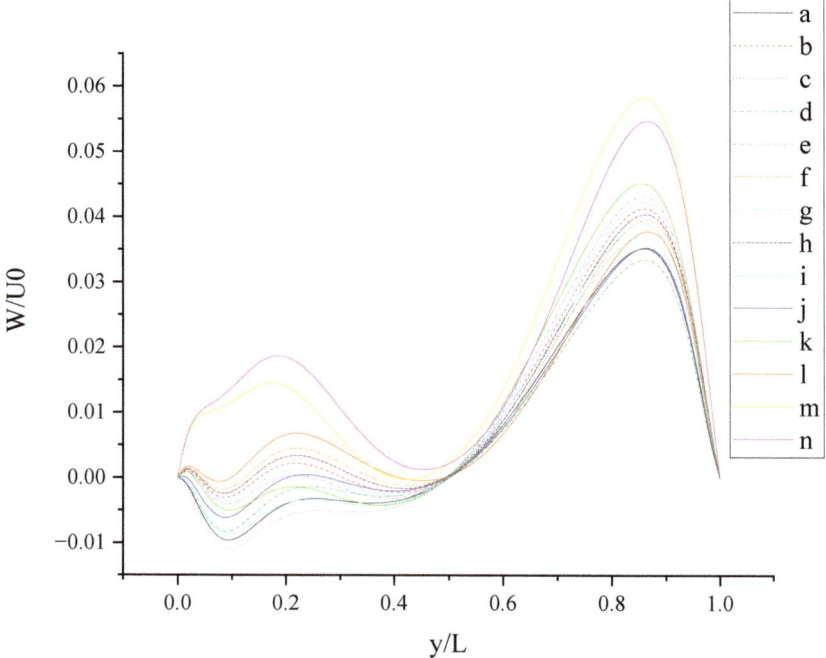

Figure 21. W along the centerline Y-axis at t = 0.25 T.

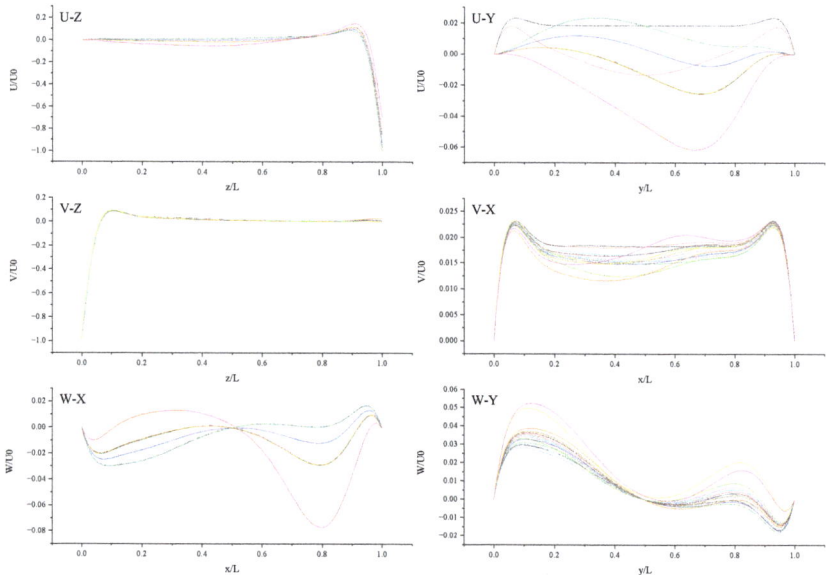

Figure 22. Centerline velocity profiles in X, Y, and Z directions at t = 0.5 T.

Table 2. Maximum vorticity magnitude at t = T, 0.25 T, 0.5 T.

Case	t	a	b	c	d	e	f	g	h	i	j	k	l	m	n
	T	11.3139	11.3139	11.4836	11.3139	11.4836	11.3139	11.3988	11.3139	11.4836	11.3139	11.6533	11.3139	11.4836	11.3139
	0.25 T	1.08977	1.20004	1.0898	1.09042	1.20004	1.20603	1.20004	1.20154	1.07988	1.08963	1.20004	1.22381	2.40009	2.40309
	0.5 T	11.3139	11.3139	11.1442	11.3139	11.1442	11.3139	11.2291	11.3139	11.1442	11.3139	10.9745	11.3139	11.1442	11.3139

5. Conclusions

The present method is validated by simulating the microchannel flow in 3D. Compared with the reference data, the present method is more accurate than the bounce-back and specular reflection slip boundary condition in LBM in Ref. [11]. The effect of anisotropic slip boundary conditions on turbulent flow is investigated by considering different slip lengths in streamwise and spanwise directions. Good agreement with DNS results shows that the present method is also accurate and stable to simulate fluid slip on 3D hydrophobic microchannel walls in a turbulent flow. The present method is effectively accurate and stable to capture velocity profiles and predict drag changes to study the effect of anisotropic slip. Then, the present method is applied to the two-sided, orthogonal, oscillating, micro-lid-driven cavity flow. Some findings are obtained from the simulation results, which can help in better understanding the anisotropic slip effect on the unsteady microflow and the design of microdevices:

The oscillating velocity of the wall has a weaker influence on W than on U and V. In most cases, large slip length has a more significant influence on velocity profiles than small slip length. However, for V along the centerline Z-axis at t = 0.25 T, the larger streamwise slip length on the top wall results in a smaller peak value with a fixed spanwise slip length. Compared with pure slip in both top and bottom walls, anisotropic slip on the top wall has a greater influence on flow, increasing the 3D mixing of flow. In short, the influence of slip on the flow field depends not only on slip length but also on the relative direction of the wall motion and the slip velocity.

Supplementary Materials: The following supporting information can be downloaded at: https://www.mdpi.com/article/10.3390/e24070907/s1. Figure S1: Contours for Velocity U, V, W and Vorticity magnitude at t = T in case (a) and case (b). Figure S2: Contours for Velocity U at t = T in cases (c–n). Figure S3: Contours for Velocity V at t = T in cases (c–n). Figure S4: Contours for Velocity W at t = T in cases (c–n). Figure S5: Contours for Vorticity magnitude at t = T in cases (c–n). Figure S6: Contours for Velocity U, V, W and Vorticity magnitude at t = 0.25 T in case (a) and case (b). Figure S7: Contours for Velocity U at t = 0.25 T in cases (c–n). Figure S8: Contours for Velocity V at t = 0.25 T in cases (c–n). Figure S9: Contours for Velocity W at t = 0.25 T in cases (c–n). Figure S10: Contours for Vorticity magnitude at t = 0.25 T in cases (c–n). Figure S11: Con-tours for Velocity U, V, W and Vorticity magnitude at t = 0.5 T in case (a) and case (b). Figure S12: Contours for Veloc-ity U at t = 0.5 T in cases (c–n). Figure S13: Contours for Velocity V at t = 0.5 T in cases (c–n). Figure S14: Contours for Velocity W at t = 0.5 T in cases (c–n). Figure S15: Contours for Vorticity magnitude at t = 0.5 T in cases (c–n). Figure S16: Contours for Velocity U, V, W and Vorticity magnitude at t = 0.75 T in case (a) and case (b). Figure S17: Contours for Velocity U at t = 0.75 T in cases (c–n). Figure S18: Contours for Velocity V at t = 0.75 T in cases (c–n). Figure S19: Contours for Velocity W at t = 0.75 T in cases (c–n). Figure S20: Contours for Vorticity magnitude at t = 0.75 T in cases (c–n).

Author Contributions: Conceptualization, W.G. and G.H.; methodology, W.G.; software, W.G.; validation, W.G. and G.H.; formal analysis, W.G. and G.H.; investigation, W.G.; resources, G.H.; data curation, W.G.; writing—original draft preparation, W.G.; writing—review and editing, W.G. and G.H.; visualization, W.G. and G.H.; supervision, G.H.; project administration, G.H.; funding acquisition, G.H. All authors have read and agreed to the published version of the manuscript.

Funding: This research was funded by the National Natural Science Foundation of China, grant number 51979115 and grant number 51679099; the Fundamental Research Funds for the Central Universities, grant number HUST.2019kfyXKJC041; and the Open Fund of Key Laboratory of Icing and Anti/De-icing, grant number IADL20190204.

Institutional Review Board Statement: Not applicable.

Informed Consent Statement: Not applicable.

Data Availability Statement: The data that support the findings of this study are available within the article.

Conflicts of Interest: The authors declare no conflict of interest.

References

1. Costantini, R.; Mollicone, J.-P.; Battista, F. Drag reduction induced by superhydrophobic surfaces in turbulent pipe flow. *Phys. Fluids* **2018**, *30*, 025102. [CrossRef]
2. Gose, J.W.; Golovin, K.; Boban, M.; Tobelmann, B.; Callison, E.; Barros, E.; Schultz, M.P.; Tuteja, A.; Perlin, M.; Ceccio, S.L. Turbulent Skin Friction Reduction through the Application of Superhydrophobic Coatings to a Towed Submerged SUBOFF Body. *J. Ship Res.* **2020**, *65*, 266–274. [CrossRef]
3. Im, H.J.; Lee, J.H. Comparison of superhydrophobic drag reduction between turbulent pipe and channel flows. *Phys. Fluids* **2017**, *29*, 095101. [CrossRef]
4. Abu Rowin, W.; Hou, J.; Ghaemi, S. Inner and outer layer turbulence over a superhydrophobic surface with low roughness level at low Reynolds number. *Phys. Fluids* **2017**, *29*, 095106. [CrossRef]
5. Naim, M.S.; Baig, M.F. Turbulent drag reduction in Taylor-Couette flows using different super-hydrophobic surface configurations. *Phys. Fluids* **2019**, *31*, 095108. [CrossRef]
6. Fuaad, P.A.; Prakash, K.A. Enhanced drag-reduction over superhydrophobic surfaces with sinusoidal textures: A DNS study. *Comput. Fluids* **2019**, *181*, 208–223. [CrossRef]
7. Patlazhan, S.; Vagner, S. Apparent slip of shear thinning fluid in a microchannel with a superhydrophobic wall. *Phys. Rev. E* **2017**, *96*, 013104. [CrossRef]
8. Chang, J.; Jung, T.; Choi, H.; Kim, J. Predictions of the effective slip length and drag reduction with a lubricated micro-groove surface in a turbulent channel flow. *J. Fluid Mech.* **2019**, *874*, 797–820. [CrossRef]
9. Tretheway, D.C.; Meinhart, C.D. Apparent fluid slip at hydrophobic microchannel walls. *Phys. Fluids* **2002**, *14*, L9–L12. [CrossRef]
10. Rothstein, J.P. Slip on Superhydrophobic Surfaces. *Annu. Rev. Fluid Mech.* **2010**, *42*, 89–109. [CrossRef]
11. Zhu, L.; Tretheway, D.; Petzold, L.; Meinhart, C. Simulation of fluid slip at 3D hydrophobic microchannel walls by the lattice Boltzmann method. *J. Comput. Phys.* **2005**, *202*, 181–195. [CrossRef]
12. Zhang, L.; Yang, S.; Zeng, Z.; Chew, J.W. Consistent second-order boundary implementations for convection-diffusion lattice Boltzmann method. *Phys. Rev. E* **2018**, *97*, 023302. [CrossRef] [PubMed]
13. Zhang, L.; Yang, S.; Zeng, Z.; Chew, J.W. Lattice model effects on the accuracy of the boundary condition implementations for the convection–diffusion lattice Boltzmann method. *Comput. Fluids* **2018**, *176*, 153–169. [CrossRef]
14. Min, T.; Kim, J. Effects of hydrophobic surface on skin-friction drag. *Phys. Fluids* **2004**, *16*, L55–L58. [CrossRef]
15. Min, T.; Kim, J. Effects of hydrophobic surface on stability and transition. *Phys. Fluids* **2005**, *17*, 108106. [CrossRef]
16. Guo, Z.; Shu, C. Lattice Boltzmann Method and Its Applications in Engineering. In *Advances in Computational Fluid Dynamics*; World Scientfic Publishing: Singapore, 2013; Volume 3, ISBN 978-981-4508-29-2.
17. Succi, S. Mesoscopic Modeling of Slip Motion at Fluid-Solid Interfaces with Heterogeneous Catalysis. *Phys. Rev. Lett.* **2002**, *89*, 064502. [CrossRef]
18. Ansumali, S.; Karlin, I.V. Kinetic boundary conditions in the lattice Boltzmann method. *Phys. Rev. E* **2002**, *66*, 026311. [CrossRef]
19. Tang, G.H.; Tao, W.Q.; He, Y.L. Lattice Boltzmann method for gaseous microflows using kinetic theory boundary conditions. *Phys. Fluids* **2005**, *17*, 058101. [CrossRef]
20. Chai, Z.; Guo, Z.; Zheng, L.; Shi, B. Lattice Boltzmann simulation of surface roughness effect on gaseous flow in a microchannel. *J. Appl. Phys.* **2008**, *104*, 014902. [CrossRef]
21. Verhaeghe, F.; Luo, L.; Blanpain, B. Lattice Boltzmann modeling of microchannel flow in slip flow regime. *J. Comput. Phys.* **2009**, *228*, 147–157. [CrossRef]
22. Kuo, L.-S.; Chen, P.-H. A unified approach for nonslip and slip boundary conditions in the lattice Boltzmann method. *Comput. Fluids* **2009**, *38*, 883–887. [CrossRef]
23. Navier, C.L.M.H. Mémoire sur les lois du mouvement des fluides. In *Mémoires de l'Académie Royale des Sciences de l'Institut de France*; Royale des Sciences de l'Institut de France: Paris, France, 1823; Volume 6, pp. 389–416.
24. Wang, K.; Chai, Z.; Hou, G.; Chen, W.; Xu, S. Slip boundary condition for lattice Boltzmann modeling of liquid flows. *Comput. Fluids* **2018**, *161*, 60–73. [CrossRef]
25. Yang, L.; Yu, Y.; Hou, G.; Wang, K.; Xiong, Y. Boundary conditions with adjustable slip length for the lattice Boltzmann simulation of liquid flow. *Comput. Fluids* **2018**, *174*, 200. [CrossRef]
26. Yang, L.; Yu, Y.; Pei, H.; Gao, Y.; Hou, G. Lattice Boltzmann simulations of liquid flows in microchannel with an improved slip boundary condition. *Chem. Eng. Sci.* **2019**, *202*, 105–117. [CrossRef]
27. Wu, D.; Wang, J.-N.; Wu, S.-Z.; Chen, Q.-D.; Zhao, S.; Zhang, H.; Sun, H.-B.; Jiang, L. Three-Level Biomimetic Rice-Leaf Surfaces with Controllable Anisotropic Sliding. *Adv. Funct. Mater.* **2011**, *21*, 2927–2932. [CrossRef]

28. Feng, L.; Li, S.; Li, Y.; Li, H.; Zhang, L.; Zhai, J.; Song, Y.; Liu, B.; Jiang, L.; Zhu, D. Super-Hydrophobic Surfaces: From Natural to Artificial. *Adv. Mater.* **2002**, *14*, 1857–1860. [CrossRef]
29. Zhu, D.; Li, X.; Zhang, G.; Zhang, X.; Zhang, X.; Wang, T.; Yang, B. Mimicking the Rice Leaf—From Ordered Binary Structures to Anisotropic Wettability. *Langmuir* **2010**, *26*, 14276–14283. [CrossRef]
30. Long, J.; Fan, P.; Jiang, D.; Han, J.; Lin, Y.; Cai, M.; Zhang, H.; Zhong, M. Anisotropic sliding of water droplets on the superhydrophobic surfaces with anisotropic groove-like micro/nano structures. *Adv. Mater. Interfaces* **2016**, *3*, 1600641. [CrossRef]
31. Rastegari, A.; Akhavan, R. On the mechanism of turbulent drag reduction with super-hydrophobic surfaces. *J. Fluid Mech.* **2015**, *773*, R4. [CrossRef]
32. Seo, J.; Mani, A. Effect of texture randomization on the slip and interfacial robustness in turbulent flows over superhydrophobic surfaces. *Phys. Rev. Fluids* **2018**, *3*, 044601. [CrossRef]
33. Rajappan, A.; Golovin, K.; Tobelmann, B.; Pillutla, V.; Abhijeet; Tuteja, A.; McKinley, G.H. Influence of textural statistics on drag reduction by scalable, randomly rough superhydrophobic surfaces in turbulent flow. *Phys. Fluids* **2019**, *31*, 042107. [CrossRef]
34. Mohamed, A.S.; Gad-el-Hak, M. Slippery surfaces: A decade of progress editors-pick. *Phys. Fluids* **2021**, *33*, 071301.
35. Abu Rowin, W.; Ghaemi, S. Streamwise and spanwise slip over a superhydrophobic surface. *J. Fluid Mech.* **2019**, *870*, 1127–1157. [CrossRef]
36. Guo, Z.; Xu, K.; Wang, R. Discrete unified gas kinetic scheme for all Knudsen number flows: Low-speed isothermal case. *Phys. Rev. E* **2013**, *88*, 033305. [CrossRef] [PubMed]
37. Bo, Y.; Wang, P.; Guo, Z.; Wang, L.-P. DUGKS simulations of three-dimensional Taylor–Green vortex flow and turbulent channel flow. *Comput. Fluids* **2017**, *155*, 9–21. [CrossRef]
38. Zhu, L.; Chen, S.; Guo, Z. dugksFoam: An open source OpenFOAM solver for the Boltzmann model equation. *Comput. Phys. Commun.* **2017**, *213*, 155–164. [CrossRef]
39. Wang, P.; Ho, M.T.; Wu, L.; Guo, Z.; Zhang, Y. A comparative study of discrete velocity methods for low-speed rarefied gas flows. *Comput. Fluids* **2018**, *161*, 33–46. [CrossRef]
40. Zhang, C.; Yang, K.; Guo, Z. A discrete unified gas-kinetic scheme for immiscible two-phase flows. *Int. J. Heat Mass Transf.* **2018**, *126*, 1326–1336. [CrossRef]
41. Yang, J.; Zhong, C.; Zhuo, C. Phase-field method based on discrete unified gas-kinetic scheme for large-density-ratio two-phase flows. *Phys. Rev. E* **2019**, *99*, 043302. [CrossRef]
42. Wang, P.; Zhu, L.; Guo, Z.; Xu, K. A Comparative Study of LBE and DUGKS Methods for Nearly Incompressible Flows. *Commun. Comput. Phys.* **2015**, *17*, 657–681. [CrossRef]
43. Boutra, A.; Ragui, K.; Benkahla, Y.K. Numerical study of mixed convection heat transfer in a lid-driven cavity filled with a nanofluid. *Mech. Ind.* **2015**, *16*, 505. [CrossRef]
44. Boutra, A.; Ragui, K.; Benkahla, Y.K.; Labsi, N. Mixed Convection of a Bingham Fluid in Differentially Heated Square Enclosure with Partitions. *Theor. Found. Chem. Eng.* **2018**, *52*, 286–294. [CrossRef]
45. Gibanov, N.S.; Sheremet, M.A.; Oztop, H.F.; Abu-Hamdeh, N. Effect of uniform inclined magnetic field on mixed convection in a lid-driven cavity having a horizontal porous layer saturated with a ferrofluid. *Int. J. Heat Mass Transf.* **2017**, *114*, 1086–1097. [CrossRef]
46. Gangawane, K.M.; Oztop, H.F.; Ali, M.E. Mixed convection in a lid-driven cavity containing triangular block with constant heat flux: Effect of location of block. *Int. J. Mech. Sci.* **2019**, *152*, 492–511. [CrossRef]
47. Azizul, F.M.; Alsabery, A.I.; Hashim, I.; Chamkha, A.J. Impact of heat source on combined convection flow inside wavy-walled cavity filled with nanofluids via heatline concept. *Appl. Math. Comput.* **2020**, *33*, 125754. [CrossRef]
48. Tissot, G.; Billard, R.; Gabard, G. Optimal cavity shape design for acoustic liners using Helmholtz equation with visco-thermal losses. *J. Comput. Phys.* **2019**, *402*, 109048. [CrossRef]
49. Sheikholeslami, M.; Vajravelu, K. Nanofluid flow and heat transfer in a cavity with variable magnetic field. *Appl. Math. Comput.* **2016**, *298*, 272–282. [CrossRef]
50. Shankar, P.N.; Deshpande, M.D. Fluid Mechanics in the Driven Cavity. *Annu. Rev. Fluid Mech.* **2000**, *32*, 93–136. [CrossRef]
51. Hammami, F.; Ben-Cheikh, N.; Ben-Beya, B.; Souayeh, B. Combined effects of the velocity and the aspect ratios on the bifurcation phenomena in a two-sided lid-driven cavity flow. *Int. J. Numer. Methods Heat Fluid Flow* **2018**, *28*, 943–962. [CrossRef]
52. Souayeh, B.; Hammami, F.; Hdhiri, N.; Alfannakh, H. Unsteady state fluid structure of two-sided nonfacing lid-driven cavity induced by a semicircle at different radii sizes and velocity ratios. *Int. J. Mod. Phys. C* **2019**, *30*, 1950060. [CrossRef]
53. Romano, F.; Kannan, P.K.; Kuhlmann, H.C. Finite-size Lagrangian coherent structures in a two-sided lid-driven cavity. *Phys. Rev. Fluids* **2019**, *4*, 024302. [CrossRef]
54. Perumal, D.A. Lattice Boltzmann computation of multiple solutions in a double-sided square and rectangular cavity flows. *Therm. Sci. Eng. Prog.* **2018**, *6*, 48–56. [CrossRef]
55. Tang, L.Q.; Tsang, T.T.H. transient solutions by a least-squares finite-element method and jacobi conjugate gradient technique. *Numer. Heat Transfer Part B Fundam.* **1995**, *28*, 183–198. [CrossRef]
56. Chew, Y.T.; Shu, C.; Niu, X.D. Simulation of unsteady incompressible flows by using taylor series expansion- and least square-based lattice boltzmann method. *Int. J. Mod. Phys. C* **2002**, *13*, 719–738. [CrossRef]
57. Amani, A.; Balcázar, N.; Naseri, A.; Rigola, J. A numerical approach for non-Newtonian two-phase flows using a conservative level-set method. *Chem. Eng. J.* **2019**, *385*, 123896. [CrossRef]

58. Blackburn, H.M.; Lopez, J.M. The onset of three-dimensional standing and modulated travelling waves in a periodically driven cavity flow. *J. Fluid Mech.* **2003**, *497*, 289–317. [CrossRef]
59. Anderson, P.D.; Galaktionov, O.S.; Peters, G.W.M.; van de Vosse, F.N.; Meijer, H.E.H. Analysis of mixing in three-dimensional time-periodic cavity flows. *J. Fluid Mech.* **1999**, *386*, 149–166. [CrossRef]
60. Huang, F.; Wang, D.; Li, Z.; Gao, Z.; Derksen, J. Mixing process of two miscible fluids in a lid-driven cavity. *Chem. Eng. J.* **2019**, *362*, 229–242. [CrossRef]
61. Wang, P.; Su, W.; Zhang, Y. Oscillatory rarefied gas flow inside a three dimensional rectangular cavity. *Phys. Fluids* **2018**, *30*, 102002. [CrossRef]
62. Wang, P.; Zhu, L.; Su, W.; Wu, L.; Zhang, Y. Nonlinear oscillatory rarefied gas flow inside a rectangular cavity. *Phys. Rev. E* **2018**, *97*, 043103. [CrossRef]
63. Wang, P.; Su, W.; Zhu, L.; Zhang, Y. Heat and mass transfer of oscillatory lid-driven cavity flow in the continuum, transition and free molecular regimes. *Int. J. Heat Mass Transfer.* **2019**, *131*, 291–300. [CrossRef]
64. Bhopalam, S.R.; Perumal, D.A.; Yadav, A.K. Computational appraisal of fluid flow behavior in two-sided oscillating lid-driven cavities. *Int. J. Mech. Sci.* **2021**, *196*, 106303. [CrossRef]
65. Peng, Y.; Shu, C.; Chew, Y. A 3D incompressible thermal lattice Boltzmann model and its application to simulate natural convection in a cubic cavity. *J. Comput. Phys.* **2004**, *193*, 260–274. [CrossRef]
66. Bhatnagar, P.L.; Gross, E.P.; Krook, M. A Model for Collision Processes in Gases. I. Small Amplitude Processes in Charged and Neutral One-Component Systems. *Phys. Rev.* **1954**, *94*, 511. [CrossRef]
67. Xu, K.; Huang, J.C. A Unified Gas-kinetic Scheme for Continuum and Rarefied Flows. *J. Comput. Phys.* **2010**, *229*, 7747–7764. [CrossRef]
68. Schäffel, D.; Koynov, K.; Vollmer, D.; Butt, H.-J.; Schönecker, C. Local Flow Field and Slip Length of Superhydrophobic Surfaces. *Phys. Rev. Lett.* **2016**, *116*, 134501. [CrossRef]
69. Guo, Z.; Shi, B.; Zhao, T.S.; Zheng, C. Discrete effects on boundary conditions for the lattice Boltzmann equation in simulating microscale gas flows. *Phys. Rev. E* **2007**, *76*, 056704. [CrossRef]
70. Guo, Z.; Zheng, C.; Shi, B. Discrete lattice effects on the forcing term in the lattice Boltzmann method. *Phys. Rev. E* **2002**, *65*, 046308. [CrossRef]
71. Junk, M.; Yang, Z. One-point boundary condition for the lattice Boltzmann method. *Phys. Rev. E* **2005**, *72*, 066701. [CrossRef]
72. Guo, W.; Liu, S.; Hou, G.; Yu, Y. A new corner boundary condition for the discrete unified gas kinetic scheme. *Int. J. Numer. Methods Fluids* **2020**, *93*, 1520–1539. [CrossRef]
73. Krastins, I.; Kao, A.; Pericleous, K.; Reis, T. Moment-based boundary conditions for straight on-grid boundaries in three-dimensional lattice Boltzmann simulations. *Int. J. Numer. Methods Fluids* **2020**, *92*, 1948–1974. [CrossRef]
74. White, F. *Viscous Fluid Flow*; McGraw-Hill: New York, NY, USA, 1974; p. 123.
75. Busse, A.; Sandham, N. Influence of an anisotropic slip-length boundary condition on turbulent channel flow. *Phys. Fluids* **2012**, *24*, 055111. [CrossRef]
76. Pope, S.B. *Turbulent Flows*; Cambridge University Press: Cambridge, UK, 2000.

Article

Hydrodynamic Behavior of Self-Propelled Particles in a Simple Shear Flow

Tingting Qi [1], Jianzhong Lin [2,*] and Zhenyu Ouyang [1]

[1] State Key Laboratory of Fluid Power Transmission and Control, Zhejiang University, Hangzhou 310027, China; 22024006@zju.edu.cn (T.Q.); ouyangzhenyu@zju.edu.cn (Z.O.)
[2] Laboratory of Impact and Safety Engineering of Ministry of Education, Ningbo University, Ningbo 315201, China
* Correspondence: mecjzlin@public.zju.edu.cn; Tel.: +86-571-87952882

Abstract: The hydrodynamic properties of a squirmer type of self-propelled particle in a simple shear flow are investigated using the immersed boundary-lattice Boltzmann method in the range of swimming Reynolds number $0.05 \leq Re_s \leq 2.0$, flow Reynolds number $40 \leq Re_p \leq 160$, blocking rate $0.2 \leq \kappa \leq 0.5$. Some results are validated by comparing with available other results. The effects of Re_s, Re_p and κ on the hydrodynamic properties of squirmer are discussed. The results show that there exist four distinct motion modes for the squirmer, i.e., horizontal mode, attractive oscillation mode, oscillation mode, and chaotic mode. Increasing Re_s causes the motion mode of the squirmer to change from a constant tumbling near the centerline to a stable horizontal mode, even an oscillatory or appealing oscillatory mode near the wall. Increasing the swimming intensity of squirmer under the definite Re_s will induce the squirmer to make periodic and stable motion at a specific distance from the wall. Increasing Re_p will cause the squirmer to change from a stable swimming state to a spiral motion or continuous rotation. Increasing κ will strengthen the wall's attraction to the squirmer. Increasing swimming intensity of squirmer will modify the strength and direction of the wall's attraction to the squirmer if κ remains constant.

Keywords: self-propelled particles; hydrodynamic properties; simple shear flow; immersed boundary-lattice Boltzmann method

1. Introduction

Various movements of self-propelled particles play an essential role in the medicinal, biophysical and engineering applications. Sperm, bacteria, protists and algae are examples of self-propelled microorganisms in nature. They achieve self-propulsion by using their own motor organs such as cilia and flagella, tail and fins, cell deformation and so on. Movement of microorganisms is associated with a variety of biological activities such as sperm swimming in mammalian cervical mucus [1], biofilm formation [2], paramecia swimming to avoid predators [3], and bacteria and algae coordinating their movement to nutrient-rich habitats [4]. The motion of self-propelled particles in the flow will be affected by the fluid motion, with the motion of self-propelled particles in the shear flow being of special importance [5–7].

Alqarni and Bearon [8] found that cells would generate a spiral swimming trajectory in the weak shear flow but could achieve a stable equilibrium direction in the strong shear flow. They also numerically simulated the trajectories of cells in a non-uniformly sheared vertical channel flow and found that helical swimming cells would aggregate toward or away from the channel center. Ishimoto and Crowdy [9] provided an analytical solution for the motion of circular self-driven particles in a simple shear flow near a non-slip wall, and demonstrated that particles couldn't migrate stably at a fixed distance from the wall, but could only oscillate periodically along the wall or move away from it. According to the results given by Ishimoto and Gaffney [10], the fluid rheology could be used to direct sperm

into the egg, and sperm moved under the combined effect of self-driving, wall constraint and fluid shear force. Jiang and Chen [11] investigated the dispersion model of dilute suspensions of self-propelled particle in a confined flow and found that the accumulation of spherical particles in shear flow would reduce overall dispersion, whereas the accumulation of rod-like self-propelled particles in shear flow would increase dispersibility because the particles were aligned with the streamlines. Brady et al. [12] simulated the stress tensor and diffusion tensor of spherical particles in the simple shear flow and pressure-driven flow. Hagen et al. [13] studied the Brownian motion of self-propelled particles in a linear shear flow, and indicated that the particles moved at a constant speed along the wave direction and were subjected to a constant torque. In addition, Wagner and Kalman [14] developed the flow-ultra-small-angle neutron scattering method for probing colloidal microstructures under steady-state flow conditions, and found that the formation of water clusters caused reversible shear thickening in colloidal suspensions due to the predominance of short-range lubrication- hydrodynamic interactions at relatively high shear rates. Siebenbürger et al. [15] conducted comprehensive research of viscoelasticity and shear flow of concentrated amorphous colloidal suspensions. Lettinga and Dhont [16] investigated the phase and flow behavior of rod-shaped particles in the shear flow, and calculated the whole phase diagram of rod-shaped particles from low concentration to two-phase area and to nematic region. Blaak et al. [17] investigated the effect of shear flow on homogeneous crystal nucleation and found that a uniform shear rate could significantly reduce crystal nucleation rate while increasing critical nucleation size. They also indicated that the nuclei orientation was inclined with respect to the shearing direction. Dhont and Nagele [18] examined the critical viscoelastic behavior of colloidal suspensions and found that the microstructural distortion generated by static shear flow had a significant impact on the spectrum of the linear viscoelastic response function.

It can be seen from the above research that there is still a lack of studies on the effects of swimming Reynolds number, flow Reynolds number and blocking rate on the hydrodynamic properties and stable equilibrium position of self-propelled particle. Therefore, the aim of this study is to numerically simulate the hydrodynamic properties of self-propelled particles moving in a simple shear flow using the lattice Boltzmann-immersed boundary method, and explore the effects of swimming Reynolds number, flow Reynolds number and blocking rate on the hydrodynamic properties and stable equilibrium position of self-propelled particle.

2. Basic Model

2.1. Squirmer Model

The squirmer model proposed by Lighthill [19] and Blake [20] has been widely used in the study of self-propelled particles. The model of two-dimensional squirmer driven with tangential surface velocity is:

$$u_\theta = B_1 \sin\theta + 2B_2 \sin\theta \cos\theta, \tag{1}$$

the squirmer's self-driving velocity is determined by the first term on the right hand side of Equation (1), $U/_{Re=0} = B_1/2$ and an irrotational velocity field with a decay rate of $1/r^2$ is generated; the second term is related to the squirmer's stress, which causes the Stokes flow to decay at a rate of $1/r$, generating vortices near the squirmer surface [21]. Squirmers are classified into three categories based on the values of $\beta = B_2/B_1 (B_1 > 0)$: puller ($\beta > 0$), pusher ($\beta < 0$), and neutral squirmer ($\beta < 0$). Puller, such as Chlamydomonas, creates thrust from the front with a breaststroke-like motion. Pusher, such as E. coli, pushes itself forward with their backward flagella [22].

Squirmer is assumed a rigid body, and the squirmer's motion is described by the Newton's second law:

$$m\frac{d^2 x_c}{dt^2} = F, \quad \frac{d(J\cdot\Omega)}{dt} = T, \tag{2}$$

where m and x_c represent the squirmer's mass and centroid position, respectively; J and Ω represent the squirmer's moment of inertia and angular velocity, respectively; F and T represent the force and torque exerted by the fluid on the squirmer, respectively.

2.2. Collision Mode

There will be an interaction between the squirmer and wall when the squirmer is close to the wall. The short-range repulsion model provided by Glowinski et al. [23] is employed to avoid the overlapping of squirmer and the wall:

$$f_r = \begin{cases} \frac{C_m}{\varepsilon}\left(\frac{d-d_{min}-\Delta r}{\Delta r}\right)e_r, & d \leq d_{min} + \Delta r \\ (0,0), & d > d_{min} + \Delta r \end{cases}, \quad (3)$$

where $\bar{C}_m = MU^2/a_0$ is the characteristic force; M, U are a_0 the squirmers' mass, velocity and radius, respectively; $\varepsilon = 10^{-4}$ is a constant positive value; d is the distance between the squirmer and the wall; $d_{min} = a_0$ is the minimum possible distance between the squirmer and the wall; $\Delta r = 2\Delta x$ represents the size of the two lattices in the numerical simulation, which is the area where the repulsion exists; e_r indicates that the center of the squirmer points to the normal direction of the wall.

3. Numerical Methods and Verification

3.1. Immersion Boundary-Lattice Boltzmann Method

The immersed boundary-lattice Boltzmann method [24,25] is utilized. In this method, the regular Euler grid is used in the flow and the lattice Boltzmann equation is solved with the velocity discrete model of DdQm to obtain the macroscopic information of the flow. The Lagrangian grid is used to model particles moving in the flow, and two sets of grids are used to exchange force and velocity information between the Lagrangian points of the particle border and the Euler points of the surrounding flow.

The N-S equation for an incompressible flow is:

$$\frac{\partial u}{\partial t} + (u \cdot \nabla)u = -\frac{\nabla p}{\rho} + \frac{\mu}{\rho}\nabla^2 u + f \quad (4)$$

$$\nabla \cdot u = 0, \quad (5)$$

where ρ, u and p are the fluid density, velocity and pressure, respectively; f is the external force exerting on the fluid.

The D2Q9 velocity model [26] is employed and the appropriate velocity vector is:

$$e_\alpha = \begin{cases} (0,0) & \alpha = 0 \\ (\pm 1, 0), (0, \pm 1) & \alpha = 1 \sim 4 \\ (\pm 1, \pm 1) & \alpha = 5 \sim 8 \end{cases}. \quad (6)$$

The corresponding single relaxed lattice Boltzmann equation with external force term is:

$$f_\alpha(x + e_\alpha \Delta t, t + \Delta t) = f_\alpha(x, t) - \frac{1}{\tau}\left[f_\alpha(x,t) - f_\alpha^{eq}(x,t)\right] + \Delta t \frac{w_\alpha \rho}{c_s^2} e_\alpha \cdot f, \quad (7)$$

where Δt is the time step of simulation; τ is the relaxation time; $f_\alpha(x,t)$ is the density distribution function of fluid particle for the velocity direction e_α in x at time t; $c_s = c/\sqrt{3} = 1/\sqrt{3}$ is the speed of sound; f is an external force; w_α is the weight function, $w_0 = 4/9$, $w_\alpha = 1/9$ for $\alpha = 1-4$, $w_\alpha = 1/36$ for $\alpha = 5-8$; f_α^{eq} is the equilibrium distribution function:

$$f_\alpha^{eq}(x,t) = \rho w_\alpha \left[1 + \frac{e_\alpha \cdot u}{c_s^2} + \frac{(e_\alpha \cdot u)^2}{2c_s^4} - \frac{u^2}{2c_s^2}\right]. \quad (8)$$

The macroscopic velocity and density of the fluid are:

$$\rho = \sum f_\alpha, \quad \rho u = \sum f_\alpha e_\alpha. \tag{9}$$

For the exchange of velocity and force information between the solid boundary and the flow, the force exerted on the solid boundary by the fluid is:

$$F(x,t) = \frac{U^d(x,t+\Delta t) - U^*(x,t+\Delta t)}{\Delta t}, \tag{10}$$

where $U^d(x,t)$ is determined by the motion of the particle. As shown in Figure 1, at the point x_b, $U^d(x_b,t)$ is the sum of translational and rotational velocities of the particle, $U^*(x_b,t)$ is obtained by interpolating the fluid around the boundary:

$$U^*(x_b,t) = \sum_f D(x_f - x_b) \cdot u^*(x_f,t), \tag{11}$$

where $u^*(x_f,t)$ is the fluid velocity at x_f without considering the external force; $D(x)$ is a two-dimensional Dirac delta function [27].

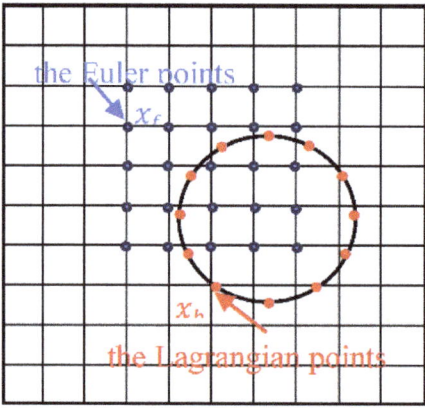

Figure 1. Distribution of Euler points and Lagrangian points.

Similar to Equation (10), the forces exerted on the fluid by the solid boundary is:

$$f(X_f,t) = \sum_b D(X_f - X_b) \cdot F(X_b,t). \tag{12}$$

where F is the force exerted on the solid boundary by fluid, D is the Dirac delta function.

3.2. Verification of Numerical Method

As shown in Figure 2, the motion of a single particle in a Newtonian shear flow is simulated to verify the validity and accuracy of the method in dealing with the fluid-particle problem. Firstly, the different periodic channel lengths (1000, 2000 and 3000) are set in the flow direction to simulate the particle trajectory, and the results are shown in Figure 3 where we can see that the results are almost the same for the three lengths, so the channel length L and width H are selected as $2000 \times 80\Delta x$ in the following simulation. The present numerical results of particle trajectory are shown in Figure 4 where the other results [28–30] are also given as a comparison, it can be seen that the results simulated by different methods agree well.

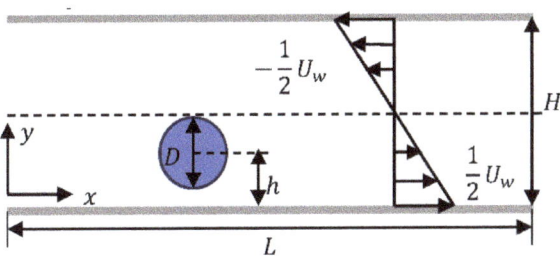

Figure 2. Particle moving in a simple shear flow.

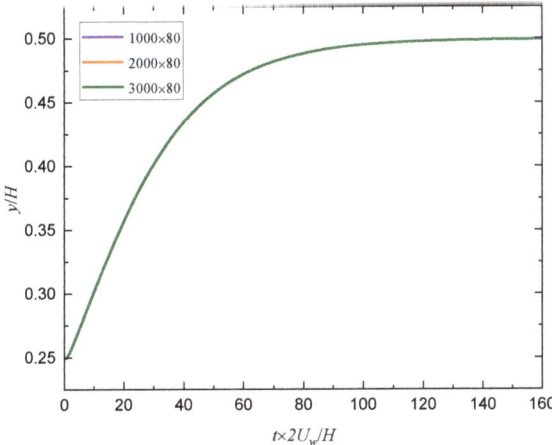

Figure 3. Particle trajectories for different channel lengths.

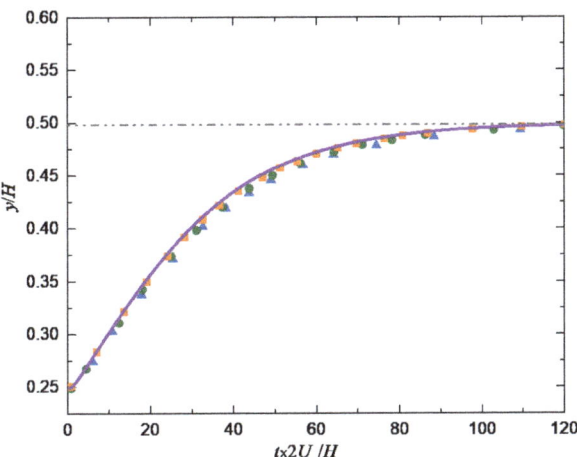

Figure 4. Comparison of particle trajectories. ▲: Ref. [28]; ●: Ref. [29]; ■: Ref. [30]; —: present result.

4. Results and Discussion

As shown in Figure 5, a squirmer with a diameter of $20\Delta x$ is released in a simple shear flow with an initial inclination angle θ and a distance h from the wall. The channel length L is set to $100D$ with D being the squirmer's diameter, the blocking rate $\kappa = D/H$, and

$\kappa = 0.25$ unless otherwise specified. The flow Reynolds number is defined as $Re_p = 2U_w H/\mu$ with U_w being the velocity difference between upper and lower walls. The swimming Reynolds number is defined as $Re_s = B_1 d/2\nu$, where B_1 is related to swimming strength as shown in Equation (1) and ν is the kinematic viscosity. No-slip and impenetrable boundary conditions are used for the upper and lower walls, and periodic boundary conditions are used at the inlet and outlet.

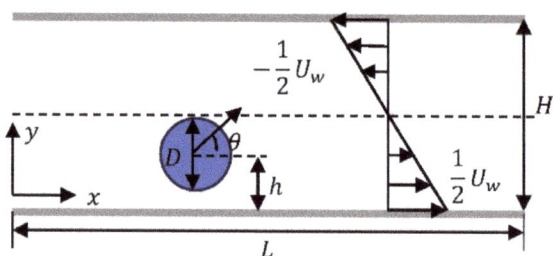

Figure 5. Initial condition of squirmer in a simple shear flow.

4.1. Effect of Initial Condition on the Squirmer's Motion

A puller with initial positions $h = 0.75\,d$, d, $1.25\,d$ and initial orientation angles $\theta = 0°$, $45°$, $90°$ is released in a simple shear flow, and the changes of trajectory and orientation angle of puller with time are shown in Figure 6. We can see that the changes of trajectory and orientation angle of puller are independent of initial conditions. Therefore, the initial position and orientation angle are set to $h = 0.75\,d$ and $\theta = 0°$, respectively, in the following simulation.

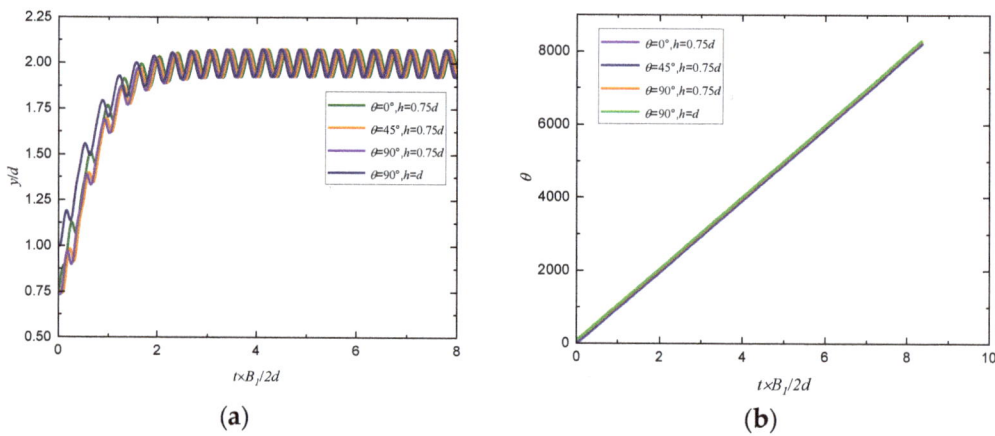

Figure 6. Changes of (**a**) trajectory and (**b**) orientation angle of a puller with time in simple shear flow ($Re_p = 80$, $Re_s = 1$, $\beta = 5$).

4.2. Effect of the Swimming Reynolds Number

To explore the effect of Re_s on the motion pattern of a squirmer swimming near the wall, a squirmer with a radius of $20\Delta x$ is released in the flow. Figure 7 shows the changes of trajectory and orientation angle of a squirmer along the flow direction for different Re_s and β, it can be seen that there exist four distinct modes for squirmer motion, i.e., horizontal mode, attractive oscillation mode, oscillation mode, and chaotic mode. When $Re_s = 0.1$, the squirmer will keep rolling as it moves to a constant position near the centerline of the channel, and will make a steady horizontal motion above ($Re_s = 1.0$, $\beta = 3$) or below ($Re_s = 0.5$, $\beta = 5$) the midline as Re_s grows.

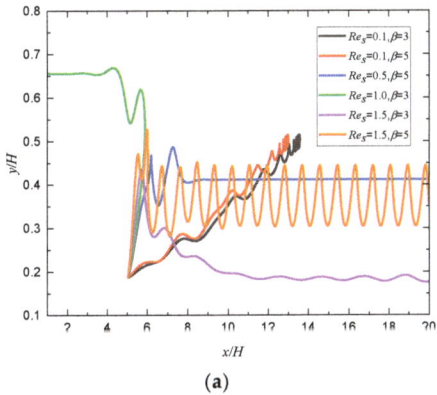 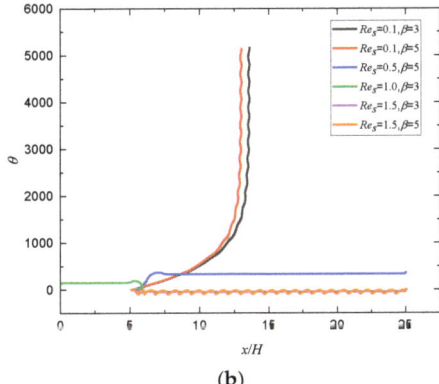

Figure 7. Changes of (**a**) trajectory and (**b**) orientation angle of a squirmer along the flow direction for different Re_s and β ($Re_p = 80$).

When Re_s continues to increase to 1.5, the repulsion force exerted on the squirmer by the wall decreases because $Re_s = B_1 d/2\nu$, the larger Re_s is, the larger d is, the smaller the repulsion force is, as shown in Equation (3), and an attractive oscillation mode ($\beta = 5$) or oscillation mode ($\beta = 3$) will be formed near the wall, which is similar to the trend of squirmer moving near the non-slip wall [10]. When β increases from 3 to 5, the squirmer will escape from the wall and make a periodic stable motion at a specific distance from the wall at $Re_s = 1.5$ because the self driving ability of squirmer is enhanced with the increase of swimming intensity. The phase diagram of Re_s and β for the transition of different modes are shown in Figure 8.

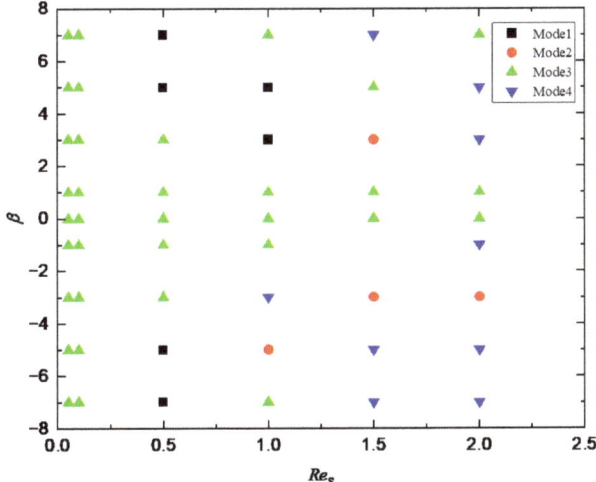

Figure 8. Phase diagram of Re_s and β for the transition of different modes. Mode 1: horizontal; Mode 2: attractive oscillation; Mode 3: oscillation; Mode 4: chaos.

4.3. Effect of the Flow Reynolds Number

Effects of Re_p and β on the motion pattern of a squirmer are shown in Figure 9 where we can see that the puller ($\beta = 7$) will move towards the outlet of the flow and form a stable trajectory below the centerline when $Re_p = 40$. However, the pusher ($\beta = -5$) will be attracted by the wall, move in the opposite direction after colliding with the wall first, and then move in the direction of the entrance across the center line, finally form a stable trajectory above the centerline. When Re_p is increased to 60, the trajectory of the pusher ($\beta = -5$) is more complicated, but eventually a stable motion pattern is formed below the centerline. As Re_p increases to 100, the trajectory of the pusher ($\beta = -5$) forms a closed loop. When Re_p continues to increase to 160, the puller ($\beta = 7$) will move to the centerline and form a spiral trajectory near the centerline. However, the pusher ($\beta = -5$) will keep rotating at a fixed position close to the centerline because an increase of Re_p means an increase in shear strength, causing the pusher to gradually change from a stable motion state to a non-stop rotating or helical motion, which is similar to the sperm swimming up and down in the airflow when the airflow to the uterus is generated in the oviduct of mammals [11]. The phase diagram of Re_p and β for the transition of different modes are shown in Figure 10.

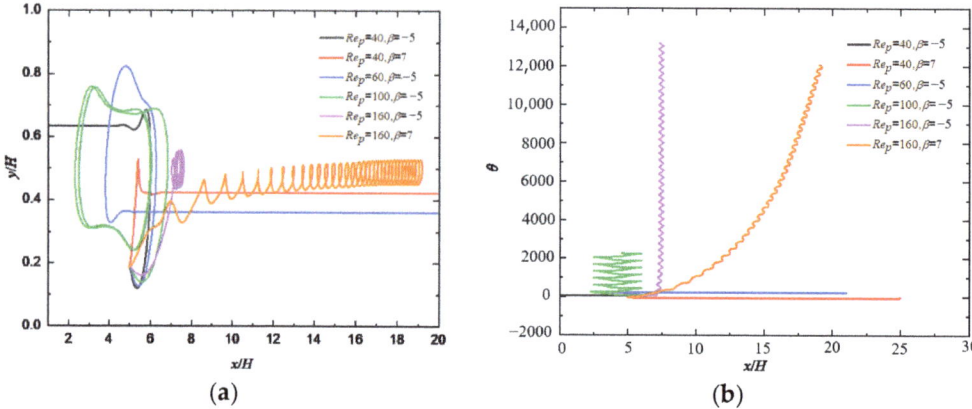

Figure 9. Changes of (**a**) trajectory and (**b**) orientation angle of a squirmer along the flow direction for different Re_p and β ($Re_s = 0.5$).

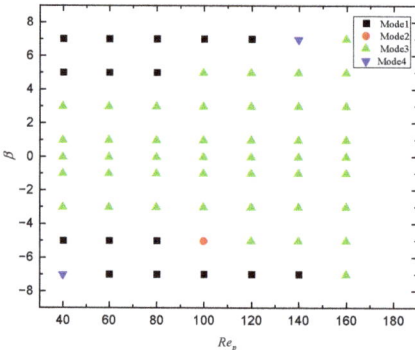

Figure 10. Phase diagram of Re_p and β for the transition of different modes. Mode 1: horizontal; Mode 2: attractive oscillation; Mode 3: oscillation; Mode 4: chaos.

4.4. Effect of the Blocking Rate

Figure 11 shows the effects of κ and β on the motion pattern of a squirmer. It can be seen that, with the increase of κ, the motion pattern of a squirmer changes from both periodic motion ($\beta = 7$) and attractive oscillation ($\beta = 5$) to the horizontal motion, and the squirmer finally moves stably near the lower wall. The reason can be attributed to that increasing κ will change the magnitude of the total moment exerted on the squirmer, making it move horizontally and stably. As κ increases from 0.2 to 0.25, it can be clearly found that the motion direction of squirmer is diametrically opposite for $\beta = 3$, the equilibrium position during stable motion also changes from below the centerline to above the centerline. Furthermore, with the increase of β, the motion pattern of squirmer changes from a horizontal mode ($\beta = 3$) near the upper wall to an appealing oscillation mode ($\beta = -5$) near the lower wall at $\kappa = 0.25$, and finally to an oscillation mode near the midline ($\beta = 7$), the direction and strength of the attraction force of the wall to the squirmer will change. The phase diagram of κ and β for the transition of different modes are shown in Figure 12.

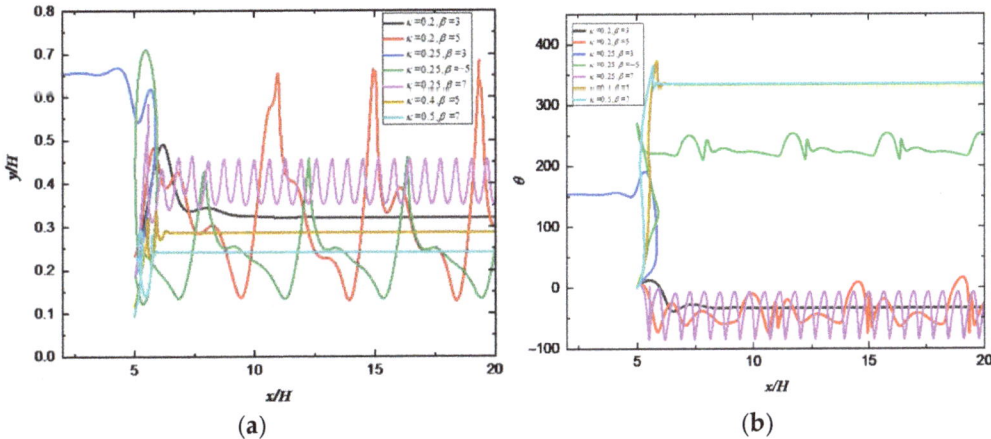

Figure 11. Changes of (**a**) trajectory and (**b**) orientation angle of a squirmer along the flow direction for different κ and β ($Re_s = 1.0$, $Re_p = 80$).

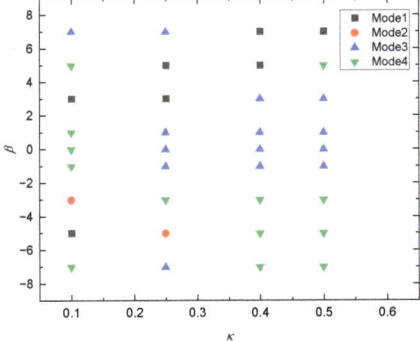

Figure 12. Phase diagram of κ and β for the transition of different modes. Mode 1: horizontal; Mode 2: attractive oscillation; Mode 3: oscillation; Mode 4: chaos.

5. Conclusions

The hydrodynamic properties of a squirmer type of self-propelled particle in a simple shear flow are investigated using the immersed boundary-lattice Boltzmann method. The present numerical results of particle trajectory are compared with the literature data, and the results agree well. The main conclusions are summarized as follows: there exist four distinct motion modes for the squirmer, i.e., horizontal mode, attractive oscillation mode, oscillation mode, and chaotic mode. The changes of trajectory and orientation angle of puller are independent of the initial conditions. Increasing Re_s causes the motion mode to change from a constant tumbling near the centerline to a stable horizontal mode, even an oscillatory or appealing oscillatory mode near the wall. Increasing β will induce the squirmer to make periodic and stable motion at a specific distance from the wall. The squirmer will form a stable pattern of horizontal motion above or below the channel centerline when $Re_p = 40 - 60$. At large Re_p, the squirmer's trajectory will become closed loop, spiral, or even chaotic. Increasing κ will strengthen the wall's attraction to the squirmer, make the squirmer's motion progressively become steady, and cause the squirmer to move from an oscillation mode to attracting oscillation mode, and finally to horizontal motion mode. Increasing β will modify the strength and direction of the wall's attraction to the squirmer. The conclusions obtained in this paper have reference value for mastering the hydrodynamic characteristics of self-propelled particles and controlling them.

Author Contributions: Conceptualization, J.L. and T.Q.; methodology, T.Q. and Z.O.; software, T.Q.; validation, Z.O.; formal analysis, T.Q. and J.L.; investigation, T.Q. and J.L.; resources, T.Q.; data curation, T.Q.; writing—original draft preparation, T.Q.; writing—review and editing, J.L.; visualization, T.Q.; supervision, J.L.; project administration, J.L.; funding acquisition, J.L. All authors have read and agreed to the published version of the manuscript.

Funding: This work was supported by the National Natural Science Foundation of China (Grant no. 12132015).

Institutional Review Board Statement: Not applicable.

Informed Consent Statement: Not applicable.

Data Availability Statement: Not applicable.

Conflicts of Interest: The authors declare no conflict of interest.

References

1. Suarez, S.S.; Pacey, A.A. Sperm transport in the female reproductive tract. *Hum. Reprod. Update* **2006**, *12*, 23–37. [CrossRef] [PubMed]
2. Pedley, T.; Kessler, J.O. Hydrodynamic Phenomena in Suspensions of Swimming Microorganisms. *Annu. Rev. Fluid Mech.* **1992**, *24*, 313–358. [CrossRef]
3. Hamel, A.; Fisch, C.; Combettes, L.; Dupuis-Williams, P.; Baroud, C.N. Transitions between three swimming gaits in *Paramecium* escape. *Proc. Natl. Acad. Sci. USA* **2011**, *108*, 7290–7295. [CrossRef]
4. Lee, T.C.; Long, D.S.; Clarke, R.J. Effect of endothelial glycocalyx layer redistribution upon microvessel poroelastohydrodynamics. *J. Fluid Mech.* **2016**, *798*, 812–852. [CrossRef]
5. Muhuri, S.; Rao, M.; Ramaswamy, S. Shear-flow–induced isotropic-to-nematic transition in a suspension of active filaments. *Europhys. Lett.* **2007**, *78*, 48002. [CrossRef]
6. Pahlavan, A.A.; Saintillan, D. Instability regimes in flowing suspensions of swimming micro-organisms. *Phys. Fluids* **2011**, *23*, 123304. [CrossRef]
7. Koch, D.L.; Subramanian, G. Collective hydrodynamics of swimming microorganisms: Living fluids. *Annu. Rev. Fluid Mech.* **2011**, *43*, 637–659. [CrossRef]
8. Alqarni, M.S.; Bearon, R.N. Transport of helical gyrotactic swimmers in channels. *Phys. Fluids* **2016**, *28*, 071904. [CrossRef]
9. Ishimoto, K.; Crowdy, D.G. Dynamics of a treadmilling microswimmer near a no-slip wall in simple shear. *J. Fluid Mech.* **2017**, *821*, 647–667. [CrossRef]
10. Ishimoto, K.; Gaffney, E.A. Fluid flow and sperm guidance: A simulation study of hydrodynamic sperm rheotaxis. *J. R. Soc. Interface* **2015**, *12*, 20150172. [CrossRef]
11. Jiang, W.; Chen, G. Dispersion of active particles in confined unidirectional flows. *J. Fluid Mech.* **2019**, *877*, 1–34. [CrossRef]
12. Swan, J.W.; Brady, J.F. Particle motion between parallel walls: Hydrodynamics and simulation. *Phys. Fluids* **2010**, *22*, 103301. [CrossRef]
13. ten Hagen, B.; Wittkowskim, R.; Lowen, H. Brownian dynamics of a self-propelled particle in shear flow. *Phys. Rev. E Stat. Nonlinear Soft Matter Phys.* **2011**, *84*, 031105. [CrossRef] [PubMed]
14. Kalman, D.P.; Wagner, N.J. Microstructure of shear-thickening concentrated suspensions determined by flow-USANS. *Rheol. Acta* **2009**, *48*, 897–908. [CrossRef]
15. Crassous, J.J.; Wittemann, A.; Siebenburger, M.; Schrinner, M.; Drechsler, M.; Ballauff, M. Direct imaging of temperature-sensitive core-shell latexes by cryogenic transmission electron microscopy. *Colloid Polym. Sci.* **2008**, *286*, 805–812. [CrossRef]
16. Lettinga, M.P.; Dhont, J.K.G. Non-equilibrium phase behavior of rod-like viruses under shear flow. *J. Phys. Condens. Matter* **2004**, *16*, S3929. [CrossRef]
17. Blaak, R.; Auer, S.; Frenkel, D.; Lowen, H. Crystal nucleation of colloidal suspensions under shear. *Phys. Rev. Lett.* **2004**, *93*, 68303. [CrossRef]

18. Dhont, J.K.G.; Nagele, G. Critical viscoelastic behavior of colloids. *Phys. Rev. E* **1998**, *58*, 7710–7732. [CrossRef]
19. Lighthill, M.J. On the squirming motion of nearly spherical deformable bodies through liquids at very small Reynolds numbers. *Commun. Pure Appl. Math.* **1952**, *5*, 109–118. [CrossRef]
20. Blake, J.R. A spherical envelope approach to ciliary propulsion. *J. Fluid Mech.* **1971**, *46*, 199–208. [CrossRef]
21. Blake, J.R. Self-propulsion due to oscillations on the surface of a cylinder at low Reynolds number. *Bull. Aust. Math. Soc.* **1971**, *5*, 255–264. [CrossRef]
22. Chisholm, N.G.; Legendre, D.; Lauga, E.; Khair, A.S. A squirmer across Reynolds numbers. *J. Fluid Mech.* **2016**, *796*, 233–256. [CrossRef]
23. Glowinski, R.; Pan, T.W.; Hesla, T.I.; Joseph, D.D.; Periaux, J. A fictitious domain approach to the direct numerical simulation of incompressible viscous flow past moving rigid bodies: Application to particulate flow. *J. Comput. Phys.* **2001**, *169*, 363–426. [CrossRef]
24. Dupuis, A.; Chatelain, P.; Koumoutsakos, P. An immersed boundary–lattice-Boltzmann method for the simulation of the flow past an impulsively started cylinder. *J. Comput. Phys.* **2008**, *227*, 4486–4498. [CrossRef]
25. Yu, Z.S.; Wu, T.H.; Shao, X.M.; Lin, J.Z. Numerical studies of the effects of large neutrally buoyant particles on the flow instability and transition to turbulence in pipe flow. *Phys. Fluids* **2013**, *25*, 043305. [CrossRef]
26. Qian, Y.H.; D'Humières, D.; Lallemand, P. Lattice BGK models for Navier-Stokes equation. *Europhys. Lett.* **1992**, *17*, 479–484. [CrossRef]
27. Peskin, C.S.; Peskin, C.S. Numerical analysis of blood flow in the heart. *J. Comput. Phys.* **1977**, *25*, 220–252. [CrossRef]
28. Feng, J.; Hu, H.H.; Joseph, D.D. Direct simulation of initial value problems for the motion of solid bodies in a Newtonian fluid Part 1. Sedimentation. *J. Fluid Mech.* **1994**, *261*, 95–134. [CrossRef]
29. Feng, Z.G.; Michaelides, E.E. Interparticle forces and lift on a particle attached to a solid boundary in suspension flow. *Phys. Fluids* **2002**, *14*, 49–60. [CrossRef]
30. Feng, Z.G.; Michaelides, E.E. The immersed boundary-lattice Boltzmann method for solving fluid–particles interaction problems. *J. Comput. Phys.* **2004**, *195*, 602–628. [CrossRef]

Article

Nonlinear Modeling Study of Aerodynamic Characteristics of an X38-like Vehicle at Strong Viscous Interaction Regions

Dingwu Jiang, Pei Wang *, Jin Li * and Meiliang Mao

Computational Aerodynamics Institute, China Aerodynamics Research and Development Center, Mianyang 621000, China; dwjiang@cardc.cn (D.J.); mlmao@cardc.cn (M.M.)
* Correspondence: wangp@mail.nwpu.edu.cn (P.W.); lijin09@cardc.cn (J.L.)

Abstract: Strong viscous interaction and multiple flow regimes exist when vehicles fly at high altitude and high Mach number conditions. The Navier–Stokes(NS) solver is no longer applicable in the above situation. Instead, the direct simulation Monte Carlo (DSMC) method or Boltzmann model equation solvers are usually needed. However, they are computationally more expensive than the NS solver. Therefore, it is of great engineering value to establish the aerodynamic prediction model of vehicles at high altitude and high Mach number conditions. In this paper, the hypersonic aerodynamic characteristics of an X38-like vehicle in typical conditions from 70 km to 110 km are simulated using the unified gas kinetic scheme (UGKS), which is applicable for all flow regimes. The contributions of pressure and viscous stress on the force coefficients are analyzed. The viscous interaction parameters, Mach number, and angle of attack are used as independent variables, and the difference between the force coefficients calculated by UGKS and the Euler solver is used as a dependent variable to establish a nonlinear viscous interaction model between them in the range of 70–110 km. The evaluation of the model is completed using the correlation coefficient and the relative orthogonal distance. The conventional viscous interaction effect and rarefied effect are both taken into account in the model. The model can be used to quickly obtain the hypersonic aerodynamic characteristics of X38-like vehicle in a wide range, which is meaningful for engineering design.

Keywords: X38-like vehicle; hypersonic; aerodynamic characteristics; viscous interaction effect; rarefied effect; modelling

1. Introduction

The viscous interaction effect, which describes the mutual interaction process between the boundary layer and the outer inviscid flow, is one of the three main effects [1] on hypersonic vehicles for ground-to-flight extrapolation. Depending on the degree of feedback from the inviscid flow on the boundary layer, strong viscous interaction and weak viscous interaction can be defined.

Traditionally, a similarity parameter, $\overline{\chi} = M_\infty^3 \sqrt{C}/\sqrt{Re}$, is used to ascertain whether an interaction region is strong or weak. $Re = \rho_e U_e x/\mu_e$ is the conventional Reynolds number based on properties, ρ_e, U_e and μ_e at the outer edge of the boundary layer: $C = \mu_w \rho_w / (\mu_e \rho_e)$. Large values of $\overline{\chi}$ correspond to the strong interaction and small values of $\overline{\chi}$ indicate a weak region. For pressure and force coefficients on simple configurations such as a flat plate or a sharp cone, a different correlation parameter, $v_\infty = M_\infty \sqrt{C}/\sqrt{Re}$, is usually used. The study of viscous interaction correlation for force coefficients derived from the space shuttle program has identified a modified viscous interaction parameter v'_∞ [2], which has been widely used in the literature to correlate the aerodynamic characteristics obtained by different means such as wind tunnel, flight, or numerical calculation. v'_∞ is defined as $v'_\infty = M_\infty \sqrt{C'}/\sqrt{Re_{L\infty}}$. $Re_{L\infty}$ is the Reynolds number based on the characteristic length of the vehicle. $C' = \mu' T_\infty / (\mu_\infty T')$. T'/T_∞ is the ratio of the reference temperature in the boundary layer to the incoming flow temperature.

Gong et al. [3] and Chen et al. [4] conducted numerical simulation and proved that for the OV-102 orbiter, v'_∞ is an accurate and effective correlation parameter for aerodynamic ground-to-flight extrapolation. Mao et al. [5] carried out correlative analyses for the viscous interaction effect based on the similarity solution for hypersonic boundary layers and concluded that the difference between the wall pressure on the surfaces of the effective body and the real body is proportional to the viscous interaction parameter at a high effective angle of attack. Hypersonic flow fields around a lifting body vehicle have been simulated by them to validate their conclusion. Han et al. [6] designed a gliding wave-rider vehicle and studied the effect of viscous interaction on the aerodynamic characteristics. It was found that the relationship between the difference of the pitching moment coefficient due to the viscous interaction and the viscous interaction parameter is nonlinear. The sign of the difference is opposite to that of the difference on the space shuttle-like vehicle, indicating that the region and intensity of the viscous interaction effects are configuration-dependent. Wang [7] proposed a joint correlative parameter to correlate experimental data with flight data for a lifting body vehicle. On the basis of experimental and numerical results of the lifting body, correlative results between joint correlative parameters with the axial force coefficient are improved efficiently compared with other parameters in terms of precision and accuracy. Zhang et al. [8] proposed a viscous interaction model of longitudinal aerodynamic coefficients under perfect gas conditions for a hypersonic wing-body configuration. The quantitative uncertainty of the prediction by the viscous interaction model is also presented in the form of relative orthogonal distance.

Molecular motion and collision at the microscopic level are two important mechanisms that determine the thermodynamic state of macroscopic fluids [9,10]. Two limiting states exist. One is the state in which the molecules are in equilibrium at all time and can be described macroscopically by the Euler equation, and the other is the state of free molecular flow without any collision between molecules. The motion of the molecules leads to viscosity. In general, the NS equation can be used when the deviation from the equilibrium state is not too great. The traditional numerical study of viscous interaction is based on the NS equation solver with the continuum assumption, so the viscous interaction model or the ground-to-flight extrapolation can only be used in the continuum regime. If the collisions between molecules are further reduced, the continuum assumption breaks down, and the so-called rarefied gas effect will appear. Rarefied gas dynamics methods are then needed to predict the rarefied effect. In views of the deviation from the thermodynamic equilibrium state, the viscous interaction effect and the rarefied gas effect are homologous. Both can be considered as the thermodynamic non-equilibrium effect. While for the viscous interaction effect flows deviate slightly from the equilibrium, for the rarefied gas effect flows deviate strongly from the equilibrium.

In fact, regardless of the amount of computation, most rarefied gas dynamics methods, such as DSMC [10] and the Boltzmann model equation solvers [11–41], can recover the NS solution in the continuum regime. Based on these methods, a viscous interaction model can be established for all flow regimes. Thus, both the traditional viscous interaction effect and the rarefied gas effect at high altitude are taken into account.

However, solving model equations in six dimensions for complex configurations at hypersonic conditions is always challenging work. Accuracy, efficiency, parallelization, robustness, memory cost, etc., are all concerns. Li [18–21] has developed a model solver called the gas-kinetic unified algorithm (GKUA). The GKUA has been validated and applied for many vehicles, such as the reusable sphere-cone satellite, the reentry spacecraft, and a complex wing-body combination shape. A total of 727 billion cells in a six-dimensional mesh and 23,800 cores on almost the largest computer systems available in China in 2015 were used in the last case [20]. Titarev [11–16] has developed an implicit parallel code, Nesvetay, in recent years. A breakthrough in Nesvetay is the adaptive velocity mesh which is almost linearly dependent on the free-stream Mach number [14]. For a M = 25 flow around the TsaGI reentry space vehicle, 18 billion six-dimensional mesh cells and only 5000 core-hours of computer time are consumed, which is state of the art. By comparison with DSMC results, Titarev also evaluated the BGK and Shakhov model equations as applied to hypersonic flows for both aerodynamics and heat transfer in [14–16]. Apart from the unstructured mesh technique used in Nesvetay, another efficient approach based on an adaptive octree velocity mesh is proposed by Baranger [17]. The octree mesh contains many fewer points than a traditional Cartesian mesh. In 2010, Xu [22] proposed the unified gas kinetic scheme (UGKS) method which is based on the integral solution of the model equation. The NS solution can be recovered from the UGKS in the hydrodynamic limit [23]. Good agreements between UGKS and DSMC results have also been achieved in rarefied regime [22–27]. Many advanced techniques such as the adaptive velocity method [28,29], implicit method [30–35], multigrid method [36], and memory-saving method [37] have been implemented. UGKS has been widely used in the simulation of flow fields from low speed to high speed, from continuum flow to rarefied flow [22–40]. For hypersonic validations and applications, Jiang [31] has conducted a UGKS simulation and verified its accuracy by comparing the pressure, stress, and heat flux distributions on an M = 25 cylinder for different regimes with DS2V results. Li [40] has conducted a kinetic blind comparative study on the aerodynamic characteristics of a complex-scaled X38-like vehicle which is the same as the one under study in the current paper. The free-stream Mach number is 8 with four different Knudsen numbers, 0.00275, 0.0275, 0.275, and 2.75. Two in-house kinetic solvers are used based on the DSMC method and UGKS method, respectively. Despite having different methods (statistical vs. deterministic) and different meshes (unstructured vs. structured), both UGKS and DSMC solvers gave similar and reasonably consistent results. The average relative errors for the lift and drag coefficients are only 0.98% and 2.01%, respectively.

Based on the above understanding and our practical experiences with UGKS in the past decade, the goal of this paper was to establish a viscous interaction model applicable to all regimes. An in-house UGKS solver was used to predict the aerodynamic characteristics of a complex X38-like configuration at high altitude (70–110 km) and high Mach number ($\geq$10). The viscous interaction correlation method derived from the space shuttle program [2] was used for reference.

The difference between the aerodynamic characteristics obtained by UGKS and the solution of inviscid Euler equations was used as the dependent variable. A prediction model relating the difference and the viscous interaction parameter was proposed. The model was evaluated using the concepts of correlation coefficient and relative orthogonal distance. Some new cases were selected and calculated by UGKS and the prediction model to verify the accuracy of the model prediction results.

2. Numerical Methods

2.1. The Inviscid Solver

The governing equations are the three-dimensional compressible Euler equations in general curvilinear coordinates. The equations are discretized based on the finite volume method and solved by the implicit LUSGS method. See [41] for more details.

2.2. The Viscous Solver

The governing equation is the Shakhov model equation [42] which can be written in non-dimensional form:

$$f_t + \mathbf{u} \cdot \nabla f = \frac{f^+ - f}{\tau}$$
$$\tau = \frac{\mu}{p\text{Re}_\infty}, f^+ = g_M + g_M(1 - \text{Pr})\frac{8\lambda^2}{5}\frac{\mathbf{c} \cdot \mathbf{q}}{\rho}\left(\lambda c^2 - \frac{5}{2}\right) \quad (1)$$
$$g_M = \rho\left(\frac{\lambda}{\pi}\right)^{\frac{3}{2}} e^{-\lambda((u-U)^2 + (v-V)^2 + (w-W)^2)}, \lambda = \frac{\gamma M_\infty^2}{2T}, \text{Re}_\infty = \frac{\rho_\infty |U_\infty| L_{ref}}{\mu_\infty}$$

Here f is the distribution function which is a function of the space $\mathbf{x}$, the particle velocity $\mathbf{u}$, and time t. τ is the collision time. g_M is the local Maxwellian distribution function. The second term in f^+ is a correction term based on the original BGK model equation in order to obtain a reasonable Prandtl number, Pr. **c** and **q** are the random velocity vector and the heat vector, respectively. μ, ρ, and p are the non-dimensional viscosity, density, and pressure, respectively. Re_∞ and M_∞ are the free stream Reynolds number and Mach number, respectively. Dimensional free stream density ρ_∞, velocity modulus $|U_\infty|$, temperature T_∞, and viscosity μ_∞ are used to obtain the non-dimensional macroscopic quantities in the following way

$$p = \frac{p^*}{\rho_\infty U_\infty^2}, \rho = \frac{\rho^*}{\rho_\infty}, \mu = \frac{\mu^*}{\mu_\infty}, T = \frac{T^*}{T_\infty}, U = \frac{U^*}{|U_\infty|}, V = \frac{V^*}{|U_\infty|}, W = \frac{W^*}{|U_\infty|}, \mathbf{q} = \frac{\mathbf{q}^*}{\rho_\infty U_\infty^3} \quad (2)$$

The superscript '*' denotes dimensional quantities. The power-law intermolecular interaction $\mu = T^\omega$ is assumed. The total length of the vehicle L_{ref} is used as scale of length. $t_\infty = L_{ref}/|U_\infty|$ is the scale of temporal variable. $\rho_\infty/|U_\infty|^3$ is used to obtain non-dimensional distribution function f.

Unless explicitly specified, all variables in the following are non-dimensional.

The relations between the macroscopic conserved quantities **Q**, the stress **P**, the heat **q** and the distribution function are

$$\mathbf{Q} = \int f \psi d\Xi \quad \psi = (1, \mathbf{u}, \frac{1}{2}\mathbf{u}^2) \quad (3)$$

$$\mathbf{P} = \int \mathbf{cc} f d\Xi \quad \mathbf{q} = \int \frac{1}{2}\mathbf{c} \cdot \mathbf{c}^2 f d\Xi \quad (4)$$

where ψ is the vector of moments and $d\Xi = dudvdw$ is the volume element in the phase space.

In UGKS, at the cell interface $(i + 1/2, j, k)$ an integral solution of the Shakhov model in the following form is used to construct the solution:

$$f_{i+1/2,j,k,l,m,n} = \frac{1}{\tau}\int_0^t f^+(x_{i+1/2} - u_l(t-t'), t', u_l, v_m, w_n) e^{-(t-t')/\tau} dt' \\ + e^{-t/\tau} f_0(x - u_l t, 0, u_l, v_m, w_n) \quad (5)$$

where $f^+ = g + g^+$ will be approximated separately. The subscripts i,j,k and l,m,n denote the indexes in three structured physical mesh directions and three Cartesian velocity mesh directions, respectively. $x' = x_{i+1/2} - u_l(t - t')$ is the particle trajectory and f_0 is the initial gas distribution function at the beginning of each time step around the cell interface $x_{i+1/2}$ at particle velocity $\mathbf{u} = (u_l, v_m, w_n)$.

As the distribution function inside each control volume is known at the beginning of each time step. f_0 can be obtained using TVD reconstruction.

$$f_{0,l,m,n} = \begin{cases} f^L_{i+1/2,j,k,l,m,n} + \sigma_{i,j,k,l,m,n} x & x \leq 0 \\ f^R_{i+1/2,j,k,l,m,n} + \sigma_{i+1,j,k,l,m,n} x & x > 0 \end{cases} \quad (6)$$

where a nonlinear limiter is used to reconstruct $f^L_{i+1/2,j,k,l,m,n}, f^R_{i+1/2,j,k,l,m,n}$ and the corresponding slopes $\sigma_{i,j,k,l,m,n}, \sigma_{i+1,j,k,l,m,n}$.

The equilibrium state g around the cell interface $x_{i+1/2}$ can be expanded with two slopes

$$g = g_0 \left[1 + (1 - H[x])\overline{a}^L x + H[x]\overline{a}^R x + \overline{A}t \right] \quad (7)$$

where $H[x]$ is the Heaviside function. g_0 is a local Maxwellian distribution located at the cell interface. It can be determined by the corresponding macroscopic flow variables. $\overline{a}^L$, $\overline{a}^R$, and $\overline{A}$ are related to the derivatives of a Maxwellian distribution in space and time. For details to obtain g_0, $\overline{a}^L$, $\overline{a}^R$ and $\overline{A}$, see [22,25,26].

With the determination of equilibrium state and the heat flux at the cell interface, the additional term g^+ in the Shakhov model can be determined.

Substituting Equations (6) and (7) into Equation (5), the gas distribution function at the cell interface with particle velocity (u_l, v_m, w_n) can be expressed as

$$\begin{aligned}
f_{i+1/2,j,k,l,m,n}&\left(x_{j+1/2}, y_j, z_k, t, u_l, v_m, w_n\right) \\
=& \left(1 - e^{-t/\tau}\right)(g_0 + g^+) \\
&+ \left(\tau\left(-1 + e^{-t/\tau}\right) + te^{-t/\tau}\right)(\overline{a}^L H[u_l] + \overline{a}^R(1 - H[u_l]))u_l g_0 \\
&+ \tau\left(t/\tau - 1 + e^{-t/\tau}\right)\overline{A} g_0 \\
&+ e^{-t/\tau}\left(f^L_{i+1/2,j,k,l,m,n} H[u_l] + f^R_{i+1/2,j,k,l,m,n}(1 - H[u_l])\right) \\
&- te^{-t/\tau}\left(\sigma_{i,j,k,l,m,n} u_l H[u_l] + \sigma_{i+1,j,k,l,m,n} u_l(1 - H[u_l])\right)
\end{aligned} \quad (8)$$

From the cell interface distribution function we can obtain the distribution function flux and macroscopic flux. We will update the macroscopic variables first with the macroscopic fluxes. Subsequently, we can immediately obtain the local Maxwellian $g_M^{\zeta+1}$ and the additional term $f^{+,\zeta+1}$ at $\zeta + 1$ time step inside each cell. Therefore, based on Equation (1) the update of distribution function in UGKS becomes

$$\begin{aligned}
\Delta f_{i,j,k,l,m,n} =& \ f^{\zeta+1}_{i,j,k,l,m,n} - f^{\zeta}_{i,j,k,l,m,n} = -\int_0^{\Delta t} \begin{bmatrix} (ff \cdot S)_{i+1/2,j,k} - (ff \cdot S)_{i-1/2,j,k} \\ +(ff \cdot S)_{i,j+1/2,k} - (ff \cdot S)_{i,j-1/2,k} \\ +(ff \cdot S)_{i,j,k+1/2} - (ff \cdot S)_{i,j,k-1/2} \end{bmatrix} dt \\
&+ \frac{\Delta t}{2}\left(\frac{f^{+\ \zeta+1}_{i,j,k,l,m,n} - f^{\zeta+1}_{i,j,k,l,m,n}}{\tau^{\zeta+1}_{i,j,k}} + \frac{f^{+\ \zeta}_{i,j,k,l,m,n} - f^{\zeta}_{i,j,k,l,m,n}}{\tau^{\zeta}_{i,j,k}}\right)
\end{aligned} \quad (9)$$

where ff is the distribution function flux across the interface and S is the interface area. The trapezoidal rule has been used for time integration of the collision time.

Equation (9) can be rearranged as

$$f^{\zeta+1}_{i,j,k,l,m,n} = \left(1 + \frac{\Delta t}{2\tau^{\zeta+1}_{i,j,k}}\right)^{-1} \left\{ -\int_0^{\Delta t} \begin{bmatrix} (ff \cdot S)_{i+1/2,j,k} - (ff \cdot S)_{i-1/2,j,k} \\ +(ff \cdot S)_{i,j+1/2,k} - (ff \cdot S)_{i,j-1/2,k} \\ +(ff \cdot S)_{i,j,k+1/2} - (ff \cdot S)_{i,j,k-1/2} \end{bmatrix} dt + \frac{\Delta t}{2}\left(\frac{f^{+\ \zeta+1}_{i,j,k,l,m,n}}{\tau^{\zeta+1}_{i,j,k}} + \frac{f^{+\ \zeta}_{i,j,k,l,m,n} - f^{\zeta}_{i,j,k,l,m,n}}{\tau^{\zeta}_{i,j,k}}\right) \right\} \quad (10)$$

This is the original explicit UGKS in [22,25].

To accelerate the convergence for steady flow, the authors of [34] introduced the implicit discrete ordinate method for an unstructured physical mesh [12,13] into UGKS. A brief introduction is given below.

Rewriting Equation (1) for f with a particle velocity $\mathbf{u} = (u_l, v_m, w_n)$ in a physical space cell (i,j,k)

$$\frac{\partial f_{i,j,k,l,m,n}}{\partial t} + u_l \frac{\partial f_{i,j,k,l,m,n}}{\partial x} + v_m \frac{\partial f_{i,j,k,l,m,n}}{\partial y} + w_n \frac{\partial f_{i,j,k,l,m,n}}{\partial z} = \frac{\left(f^+_{i,j,k,l,m,n} - f_{i,j,k,l,m,n}\right)}{\tau} \quad (11)$$

Treating the loss term of collision integral semi-implicitly and the gain term explicitly we can find

$$\begin{aligned}
\left(1 + \Delta t \cdot \frac{1}{\tau^{\zeta}} + \Delta t \cdot \mathbf{u}_{l,m,n} \nabla\right)(\Delta f)_{i,j,k,l,m,n} &= \Delta t \cdot R^{\zeta}_{i,j,k,l,m,n} \\
R^{\zeta}_{i,j,k,l,m,n} &= -u_l \frac{\partial f^{\zeta}_{i,j,k,l,m,n}}{\partial x} - v_m \frac{\partial f^{\zeta}_{i,j,k,l,m,n}}{\partial y} - w_n \frac{\partial f^{\zeta}_{i,j,k,l,m,n}}{\partial z} + \frac{1}{\tau^{\zeta}}(f^+ - f) \\
&= -R' + \frac{1}{\tau^{\zeta}}(f^+ - f)
\end{aligned} \quad (12)$$

where R' is the net cell flux averaged over the evolution time step, which can be expressed as

$$R' = \frac{1}{\Delta \tilde{t}} \int_0^{\Delta \tilde{t}} \begin{bmatrix} (ff \cdot S)_{i+1/2,j,k} - (ff \cdot S)_{i-1/2,j,k} \\ +(ff \cdot S)_{i,j+1/2,k} - (ff \cdot S)_{i,j-1/2,k} \\ +(ff \cdot S)_{i,j,k+1/2} - (ff \cdot S)_{i,j,k-1/2} \end{bmatrix} dt \tag{13}$$

The evolution time step $\Delta \tilde{t}$ is determined by the following

$$\Delta \tilde{t} \leq \frac{\Delta t_{\min}}{CFL} \tag{14}$$

where $\Delta t_{\min}$ is the minimum marching time step determined by the stability condition. CFL is the CFL number.

Equation (12) can be further written as

$$\begin{aligned} &\left(1 + \Delta t \cdot \tfrac{1}{\tau^{\zeta}}\right)(\Delta f)_{i,j,k,l,m,n} \\ &+ \frac{\Delta t}{|V_{i,j,k}|} \sum_{ii=1}^{6} (\mathbf{u}_{l,m,n} \cdot \mathbf{n}_{ii}) \cdot \left|S_{i,j,k,ii}\right| \cdot FF\left((\Delta f)_{i,j,k,l,m,n}, (\Delta f)_{i1,j1,k1,l,m,n}\right) \\ &= \Delta t \cdot R^{\zeta}_{i,j,k,l,m,n} \end{aligned} \tag{15}$$

where the subscript ii indicates the six faces of the physical cell (i,j,k). $S_{i,j,k,ii}$ is the area of the iith face. $V_{i,j,k}$ is the cell volume. The subscript $(i1,j1,k1)$ indicates the cell which shares the iith face with cell (i,j,k). $\mathbf{n}_{ii}$ is the outer normal vector of the iith face.

$$\begin{aligned} &FF\left((\Delta f)_{i,j,k,l,m,n}, (\Delta f)_{i1,j1,k1,l,m,n}\right) \\ &= \tfrac{1}{2}\left[(\Delta f)_{i,j,k,l,m,n} + (\Delta f)_{i1,j1,k1,l,m,n}\right] \\ &+ \tfrac{1}{2} sign(\mathbf{u}_{l,m,n} \cdot \mathbf{n}_{ii})\left[(\Delta f)_{i,j,k,l,m,n} - (\Delta f)_{i1,j1,k1,l,m,n}\right] \end{aligned} \tag{16}$$

Substituting Equation (16) into Equation (15), we can obtain

$$\begin{aligned} &\left(1 + \Delta t \cdot \tfrac{1}{\tau^{\zeta}}\right)(\Delta f)_{i,j,k,l,m,n} \\ &+ \frac{\Delta t}{|V_{i,j,k}|} \sum_{ii=1}^{6} (\mathbf{u}_{l,m,n} \cdot \mathbf{n}_{ii}) \cdot \left|S_{i,j,k,ii}\right| \left[\tfrac{1}{2}(1 + sign(\mathbf{u}_{l,m,n} \cdot \mathbf{n}_{ii})) \cdot (\Delta f)_{i,j,k,l,m,n}\right] \\ &+ \frac{\Delta t}{|V_{i,j,k}|} \sum_{ii=1}^{6} (\mathbf{u}_{l,m,n} \cdot \mathbf{n}_{ii}) \cdot \left|S_{i,j,k,ii}\right| \left[\tfrac{1}{2}(1 - sign(\mathbf{u}_{l,m,n} \cdot \mathbf{n}_{ii})) \cdot (\Delta f)_{i1,j1,k1,l,m,n}\right] \\ &= \Delta t \cdot R^{\zeta}_{i,j,k,l,m,n} \end{aligned} \tag{17}$$

After a simple deformation, it can be written as

$$\begin{aligned} &\left[1 + \Delta t \cdot \tfrac{1}{\tau^{\zeta}} + \Delta t \cdot b_{i,j,k,l,m,n}\right](\Delta f)_{i,j,k,l,m,n} \\ &+ \sum_{ii=1}^{6} \Delta t \cdot c_{i,j,k,l,m,n} \cdot (\Delta f)_{i1,j1,k1,l,m,n} = \Delta t \cdot R^{\zeta}_{i,j,k,l,m,n} \\ &b_{i,j,k,l,m,n} = \sum_{ii=1}^{6} (\mathbf{u}_{l,m,n} \cdot \mathbf{n}_{ii}) \cdot (1 + sign(\mathbf{u}_{l,m,n} \cdot \mathbf{n}_{ii})) \frac{|S_{i,j,k,ii}|}{2|V_{i,j,k}|} \\ &c_{i,j,k,l,m,n} = (\mathbf{u}_{l,m,n} \cdot \mathbf{n}_{ii}) \cdot (1 - sign(\mathbf{u}_{l,m,n} \cdot \mathbf{n}_{ii})) \frac{|S_{i,j,k,ii}|}{2|V_{i,j,k}|} \end{aligned} \tag{18}$$

Continuing to deform

$$(\Delta f)_{i,j,k,l,m,n} + \sum_{ii=1}^{6} \Delta t \cdot z_{i,j,k,l,m,n} \cdot (\Delta f)_{i1,j1,k1,l,m,n} = \frac{\Delta t}{\chi_{i,j,k,l,m,n}} \cdot R_{i,j,k,l,m,n}^{\zeta}$$
$$\chi_{i,j,k,l,m,n} = 1 + \Delta t \cdot \frac{1}{\tau^{\zeta}} + \Delta t \cdot b_{i,j,k,l,m,n} \quad (19)$$
$$z_{i,j,k,l,m,n} = \frac{c_{i,j,k,l,m,n}}{\chi_{i,j,k,l,m,n}}$$

Writing in matrix form

$$(\mathbf{I} + \Delta t \cdot \mathbf{Z}_{l,m,n}) \cdot (\Delta \mathbf{f})_{l,m,n} = \Delta t \cdot \mathbf{X}_{l,m,n}^{-1} \cdot \mathbf{R}_{l,m,n}^{\zeta}$$

$$(\Delta \mathbf{f})_{l,m,n} = \begin{pmatrix} (\Delta f)_{1,1,1,l,m,n} \\ (\Delta f)_{2,1,1,l,m,n} \\ \cdots \\ (\Delta f)_{NI-1,NJ-1,NK-1,l,m,n} \end{pmatrix} \quad \mathbf{R}_{l,m,n}^{\zeta} = \begin{pmatrix} R_{1,1,1,l,m,n}^{\zeta} \\ R_{2,1,1,l,m,n}^{\zeta} \\ \cdots \\ R_{NI-1,NJ-1,NK-1,l,m,n}^{\zeta} \end{pmatrix} \quad (20)$$

$$\mathbf{X}_{l,m,n} = \begin{pmatrix} \chi_{1,1,1,l,m,n} & 0 & \cdots & 0 \\ 0 & \chi_{2,1,1,l,m,n} & \cdots & 0 \\ 0 & 0 & \cdots & 0 \\ 0 & 0 & \cdots & \chi_{NI-1,NJ-1,NK-1,l,m,n} \end{pmatrix}$$

where $(\mathbf{I} + \Delta t \cdot \mathbf{Z}_{l,m,n})$ is a seven-diagonal matrix. *NI*, *NJ*, and *NK* are the total points in the *i*, *j*, and *k* directions of a block in the structured physical mesh, respectively. Applying the LU decomposition yields

$$\mathbf{I} + \Delta t \cdot \mathbf{Z}_{l,m,n} = \mathbf{L}_{l,m,n} \cdot \mathbf{U}_{l,m,n} + \bigcirc(\Delta t^2) \quad (21)$$

$\mathbf{L}_{l,m,n}$, $\mathbf{U}_{l,m,n}$ are both matrices.

$$l_{pq} = \begin{cases} \Delta t \cdot z_{pq} & p < q \\ 0 & p > q \end{cases}$$
$$u_{pq} = \begin{cases} 0 & p < q \\ \Delta t \cdot z_{pq} & p > q \end{cases} \quad (22)$$
$$l_{pp} = u_{pp} = 1$$

The final form of the implicit UGKS is

$$\mathbf{L}_{l,m,n} \cdot \mathbf{U}_{l,m,n} \cdot (\Delta \mathbf{f})_{l,m,n} = \Delta t \cdot \mathbf{X}_{l,m,n}^{-1} \cdot \mathbf{R}_{l,m,n}^{\zeta} \quad (23)$$

By performing direct and backward substitutions in a structured physical mesh, $(\Delta f)_{i,j,k,l,m,n}$ can be found. We can then obtain the distribution function $f_{i,j,k,l,m,n}$ at time step $\varsigma + 1$. After that, macroscopic variables can be obtained with Equations (3) and (4).

The tests [34] on the flows over a cylinder with different free stream Mach numbers showed that the above implicit method can give the same result as the original explicit method with a properly chosen evolving time step. Meanwhile, the computational efficiency can be improved by 1~2 orders.

Due to the explicit treatment of $f_{i,j,k,l,m,n}^+$ in the above method, slow convergence exists in small Knudsen number cases. To further accelerate the convergence, Zhu et al. [35] proposed a macroscopic variable prediction technique to deal with $f_{i,j,k,l,m,n}^+$ in their implicit UGKS, which is proved to be efficient in all flow regimes.

Under the support of the National Numerical Wind Tunnel Program, an aerodynamic characteristics prediction software applicable for multiple flow regimes called NNW-UGKS [38] has been established, and the viscous flow in the current paper was simulated by this software. Decomposition both in the physical and velocity meshes is applied for

MPI parallelism, which is similar to the one in [39]. The composite Newton–Cotes quadrature formula which can be used for any kinds of flow simulation including the current hypersonic or highly non-equilibrium flows, was chosen for integration.

The diffusive reflection wall boundary condition and perfect gas assumption was used.

3. Results and Modeling

As a demonstrator of the Crew Return Vehicle (CRV), the X38 vehicle has a number of advantages, such as relatively high lift-to-drag ratio and volumetric efficiency [43]. Although the X38 project has long been terminated, research on similar shapes still continues.

The sketch of the vehicle is shown in Figure 1. The reference length of the vehicle, L_{ref}, is 4.67 m.

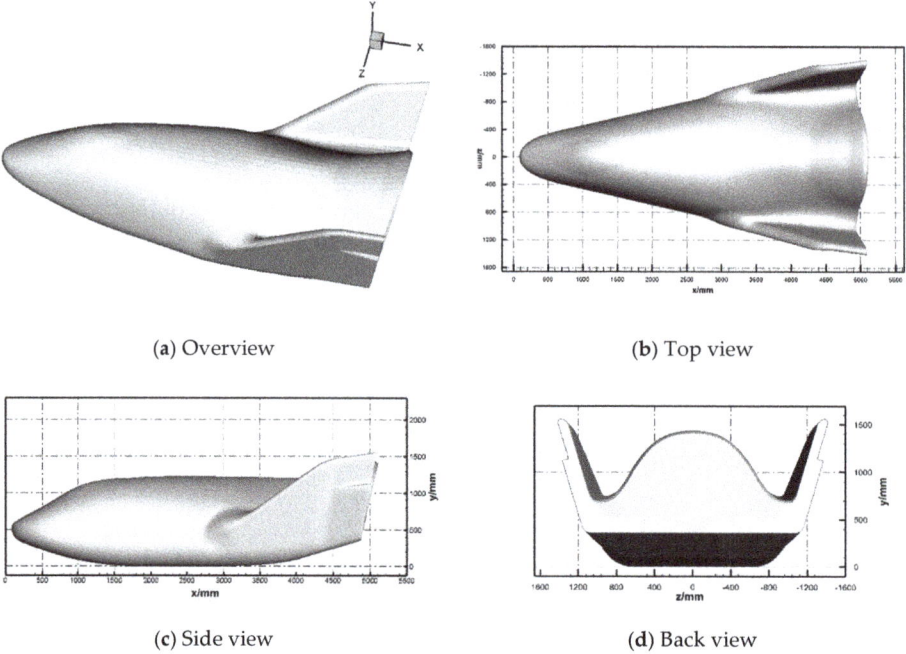

(a) Overview (b) Top view

(c) Side view (d) Back view

Figure 1. Sketch of the X38-like vehicle.

Free-stream conditions are given in Table 1. A total number of 24 cases and 4 cases are simulated by viscous and inviscid solvers, respectively. The structured physical mesh is illustrated in Figure 2. The number of cells is 334,434 for altitudes lower than 110 km. For 110 km, the outer boundary is not large enough and additional 82,656 cells were added. The minimum distance near the wall is 1.67 mm which is nearly two times and 0.3% of the free stream mean free paths of 70 km and 110 km, respectively. The velocity mesh is $65 \times 65 \times 65$ and $81 \times 81 \times 81$ for M = 10 and M = 15, respectively, ranging from $-2.5|U_\infty|$ to $2.5|U_\infty|$.

Table 1. Free-stream conditions.

Height/km	Mach Number	Angle of Attack/Degrees	Solvers
70, 80, 85, 90, 100, 110	10	20, 30, 40	inviscid, viscous
70, 80, 85, 90, 100, 110	15	20	inviscid, viscous

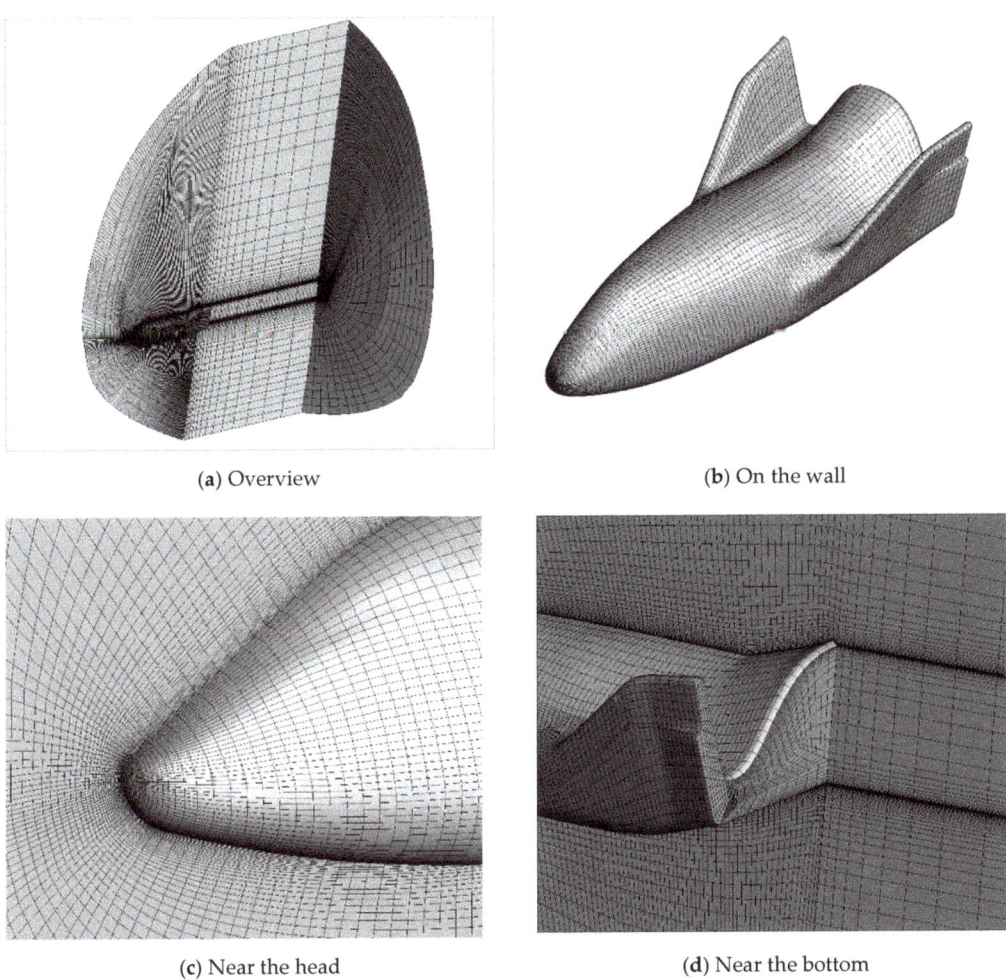

Figure 2. Structured multi-block physical mesh.

To conduct a thorough mesh convergence for such a problem is almost impossible. As is shown in our previous paper [40] for a 1:16.7 scaled model, good agreements with the DSMC results can be obtained for four different free stream conditions. For the DSMC method, the cell size should be adjusted according to the free stream condition to be smaller than the local mean free path of particles. While for UGKS method, the same physical structured mesh can be used for different free stream conditions. This may be due to the coupling mechanism of the particle transport and collision in UGKS method. The cell size can be larger than the mean free path of particles.

3.1. Flow Field Characteristics

Figure 3 shows the pressure contour of the flow field and the velocity vector on the symmetry plane at two altitudes. For sake of clarity, the grid in the vector diagram is one out of three. The viscous boundary layer can be clearly distinguished from the figure. With the increase in altitude, the shock stand-off distance and the thickness of boundary layer increase, and the wall slip velocity, increases obviously.

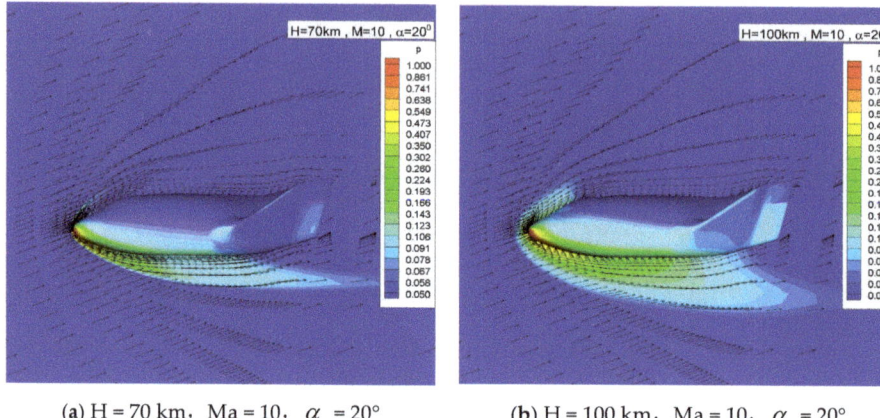

(a) H = 70 km, Ma = 10, α = 20° (b) H = 100 km, Ma = 10, α = 20°

Figure 3. Velocity vector and pressure contour.

Figure 4 shows the streamlines on the symmetry plane and near the body surface. No flow separation on the windward and leeward sides can be observed. At 70 km, there is a small separation at the bottom. At 100 km, no separation exists due to the smaller bottom adverse pressure gradient.

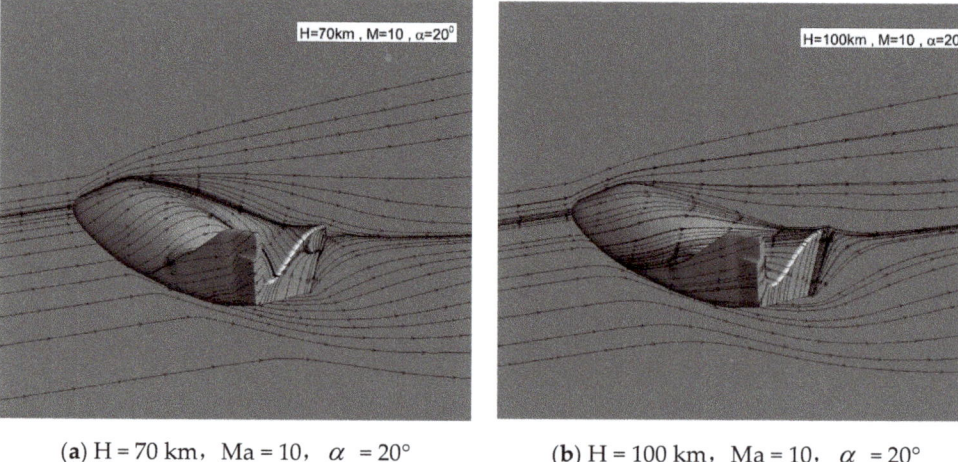

(a) H = 70 km, Ma = 10, α = 20° (b) H = 100 km, Ma = 10, α = 20°

Figure 4. Streamlines on the symmetry plane and near the body surface.

Figure 5 shows the local Knudsen number distribution on the symmetry plane and near the body surface at two altitudes.

The local Knudsen number is defined [44] as

$$Kn_{GLL} = \frac{l_{mfp}}{\rho/|\nabla \rho|} \tag{24}$$

where l_{mfp} is the local mean free path. The Knudsen number of this form has a great physical meaning. Traditionally, different flow regimes are defined according to the Knudsen numbers [10]. For continuum regime, Kn is smaller than 0.01. For a transitional regime, Kn ranges between 0.01 and 10. When Kn is larger than 10, the flow is considered as free-molecular. Thus, when Kn_{GLL} is much less than unity the flow can be regarded as locally slightly perturbed from equilibrium which is a fundamental assumption of the NS equations. Therefore, it is an appropriate parameter to indicate the degree of non-equilibrium.

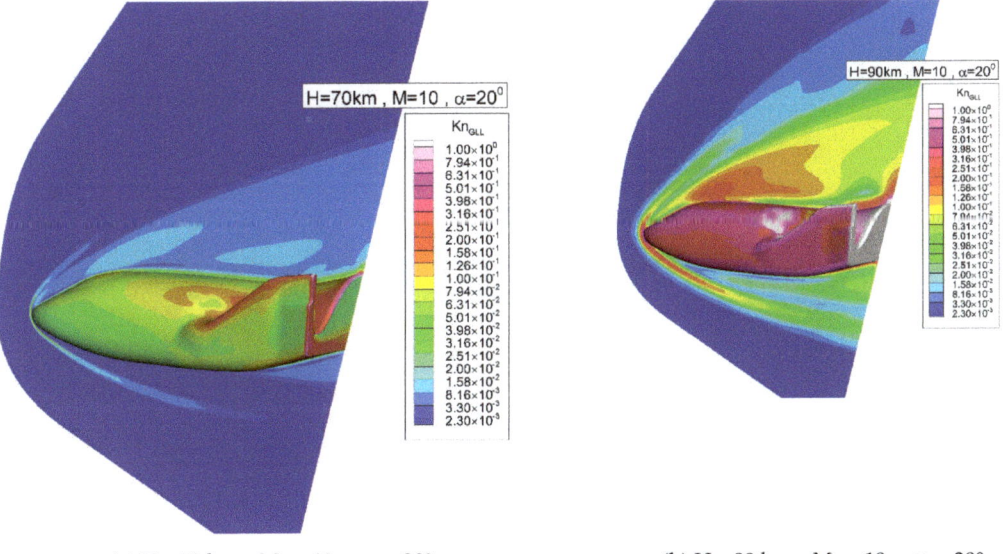

(a) H = 70 km, Ma = 10, α = 20° (b) H = 90 km, Ma = 10, α = 20°

Figure 5. Local Knudsen number distribution on the symmetry plane and near the body surface.

Figure 6 shows the local Knudsen number comparison along the y = 500 mm line in front of the vehicle. The local Knudsen number is large inside the bow shock which usually locates in the first peak from left, and near the wall which has been marked on the right. Even at 70 km, the local Knudsen number near the wall and inside the shock is on the order of 0.01, where the continuum assumption may break down. Thus, it is necessary to use UGKS for simulation.

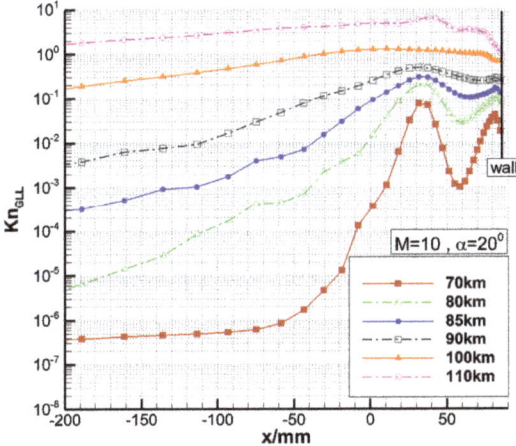

Figure 6. Local Knudsen number comparison along the y = 500 mm line.

Figure 7 shows the comparison of the pressure distribution on the centerlines. The pressure distribution on the windward centerline shows an increasing trend with the increase in altitude. While on the leeward centerline it increases first and then decreases with the increase in altitude. The magnitude is about an order smaller than that on the windward centerline.

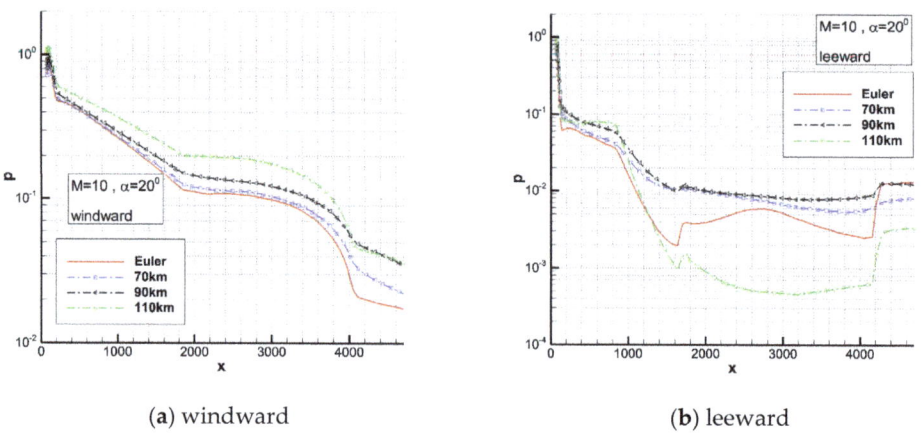

(a) windward (b) leeward

Figure 7. Comparison of pressure on the centerlines.

Figure 8 shows the variation in the pressure change, Δp, due to viscous interaction at several typical stream-wise positions on the centerlines.

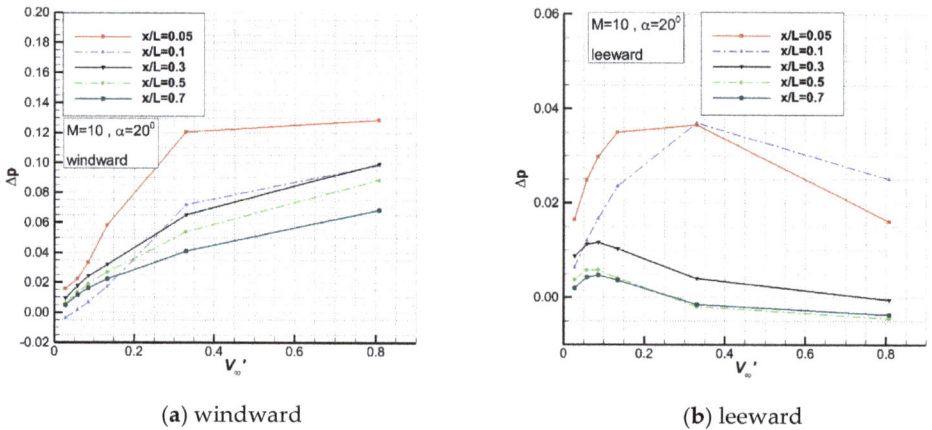

(a) windward (b) leeward

Figure 8. Variation in pressure change on the centerlines with viscous interaction parameter.

In early research on simple configurations, figures similar to Figure 8 have been frequently given and linear relationships have been obtained. For the current complex vehicle, in the range of 70~85 km and X/L = 0.1~0.5, there is a good linear relationship between the pressure change and the viscous interaction parameter on the windward side for 20 degrees angle of attack. In other areas and the whole leeward side, no good linear relationships can be seen.

3.2. Aerodynamic Characteristics and Viscous Interaction Modelling

Figure 9 shows the aerodynamic force coefficients computed by the Euler and UGKS solvers. For the UGKS results, the contributions of the pressure and friction are separated. With the increase in the viscous interaction parameter, the axial force and the normal force coefficients increase, and the pressure part and viscous part also increase at the same time. For the axial force, the viscous part increases rapidly as the altitude increases, from 34% at 70 km to 87% at 110 km. At 80 km and above, the viscous part exceeds the pressure part. For the normal force, the pressure part is dominant, decreasing from 95% at 70 km to 74% at 110 km, and the viscous part is relatively small.

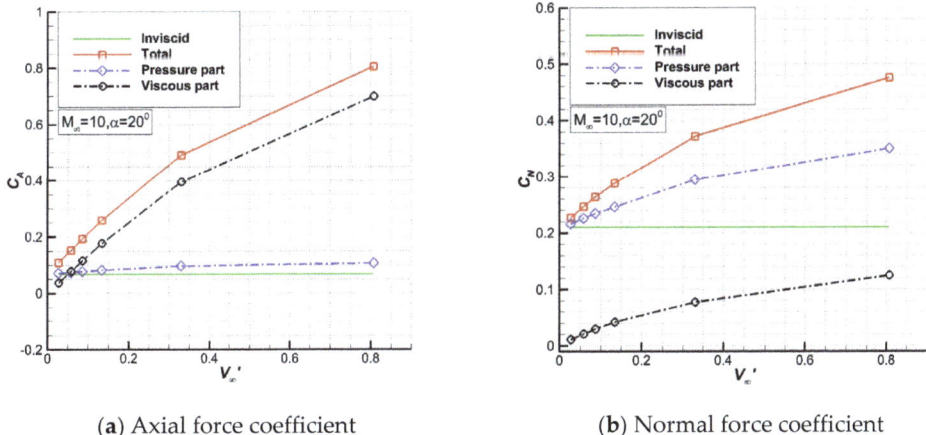

(**a**) Axial force coefficient (**b**) Normal force coefficient

Figure 9. Aerodynamic force coefficients for different v'_∞.

Figure 10 shows the viscous force coefficients with the third viscous interaction parameter. Note that the viscous force coefficient is defined as the quantity due to viscous interaction [45] which is equal to the difference between UGKS and Euler solutions. Thus, it is different from the viscous part of UGKS.

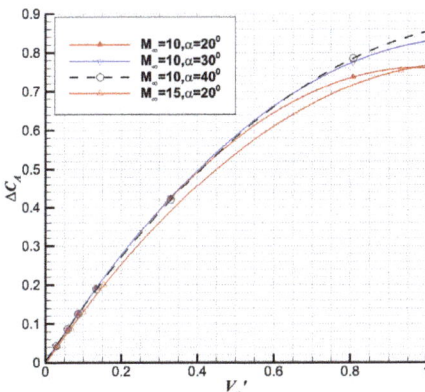

Figure 10. The viscous axial force coefficient vs. v'_∞.

At an altitude less than 100 km where v'_∞ is about 0.33 (M = 10), the viscous axial force coefficient has a weak linear relationship with the third viscous interaction parameter. The higher the altitude is, the more serious the deviation from the linear relationship is. In order to correlate the results for all ranges of calculation, it is assumed that the change in the aerodynamic coefficients due to the viscous interaction satisfies the following relationship:

$$\Delta C(v_\infty', M_\infty, \alpha) \approx a(M_\infty, \alpha) + b(M_\infty, \alpha)v_\infty' + c(M_\infty, \alpha)v_\infty'^2 \quad (25)$$

As a preliminary study, it is further assumed that

$$\begin{aligned} a(M_\infty, \alpha) &\approx a_0 + a_1(M_\infty) + a_2(\alpha) \\ b(M_\infty, \alpha) &\approx b_0 + b_1(M_\infty) + b_2(\alpha) \\ c(M_\infty, \alpha) &\approx c_0 + c_1(M_\infty) + c_2(\alpha) \end{aligned} \quad (26)$$

According to the calculated aerodynamic force coefficients and the parameters in Equation (26), the following expression of the viscous axial force coefficient can be obtained by fitting with the least square method,

$$\begin{aligned} \Delta C_A(v_\infty', M_\infty, \alpha) &\approx a^A(M_\infty, \alpha) + b^A(M_\infty, \alpha) \cdot v_\infty' + c^A(M_\infty, \alpha) \cdot v_\infty'^2 \\ a^A &= -1.26 \times 10^{-2} - \frac{3.21 \times 10^{-3}}{M_\infty^2} + 6.14 \times 10^{-4} \cdot \alpha - 5.38 \times 10^{-6} \cdot \alpha^2 \\ b^A &= 1.31 + \frac{2.72 \times 10^1}{M_\infty^2} - 2.23 \times 10^{-4} \cdot \alpha - 7.08 \times 10^{-5} \cdot \alpha^2 \\ c^A &= -0.787 - \frac{2.81 \times 10^1}{M_\infty^2} + 1.69 \times 10^{-2} \cdot \alpha - 1.36 \times 10^{-4} \cdot \alpha^2 \end{aligned} \quad (27)$$

From the expressions of a^A, b^A, and c^A, we can conclude that the effect of Mach number can be ignored under the condition of high Mach number. In fact, the effect of Mach number may be mainly reflected in the viscous interaction parameter.

Usually, Equation (27) is called a viscous interaction model for the axial force coefficient. Models for other viscous force coefficients can be obtained in a similar way.

Figure 11 shows the correlation curve between the viscous interaction model prediction data which is represented by suffix '_ model' and the numerical simulation data which is represented by suffix '_ UGKS'. The data are basically distributed near the correlation line at different angles of attack and Mach numbers. It can be seen that the correlation between the data is good.

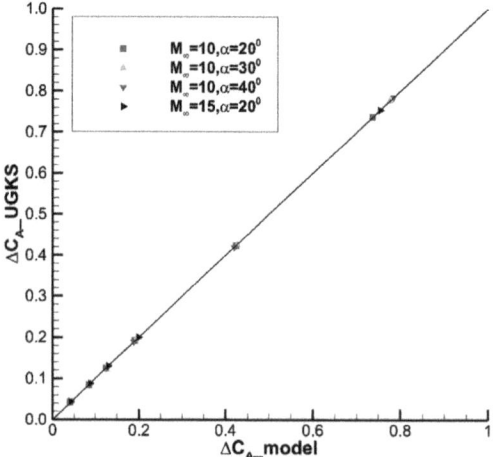

Figure 11. Correlation between viscous interaction model and numerical simulation results.

The Pearson Correlation Coefficient r, which is widely used in statistics, is chosen to characterize the degree of correlation between the aerodynamic prediction data and the numerical simulation data, and its expression is

$$r = \frac{\sum_{i=0}^{n}(x_i-\bar{x})(y_i-\bar{y})}{\sqrt{\sum_{i=0}^{n}(x_i-\bar{x})^2 \cdot \sum_{i=0}^{n}(y_i-\bar{y})^2}} \qquad (28)$$

The closer r is to 1, the better agreement between the predicted values of the model and the numerical results we obtain. The Pearson correlation coefficients of axial force, normal force and pitching moment are 0.999996, 0.999973, and 0.999863, respectively. They are all very close to 1, indicating that the correlation between the predicted data and the numerical simulation data is very good.

In order to further assess the viscous interaction model, the relative orthogonal distance, dr_i, is defined to characterize the relative degree of deviation of the data from the correlation curve, as shown in the following,

$$dr_i = \frac{d_i}{x_r} \qquad (29)$$

The dr_i of the viscous axial force is shown in Figure 12. The maximum fitting deviation is only 1.8%.

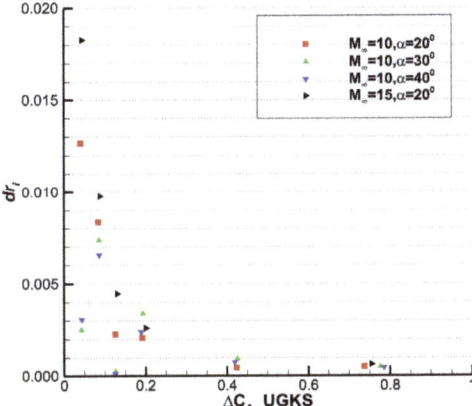

Figure 12. Relative orthogonal distance of the viscous axial force coefficient.

Finally, the accuracy of the prediction model is preliminarily evaluated. The UGKS and the viscous interaction models are used to calculate two new cases with altitudes equal to 80 km and 90 km, respectively. The angle of attack is 30 degrees with a Mach number of 15. The results and relative errors are shown in Table 2. The relative error of viscous axial force is small partially due to its large magnitude. While the error of viscous pitching moment is large due to its small magnitude compared with the viscous axial force. However, the relative error of the pitching moment itself is small. Taking the 80 km case as an example, the relative error of predicted viscous pitching moment is 9.87%. However, the pitching moments obtained by UGKS simulation and predicted by the model are -0.2158 and -0.2180, respectively, resulting in a relative error of only 1.01%.

Table 2. Comparison between model predictions and UGKS simulation results.

No	Altitude (km)	UGKS Simulation			Model Prediction			Relative Error		
		dCA	dCN	dCm	dCA	dCN	dCm	dCA	dCN	dCm
1	80	0.0918	0.0448	−0.0221	0.0904	0.0486	−0.0243	−1.58%	8.66%	9.87%
2	90	0.2056	0.1019	−0.0477	0.1993	0.1064	−0.0516	−3.07%	4.47%	8.18%

4. Conclusions

Hypersonic viscous and inviscid flow fields around the X38-like vehicle are simulated by UGKS solver and Euler solver, respectively. Viscous force coefficients at different altitudes, Mach numbers, and attack angles are obtained by subtracting the two solutions and correlated by the third viscous interaction parameter. A nonlinear viscous interaction model of force coefficients is established, and some preliminary conclusions are as follows,

(1) For the X38-like vehicle, the contribution of the viscous part to the axial force coefficients increases rapidly with altitude, and reaches 87% at 110 km for the typical conditions, with Ma = 10 and AOA = 20. The contribution of the viscous part to the normal force coefficients is small, and can only reach 26% at 110 km.

(2) For complex configurations such as the current X38-like vehicle, the changes of wall pressure and aerodynamic coefficients due to viscous interaction cannot be expressed linearly with the viscous interaction parameters in the whole flow field.

(3) A viscous interaction model can be established by taking the viscous interaction parameters as the independent variables combined with the inviscid solution and the viscous solution, which is helpful to quickly obtain the aerodynamic characteristics at moderate to high altitudes and has certain application value in engineering design.

In this paper, the idea of modeling the viscous interaction based on UGKS solver is applied to the X38-like vehicle, and a satisfactory result has been achieved. The prediction model can take into account both the viscous interaction effect and rarefied gas effect. However, the Cartesian velocity mesh in our UGKS solver causes huge waste both in computation and memory. The next step is to introduce an unstructured velocity mesh into our solver to reduce the cost and give a more accurate prediction model for more complex configurations.

Author Contributions: Conceptualization, D.J. and M.M.; methodology, D.J.; software, D.J. and P.W.; validation, D.J., P.W. and J.L.; formal analysis, D.J.; investigation, P.W.; resources, P.W.; data curation, P.W.; writing—original draft preparation, D.J.; writing—review and editing, D.J.; visualization, P.W.; supervision, M.M. and J.L.; project administration, M.M.; funding acquisition, M.M. All authors have read and agreed to the published version of the manuscript.

Funding: This research was funded by NSFC, grant number 11972362, and NNW, grant number NNW-CFD-4.

Institutional Review Board Statement: Not applicable.

Informed Consent Statement: Not applicable.

Data Availability Statement: The datasets used or analyzed during the current study are available from the corresponding author on reasonable request.

Conflicts of Interest: The authors declare no conflict of interest.

References

1. Anderson, J.D. *Hypersonic and High-Temperature Gas Dynamics*, 2nd ed.; American Institute of Aeronautics and Astronautics Inc.: Reston, VA, USA, 2006; pp. 375–462.
2. Wilhite, A.W.; Arrington, J.P.; McCandless, R.S. Performance aerodynamics of aero-assisted orbital transfer vehicles. In Proceedings of the 22nd Aerospace Sciences Meeting, AIAA Paper84-0406, Reno, NV, USA, 9–12 January 1984.
3. Gong, A.L.; Zhou, W.J.; Ji, C.Q.; Yang, Y. Study on Correlation of Hypersonic Viscous Interaction. *J. Astronaut.* **2008**, *29*, 1706–1710. (In Chinese)

4. Chen, J.Q.; Zhang, Y.R.; Zhang, Y.F.; Jie, F. Review of correlation analysis of aerodynamic data between flight and ground prediction for hypersonic vehicle. *Acta Aerodyn. Sin.* **2014**, *32*, 587–599. (In Chinese) [CrossRef]
5. Mao, M.L.; Wan, Z.; Chen, L.Z.; Chen, L. Study of hypersonic viscous interaction. *Acta Aerodyn. Sin.* **2013**, *31*, 137–143. (In Chinese)
6. Han, H.Q.; Zhang, C.A.; Wang, F.M. Study on multi-physical effects of hypersonic gliding wave rider vehicles. *Acta Aerodyn. Sin.* **2014**, *32*, 101–108. (In Chinese) [CrossRef]
7. Wang, G. Method of Data Correlation for Hypersonic Viscous Interaction Effect. Ph.D. Thesis, China Aerodynamic Research and Development Center, Mianyang, China, 2016. (In Chinese).
8. Zhang, Y.; Zhang, Y.; Xie, J.; Chen, J. Study of viscous interaction effect model for typical hypersonic wing-body figuration. *Acta Aerodyn. Sin.* **2017**, *35*, 186–191. (In Chinese)
9. Vincenti, W.G.; Kruger, C.H., Jr. *Introduction to Physical Gas Dynamics*; Wiley Press: New York, NY, USA, 1975.
10. Bird, G.A. *Molecular Gas Dynamics and the Direct Simulation of Gas Flows*; Oxford University Press: New York, NY, USA, 1994.
11. Titarev, V.A. Numerical method for computing two-dimensional unsteady rarefied gas flows in arbitrarily shaped domains. *Comput. Math. Math. Phys.* **2009**, *49*, 1197–1211. [CrossRef]
12. Titarev, V.A. Implicit Unstructured-Mesh Method for Calculating Poiseuille Flows of Rarefied Gas. *Commun. Comput. Phys.* **2010**, *8*, 427–444. [CrossRef]
13. Titarev, V.A. Efficient Deterministic Modelling of Three-Dimensional Rarefied Gas Flows. *Commun. Comput. Phys.* **2012**, *12*, 162–192. [CrossRef]
14. Titarev, V.A. Application of model kinetic equations to hypersonic rarefied gas flows. *Comput. Fluids* **2018**, *169*, 62–70. [CrossRef]
15. Titarev, V.A.; Frolova, A.A.; Rykov, V.A.; Vashchenkov, P.; Shevyrin, A.; Bondar, Y. Comparison of the Shakhov kinetic equation and DSMC method as applied to space vehicle aerothermodynamics. *J. Comput. Appl. Math.* **2020**, *364*, 112354. [CrossRef]
16. Titarev, V.A. Application of the Nesvetay Code for Solving Three-Dimensional High-Altitude Aerodynamics Problems. *Comput. Math. Math. Phys.* **2020**, *60*, 737–748. [CrossRef]
17. Baranger, C.; Claudel, J.; Hérouard, N.; Mieussens, L. Locally refined discrete velocity grids for stationary rarefied flow simulations. *J. Comput. Phys.* **2014**, *257*, 572–593. [CrossRef]
18. Li, Z.H.; Zhang, H.X. Study on gas kinetic algorithm for flows from rarefied transition to continuum using Boltzmann model equation. *Chin. J. Theor. Appl. Mech.* **2002**, *34*, 145–155. (In Chinese)
19. Li, Z.H.; Jiang, X.Y.; Wu, J.L.; Peng, A.P. Gas-kinetic unified algorithm for Boltzmann model equation in rotational nonequilibrium and its application to the whole range Flow regimes. *Chin. J. Theor. Appl. Mech.* **2014**, *46*, 336–351. (In Chinese)
20. Li, Z.H.; Wu, J.L.; Jiang, X.Y.; Wu, J.L.; Bai, Z.Y. A massively parallel algorithm for hypersonic covering various flow regimes to solve Boltzmann model equation. *Acta Aeronaut. Et Astronaut. Sin.* **2015**, *36*, 201–212. (In Chinese)
21. Li, Z.H.; Peng, A.P.; Zhang, H.X.; Yang, J.Y. Rarefied gas flow simulations using high-order gas-kinetic unified algorithms for Boltzmann model equations. *Prog. Aerosp. Sci.* **2015**, *74*, 81–113. [CrossRef]
22. Xu, K.; Huang, J.C. A unified gas-kinetic scheme for continuum and rarefied flows. *J. Comput. Phys.* **2010**, *229*, 7747–7764. [CrossRef]
23. Liu, C.; Xu, K. Direct modelling methodology and its applications in multiscale transport process. *Acta Aerodyn. Sin.* **2020**, *38*, 197–216. (In Chinese)
24. Xu, K.; Chen, S.Z. Gas kinetic scheme in hypersonic flow simulation. *Acta Aeronaut. Et Astronaut. Sin.* **2015**, *36*, 135–146. (In Chinese)
25. Xu, K.; Huang, J.C. An improved unified gas-kinetic scheme and the study of shock structures. *IMA J. Appl. Math.* **2011**, *76*, 698–711. [CrossRef]
26. Huang, J.C.; Xu, K.; Yu, P.B. A Unified Gas-Kinetic Scheme for Continuum and Rarefied Flows II: Multi-Dimensional Cases. *Commun. Comput. Phys.* **2012**, *12*, 662–690. [CrossRef]
27. Liu, S.; Yu, P.B.; Xu, K.; Zhong, C. Unified gas-kinetic scheme for diatomic molecular simulations in all flow regimes. *J. Comput. Phys.* **2014**, *259*, 96–113. [CrossRef]
28. Chen, S.Z.; Xu, K.; Lee, C.; Cai, Q. A unified gas kinetic scheme with moving mesh and velocity space adaptation. *J. Comput. Phys.* **2012**, *231*, 6643–6664. [CrossRef]
29. Yu, P.B. A Unified Gas Kinetic Scheme for All Knudsen Number Flows. Ph.D. Thesis, The Hong Kong University of Science and Technology, Hong Kong, China, 2013.
30. Liu, S. Unified Gas Kinetic Scheme. Ph.D. Thesis, Northwestern Polytechnical University, Xi'an, China, 2015. (In Chinese).
31. Jiang, D.W. Study of the Gas Kinetic Scheme based on the Analytic Solution of Model Equations. Ph.D. Thesis, China Aerodynamic Research and Development Center, Mianyang, China, 2016. (In Chinese).
32. Zhu, Y.J. Construction and Application of the Implicit Algorithm of the Unified Gas Kinetic Scheme. Master's Thesis, Northwestern Polytechnical University, Xi'an, China, 2016. (In Chinese).
33. Yuan, R.F. Application and Study of Multiscale Kinetic Method Applicable for All Flow Regimes. Ph.D. Thesis, Northwestern Polytechnical University, Xi'an, China, 2021. (In Chinese).
34. Mao, M.L.; Jiang, D.W.; Li, J.; Deng, X.G. Study on implicit implementation of the unified gas kinetic scheme. *Chin. J. Theor. Appl. Mech.* **2015**, *47*, 822–829.
35. Zhu, Y.J.; Zhong, C.W.; Xu, K. Implicit unified gas-kinetic scheme for steady state solutions in all flow regimes. *J. Comput. Phys.* **2016**, *315*, 16–38. [CrossRef]

36. Chen, S.; Zhang, C.; Zhu, L.; Guo, Z. A unified implicit scheme for kinetic model equations. Part I. Memory reduction technique. *Sci. Bull.* **2017**, *62*, 119–129. [CrossRef]
37. Zhu, Y.J.; Zhong, C.W.; Xu, K. Unified gas-kinetic scheme with multigrid convergence for rarefied flow study. *Phys. Fluids* **2017**, *29*, 096102. [CrossRef]
38. Jiang, D.; Mao, M.; Li, J.; Deng, X. An implicit parallel UGKS solver for flows covering various regimes. *Adv. Aerodyn.* **2019**, *1*, 8. [CrossRef]
39. Li, S.Y.; Li, Q.B.; Fu, S.; Xu, J. The high performance parallel algorithm for unified gas-kinetic scheme. In Proceedings of the 30th International Symposium on Rarefied Gas Dynamics, Glasgow, UK, 23–27 July 2016.
40. Li, J.; Jiang, D.W.; Geng, X.R.; Chen, J. Kinetic comparative study on Aerodynamic Characteristics of Hypersonic Reentry Vehicle from Near-continuous Flow to Free Molecular Flow. *Adv. Aerodyn.* **2021**, *3*, 10. [CrossRef]
41. Yoon, S.; Jameson, A. Lower-upper symmetric-Gauss-Seidel method for the Euler and Navier-Stokes equations. *AIAA J.* **1988**, *26*, 1025–1026. [CrossRef]
42. Shakhov, E.M. Generalization of the Krook Kinetic Equation. *Fluid Dyn.* **1968**, *3*, 95–96. [CrossRef]
43. Tang, W.; Feng, Y.; Ning, Y.; Gui, Y.W. Aerodynamics configuration conceptual design for X-38 analog lifting body transporter. *Acta Aerodyn. Sin.* **2011**, *29*, 555–558. (In Chinese)
44. Wang, W.L.; Boyd, I.D. Predicting continuum breakdown in hypersonic viscous flows. *Phys. Fluids* **2003**, *15*, 91–100. [CrossRef]
45. Maus, J.; Griffith, B.; Tolbert, D.; Best, J. Understanding space shuttle flight data by use of wind tunnel and CFD results. In Proceedings of the 2nd Flight Testing Conference, AIAA Paper83-2745, Las Vegas, NV, USA, 16–18 November 1983.

MDPI\
St. Alban-Anlage 66\
4052 Basel\
Switzerland\
Tel. +41 61 683 77 34\
Fax +41 61 302 89 18\
www.mdpi.com

Entropy Editorial Office\
E-mail: entropy@mdpi.com\
www.mdpi.com/journal/entropy

www.ingramcontent.com/pod-product-compliance
Lightning Source LLC
LaVergne TN
LVHW070435100526
838202LV00014B/1601